Extraterres

Catholic Imagination

Extraterrestrials in the Catholic Imagination:

Explorations in Science, Science Fiction and Religion

Edited by

Jennifer Rosato and Alan Vincelette

Cambridge
Scholars
Publishing

Extraterrestrials in the Catholic Imagination:
Explorations in Science, Science Fiction and Religion

Edited by Jennifer Rosato and Alan Vincelette

This book first published 2021. The present binding first published 2023.

Cambridge Scholars Publishing

Lady Stephenson Library, Newcastle upon Tyne, NE6 2PA, UK

British Library Cataloguing in Publication Data
A catalogue record for this book is available from the British Library

ISBN (10): 1-5275-9674-5
ISBN (13): 978-1-5275-9674-0

TABLE OF CONTENTS

LIST OF ILLUSTRATIONS

PREFACE

St. John's Seminary in Camarillo, California was one of forty-two seminaries selected to receive a Science for Seminaries grant from the American Association for the Advancement of Science (AAAS) during the time period of 2014-2021. This project was established by the AAAS Dialogue on Science, Ethics, and Religion (DoSER) program, in partnership with the Association of Theological Schools (ATS), to assist seminaries in integrating science into their core curricula, providing seminary students and faculty familiarity with the scientific method and achievements, and preparing future faith leaders to engage their congregants in dialogues regarding science and technology.

St. John's Seminary was particularly interested in acquiring such a grant because an increasing number of seminarians enter each year who have degrees in a scientific field (currently around 15% of the student body), as do many practicing and fallen away Catholics. Lack of proficiency in and knowledge of the sciences and technology has left fellow students, faculty, and graduates ill-prepared to converse about ethical or social implications of new discoveries or perceived conflicts involving philosophy, theology, and science.

As part of its Science for Seminaries grant initiatives, St. John's Seminary held a series of lectures and a conference on the topic of space in the Catholic imagination in the spring semester of 2020. This brought together astronomers, physicists, philosophers, theologians, and science fiction authors to discuss medieval Catholic views of the cosmos; current knowledge about the existence of exoplanets, their suitability for life and how such life might evolve; how the existence of intelligent life elsewhere in the universe would impact theology; and how Catholic science fiction authors have imagined life and religion on other worlds.

Several of these talks have been reworked and collected into this volume, and a few additional invited papers have been incorporated, as a resource for future seminarians, church leaders, and indeed for anyone interested in how Christians past and present have conceived of issues involving the cosmos and alien life forms.

Included herein are papers written by Christian astronomers, physicists, and biologists about our current state of knowledge regarding the likelihood and possible nature of life outside of our solar system; discussions by

Catholic philosophers and theologians on the medieval picture of the cosmos and its misrepresentations, as well as theological issues pertaining to the existence of intelligent life on exoplanets; and finally, presentations by Catholic science fiction authors on how science fiction has dealt with issues of religion and conceived of alien life forms, religion, and salvation.

The editors of this volume wish to thank those who contributed papers to this volume; those who contributed artwork (Daniel Vega, Chris Decaen, and Margaret Youngblood); those who gave talks not included in this collection (Kevin Brennan, Paul Ford, Timothy Pawl, Karin Öberg, and Mary Oksala); those who served as scientific advisors (Erin Smith and Mark Oksala once again) or theological advisors (Paul Louis Metzger and Robert Spitzer, S. J.) for the grant; those who assisted in bringing the conference to fruition (Luke Dysinger, Kevin Brennan once again, George Perez, Janice Daurio, Julia Scalise, John O'Brien, Anthony Lilles, Marco Durazo, Dan Schwala, and Archbishop José Gomez); and finally staff members of AAAS who assisted St. John's Seminary in these endeavors (John Slattery, Curtis Baxter, Jennifer Wiseman, and Lilah Sloane-Barrett). And finally, a warm thanks to fellow students, faculty, board members, and guests who were able to attend and contributed to one of the lectures on space in the Catholic imagination held in the spring semester of 2020.

Jennifer Rosato and Alan Vincelette

INTRODUCTION

JENNIFER ROSATO

A memorable scene from Cy Kellett's science fiction novella *Ad Limina* portrays a conversation that takes place on a space station between the first bishop of Mars and a character named Doug, who is the result of a successful experiment in which scientists induced a human brain to live within the body of an ape. Doug thinks and speaks like a human, and early in the conversation he firmly tells the bishop, "I am not an ape. . . . I am probably as human as you are." But despite this confident proclamation, it becomes clear that Doug is not used to being accepted as a human being. Hence Doug is surprised and grateful when the bishop asks him if he is a religious person: "Thank you, bishop, for referring to me as a person. Some people take a long time to see past appearances."

In fact, over the course of several pages, the reader discovers that Doug himself is not truly sure who or what he is. "Am I a child of God?" he asks the bishop, poignantly, or does his artificial origin prevent him from holding that status? Finally, Doug revisits and poses the question that his early assertion dodged: is his life is marked by the unique dignity and moral worth accorded to human beings? "But bishop," says Doug, "you are avoiding the key question—am I human? I believe I am; I am certainly sentient in a human way, does that—" When the bishop cuts him off to discuss the relationship between sentience and personhood, Doug poses his question again: "I have thought of myself as human. But since I have been thinking about God, I have felt unsure about . . . about whether I was human in a . . . religious way. Does that make sense?"[1]

As a character, Doug fills a familiar enough role in the world of science fiction. After all, it is a common technique of the genre to imagine as persons beings whose physical appearance, customs, attitudes, and history are completely foreign to our own. Whether they arise as a result of experimentation, exploration, or invasion, these beings allow authors and readers to consider real questions—about what it means to be human or a

---

[1] Cyril Jones-Kellett, *Ad Limina: A Novella* (March 7 Media, 2013), Kindle edition, loc. 1245–1313.

person, who we are in the context of the vast universe, how intelligent life ought to be treated, and so on—in an utterly artificial setting that nevertheless seems to foreshadow true possibilities. Doug, then, is hardly out of place in the world of science fiction. But the fact that his questions are also religious ones—questions about whether God loves him and has a plan for him; whether he was created only by the hands of scientists or also, in some other sense, by the Hand of the Creator; and ultimately whether he can be baptized—makes him a much rarer figure. Yet these questions are natural from a Catholic perspective. They are questions that arise spontaneously when believers participate imaginatively in the world created by the authors of science fiction, and they are questions that would arise with pressing force for Christians if we actually did encounter nonhuman or extraterrestrial intelligent life.

The essays in this volume also aim to consider these sorts of questions. Instead of adopting a narrative context, however, the authors of the contributions here offer nonfictional approaches to the central theme announced in the title, *Extraterrestrials and the Cosmos in the Catholic Imagination*. How, they consider, have Catholics in the past thought about space and aliens of all sorts, not only in philosophical and theological texts but also in literature? How should Catholics today think about these topics, in light of contemporary scientific knowledge as well as our doctrinal commitments?

It is both a peculiarity and a strength of the book that it treats its central topic from a multidisciplinary approach, since it is clear even upon first reflection that such a topic will naturally lead to questions that concern not only the theologian and the philosopher, but also the natural scientist, the man or woman of letters, the historian, and others. While multi- and inter-disciplinary approaches are often enough praised, publications that actually invite commentary from authors with varied areas of expertise are not as common. The breadth of this volume arose out of the decision, first, to pursue an open-ended discussion of the topic by inviting a wide variety of speakers to the series of lectures and conference held at St. John's in the spring of 2020, and the commitment to this decision was first and foremost Alan Vincelette's. Indeed, it is hard to imagine that anyone without Vincelette's unique background in both biology and philosophy, as well as his years of experience teaching at a Catholic seminary, would have had the ingenuity or the competence to conceive and organize such a series. It is thanks to the variety of speakers' perspectives, all coming at the central topic from a different angle, that we were able to conceive this volume as a means of organizing and sharing that open-ended discussion. As noted in the Preface St. John's Seminary also was the beneficiary of a Science for

Seminaries grant from the Association for the Advancement of Science that provided the funding for this speaker series and conference.

The papers in this book have been arranged into three sections, each of which roughly corresponds to a different mode of inquiry by means of which one might consider our topic. In Part One, the authors approach the topic from the standpoint of the natural sciences, inquiring into the nature of the universe and what we know about the life contained therein. Here it should be noted that there is nothing distinctively Catholic or Christian about scientific inquiry into the nature of space *per se*. Nevertheless, attention to the sciences is pertinent because Catholics will need to know something about the structure of the universe if we are to appreciate important Catholic teachings, such as the claim that our God is Creator of all things and author of all life, or to raise theological questions about how we would understand the teaching that all salvation is through Christ and His Church if it should turn out that there are other rational beings in the universe. Further, the ways that faithful Catholics today, like our predecessors before us, envision the place of the human person in the cosmos is informed by the harmonious union of knowledge acquired both through reason and by faith. In this way, the essays in the first section of the book, though they could stand alone, also prepare the way for Parts Two and Three, wherein Christian topics are considered directly.

Jeffrey Zweerink opens the volume with his essay "Is There Life Out There?" in which he addresses the question of whether it is likely that intelligent extraterrestrial forms of life exist, given what we know about our own Solar System and the conditions that might obtain on exoplanets. He explains the techniques that astronomers use to search for exoplanets and clarifies what is meant when they talk about the habitability of various planets. In the end, Zweerink argues that Earth's capacity to host life is likely unique, but also emphasizes that many more pertinent scientific discoveries remain to be made when it comes to the question of life out there.

Next, Carol Day's "Other Worlds and the Scientific Imagination" opens with a discussion of the scientific imagination, or the way in which the "stories" developed on the basis of scientific data shape our understanding of that data, supplementing what is most abstract or obscure in our reasoning with images that in turn direct our future research. Hence, when it comes to speculating on the possibility of life on other planets, Day reminds us to be careful to avoid "an undisciplined use of the imagination" since "nothing is so opposed to scientific objectivity as a strong desire to find a particular answer." Day goes on to summarize current consensus as regards the origin and nature of galaxies, stars, and the Solar System, as well as the conditions under which life flourishes on Earth and whether those conditions might be found also on exoplanets. She points out that given what we know about the conditions necessary for life to arise on Earth complex life on exoplanets is likely to be rare.

In "Limitations of Life Considered: The Likelihood of Complex Multicellular Life on Earth-Like Exoplanets," Alan Vincelette appeals to what we know about the mechanisms of evolution on Earth in order to suggest that complex life on other planets might turn out to take surprisingly similar forms as life does here. In the first part of the paper, Vincelette introduces us to the phenomenon of convergent evolution, or the tendency for species of distinct evolutionary lineages to acquire similar adaptations over time when they are forced to survive in similar biological niches. Having discerned this tendency, we can see that the overall history of life is not completely random, but has rather been guided in fairly regular patterns by environmental pressures, and is likely to be guided in similar ways by similar environmental pressures on other planets. Vincelette engages in detail with the work of several recent scientists who have debated the true significance of convergent evolution and is ultimately optimistic about the possibility that the complex characteristics we think are essential to humans might also have evolved elsewhere in the universe. As a supplement to his essay, published as an appendix at the end of the book, Vincelette offers a taxonomy of 81 basic mammalian forms that have arisen as a result of convergent evolution. He proposes that such a taxonomy, based on generalized body types, would be more helpful in categorizing extraterrestrial life than other systems that prioritize the evolutionary relationships that unfolded here on Earth.

The essays in Part Two of the volume explore how Catholics, both recently and over the centuries, have imagined the possibility of extraterrestrial life and its significance in light of Christian faith. These shorter selections introduce us to aspects of the Catholic intellectual and literary tradition that touch on these topics. In fact, the authors of the six chapters in this section have all contributed to that tradition themselves by writing successful works of science fiction.

Robert Chase's essay, "From the Antipodes to Infinity" opens the section by documenting and then refuting the popular assumption that Christian faith would crumble if extraterrestrials were to be discovered. In fact, Chase argues, a brief survey of key figures from St. Augustine to Pope Francis reveals that Catholics are generally quite at ease with the possibility of extraterrestrials. Chase closes by contrasting the ways in which three works of Catholic science fiction—Mary Doria Russell's *The Sparrow*, Michael Flynn's *Eifelheim*, and Chase's own *The Game of Fox and Lion*—

envision what human interaction with other intelligent beings would look like.

Michael Flynn's "Sciopods, Blemyae, and the Green Children of Woolpit: 'Aliens' in the Catholic Imagination, Premodern Era," fills in some of the gaps left by Chase's survey and introduces us to various strange but rational beings described in texts by premodern Catholics such as John Mandeville and Ralph of Coggeshall. What are we to make of these stories of 'alien' beings, such as the sciopods who hop on one large foot, or the race of beings who have the bodies of men and the heads of dogs, or the two green-skinned children who crawled out of a pit in a village in Suffolk one day speaking a foreign language? Flynn himself adopts St. Augustine's position on the matter: we're not bound to believe everything we hear, but if these beings do exist, and if they have intellect and will, then "they would be just like any other species of man."

While both the possibility of extraterrestrial life and our modern understanding of the universe's vast size are sometimes taken to be significant challenges to the Christian account of creation, original sin, and salvation, anyone who actually examines these ostensible arguments against Christianity will discover that they are neither new nor convincing—at least, such is the position that John C. Wright defends in "What Has Outer Space to Do with Christ?" In fact, these challenges aren't arguments at all, but rather ways of telling a story about who man is, traceable more clearly to the science fiction of authors such as Arthur Clarke and Carl Sagan than to actual science fact. Wright suggests that what is needed in response is better storytelling: epics "set against the backdrop of all the width of starry space" wherein the basic doctrinal commitments of a Christian worldview form a framework within which the science fiction author's creative imagination weaves truthful fiction.

Next, Cy Kellett reflects on two classic examples of Catholic science fiction in his "Science Fiction and Religion": Walter Miller's *A Canticle for Leibowitz* and Walker Percy's *The Thanatos Syndrome*. As he sees it, both of these books, as well as his own *Ad Limina*, represent the "insanity" of modern Western society, which over the past several centuries abandoned first Christ and then reality itself. Kellett's brief narrative of decline situates the novels, each of which reminds us in its own way that advanced technology does not save us from moral failure, and encourages us to reflect anew on what it means to be human.

The fact that Catholic science fiction authors generally critique contemporary society shouldn't mean their stories are merely didactic exercises or thinly veiled metaphors for current sociopolitical concerns. Tim Powers reminds us of this at the start of his "Catholic Questions in Science

Fiction and Fantasy." Good stories must be convincing simply as stories first, and the supernatural elements in science fiction and fantasy need to grip as frighteningly, imaginatively plausible if they are to achieve their purpose. Powers proposes that, while science fiction and fantasy are just fiction, the supernatural is real, and Christian readers may be better prepared to envision the true supernatural elements of the Gospels having imaginatively taken the mere fictions as seriously as possible. After all, we Catholics hold that such supernatural realities as transubstantiation, the Resurrection, demons, and man's immortal soul are no mere metaphors.

The final chapter of Part Two comprises a dialogue between Flynn, Powers, and Wright, and is derived from the actual discussion these authors shared during the Q&A session at the close of the conference in May 2020. In the selections recorded here, the authors reflect on why science fiction today is typically inhospitable to religion; on how their own science fiction work incorporates real-world facts; and on the way that science fiction and fantasy stories function convincingly both as stories and as ways of reflecting on philosophical and theological truths.

The third and final part of this volume includes three essays in which Catholic philosophers consider questions raised by the possibility of extraterrestrial life and our contemporary scientific understanding of the cosmos. The first paper assesses the implications of the Copernican revolution for philosophical and theological anthropology, while the second and third reflect on how Christians should think about the possible ways in which intelligent extraterrestrial life could fit into God's plan of salvation.

In "Human Significance for the Medieval Mind," Alan Vincelette aims to refute the popular myth "that medieval cosmology placed humans on a pedestal which the Copernican theory pulled out from under them." Here Vincelette documents the ways in which patristic, medieval, and Renaissance Christians conceived man's place in the cosmos. While individual thinkers vary in their degree of optimism regarding human dignity, they all situate man in a middle place between angels and the lower animals, seeing in him a being created in the image of God whose earthly existence is nevertheless a foul and painful experience filled with poverty, disease, suffering, and ultimately death. Neither, Vincelette goes on to argue, does the commitment to geocentrism signify that premoderns thought of the Earth as the most important or noblest place in the universe; to the contrary, he documents instances in which premodern thinkers went out of their way to correct the false implication that the Earth's geographical centrality might challenge the superior dignity and significance of the heavens. In the last section of the paper, Vincelette offers his account of how the relative size and position of men in the universe came to be seen, over the course of the modern period, both as evidence of humans' cosmic insignificance and, contrary to the historical record, as a challenge to the premodern conception of human worth.

The final two chapters of this book take up the topic of how we should understand the potential or actual existence of intelligent extraterrestrials in the context of the Christian account of salvation history. In "Christianity and Intelligent Extraterrestrials," Marie George asks first whether Christianity is incompatible with the possibility that intelligent extraterrestrial life exists. Answering no, George goes on to consider whether Christianity renders the existence of extraterrestrials likely or unlikely. Central to George's deliberation are key passages of Scripture which, she argues, teach that Christ's incarnation on Earth is the central event of cosmic history and suggest Christ took on human flesh precisely because he wanted to share the lineage of those who would be saved by His sacrifice. George concludes that theological considerations do seem to render the existence of either fallen or unfallen extraterrestrial existence implausible, but they do not definitively rule it out, nor would the real existence of these creatures undermine the Christian understanding of the special place humans hold in the cosmos.

The final essay of Part Three is Janice Daurio's "Are Extraterrestrials Saved?" In this piece, Daurio asks what significance the Christian story would have for intelligent extraterrestrial beings, assuming they exist. Daurio argues forcefully that if such extraterrestrials are persons, then they are just as capable of receiving salvation through Christ's death on Calvary as human persons are. The question of whether such extraterrestrials are in fact persons, claims Daurio, cannot be decided until we actually encounter such beings. If upon encounter there should be ambiguity about the fact, however, Daurio suggests that we should treat extraterrestrials as persons until proven otherwise, lest we end up repeating moral abominations of the past in which various individuals and groups of humans were treated as non-persons.

In closing, I would simply like to draw attention to the artwork included in the volume and placed at the beginning of each section. The pieces by Chris Decaen, Daniel Vega, and Margaret Youngblood, both contemplative and whimsical in tone, are a fitting addition to a volume that invites the reader to consider how the Catholic imagination envisions outer space and extraterrestrial life. It remains to be seen whether there are ever Donut Sundays at a station church in orbit or whether Carmel ever includes winged aliens, but the evangelical spirit that foresees Christ's truth extending beyond our present understanding and to the farthest reaches of the universe can inspire us even now.

PART ONE:

SCIENCE AND THE EXTRATERRESTRIAL INTELLIGENCES QUESTION

Figure 0-1: Green Extraterrestrial with Scriptures, Margaret Youngblood.

CHAPTER ONE

IS THERE LIFE OUT THERE?

JEFFREY ZWEERINK

> Although making no claims about whether extraterrestrials exist, I shall cite evidence to show that they have long since invaded and that their efforts can be uncovered by historical research.[1]

Is there anybody who is *not* fascinated with the idea of life beyond Earth? Consider the runaway success and continued buzz over blockbuster movies such as the Marvel Cinematic Universe, *Star Wars*, and *Star Trek* franchises, *E.T. the Extra-Terrestrial*, *Independence Day*, and others. Sure, the entertainment value is great, but also the prospect of extraterrestrial (ET) life fills our imaginations. "What if" scenarios make for great sport and scientific inquiry.

We tend to think of this fascination as a recent phenomenon, but debates about the existence of ET life date back millennia. At the start of the scientific revolution, Galileo and Kepler (both Christians) argued on opposite sides of the debate. Kepler thought that ETs populated the recently discovered moons of Jupiter whereas Galileo (who discovered the moons) believed life existed only on Earth. According to historians the discussion about alien life existed before Christ walked the Earth. Thus, it would not surprise me to find that Adam and Eve pondered the existence of life beyond Earth!

Exploring the Solar System

In recent years, science has developed the capacity to investigate whether life might exist out there.[2] And while we don't yet have the technology to

---

[1] Michael J. Crowe, ed., *The Extraterrestrial Life Debate, Antiquity to 1915: A Source Book* (Notre Dame: University of Notre Dame Press, 2008), xvi.
[2] Much of the material in this paper draws upon research for my book *Is There Life Out There?* (Corvina, CA: RTB Press, 2017), where you can find more details and references to the scientific literature.

find life necessarily, we do possess the tools to discuss how many planets there are, what kinds of stars they orbit, and whether they might be habitable. Based on current research, a potentially habitable planet will be rocky like Earth and it will orbit its star at an appropriate distance.

Before exploring what exists beyond our Solar System, it's worth looking at the Solar System itself because it provides a frame of reference for what we might find beyond the Sun. As shown in Figure 1-1, eight planets orbit the Sun: Mercury, Venus, Earth, Mars, Jupiter, Saturn, Uranus, and Neptune. The first four are rocky planets that orbit relatively close to the Sun, whereas the last four, comprised dominantly of ice and gas, are much larger and orbit farther from the Sun. An abundance of smaller bodies—called Kuiper Belt objects and appearing as dots in the figure— resides beyond the orbit of Neptune out to the Oort cloud, which is the boundary of our Solar System.

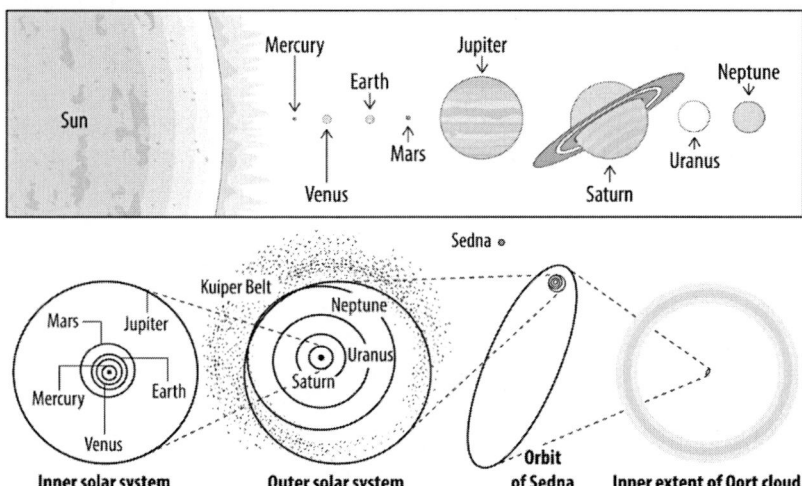

Figure 1-1: Basic structure of the Solar System. All eight planets reside in nearly circular orbits. The planetoid Sedna has an elongated orbit. Credit: Reasons to Believe.

I highlight this solar system structure because astronomers had long thought that planetary systems discovered around other stars would look largely like the Solar System. This similarity, called the Copernican principle, embodies the belief that our Solar System is ordinary in its

location, structure, composition, and the life—found only on Earth so far—
that resides here.

How Do Scientists Find Exoplanets?

The most important scientific advance in the search for life elsewhere in the
universe is the relatively recent capacity to detect planets around other stars.
Until the early 1990s, astronomers knew only of the eight planets orbiting
the Sun although they expected that planets existed around most stars. In the
time since the first confirmed discovery in 1992, astronomers have
discovered thousands of exoplanets—planets orbiting a star other than the
Sun. Astronomers use several techniques to detect exoplanets, and each
method has advantages and limitations. Four are worthy of mention.

Radial Velocity: An orbiting exoplanet exerts a gravitational pull on its
host star, causing the star to move toward and away from Earth. By mapping
the star's motion, astronomers can determine the minimum mass and the
orbital characteristics of the exoplanet. Until recently, this was the most
prolific exoplanet-finding technique available to researchers. However, this
technique provides no other information, and the current technology cannot
find Earth-sized planets on Earth-like orbits when looking at Sun-like stars.

Transit: This technique looks for dips in the amount of detected
starlight resulting from a planet passing in front of the star. Transits allow
astronomers to determine the orbital characteristics, planet size, and mass
(when combined with radial velocity). Occasionally, light from the planet
itself can be measured during the transits. Using this technique, the Kepler
mission discovered over 2,500 exoplanets. Even with current technology,
this technique has the potential to discover a planet similar to Earth. While
more information comes from transits, they occur less frequently. Also, this
process works only for exoplanetary systems with the correct alignment
with Earth.

Gravitational Lensing: Occasionally, a star and an associated planet
will pass in front of a background star. For specific alignments, the star and
planet gravitationally lens (enhance the view of) the background star,
causing a brief but dramatic increase in detected light. While gravitational
lensing searches have detected only a dozen or so planets thus far, it is the
only technique capable of finding Earth-mass planets around stars with
masses similar to the Sun.

Direct Detection: This method seeks to directly detect the light coming from an exoplanet. To see the exoplanet's light, an instrument must block the host star's light because the latter is a million to a billion times brighter. One limitation of the method is that current technology allows astronomers to detect only Jupiter-class planets orbiting relatively far (more than 10 times the Earth-Sun distance) from their host stars. However, one distinct advantage is that the light from the planet carries ample information about the planet size, temperature, orbit, and atmosphere. Several ground-based and space telescopes seek to directly image an Earth-like planet with an Earth-like orbit around a Sun-like star.

Figure 1-2 shows the sensitivity (shaded areas) of the different techniques as a function of mass and orbital period. As seen by the location of the Solar System planets, the techniques are not generally capable of detecting exoplanets like Earth; i.e., those with the capacity to support life (only Jupiter shows up). But that does not mean that astronomers cannot extract some interesting information related to the search for life.

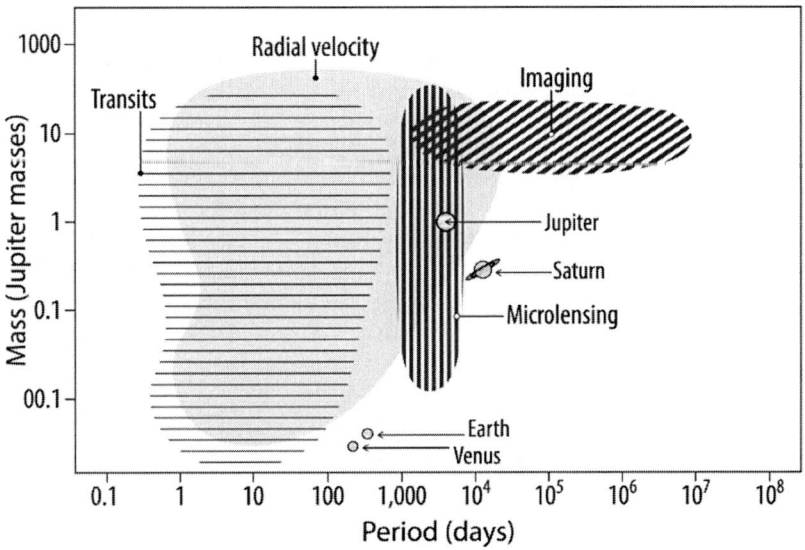

Figure 1-2: The different techniques find exoplanets of different sizes and orbits. Solar System planets are shown for reference. Notice that with the current technology, astronomers would have great difficulty detecting most of the exoplanets in a system resembling the Solar System. Credit: Reasons to Believe.

For example, the data (for all detection methods) shows that exoplanets with smaller masses are exponentially more abundant than more massive exoplanets. Furthermore, the number of confirmed exoplanet discoveries has grown exponentially over the past three decades to well over 4,000.[3] Using these facts, and accounting for the details of each detection method, astronomers have calculated that the Milky Way galaxy contains ~160 billion exoplanets with masses like Neptune or larger. When shrinking the mass to something Earth-like, the number of exoplanets grows to more than 400 billion!

Planet Migration and Harsh Environments

Given the incredible number of Earth-sized exoplanets, will the detection of life be inevitable? Probably not. The discoveries highlight a strong word of caution about the hopes of finding life beyond Earth. Remember, the Solar System consists of four rocky planets closer to the Sun and four more-distant gaseous planets—all of which orbit the Sun on nearly circular paths.

However, the first large group of exoplanets discovered looked nothing like this. Of the first 200 detections, more than half were "hot Jupiters"—gaseous, not rocky, exoplanets the size of Jupiter but with orbits much smaller than Earth's! This discovery caused some consternation because our understanding of planet formation precludes objects of this size forming so close to a star. Eventually, astronomers recognized that most, if not all, planetary systems undergo a period of migration where the planets drift inward or outward from their place of birth. A planet the size of Jupiter migrating from its birthplace (at least 5 times the radius of Earth's orbit for a Sun-like star) to an orbit less than the size of Earth's would completely disrupt the process of planet formation. It would likely preclude the formation of any rocky planets capable of hosting life.

Some exoplanet finds point to an even more disruptive form of migration. In the Solar System, the Sun rotates and all the planets revolve in the same direction. In most instances, this trend extends to the planetary rotations and even to the motion of planetary moons. However, some Jupiter-sized exoplanets orbit in a *different* direction than the host star. The migration required to produce this disparity occurs over a timescale (tens of millions of years) much longer than the period in which rocky planets can

---

[3] See exoplanet.eu/, exoplanets.nasa.gov/exoplanet-catalog/, and in addition exoplanetarchive.ipac.caltech.edu/ for some catalogs that allow you to see all the detected exoplanets and their properties.

form. Also, the strong gravitational influences of such migration ensure that no rocky exoplanets exist in these environments.

One particular exoplanet highlights the diversity of environments found so far. The exoplanet known as HIP 13044b formed in another galaxy more than 6 billion years ago.[4] Its host star, HIP 13044, exhausted its nuclear fuel and died. (Or, in technical terms, the star ascended the horizontal giant branch.) The Sun will experience a similar death in 5–6 billion years, which will cause it to expand in size beyond Earth's current orbit! HIP 13044b survived this death (so far) and the process in which the Milky Way galaxy ingested its host dwarf galaxy. Based on this discovery, astronomers think our Solar System's outer planets may face a similar danger when our Sun dies. Astronomers truly make some amazing discoveries!

Are Any Known Exoplanets Habitable?

With little effort, astronomers can easily dismiss most of the discovered exoplanets as potential life sites because they orbit their host star outside the "habitable zone." The habitable zone is the region around a star where a hypothetical planet would receive enough stellar radiation to keep all water from freezing, but not so much radiation that all the water would evaporate. A long-standing supply of liquid water is seen as a key feature of the habitable zone. However, keep in mind that some disagreement exists among astronomers as to the proper way to define the habitable zone. Additionally, just because an exoplanet orbits in the habitable zone doesn't mean that the exoplanet could host life. The atmosphere and size of the planet dramatically affect habitability.

Looking at Earth's Neighbors for Clues

Many definitions of the habitable zone, when applied to the Solar System, would include Mars and Venus. The proximity of these two planets to Earth permits a closer investigation, which reveals that neither currently holds much promise for hosting life. Venus has a mass about 20% smaller than Earth's and orbits 30% closer to the Sun. That might not look like much of a difference, but the surface temperature of Venus exceeds 750°F. A piece of paper on Venus would spontaneously burst into flames—if the planet's atmosphere contained any oxygen. Even though smaller in mass, Venus experiences an atmospheric pressure almost 100 times greater than Earth's. The recent excitement surrounding the discovery of phosphine gas on

---

[4] See exoplanet.eu/catalog/hip_13044_b/ for more details on this exoplanet.

Venus—a gas produced uniquely by life on Earth—does not change the inherent hostility of Venus to originating and hosting life. If scientists eventually discover life on Venus or anywhere else in the Solar System, such evidence strongly demonstrates the robustness of Earth's life as it moves around the Solar System.

Mars is a barren, frozen wasteland. With a mass one-tenth that of Earth's, the red planet's atmospheric pressure is one *fiftieth* that of the top of Mount Everest. Mars's small mass also makes it unable to hold on to its water as it seeks to escape into space. However, the data shows that Mars *did* have abundant water in the past. NASA's *Spirit* rover found formations of 90% (or more) pure silica just below the surface. The best (and maybe only) process for producing such formations are streams with dissolved silicates feeding a body of standing water where the silica can precipitate to the bottom. Also, NASA's *Phoenix* lander found water-ice cubes as it dug a few inches into the Martian surface.

Planetary models and observational data both indicate that Earth, Mars, and Venus all started with an abundance of water. Today, Earth exhibits an extraordinary water cycle that sustains a thriving array of abundant and diverse life. Neither Mars nor Venus shows any hint of stable liquid water, much less a water cycle.

As mentioned earlier, astronomers now know that the planet formation process includes a period where planets migrate from their birthplace. The Solar System is no exception. Theoretical and observational evidence show that the migration era revealed an unusual process that greatly enhanced Earth's capacity to host complex life. Figure 1-3 shows three panels representing the time just before migration, a snapshot during migration, and the effects of migration. Only the orbits of the four gaseous planets are shown. The best planet formation models indicate that the orbits of Jupiter and Saturn begin moving toward the Sun (much like the process of forming the hot Jupiters mentioned earlier). However, the motion halts and reverses direction. As Jupiter moves back near its starting point, the orbits of the remaining three gas giants destabilize briefly and move even farther from the Sun. The net effect of this migration produces three interesting results.

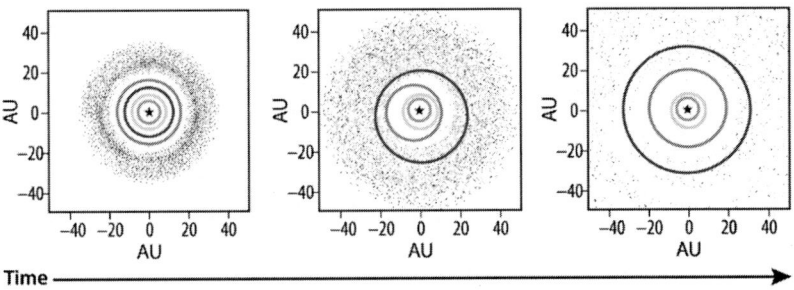

Figure 1-3: Effects of planetary migration in the Solar System. The four circles represent the migrations of Jupiter, Saturn, Uranus, and Neptune. Credit: Reasons to Believe.

First, the orbits of Neptune and Uranus (the outer two circles) switch places. Although interesting, this probably has no impact on Earth's habitability. Second, the orbits of the four gas giants become more widely separated. This increased separation will tend to minimize various orbital resonances that destabilize the smaller bodies (like rocky planets, asteroids, etc.) in the inner Solar System. Third, the migration causes a period known as the late heavy bombardment (LHB) that thins the dense cloud of debris remaining from the Solar System formation by a factor of ~1,000. Because the amount of debris (asteroid and comet material) decreases by such a large factor, the rate of meteor impacts on Earth also drops by a similar factor.

To understand the significance of this reduction, consider the impact 66 million years ago that caused the dinosaurs (and much other life) to go extinct. Scientists estimate that similar impacts happen every 50–100 million years. Without the LHB, which happened about 4 billion years ago, these extinction-causing impacts would happen every 50–100 *thousand* years. For reference, that is the timescale for humanity's residency on Earth. One would seriously question if a planet experiencing extinction-level impacts every 50–100 thousand years could host the complex life seen so abundantly throughout Earth.

Earth's Unlikely Life-Friendly Transitions

When looking at all the data, Earth alone appears amazingly designed for life. At least several powerful processes have affected the planet, and especially its habitability. Astronomically, the Sun's luminosity (brightness) started 30–40% smaller than today and has steadily grown to its current value. Geologically, Earth started covered in water but today continents make up 30% of its surface. Free oxygen comprises 21% of the atmosphere today but was virtually nonexistent for the first ~2 billion years of Earth's history. Biologically, the transitions required to go from relatively simple, single-celled organisms to complex animals (like humans) radically transformed Earth's environment.

Any one of these processes had the potential to demolish Earth's capacity to host life. Yet, over the 4.5 billion years in which they occurred, the average global temperature remained solidly within a 20°C window that enabled a thriving biosphere. The scientific data increasingly demonstrates that Earth repeatedly came dangerously close to becoming uninhabitable from the same processes that made Venus and Mars hostile to life. Such a finding leads me to expect that our search for habitable exoplanets will yield a wealth of planets that appear habitable at first, but upon further study will be uninhabitable for a variety of reasons.

What if We Find Life beyond Earth?

This essay presents a case that Earth is likely unique in its capacity to host human life. Often this case involves arguing for evidence of design that points to the Christian God. Usually those arguments entail some probabilities. Without some caution, this line of argumentation can lead one to conclude that the discovery of extraterrestrial life—a highly improbable event that, in this case, turns out to be true—would argue against Christianity. But this is incorrect.

Well before science had the capacity to explore life beyond Earth, Christians had wrestled with the idea. The main issue relates to the grand redemption story described in Scripture, which can be summarized as follows. God created the universe and the first humans, Adam and Eve, placing them in the garden fashioned on Earth. The first couple rebelled against God's command, subjecting themselves and their posterity to a life of futility. The second person of the Godhead took on human form and became a man, Jesus Christ. After living a sinless life, Jesus atoned for humanity's sin by dying on the cross and resurrecting from the grave on the third day. He now sits on the throne until returning to judge the world and usher in the new creation.

Would the discovery of life (sentient life like humanity) out there undermine any of the story? In short, Christian scholarship says no. In fact, Christian thinkers have proposed at least five options (in no particular order) that provide a broader context for the redemption story.

1. Jesus's work here brings redemption for all sentient extraterrestrial life. One could imagine that the Scripture revealed on other planets with intelligent life says that Christ existed on Earth rather than specifically visiting their exoplanet.
2. Jesus incarnates on each planet. This idea recognizes that while humans are made in God's image, we don't fully reflect his image. If Jesus could take on a human nature without changing, maybe he took on a Klingon (or any alien) nature also.
3. God has another means of redemption for other sentient life. We don't know what this alternative means might be, but we only know of Christ's redemption because God revealed it to us.
4. No redemption is possible for other life out there. This seems to be the fate of the angelic realm.
5. No redemption is necessary for other life out there. Perhaps there exists intelligent life that never rebelled.

Considering any of these possibilities may bring some level of apprehension. The main point is not to debate which one might be correct. Rather, it is simply to demonstrate that Christianity is a robust worldview (although so much more) that can easily accommodate an incredible discovery like extraterrestrial live in the universe!

Exciting Times Lie Ahead

With the discovery of the first exoplanet in 1992, science definitively marked its place in the quest to find life in the universe. As the search continues, we've learned at least two things. One, Earth-sized planets abound in the Milky Way galaxy. We know of thousands and have the potential to explore millions of times more than that! Two, at the same time, the remarkable features of Earth point to a Creator or Designer who fashioned this planet for a purpose. The fact that these two scientific finds exist in some degree of tension highlights how fascinating the search for extraterrestrial life will be.

Is there life out there? It is a great scientific question *and* a great theological question. It may be decades before science provides more data for an answer, but I can guarantee that the journey will be exhilarating.

CHAPTER TWO

OTHER WORLDS AND THE SCIENTIFIC IMAGINATION[1]

CAROL A. DAY

Before I begin to talk about the search for planets orbiting other stars and the prospects for finding habitable planets beyond the Earth, I'd like to say a little about the role of imagination in natural science. This may seem out of place, but I thought it would be appropriate to connect my lecture to the general topic of this course, "Space and the Catholic Imagination." You will have noticed that the title of my lecture refers to the scientific, not the Catholic imagination, and you may wonder what I mean by the scientific imagination. All I mean by that phrase is the imagination as it functions in scientific thought and investigation. The scientific imagination is not Catholic, nor does it belong to any sect, philosophy or ideology, although it may be influenced by any of these. The well-functioning scientific imagination is, however, proper to a mind ordered according to right reason and so belongs in a way to the Church, as do all good things. In that sense only can we call it Catholic.

Science is not just a collection of data, equations and models. If it were only that, no one but scientists would be much interested in it. Science also includes what I think we should call stories, not meaning any disrespect by the term. We want to know things; that is part of being human. When we read an article in a popular scientific journal or a book for the general public, we are being told a story, by which I mean a summary account either of what is generally thought about the subject in question or about some new discovery or hypothesis. By no means do I mean to imply that a story in my sense is something "made-up" or that it has no relation to reality. Rather, it is an attempt to put into words in a more or less simplified manner what a scientist or group of scientists are thinking about the subject. A good story

---

[1] The following is based on a lecture delivered at St. John's Seminary in Camarillo, CA on March 4, 2020.

will have some details and also a certain amount of reasoning or argument, more or less as the reader is expected to have a stronger or weaker background in the subject. To see what I mean by a scientific story by way of contrast, one might read about a subject, for example black holes, first in *Sky & Telescope* or *Scientific American* and then in the *Astrophysical Journal*.

It would be wrong to think that stories, in my sense, have no importance for professional scientists. Leaving aside the obvious point that a professional in one field may have an amateur's interest in another quite different branch of science, even in one's own field of expertise stories are useful and may sometimes even be necessary.[2] Whatever is very abstract or conceptually obscure in our explanations must be supplemented by the imagination, especially for the sake of the uninitiated. We cannot tell the story of quantum mechanics, for example, to the general public by giving them the Schrödinger equation or telling them about Hilbert spaces. We might ask them instead to imagine something of no determinate size or location that is in flux such that if you look at it one way it looks like a particle and in another way it looks like a wave, or we might even tell them a story about a cat in a box. Even the scientist cannot think in terms of the story, as distinct from the technicalities of the theory and its calculations, without forming some kind of image.

Scientific knowledge seems to be characterized above all by careful observation and strict reasoning. Our ideas about some things in the natural world, however, cannot be deduced by logical reasoning from prior scientific knowledge or induced from experience. This is especially true of unrepeatable or as far as we know unrepeated things. These things need to be approached both from the standpoint of science and of philosophy. Both deductive and inductive reasoning may be involved in coming up with the story, but they do not give us sufficient detail to be fully satisfying, nor are they without their puzzles and paradoxes. Whatever gaps are left in our reasoning must be filled in by the imagination. The larger the scope, the greater the gaps are likely to be.

---

[2] This seems to have been the view of Werner Heisenberg, who wrote: "The physicist may be satisfied when he has the mathematical scheme and knows how to use it for the interpretation of the experiments. But he has to speak about his results also to nonphysicists who will not be satisfied unless some explanation is given in plain language, understandable to anybody. Even for the physicist the description in plain language will be a criterion of the degree of understanding that has been reached" (*Physics and Philosophy: The Revolution in Modern Science* [London: George Allen & Unwin LTD, 1958], 145–46). Plain non-technical language is a distinguishing mark of a scientific story.

So, here are a few things I think we should keep in mind. First, thinking and imagining go hand in hand in human thought, both scientific and otherwise. We can see a two-fold movement between them, from reasoning to imagining and from imagining to reasoning. Scientific observation and experiment, like other forms of experience, provide raw material for our imagination. This is obvious. Perhaps less obvious, but just as true, is that the imagination guides what kinds of questions scientists ask and where and how they look for answers. Here is an example of what I have in mind. Albert Michelson decided to measure the speed of light with respect to the electromagnetic ether, the elastic substance that was supposed to be the medium for light waves. Since the ether could not be directly observed, it had to be imagined. Michelson invented an experimental set-up to detect the motion of light relative to this imagined medium. What his experiment helped to show was that there is no such ether. Bare logic cannot produce a sophisticated experimental apparatus; this calls for creativity.[3] We see in this example that the very thing being sought in this experiment was a product of the imagination and the way of seeking it involved the creative imagination of the experimenter.

The second thing to keep in mind is that the scientific imagination is, or at least should be, different from the imagination of the novelist or other creative artist. The scientist must often posit things that are not directly seen, such as the ether that most physicists of Michelson's day believed in. But the scientist does not have the freedom of the artist, since his imagination must be governed by prior knowledge and reasonable hypotheses about the physical world and must be subject to experimental test as well as to logical examination. The scientific imagination gives rise to models that are meant to explain some aspect of reality. Atoms, for example, were imagined by John Dalton as invisible and indestructible bits of matter capable of hooking on to one another to make chemical compounds. These imagined atoms were able to explain some things known to the chemist, such as the law of definite proportions. Later, when the chemical atoms were known to be composed and not simple, they were imagined as tiny solar systems with electrons orbiting a nucleus made up of protons and electrons. Later still, the electrons themselves could be imagined in more than one way, as standing waves or as clouds of probability. My point is that, as we learn more, our way of imagining the constituents of the world must change, but without changing their character as images.

---

[3] For example, after some failed trials Michelson realized that the way to protect the apparatus from vibration caused by traffic outside the lab was to float it in a pool of mercury.

The third thing to keep in mind is that the imagination may be used well or badly in the search for knowledge. Good use of the imagination involves both creativity and restraint. To these two characteristics we might also add honesty, or to put it more bluntly, a due skepticism about our own imaginings. This becomes especially important when evidence is scarce and when we are dealing with historical events such as the origin of the universe or the appearance of life on Earth. I want to emphasize this point, since I believe that an undisciplined use of the imagination is common in books and articles about the possibility of life, especially intelligent life, in the universe. The desire to speculate whether we are alone in the universe is understandable. On the other hand, nothing is so opposed to scientific objectivity as a strong desire to find a particular answer. The Catholic scientist will incline to be cautious where many others proceed with the expectation of finding a positive answer, knowing that the creation of life is God's prerogative.[4] It is right to inquire, but we should withhold judgment until and if convincing evidence appears.

Part One: The Origin of Galaxies and of Stars

When it comes to the story of the universe as a whole, we are somewhat handicapped in that we have only one example to study and we are unable to experiment directly on it. The situation is not altogether hopeless, however. As for experiment, the work of the particle physicists is helpful, together with the many amazing discoveries that have been made by astronomers using ground and space-based telescopes. There is one advantage that we have in studying the origin of cosmos, in comparison to the other great mystery, the origin and evolution of life. Because of the finite speed of light, we can see what the universe looked like at various stages in its development. In the great story called evolution, we do have fossils from the past, but these are static. In astronomy, we get to see our subject in action now and in the past, going back to near the very beginning. We are also helped by the fact that some pieces of the story are supplied by theories that are subject to verification or falsification by experiment, such as general relativity.[5] So, making use both of historical and dynamical observation and reasonably well-established physical theories, we are able to tell a plausible story about the origin and evolution of the cosmos. At first the story was

---

[4] It is only fair to point out that Catholic theology does acknowledge the existence of intelligent forms of life other than human, and they are called angels.

[5] It is of course true for the theory of evolution that laboratory experiments as well as field work in geology are relevant to the development and refinement of the theory.

contrived to explain only a few very simple facts. Now the story is being refined and advanced by trying to fit in more and more details about the structure of the universe. We must keep in mind that our story is provisional. It is always possible for it to be radically modified or even overturned, as has happened so often to other stories.

Here, then, is a story of origins: "Before the Sun was formed or the Earth came into existence, there was the Big Bang."[6] Cosmologists are tying themselves in knots these days over details concerning the Big Bang, or even whether there was a Big Bang.[7] There is a great deal of uncertainty among cosmologists about what may or may not have happened in the first unimaginably small fraction of time. Fortunately for our purposes, the part of cosmology relevant to the formation of the Solar System and of other star systems is more solidly established.

At some point, probably at about 1 second after the beginning, there was a sudden outward expansion of hot matter and energy in a small region of space in which, as it cooled, various kinds of particles appeared by a process analogous to the condensation of water vapor. It is important to note that this expansion did not consist in things flying away from each other. Rather it was space itself that was expanding and cooling, and the energy of the radiation and of the particles that condensed out was drawn from the energy of this space. So you see that in this theory space is something and not nothing. Since then the expansion has been carrying on at an ever-increasing rate, a profound mystery. The cause of this is given a name, dark energy, but no one knows what it is or what if anything causes it.

As time passed, various kinds of matter condensed out of the primordial cosmic energy, not all at once, but in an order determined by the temperature required to form each kind of particle and to allow it to be stable. Among the particles formed early on, while the universe was still very hot, the most common were protons, which are hydrogen nuclei. Thus hydrogen was the first element formed in abundance, and it was and still is the most abundant substance in the universe. The next substances to be formed were deuterium, which is hydrogen with a neutron as well as a proton in its nucleus, helium and trace amounts of lithium, the third element on the periodic table.[8]

---

[6] The standard account of the Big Bang and the subsequent development of the early universe may be found in any recent textbook of astrophysics and of course on the internet.

[7] For a popular account of the controversy, see Faye Flam, "What Came Before the Big Bang?," *Sky & Telescope*, February 2019, 16–21.

[8] One of the puzzles about this story is what happened to the anti-matter that should have been formed along with the matter. For some reason there must have been an

Good evidence points to the homogeneity of the cosmos up to the time when this sort of matter first appeared. For some reason not perfectly understood, when this material came into being, it was not uniformly distributed but was organized into immense string-like filaments with empty spaces between them. The first stars began to form within these filaments. Denser clumps of matter could attract other matter, thus increasing the mass of the clump. In addition, clumps of matter could collide and join together. By some combination of these two processes the stars and the galaxies they composed came into being.

The material making up the first stars was not as diverse of that from which later generations of stars were formed. Once the first generation of stars formed and heated up as they collapsed in on themselves by gravity, they began to shine by nuclear fusion, thus producing more elements. Of these, oxygen was the most abundant. As the early stars died off, the elements synthesized in their interiors were released into space. Water soon came into being from reactions between the original hydrogen and the newly formed oxygen. This water was largely in the form of ice.[9]

Why ice rather than water vapor? Whenever a chemical bond is formed, energy is released in the form of heat. For the hydrogen and oxygen atoms to stick together very long, there needs to be something to absorb the heat liberated by their reaction. Otherwise this heat would soon cause the newly formed molecule to break apart. Thus solid grains of matter served to absorb this heat, and in doing so came be to be coated with thin layers of water molecules, constituting an amorphous form of ice. Because hydrogen and oxygen are abundant and very reactive, water is one of the most abundant molecules in the universe.

As new generations of stars were formed from the primordial hydrogen and helium and the remnants of earlier stars, even more elements came into existence by nuclear fusion. The heavier the element, the more energy required to produce it. Stellar fusion of the heavier elements is powered by

---

imbalance, such that after all the annihilation events there was left a great deal of matter.

[9] This has been established by examination of absorption lines in the spectra of interstellar molecular clouds. For an account of the formation of water ice in the interstellar medium, see N. Miyauchi et al., "Formation of hydrogen peroxide and water from the reaction of cold hydrogen atoms with solid oxygen at 10 K," *Chemical Physics Letters* 456, no. 1–3, (April 2008): 27–30. https://doi.org/10.1016/j.cplett.2008.02.095. More recent research suggests that water in the gaseous phase may have also been formed very early on. See Tel Aviv University, "Water was plentiful in the early universe," *Phys.org*, May 13, 2015, https://phys.org/news/2015-05-plentiful-early-universe.html.

the energy liberated when the star begins to collapse late in the stage of its evolution. In ordinary stars, which fade away rather than dying spectacularly as novae or supernovae, the end product of this process is iron. Something more violent is required to get past the energy barrier that makes iron stable. This violence may be the explosion of a supernova. The heavier elements can be forged in these explosions and also spread far and wide around the remnant of the exploded star. It is now also thought that some of the heavy elements may be formed in the recurring eruptions of binary star systems in which one star is consuming matter from the other. This is called a nova. Now it took a long time for all these things to happen. Only after the birth and death of several generations of stars would there be enough of these elements floating around to allow for a planet like Earth.

Part Two: Our Solar System

A newly-forming star is typically surrounded by a disk of gas and dust not close enough to the center of attraction to be drawn in, but close enough to rotate about it. From this leftover material planets can be formed, along with smaller objects such as moons, asteroids and comets. At the center of the cloud of interstellar gas and dust that was to become our Solar System was a dense concentration of matter which grew ever greater as it attracted more and more matter to itself by its gravity. There may have been more than one such concentration. Some think that Jupiter and Saturn started to form in the same way as the Sun and only failed to become stars because they did not accumulate enough mass. This is suggested by the fact that their chemical composition is very like the Sun's. Elsewhere in the galaxy, many of the interstellar clouds formed two or even more stars in orbit about one another. Binary and other multiple stars are very common. The nearest star, Alpha Centauri, is a triple. Jupiter is almost massive enough to have become a star. The key to becoming a star rather than just a large planet is that the precursor have enough mass to generate enough heat when it collapses in on itself to start a nuclear reaction in its interior. Jupiter falls a little short of this threshold.

The matter not used up in forming the Sun, Jupiter and Saturn was available for the making of other inhabitants of the Solar System. The formation of these planets seems to have occurred in several stages. The first was the condensing of solid grains out of smaller particles; next came the aggregation of grains into large bodies called planetesimals; finally, there was the building up of even larger bodies by collision of planetesimals; these were the proto-planets, which evolved into the planets as we know them today. The process I have outlined is consistent with classical mechanics, and it is studied in detail by computer modeling.

The nebula from which the Sun and planets formed was rotating, which is typical of celestial bodies of all sorts. A rotating object has what is called angular momentum and, like linear momentum, it is a conserved quantity. The consistent pattern of rotation seen in the Sun and planets is a result of this original rotation. As the interstellar cloud began to collapse under its own gravity, it began to spin faster and faster. A collapsing body tends to flatten. Even the Earth bulges at the equator and is flattened at the poles. Loosely organized matter flattens out without the constraint of solidity, and so the cloud which was the proto-Solar System flattened into a disk. This is the reason why the planets, for the most part, orbit the Sun in nearly the same plane. The exceptions presumably resulted from near encounters or collisions with other bodies, with which they shared some of their angular momentum. The history of the Solar System has been a complex and often violent affair. This is likely to be true of other planetary systems as well, and it is quite possible that not all planets move in the same orbit in which they were formed.

Most of the collapsing matter went into the central body, since there the gravitational force is strongest, but most of the angular momentum of the original cloud now belongs to the planets, especially to Jupiter and Saturn. This fact requires explanation, since basic dynamics alone would not predict it.[10] Possible explanations are that that most of the Sun's angular momentum was transferred outward by means of the solar wind or by its strong magnetic field, which may have served as a brake on the Sun's rotation. However it came about, the Earth's year, long but not too long, together with the tilt of its axis to the plane of its orbit, allows for a succession of seasons. This is one of many factors that contribute to the flourishing of life as we know it.

The location of a planet relative to its star is a crucial factor in determining its properties. As we shall see, not all stars are alike, so the fact that the gas and ice giants in the Solar System lie far from the Sun does not imply that this will be the case for all stars. I will say more about this later. The character of a given planet depends in part on the temperature of the region in which it forms, but also on the chemical composition of the environment in which it forms. Unlike the temperature at various distances from the star, which is easy to compute, the chemical environment is not

---

[10] For a very interesting discussion of this issue, as it applies to the Solar System and to exo-planetary systems, see Stacy Ann Irwin, "Analysis of Angular Momentum in Planetary Systems and Host Stars" (PhD diss., Florida Institute of Technology, 2015).

predictable by theory but must be determined by observations on a case by case basis.

A fundamental concept of exobiology is that of the habitable zone around a planet. This has been defined as the region of space where it is possible for water to exist in liquid form. We have already seen that water is common in the universe, and it has been detected in many places in the Solar System. For the water to exist in liquid form requires, of course, that it be within a narrow range of temperature, from 0 to 100 degrees Celsius. Given the temperature and size of a star, it is easy to locate its habitable zone. For the Sun, the habitable zone as defined above includes only the Earth, though it is possible that Mars once occupied this zone. The notion of the habitable zone needs to be broadened if we take into account the so-called extremophiles, microbial life which has been discovered to exist on Earth in extreme environments. It is possible that this kind of life might exist on Venus or Mars or elsewhere. But if we are interested in more complex forms of life, the original definition will serve.

There are also habitable and uninhabitable zones in our galaxy. There are for example regions where space is continually being bombarded with ionizing radiation. Our location out in one of the spiral arms makes us relatively safe from this. As long as no supernova or other extremely violent event happens near us, we do not have to worry so much about the surface of the Earth being sterilized by such radiation.[11] There will also be times in the history of the universe not suited to the presence of life, as when not enough of the elements needed to support biology existed. Again, we are fortunate to be orbiting a star formed after at least a few earlier generations.

Let's take a closer look now at the planets in the Solar System, with a view to understanding some of the possibilities for the properties of planets orbiting other stars. First, a definition: the Solar System is the collection of objects whose motions are primarily governed by the gravitational field of our star, the Sun. It has denizens of various sorts, notably planets, moons, asteroids and comets, but also dust and gases of various kinds. The number of planets has varied as the criteria for planet-hood have changed from time to time, but the current number is eight, with Pluto put into the newly invented category of "Dwarf Planet."[12] I bring this up to show that there is some arbitrariness in the definition of a planet. One necessary criterion, however, is that it orbit the Sun directly and not some other body in the Solar

---

[11] If we assume that we keep intact our ozone layer, that is, since it provides us with a great deal of protection.

[12] It was after the discovery of another body much like Pluto in the Kuiper Belt (a region similar to the asteroid belt out past the orbit of Neptune) that led to the invention of this new category.

System. It must be large enough to be spherical and massive enough to have swept its orbit clear of other bodies. Pluto fails this last requirement.

The Sun's planets may be divided into two groups, the rocky worlds called terrestrial planets, and the giants. There are two subgroups of the latter, gas giants and ice giants. Terrestrial planets are relatively small and they may or may not have atmospheres. They may or may not have moons orbiting them, but if they do, they are few. In the Solar System the terrestrial planets are Mercury, Venus, Earth, and Mars. Mercury is a small planet with a density that suggests it has a greater proportion of metals than other terrestrial planets. In some ways, Mercury is similar to our Moon, though of course it is much hotter on its sunward side, and whereas the Moon's rotation period is the same as its orbital period, so that it keeps the same face to the Earth, Mercury's periods are in resonance with a two to one ratio. This means that its solar day is twice the length of its orbital period. Its day is long and hot and its night long and cold. It seems to have a very thin atmosphere and a weak magnetic field., and in this way it differs from the Moon. Why it has either is not well understood. Mercury has no moon. Venus is about the same size as the Earth but, being closer to the Sun, is much hotter. It is too hot to have liquid water, and its surface is known to be dry. It has an atmosphere composed mostly of carbon dioxide. It has a cratered surface, like Mercury and the Moon, and it has a history of volcanic eruptions. Venus has no moon. The interior of the planet seems to be similar to Earth's, so it's apparent lack of a magnetic field is puzzling.

Mars is in some ways the most Earth-like of the planets, but not very. Being much smaller, it cannot retain as much atmosphere as the Earth does, though it does have a thin one. The composition of its atmosphere is unlike the Earth's and its interior seems to be different as well. Whether it will prove to have or to have had some kind of simple life is still an open question. Being much father out it is colder than Earth, too cold to be in the habitable zone, but it might have been there once. It does have water in the form of ice, and it once had liquid water flowing on its surface. It has two small moons. Mars has a very weak magnetic field; there are indications of volcanic activity, with some uplifting and faulting. Between Mars and the outer planets we have the asteroid belt, a region of rocky bodies of various sizes which did not coalesce into a planet.

The gas giants, also known as Jovian planets, are Jupiter and Saturn. Uranus and Neptune are the ice giants. The chemical composition of the Jovian planets resembles that of the Sun. Jupiter and Saturn differ from one another in many ways, but what they have in common is a thin atmosphere of light gases such as hydrogen, helium, ammonia and methane, a deep ocean of liquid hydrogen with a layer of metallic liquid hydrogen beneath it, and probably a small rocky core. Of course we have not been able to see beneath the surface, but computer models suggest this structure; the metallic hydrogen would be the source of these planets' significant magnetic fields. The Jovian planets have numerous moons, as well as rings, although only Saturn's rings are easily seen. The rings are made of unconsolidated rocky matter, either material that failed to coalesce into moons or the remnants of moons that have been torn apart.

Uranus and Neptune resemble each other in size and composition, both being considerably smaller, as well as colder, than Jupiter and Saturn. Both have a bluish or greenish color, but Neptune has a more complex appearance than Uranus. Their rocky cores are relatively larger than what we find in the Jovian planets and their atmospheres, composed of molecular hydrogen, are relatively larger. In between the core and the atmosphere is a layer of ice. There are some interesting differences between these two planets. Uranus, for example, is unique in that its axis of rotation lies nearly in the plane of its orbit. This is clearly a sign of some violence done to it in the past. On the other hand, Uranus has a very normal looking set of moons orbiting in its plane of revolution, while Neptune's moons do not share a common plane, suggesting that they are captured objects. Recent studies suggest that Uranus once suffered a grazing collision with a body one to three times the mass of the Earth, while Neptune may have suffered a head-on collision with a similarly sized body.[13] This could account for the fact that Neptune has an internal heat source while Uranus does not. Uranus, but not Neptune, is known to have a magnetic field, but one much weaker than Saturn's. From the sampling of planets in our Solar System with deep gaseous atmospheres, we can get a fair idea of the variety we can expect in such planets.

Finally, there is Pluto. Pluto, demoted by the International Astronomical Union to the status of Dwarf Planet, seems from a distance to be much like other bodies in the outer reaches of the Solar System, though it would be one of the largest of those known. Out there we find planetesimals or small planetary bodies that never had a chance to grow to the size of planets and still farther out a vast reservoir of comets. Since Pluto is so small and so far from Earth, little has been known about it until recently, when the flyby of the New Horizons spacecraft sent back to Earth high resolution photographs of the planet and its moons. Pluto is more complex than anyone had imagined, so much so that one of the principal investigators said that "what the data revealed didn't surprise us. It shocked us."[14] It was already known

[13] Paul Scott Anderson, "Why Neptune and Uranus are different," *EarthSky*, February 9, 2020, https://earthsky.org/space/why-neptune-uranus-different-collisions.
[14] James Green, manager of NASA's solar-system exploration division, as quoted in J. Kelly Beatty,

that the spin axis of Pluto is swung over with respect to its orbital plane by 120°. (Compare this to the Earth's more typical orbital tilt of 23½°) This is one of the signs that something large collided with Pluto sometime in the past. There were also signs of ice on the surface of the planet. New Horizons has confirmed the presence of ices of nitrogen, methane, and carbon monoxide in addition to water ice and has measured their distribution over the surface. The complexity of its icy topography was surprising, but the truly shocking discovery was that Pluto seems to be geologically active. This means that radioactive elements in its core are still releasing heat. Two things we can infer from the example of Pluto is how rich the possibilities are for the characteristics and histories of planets and how difficult it is to know much about them from a distance, even a distance so tiny on the cosmic scale as that from Earth to the limits of the Solar System.

Part Three: Rare Earth

This brings us to our own world, a rocky planet lying in the habitable zone, between Venus and Mars. Being in the habitable zone is a necessary condition for life on Earth, but it is far from being sufficient. Peter Ward and Donald Brownlee, who wrote a very interesting book assessing the probability of complex life, that is to say plants or animals, elsewhere in the galaxy, make a compelling case that such life is likely to be rare.[15]

It would take too long to survey all the features that make planets not only habitable by plants and animals but also such that human life can exist and flourish. I do want to point out some of the more important of these features, since these should be kept in mind when we speculate about the possibility of complex life on other worlds. Most of these are ignored in the more enthusiastic accounts, especially in the popular press. One crucial factor is the chemical composition of the Earth, and this is important in several respects. First, Earth has a sufficient quantity of carbon and other elements needed to support life as we know it. Its most abundant elements, silicon, magnesium and iron, together with their oxidized compounds, provide for its rocky character, and the liquid iron in its core is the source of its magnetic field. Its atmosphere is also intimately involved in living

---

"Pluto's Amazing Story," *Sky & Telescope*, October 2016, 12.

[15] Peter D. Ward and Donald Brownlee, *Rare Earth: Why Complex Like is Uncommon in the Universe* (New York: Springer-Verlag, 2000). This work is the source for details about the features of the Earth and Solar System that are favorable to life, except where elsewhere noted. Ward is Professor of Geological Sciences at the University of Washington, Seattle, and Brownlee is Professor of Astronomy at the same institution.

processes, especially in its balance of oxygen and carbon dioxide which is maintained by animal and plant respiration. Without sufficient mass, Earth would not be able to retain its atmosphere over a long period of time. It has enough water to sustain life while having little enough to allow for large land masses on which many and diverse forms of life can flourish. Just as important but not as obvious is its copious supply of heavy metals in its core, mantle and crust. The radioactive elements generate the heat needed to drive plate tectonics and to make the Earth warmer than it otherwise would be. Besides the roles already mentioned, two metals, iron and copper, play an important role for animals as blood pigments. The richness of the Solar System in heavy metals is very unusual, as recent studies have shown. This is one reason for suspecting that complex life elsewhere is likely to be rare.

If we assume that life took millions of years to evolve on Earth, it is essential that its orbit was stable and that its surface was protected from catastrophic collisions for that period of time. It is thought that collisions with large asteroids or comets caused a number of extinction events, but even worse things seem to have happened to the Earth long ago. According to the currently accepted model, Earth acquired its satellite, the Moon, because of a collision with a Mars-sized body some 3–4 billion years ago. Before the Apollo mission brought back rocks from the lunar surface for scientists to study, it was thought that the Moon either formed by accretion along with the Earth, was captured by the Earth when it came too close, or was spun off from the Earth while our planet was in a molten state. Barbuzano summarizes the evidence in these words:

> Chemically, the Moon looks like what you'd expect after vaporizing Earth material and letting it condense in the vacuum of space. It lacks most of the easily vaporized elements regularly found in meteorites and terrestrial rocks, including water and hydrogen, and has little iron. The oldest rocks on the Moon . . . are almost completely devoid of heavy metals and must have formed after a global event melted the entire Moon, allowing these buoyant rocks to float to the top of a magma ocean and solidify on its surface as the Moon's original frothy crust.[16]

By the mid-1980s this hypothesis became generally accepted, and the hypothetical impactor was given the name Theia. The original way of imagining the impact as a grazing collision has not stood up to further evidence, but it seems agreed that something more of a head-on collision or perhaps a collision with several bodies, brought about the formation of the

---

[16] Javier Barbuzano, "The Moon Mess," *Sky & Telescope*, August 2018, 26.

Moon, and at the same time affected the composition of the Earth, especially by contributing to the iron content of its core.

The fact that we have such a large satellite orbiting our planet is at least helpful and perhaps necessary for the presence of complex life on Earth. One way it contributes is by stabilizing the angle of tilt of the Earth's axis to the plane of the ecliptic. This is important because it causes a consistency in the cycle of the seasons over a long period of time. The tides caused by the Moon also had an important effect on the Earth. In the giant impactor hypothesis, the Moon formed much closer to the Earth than it is now, only about 15,000 miles away. The Earth would have been spinning so fast that the day was only 5 hours long. But because of tidal friction caused by the Moon, our satellite moved outwards and, to conserve angular momentum, the Earth's spin rate would have decreased to the present 24-hour day. It is also possible that the heating caused by the tidal friction due to the nearby Moon contributed to the onset of plate tectonics on Earth.

Why is it important that the Earth have plate tectonics? This phenomenon is responsible for the existence of mountain chains and ocean basins. This topography makes possible the great biodiversity that we have on Earth, by isolating regions from each other long enough for plants and animals to evolve in isolation. Biodiversity is a good counter to mass extinctions. But there is more to the story than that. Ward and Brownlee describe other crucial effects of tectonics.

The turning over of the Earth's crust and mantle is important for maintaining liquid water on the surface of the Earth. Tectonics also plays an important role by helping to keep in check the amount of carbon dioxide in the atmosphere and thus the average temperature of our planet. As Ward and Brownlee explain, "Without plate tectonics, Earth might look much as it did during the first billion and a half years of its existence: a watery world, with only isolated islands dotting its surface. Or it might look even more inimical to life; without continents, we might by now have lost the most important ingredient for life, water, and in doing so come to resemble Venus."[17] But these days we don't need to be reminded about the possibly disastrous effects of the buildup of greenhouse gases in our atmosphere. Finally, tectonics is intimately involved with the production and maintenance of Earth's magnetic field. Without this field to shield us, we would be constantly under attack from lethal cosmic radiation and solar wind, which would degrade our atmosphere, as they have done on Mars.

In many ways Jupiter has a prominent role in the Solar System. Its gravitational influence kept the asteroids in the belt between it and Mars

---

[17] Ward and Brownlee, *Rare Earth*, 194.

from coalescing into a planet and probably prevented Mars from growing to a size more nearly like that of Earth and Venus. It was responsible for clearing the inner Solar System of material leftover from the formation of the planets, and it continues to deflect objects coming near it into paths taking them outward. It has been estimated that if it weren't for the influence of Jupiter, collisions of objects 10 km in diameter with Earth might be 10,000 times as frequent as they now are. The current impact rate is one such collision every 100 million years or so. Ward and Brownlee point out that we are fortunate to have Jupiter and Saturn in our Solar System, but we are also fortunate that they are not much bigger than they are or closer together, and that we don't have a third planet of that size. Computer simulations reveal that, in those scenarios, the planetary system becomes unstable and is torn apart by its largest inhabitants.[18]

I have gone over all too briefly some of the characteristics of Earth that make plant and animal life possible. It is likely that even more special conditions have made possible the increase of human population and the growth of civilizations, most notably conditions favorable to agriculture. Although we must keep an open mind about how living beings might differ from those we know on Earth, a study of what makes life possible and indeed flourishing here must be our starting point, and in some cases we can be sure about conditions that would make biological life impossible. As astronomers, we have nothing to say about the kinds of creatures that are sometimes presented in science fiction, such as Star Trek's Q or its mysterious cloud-like creatures existing in space.

Part Four: Exoplanets

Let us now leave our Solar System behind and look out to see what other planetary systems we can find. Our knowledge of our own star and its planets will provide a template for speculation about other worlds. We will not be able to see or understand what we are seeing out there nearly as well as we can see and understand our own neighborhood. As challenging as it is to fully understand the Solar System, it is much more difficult to know much about other stellar systems. With new data continuing to come in, and with older and newer data being just now analyzed, it is impossible for a lecture or book to be up to date. It will be most useful, then, to concentrate on the tools and techniques available for the search and on the properties of stars that might make them suitable or hostile for the existence of planets and for their possible habitability. I will also summarize some of the results

---

[18] Ward and Brownlee, *Rare Earth*, 240.

of current research. I have cited sources that are readily available to all interested persons, and by consulting the latest issues of these astronomical magazines and websites, one can keep abreast of the latest results, hypotheses and speculations.

Heather Knutson of California Institute of Technology very honestly explains why it is not easy, not perfectly straightforward, for astronomers to understand the ways different kinds of planetary systems can be formed. Results coming from the Kepler space telescope have revealed that some of the planets found by the survey are not acting as they "should", based on the received model of planet formation. This model assumes a simple and orderly progression of cause and effect, neglecting random factors. The data indicate that chance events in the past history of various planetary systems are more important than was once thought:

> It's like saying if you have a dice [*sic*] and roll it only once, that you know everything about the dice. . . . You don't know anything until you roll it a bunch of times, and then you understand that there are six different possible numbers that you can get, and the probability is the same for each. So in a way that's what we are trying to do with exoplanets as well. We're trying to roll the dice a bunch of times [and] see all the possible outcomes, so that we can understand which things are more likely and less likely, and then develop stories to explain the different routes that you can go down in forming planets.[19]

The first step in the process is the discovery of these planets, and the next is the attempt to determine their properties. As one might suspect, our indications of the existence of planets orbiting a star are almost always indirect. There are three methods which have been used to search for planets orbiting other stars. The first is direct imaging. Just as astronomers can simulate a solar eclipse by blocking the light of the Sun's disk, so they can block the light from a star to see what may lie near it. To detect a planet in this way requires that it be distant from its star and bright enough to stand out against the background light. This method favors planets in distant orbits about stars near us. Relatively few planets will be detectable by this method.

Another technique is to measure changes in the velocity of a star directly towards or away from us. This is done by looking at the way lines in the spectrum of the star shift their frequency with time. This is the visual equivalent of the Doppler effect for sound, the changing in pitch of a siren, for example, as an ambulance speeds first towards you and then away. In

---

[19] Heather Knudson, quoted in Shannon Hall, "The Secrets of Super-Earths," *Sky & Telescope*, March 2017, 27.

the case of light, a red-shift of the spectral lines indicates motion away while a blue-shift indicates motion towards the observer. The red- or blue-shift of a star is easily detected. Any body orbiting the star will cause it to periodically speed up and slow down in the direction of the line of sight and if the effect is great enough, this will reveal its presence in the star's spectrum. Some stars have been discovered to have a companion star in this way. The more massive the orbiting body and the closer it is to its star, the stronger the effect. This method is therefore not very useful in looking for roughly Earth-sized bodies or for planets in orbits far from their stars. Rather, it favors the detection of Jupiter- or Neptune-like bodies orbiting close to their stars.

A third method is able to detect planets more like the Earth, although only those relatively close to their stars are likely to show up this way. This is the transit method. If our line of sight to the star passes through the orbital plane of the exoplanet, it is possible to detect dips in the amount of light coming from the star as the planet passes in front of it. Transits caused by the passage of Mercury or Venus between us and the Sun happen from time to time, though not often; you may have heard about or seen the transit of Mercury which recently occurred. Since these transits are rare, it is important to look at a lot of stars and then use statistical methods to infer how many planets of a given sort exist from the number of those detected. The two missions launched by NASA to look for exoplanets using the transit method were Kepler and TESS. The Kepler Mission was launched in 2009 on a nine-year mission; its primary mission was to survey a limited region of the sky for exoplanets. This search was not limited to stars near the Earth. Before the mission was over, Kepler had examined about half a million stars, with over 150,000 monitored for planetary transits.[20]

The second and more extensive planet-hunting satellite is TESS, which is short for Transiting Exoplanet Survey Satellite. TESS was launched into orbit on April 18, 2018, and its mission continues. Unlike Kepler, Tess will survey the whole sky but only for bright nearby stars. Stars with planets that look interesting will be singled out with a view to future follow-up studies using other techniques, such as the radial velocity method. By combining the results of different studies, a more complete picture of these planets can be formed.

A fourth method should be mentioned, the use of computer simulations. This is a method astronomers use to test hypotheses about how objects or groups of objects may change with time. Observational data can be subject

---

[20] David Dickenson, "The Kepler Space Telescope Comes to an End," *Sky & Telescope*, February 2019, 12.

to various conditions and constraints and allowed to evolve under the action of known forces and interactions. In this era of "big data" and fast super-computers, this has become a valuable tool for astronomers.

The most important member of a planetary system is its star. The nature of the star, its own life history and the region of the galaxy where it is found, has a decisive effect on the possibilities for the planets that surround it. The literature about exoplanets assumes a basic knowledge of stars, so it will be good to say a little about them before going on to planets. There is a taxonomy of stars just as there is of plants and animals. The most useful depiction of various classes of stars (which unlike plants and animals are designated by letters and numbers rather than by names) is the Hertzsprung-Russell, or H-R Diagram. This diagram shows that stars fall into distinct groups based upon their luminosity, that is, their absolute brightness, and their temperature. The luminosity is a measure of the energy output of the star. The temperature is often represented by what is called the spectral class, a description of the star in terms of some of the features of its spectrum. The spectral classes are designated by the letters OBAFGKM.[21] The spectral type is correlated with the temperature of the star and so is often used as the horizontal axis of the diagram.[22] The hottest stars are class O and the coolest are class M. The literature on exoplanets makes use of this classification in discussing what kind of stars are most likely to have habitable planets.

Stars are not distributed randomly over the H-R Diagram but form distinct patterns. Most stars fall along what is called the main sequence, a belt running from the upper left of the diagram (luminous and hot) to the lower right (less luminous and cooler.) Below the main sequence are the white dwarfs stars, while the lower end of the main sequence contains the red dwarf stars. The fact that the dwarfs appear in different parts of the diagram indicates different stages in the life history of stars. The place of a star on the H-R diagram is not fixed. A star evolves, or to speak more accurately it ages, and so its place on the diagram changes with time. Not all kinds of stars go through the same changes. What happens to the star as it ages depends upon its mass, for this determines the kinds and rates of nuclear reactions that go on within it. A red dwarf, for example, has relatively low mass, just enough to stoke the nuclear fires. That is why it is

---

[21] There is of course a reason for these odd designations, which were given when the various kinds of stars were not sorted out very well. The student quickly learns (or used to learn) them using the mnemonic, "O be a fine girl (or guy), kiss me."

[22] I am glossing over many details. The temperature may be represented by the color index, which is the difference of temperature measured at two reference frequencies. Depictions of the diagram are readily found on the Internet.

relatively cool and red in color. Its history as a star ends in an unspectacular way when it runs out of fuel. A white dwarf, on the other hand, represents an advanced stage of a massive star that has blown off much of its mass and has collapsed down into a small but very hot star. Above the main sequence are the giant and supergiant stars. Their temperature and luminosity vary, in accordance with their initial mass and where they are in the aging process.

The Sun falls into class G on the main sequence and is often referred to as a yellow dwarf. It is sometimes said that our Sun is an average star because of its position in the middle of the H-R diagram, but this claim is misleading. If we consider the number of stars in each category, we see that our Sun is far from average. Its mass, though much less than that of the heaviest stars, is well above the median. Of the 200 billion stars in our galaxy, about 10% resemble the Sun. Not surprisingly, these have been of special interest to planetary researchers. Notwithstanding the fact that the one inhabited planet we know of orbits the Sun, concentrating on Sun-like stars is problematic, and not only because they are uncommon. One of Kepler's secondary missions has some relevance to the problem of potentially habitable exo-planets about Sun-like stars, as well as to the possible future history of the Earth. Shannon Hall gives a sobering picture, not only with regard to other planetary systems but even with regard to our own:

> Because astronomers can use Kepler to glean a star's mass, size and age, they can then cherry-pick the stars that look exactly like the Sun in order to study how they behave. The results have been unnerving. Although our Sun has a relatively quiet life . . . some of the Sun-like stars imaged with Kepler are anything but peaceful. Instead, they emit *superflares*—giant blasts of radiation that are up to 10,000 times stronger than the strongest flares we've seen on the Sun.[23]

In 1859 a great flare erupted on the Sun, giving rise to auroras visible as far south as the Caribbean. It is estimated that it also destroyed about 5% of Earth's ozone layer. If such a flare were to occur today, it would knock out power grids all over the Earth and cause untold economic and social damage. A flare thousands of times more intense would no doubt produce mass extinctions. So stars like the Sun may not be the best candidates for having habitable planets.

Current research centers on stars that are more common than the Sun. A focus of interest has been the red dwarf, or dwarf M-class stars, since these

---

[23] Shannon Hall, "Kepler's Unknown Legacy," *Sky & Telescope*, January 2018, 24–25.

are the most common in our galaxy. Of the 52 known stars that lie within 5 parsecs (16.3 light years) of the Sun, 50 are red dwarfs. These stars are much smaller and much less massive than the Sun, and as a result, their habitable zones are much closer in. Many of the exoplanets that have been discovered revolve around red dwarfs. Among systems of particular interest, as being relatively close to us and thus good candidates for more detailed study, are Proxima Centauri, the closest star to the Sun, and Trappist-1, which is known to have several planets circling it. Red dwarf stars pose clear difficulties (for example, they are given to emitting strong flares) but also possible advantages for life.[24] More recently, interest has shifted towards orange dwarfs, the K class stars which lie between red and yellow dwarfs in mass and temperature.[25]

The final catalogue released by the Kepler team contains 4,034 possible exoplanets, and of these 2,335 have been confirmed. Of these, 50 are suspected to be nearly Earth-size and orbit in their star's habitable zone, and of these 30 have been verified.[26] This amounts to 1.3% of confirmed cases. Most such planets will be missed by transit observations, since the angle of the line of sight of the planet is not suitable, so there should be many more cases than those detected. But since estimates from this data using computer simulations and statistical analysis range from 1 in 33 stars having such planets to 1 in 2, we can see how difficult it is to draw clear conclusions.[27] We must also keep in mind that being in the habitable zone is only a very rough way of finding candidates for living worlds. It is a little like saying that a substance which is yellow and solid at room temperature might be gold. It is much better to say that not being in the habitable zone is a contraindication for life than that being in the zone is a reason for optimism.

It is expected that many planetary systems will be detected by the new and still ongoing TESS mission. By selectively observing stars nearer Earth, we can have a better idea of the environment in which they formed. This

---

[24] For a good introduction to this topic, see Igor Pablubski and Aomawa Shields, "Red Dwarf Habitability Recipe," *Sky & Telescope*, August 2019, 34–40.

[25] Anderson, "Why Neptune and Uranus are different."

[26] Shannon Hall, "Kepler Team Releases Final Catalogue," *Sky & Telescope*, October 2017, 10.

[27] See, for example, the study described in Paul Scott Anderson, "Wow! What if 1 in 4 sunlike stars has an earth?," *EarthSky*, August 23, 2019, https://earthsky.org/space/earth-like-exoplanets-orbit-one-in-four-sun-like-stars. Anderson explains that Eric Ford of Penn State wrote a computer program which simulates "universes" of stars and "observes" them to see how many would be discovered by Kepler in each "universe". Based on statistical studies he expects from 1 in 33 to 1 in 2 to have such planets. This is a great example of enthusiasm based on rather sketchy reasoning.

mission will also give astronomers a better list of candidates for further study using other methods. If a planet is found to have an atmosphere, investigation of the composition as well as density of that atmosphere may give clues to whether life might be present. The attempt to isolate what are called biosignatures in this data will be an important part of future studies of these planets. New methods for detecting oxygen in planetary atmospheres, for example, will allow the James Webb telescope to examine some of the dwarfs within 5 parsecs to see if oxygen can be detected.[28] The James Webb telescope is scheduled to be launched some time in 2121. Although an excess of oxygen would be harmful to life, the presence of a lesser amount in the atmosphere might be a sign that the planet is inhabited. It is difficult to rule out non-biological sources for the oxygen in a planetary atmosphere, but there may well be cases where the biological explanation is the most likely.

The study of exoplanet atmospheres is in its infancy. For now, what can be established with most confidence is the size and mass of an exoplanet, and its distance from its star. Since the planet's density can be calculated from its size and mass, astronomers can conjecture whether it is mostly rocky or mostly gaseous. Most of the exoplanets that have been confirmed fall in size somewhere between Earth and Neptune.[29] Neptune has nearly 4 times the diameter of Earth and is approximately 17 times more massive. At first the planets falling into this category were lumped together as "super-Earths," suggesting that they might be Earth-like. After Kepler, it was realized that these planets apparently fall into two subgroups, with a gap between 1.75–2 Earth diameters and 2–4 Earth diameters.[30] The larger planets were dubbed "mini-Neptunes" and the smaller ones retain the name "super-Earths." Of these, the mini-Neptunes seem to be the more common. Taken together, mini-Neptunes and super-Earths appear to be the most common kind of planet in our galaxy.[31] It is interesting that the Solar System

---

[28] Paul Scott Anderson, "A new way to detect oxygen in exoplanet atmospheres," *EarthSky*, January 17, 2020, https://earthsky.org/space/new-technique-oxygen-exoplanet-atmospheres-jwst.

[29] About one in three systems with planets discovered by Kepler fall into this range. In comparison, only one in every 50 planetary systems has a planet the size of Jupiter or Saturn (Hall, "The Secrets of Super-Earths," 28).

[30] Hall, "The Secrets of Super-Earths," 22.

[31] Sara Seager, "TESS: The Transiting Exoplanet Hunter," *Sky & Telescope,* March 2018, 27. We should remember though that these are among the planets most likely to be found by our methods. See also the informative summary of some of the latest results of studies of these intermediate planets in the article on the Planetary Society's website: Hannah Wakeford, "The Skies of Mini-Neptunes: Sniffing the

does not have one. Super-Earths are of great interest to those who hope to find life on other worlds, but it is far from true that being a super-Earth makes a planet a good candidate for being habitable. Planets larger than two times the diameter of the Earth are probably not habitable, at least by life as we understand it. This rules out the mini-Neptunes as good candidates for life. The diameter and mass of a planet is only one small part of the story. Astronomers hope that the James Webb telescope will help them to understand more about both super-Earths and mini-Neptunes.

In conclusion, the study of exoplanets is off to a good start but there is much more left to do. So far, no star like the Sun has been found with a system of planets like that which we inhabit. Although there may be others like ours, the evidence suggests they will not be common. On the other hand, there is reason to think that some may well be suitable for habitation by at least primitive forms of life. The search should and will continue, but science is not well served by exaggerations and by overly active imaginations driven by hopes that we are not alone.

Air of Other Worlds to Learn How Planets Formed and Evolved," *The Planetary Report*, March 2019, https://www.planetary.org/articles/the-skies-of-mini-neptunes.

CHAPTER THREE

LIMITATIONS OF LIFE CONSIDERED: THE LIKELIHOOD OF COMPLEX MULTICELLULAR LIFE ON EARTH-LIKE EXOPLANETS[1]

ALAN VINCELETTE

Astronomers have now detected thousands of exoplanets, a few of which even occur in the habitable zone and are candidates for life.[2] There have also been suggestions of planetary atmospheres and water on exoplanets.[3] As technology improves and more searches are undertaken this number is sure to increase exponentially. We also know that some developing stars contain a broth of complex organic molecules, the fundamental ingredients of life.[4] We don't fully understand the process of the origin of life yet and so don't have a grasp of how easily life might originate on these exoplanets. But there certainly is a possibility of unicellular life occurring if not

---

[1] I would like to thank the various biologists and geologists who served as my mentors and teachers in the past, all of whom have contributed to these debates with their research: Joel Cracraft, Michael Woodburne, David Reznick, and Mary Droser.

[2] NASA lists over 4000 exoplanet discoveries at the moment, around twenty of which are rocky and located in the habitable zone ("Exoplanet Exploration: Planets Beyond Our Solar System," *NASA*, accessed March 21, 2020 at https://exoplanets. nasa.gov/; "Habitable Exoplanets Catalog," *Planetary Habitability Laboratory*, accessed March 21, 2020 at http://phl.upr.edu/projects/habitable-exoplanets-catalog).

[3] One recent study reports evidence of water on an exoplanet in the habitable zone (Angelo Tsiaras, et al., "Water Vapour in the Atmosphere of the Habitable-Zone Eight-Earth-Mass Planet K2-18 b," *Nature Astronomy* 3, no. 12 (2019): 1086–1091. Detailed information, however, will likely have to wait until the launch of planned telescopes such as LUVOIR or HabEx that can detect various biosignatures in the decades to come.

[4] See Karin I. Öberg, et al., "The Comet-Like Composition of a Protoplanetary Disk as Revealed by Complex Cyanides," *Nature* 520, no. 7546 (2015): 198–201.

multicellular.[5] If multicellular life evolves on exoplanets we can anticipate it would also involve some of the evolutionary processes we observe on Earth. Hence there is a possibility of the evolution of quite complex and highly evolved creatures. This paper will accordingly speculate on how likely it is that life will occur on other planets and will take similar forms to those found on Earth.

Convergent Evolution in Plants, Invertebrates, and Lower Vertebrates

There has been an ongoing debate in biology about the degree to which evolution has a directionality, or at least predictability. Defenders of the predictability of evolution advocate for their position on the basis of the tendency for evolution independently to achieve similar morphological forms (i.e. for what is called convergent evolution, evolution of analogues, or homoplasy).[6] For there are a limited number of environmental realms and

---

[5] Some scientists have argued multicellular life will be relatively rare elsewhere in the cosmos. For example, see Peter D. Ward and Donald Brownlee, *Rare Earth: Why Complex Life is Uncommon in the Universe* (New York: Copernicus, 2003); Simon Conway Morris, *Life's Solution: Inevitable Humans in a Lonely Universe* (Cambridge: Cambridge University Press, 2004); John Gribbin, *Alone in the Universe: Why Our Planet Is Unique* (Hoboken: Wiley, 2011); David Waltham, *Lucky Planet* (New York: Basic Books, 2013); Hugh Ross, *Improbable Planet: How Earth Became Humanity's Home* (Grand Rapids: Baker Books, 2016).
Others are more optimistic, including Julian Chela-Flores, *The New Science of Astrobiology: From Genesis of the Living Cell to Evolution of Intelligent Behavior in the Universe* (Dordrecht: Kluwer, 2001); Christian de Duve, *Life Evolving: Molecules, Mind, and Meaning* (Oxford: Oxford University Press, 2002); Giancarlon Genta, *Lonely Minds in the Universe* (New York: Copernicus Books, 2007); Athena Coustenis and Thérèse Encrenaz, *Life Beyond Earth: The Search for Habitable Worlds in the Universe* (Cambridge: Cambridge University Press, 2013); Jeffrey Bennett and Seth Shostak, *Life in the Universe* (London: Pearson, 2016); Jeff Zweerink, *Is There Life Out There?: A Christian Astrophysicist Answers Common Questions about the Search for Life-Friendly Planets* (Covina: RTB Press, 2017).
[6] Michael J. Sanderson and Larry Hufford, eds., *Homoplasy: The Recurrence of Similarity in Evolution* (London: Academic Press, 1996); Conway Morris, *Life's Solution*; Jeff Arendt and David N. Reznick, "Convergence and Parallelism Reconsidered: What Have We Learned about the Genetics of Adaptation?," *Trends in Ecology and Evolution* 23 (2008): 26–32; Simon Conway Morris, ed., *The Deep Structure of Biology: Is Convergence Sufficiently Ubiquitous to Give a Directional Signal* (West Conshohocken: Templeton Foundation Press, 2008); George R. McGhee, Jr., *Convergent Evolution: Limited Forms Most Beautiful* (Cambridge: M.I.T. Press, 2011); Kevin Arbuckle, Cheryl M. Bennett, and Michael P. Speed, "A

hence a likelihood of organisms taking on similar adaptations to similar environmental biomes and niches. So subterranean creatures tend to reduce their optical adaptations and limb structure and emphasize digging adaptations, land animals tend to develop adaptations for walking and running (cursorial) or climbing trees (arboreal), water-dwelling animals tend to develop fins, webbing, paddle-like structures, or a form of jet propulsion, and creatures that live in the air tend to develop wings. Paralleling this there are limited sources of nutrition and modes of gustation, and so animals tend to develop similar adaptations for herbivory, carnivory, omnivory, filter-feeding, etc. Indeed it has become more and more clear that any trait that is highly-adapted for and closely-linked to a particular way of life is a poor candidate for phylogenetic systematics as it may have independently arisen in different lineages and not be reflective of common descent. Rather most useful for phylogenetic classification schemes are shared features and basic body traits that are independent of lifestyle or adaptable to a multitude of lifestyles.

As a matter of fact, we find a great, one might say astonishing, degree of convergent evolution in fossil and living creatures. Plant species that occupy a desert biome converge on a succulent body-type with the development of hardened and thickened stems, and a thinning and hardening of leaves into spines, such as with the families Euphorbiaceae and Asphodelaceae of South Africa and Cactaceae of North America.[7] The pitcher plant trap has also

---

Simple Measure of the Strength of Convergent Evolution," *Methods in Ecology and Evolution* 5, no. 7 (2014): 685–693; Simon Conway Morris, *The Runes of Evolution: How the Universe became Self-Aware* (West Conshohocken: Templeton Foundation Press, 2015); C. Tristan Stayton, "The Definition, Recognition, and Interpretation of Convergent Evolution, and Two New Measures for Quantifying and Assessing the Significance of Convergence," *Evolution* 69, no. 8 (2015): 2140–2153; Pierre Pontarotti, ed., *Evolutionary Biology: Convergent Evolution, Evolution of Complex Traits, Concepts and Methods* (Dordrecht: Springer, 2016); Anurag A. Agrawal, "Toward a Predictive Framework for Convergent Evolution: Integrating Natural History, Genetic Mechanisms, and Consequences for the Diversity of Life," *American Naturalist* 190 (2017): 1–12; Kristin M. Lee and Graham Coop, "Population Genomics Perspectives on Convergent Adaptation," *Philosophical Transactions of The Royal Society B: Biological Sciences* 374, no. 1777 (2019): 20180236; George R. McGhee, Jr., *Convergent Evolution on Earth: Lessons for the Search for Extraterrestrial Life* (Cambridge: M.I.T. Press, 2019); Russell Powell, *Contingency and Convergence: Toward a Cosmic Biology of Body and Mind* (Harvard: MIT Press, 2020).

[7] Gordon H. Orians and Otto T. Solbrig, eds., *Convergent Evolution in Warm Deserts: An Examination of Strategies and Patterns in Deserts of Argentina and the United States* (Stroudsburg: Dowden, Hutchinson, and Ross, 1977); R. M. Cowling and B. M. Campbell, "Convergence in Vegetation Structure in the Mediterranean

evolved independently in the carnivorous plant families Nepenthaceae and Sarraceniaceae.[8] Similar pollen and seed-dispersal mechanisms have also evolved independently in different plant families, such as nectar-filled tubular structures for dispersal of pollen by insects or birds in Orchidaceae, Ranunculaceae, and Tropaeolaceae, or plumed seeds for wind dispersal in Apocynaceae and Asteraceae.[9]

Within invertebrate lines, both bees [Superfamily Apoidea of the Order Hymenoptera] and flower beetles [Superfamily Meloidea of Order Coleoptera] have converged on long proboscis-shaped mouths for collecting nectar from flowers.[10] Pill bugs [Family Armadillidiidae of Order Isopoda] and pill millipedes [Order Glomerida] have independently evolved the same defensive system consisting of multi-segmented armored body-plates and the ability to roll up into a ball.[11] And the mantis body form consisting of an elongated body, a long prehensile neck, and large raptorial forelimbs, has evolved in true praying mantises [Order Mantodea] as well as in mantidflies

---

Communities of California, Chile and South Africa," *Vegetatio* 43 (1980): 191–197; R. M. Cowling and E. T. F. Witkowski, "Convergence and Non-Convergence of Plant Traits in Climatically and Edaphically Matched Sites in Mediterranean Australia and South Africa," *Animal Ecology* 19, no. 2 (1994): 220–232; Leonardo O. Alvarado-Cárdenas, et al., "To Converge or Not to Converge in Environmental Space: Testing for Similar Environments Between Analogous Succulent Plants of North American and Africa," *Annals of Botany* 111, no. 6 (2013): 1125–1138.

[8] Aaron M. Ellison and Nicholas J. Gotelli, "Energetics and the Evolution of Carnivorous Plants: Darwin's 'Most Wonderful Plants in the World'," *Journal of Experimental Botany* 60, no. 1 (2009): 19–42; Chris J. Thorogood, Ulrike Bauer, and Simon J. Hiscock, "Convergent and Divergent Evolution in Carnivorous Pitcher Plant Traps," *New Phytologist* 217, no. 3 (2018): 1035–1041.

[9] See McGhee, *Convergent Evolution*, 115–134, as well as: Karl J. Niklas, "Convergence and Divergence," *The Evolutionary Biology of Plants* (Chicago: University of Chicago Press, 1997), 303–348; Andrea Bennici, "Convergent Evolution in Plants," *Rivista di Biologia* 96, no. 3 (2003): 485–489; Anthony Trewavas, "Convergent Evolution Is Common in Plant Systems," *Plant Behaviour and Intelligence* (Oxford: Oxford University Press, 2014), 53–64.

[10] Harald W. Krenn, John D. Plant, and Nikolaus U. Szucsich, "Mouthparts of Flower-Visiting Insects," *Arthropod Structure and Development* 34, no. 1 (2005): 1–40; Andreas P. Wilhelmi and Harald W. Krenn, "Elongated Mouthparts of Nectar-Feeding Meloidae (Coleoptera)," *Zoomorphology* 131, no. 4 (2012): 325–337.

[11] Jan Philip Oeyen and Thomas Wesener, "A First Phylogenetic Analysis of the Pill Millipedes of the Order Glomerida, with a Special Assessment of Mandible Characters (Myriapoda, Diplopoda, Pentazonia)," *Arthropod Structure and Development* 47, no. 2 (2018): 214–228.

[Family Mantispidae of Order Neuroptera].[12] Finally in gastropods the limpet coned shell structure has evolved in parallel in true limpets [Family Patellidae], pulmonated false limpets [Family Siphonariidae], and freshwater limpets [Family Planorbidae].[13]

When we come to the lower vertebrates, we find stark examples of convergent evolution in fish, amphibians, reptiles, and birds. Benthic and burrowing fish including gobies [Order Gobiiformes of Class Actinopterygii], lampsuckers [Order Scorpaeniformes], and sand eels [Order Trachiniformes of Class Actinopterygii] have independently evolved elongated bodies and dorsal fins,[14] whereas other bottom-dwelling and burrowing fish have converged on a form with flattened bodies and elongated pectoral fins as with stingrays [Order Myliobatiformes of Class Chondrichthyes], skates [Order Rajiiformes of Class Chondrichthyes], rhananid placoderms [Order Rhenanida of Class Placodermi], and to a degree in the diplocaulid lepospondyl amphibians [Order Nectridea].[15] Cichlids [Order Cichliformes of Class Actinopterygii] and sunfish [Family Centrarchidae of Order Perciformes of Class Actinopterygii] likewise have converged on compressiform bodies that are flattened horizontally.[16] Carnivorous fishes, like sawfishes [Family Pristidae or Order Rhinopristiformes of Class Chondrichtyes] and sawsharks [Family Pristiophoridae of Order Pristiophoriformes of Class Chondrichthyes] independently evolved an

---

[12] Kurt E. Redborg, "Biology of the Mantispidae," *Annual Review of Entomology* 43 (1998): 175–194.

[13] Geerat J. Vermeu, "The Limpet Form in Gastropods: Evolution, Distribution, and Implications for the Comparative Study of History," *Biological Journal of the Linnean Society* 120 (2017): 22–37. For more examples of convergent evolution in invertebrates see Janet Moore and Pat Willmer, "Convergent Evolution in Invertebrates," *Biological Reviews of the Cambridge Philosophical Society* 72, no. 1 (1997): 1–60.

[14] Kirk Winemiller, "Ecomorphological Diversification in Lowland Freshwater Fish Assemblages from Five Biotic Regions," *Ecological Monographs* 61, no. 4 (1991): 343–464.

[15] Neil C. Aschliman, et al., "Body Plan Convergence in the Evolution of Skates and Rays (Chondrichthyes: Batoidea)," *Molecular Phylogenetics and Evolution* 63, no. 1 (2012): 28–42.

[16] Carmen G. Montaña and Kirk O. Winemiller, "Evolutionary Convergence in Neotropical Cichlids and Nearctic Centrarchids: Evidence from Morphology, Diet, and Stable Isotope Analysis," *Biological Journal of the Linnean Society* 109 (2013): 146–164.

elongated rostrum for capturing prey and a fusiform body shape.[17] And the elongated and mostly finless eel form has evolved independently in brook lampreys [Order Petromyzontiformes of Class Cephalaspidomorphi], neotropical swamp eels [Order Synbranchiformes of Class Actinopterygii], and true eels [Order Anguilliformes of Class Actinopterygii].[18] Similarly, the streamlined fast-swimming forms of pelagic carnivorous fishes has evolved several times in lamnid sharks [Order Lamniformes of Class Chondrichthyes], ichthyosaurs [Order Ichthyosauria of Class Reptilia], and dolphins [Family Delphinidae of Order Artiodactyla of Class Mammalia].[19] Finally, the convergent adaptive radiations of different lines of African cichlid fishes and glacial stickleback fishes are a much-studied phenomena.[20]

When we come to lower land vertebrates we find a repeated loss of appendages in the legless caecilians [Family Caeciliidae of Clade Apoda of Order Gymnophiona of Class Amphibia], worm lizards [Family Amphisbaenidae of Clade Amphisbaenia of Order Squamata of Class Reptilia], glass and legless lizards [Families Anguidae and Pygopodoidea of Order Squamata of Class Reptilia], and snakes [Suborder Serpentes of Order Squamata of Class Reptilia], each having occurred convergently.[21]

---

[17] Charlie J. Underwood, et al., "*Sclerorhynchus atavus* and the Convergent Evolution of Rostrum-Bearing Chondrichthyans," *Geological Society London Special Publications* 430 (2015): 129–136.

[18] S. Elizabeth Alter, et al., "Molecular Phylogenetics Reveals Convergent Evolution in Lower Congo River Spiny Eels," *BMC Evolutionary Biology* 15 (2015): 1–12.

[19] Rahul Bale, et al., "Convergent Evolution of Mechanically Optimal Locomotion in Aquatic Invertebrates and Vertebrates," *PLoS Biology* 13, no. 4 (2015): e1002123; Maria Chikina, Joseph D. Robinson, and Nathan L. Clark, "Hundreds of Genes Experienced Convergent Shifts in Selective Pressure in Marine Mammals," *Molecular Biology and Evolution* 33, no. 2 (2016): 2182–2192; Theagarten Lingham-Soliar, "Convergence in Thunniform Anatomy in Lamnid Sharks and Jurassic Ichthyosaurs," *Integrative and Comparative Biology* 56, no. 6 (2016): 1323–1336. See also R. Brian Langerhans and Thomas J. DeWitt, "Shared and Unique Features of Evolutionary Diversification," *The American Naturalist* 164, no. 3 (2004): 335-349.

[20] Thomas D. Kocher, et al., "Similar Morphologies of Cichlid Fish in Lakes Tanganyika and Malawi Are Due to Convergence," *Molecular Phylogenetics and Evolution* 2 (1993): 158–165; Howard D. Rundle, et al., "Natural Selection and Parallel Speciation in Sympatric Sticklebacks," *Science* 287, no. 5451 (2000): 306–308; Moritz Muschick, et al., "Convergent Evolution within an Adaptive Radiation of Cichlid Fishes," *Current Biology* 22, no. 24 (2012): 2362–2368; Marco Colombo, et al., "The Ecological and Genetic Basis of Convergent Thick-Lipped Phenotypes in Cichlid Fishes," *Molecular Ecology* 22 (2013): 670–678.

[21] James C. O'Reilly, Dale A. Ritter, and David R. Carrier, "Hydrostatic Locomotion in a Limbless Tetrapod," *Nature* 386, no. 6622 (1997): 269–272; Maureen Kearney

Independent lines of vertebrates have also evolved winged-flight as with pterosaurs [Order Pterosauria of Clade Ornithodira], birds [Class Aves of Clade Avemetatarsalia], and bats [Order Chiroptera of Class Mammalia].[22] For that matter, lizards have independently evolved the ability to glide with wings a number of times as in flying dragons [Genus *Draco* of Family Agamidae of Order Squamata], kuehnosaurids [Family Kuehneosauridae of Order Squamata], *Coelurosauravus* [Family Weigeltisauridae of Order Squamata], *Mecistotrachelos* [Clade Archosauromorpha], as well as *Sharovipteryx* [Family Sharovipterygidae of Order Protorosauria].[23]

In addition to these quite dramatic examples, several other examples of convergence could be cited in vertebrates. Ankylosaurs [Family Ankylosauridae of Order Ornithischia of Clade Dinosauria], armadillos [Family Chlamyphoridae of Order Cingulata of Class Mammalia], and pangolins [Order Pholidota of Class Mammalia] have all independently

---

and Bryan L. Stuart, "Repeated Evolution of Limblessness and Digging Heads in Worm Lizards Revealed by DNA from Old Bones," *Proceedings of the Royal Society of London B: Biological Sciences* 271 (2004): 1677–1684; John J. Wiens, Matthew C. Brandley, and Tod W. Reeder, "Why Does a Trait Evolve Multiple Times within a Clade?: Repeated Evolution of Snakelike Body Form in Squamate Reptiles," *Evolution* 60, no. 1 (2006): 123–141; Matthew C. Brandley, et al., "Rates and Patterns in the Evolution of Snake-Like Body Form in Squamate Reptiles: Evidence for Repeated Re-Evolution of Lost Digits and Long-Term Persistence of Intermediate Body Forms," *Evolution* 62, no. 8 (2008): 2042–2064; Gen Morinaga and Philip Bergmann, "Convergent Body Shapes Have Evolved Via Deterministic and Historically Contingent Pathways in Lerista Lizards," *Biological Journal of the Linnean Society* 121, no. 4 (2017): 858–875; Philip J. Bergmann and Gen Morinaga, "The Convergent Evolution of Snake-Like Forms by Divergent Evolutionary Pathways in Squamate Reptiles," *Evolution* 73, no. 3 (2019): 481–496; Philip J. Bergman et al., "Convergent Evolution of Elongate Forms in Craniates and of Locomotion in Elongate Squamate Reptiles," *Integrative and Comparative Biology* 60 (2020): 190–201.

[22] David E. Alexander, *On the Wing: Insects, Pterosaurs, Birds, Bats and the Evolution of Animal Flight* (Oxford: Oxford University Press, 2015); Georg Glaeser, Hannes F. Paulus, and Werner Nachtigall, *The Evolution of Flight* (Dordrecht: Springer, 2017).

[23] Claudia Luke, "Convergent Evolution of Lizard Toe Fringes," *Biological Journal of the Linnean Society* 27, no. 1 (1986): 1–16; G.L. Dyke, et al., "Flight of Sharovipteryx: The World's First Delta-Winged Glider," *Journal of Evolutionary Biology* 19 (2006): 1040–1043; N.C. Fraser, et al., "A New Gliding Tetrapod (Diapsida: Archosauromorpha) from the Upper Triassic (Carnian) of Virginia," *Journal of Vertebrate Paleontology* 27 (2007): 261–265; J.A. McGuire and R. Dudley, "The Biology of Gliding in Flying Lizards (Genus *Draco*) and their Fossil and Extant Analogs," *Integrative and Comparative Biology* 51, no. 6 (2011): 983–990.

evolved armored body plates, and indeed within the armadillo family the glyptodonts [Subfamily Glyptodontidae] also involved spiked tail clubs resembling those of ankylosaurids.[24] Beaks evolved independently in ceratopsian dinosaurs [Family Ceratopsidae of Order Ornithischia of Clade Dinosauria] and birds [Class Aves], as did bills on hadrosaurian dinosaurs [Family Hadrosauridae of Order Ornithischia of Clade Dinosauria], ducks [Family Anatidae of Order Anseriformes of Class Aves], and the platypus [Family Ornithorhynchidae of Order Monotremata of Class Mammalia], the similarities reflected in the Latin classificatory names. Reptiles have also converged on the crocodilian form more than once, namely, in crocodiles proper [Order Crocodilia of Class Reptilia], phytosaurs [Order Phytosauria of Class Reptilia], champsosaurs [Family Champsosauridae of Order Choristodera of Class Suropsida], eosuchians [Family Tangasauridae of Class Reptilia], mesosaurs [Family Mesosauridae of Order Mesosauria], and archegosaurian amphibians [Family Archegosauridae of Order Temnospondyli of Class Amphibia].[25] Finally the convergent adaptive radition of anolis lizards has been much-publicized.[26]

Within avian evolution [Class Aves] an argument has recently been made that convergent evolution has occurred among the large flightless cursorial species such as ostriches [Order Struthioniformes], emus [Order Casuariiformes], rheas [Order Rheiformes], eogruids [Family Eogruidae

---

[24] Victoria M. Arbour and Philip J. Currie, "Ankylosaurid Dinosaur Tail Clubs Evolved through Stepwise Acquisition of Key Features," *Journal of Anatomy* 227, no. 4 (2015): 514–523; Frédéric Delsuc et al., "The Phylogenetic Affinities of the Extinct Glyptodonts," *Current Biology* 26, no. 4 (2016): R155–R156; Victoria M. Arbour and Lindsay E. Zanno, "Tail Weaponry in Ankylosaurs and Glyptodonts: An Example of a Rare but Strongly Convergent Phenotype," *The Anatomical Record* 303, no. 4 (2020): 988–998.

[25] Paul C. Sereno and Andrea B. Arcucci, "The Monophyly of Crurotarsal Archosaurs and the Origin of Bird and Crocodile Ankle Joints," *Neues Jahrbuch für Geologie und Paläontologie* 180 (1990): 21–52; Stephan Lautenschlager and Richard J. Butler, "Neural and Endocranial Anatomy of Triassic Phytosaurian Reptiles and Convergence with Fossil and Modern Crocodylians," *PeerJ* 4, no. 7 (2016): e2251.

[26] Jonathan B. Losos, et al., "Contingency and Determinism in Replicated Adaptive Radiations of Island Lizards," *Science* 279, no. 5359 (1998): 2115–2118; D. Luke Mahler, Travis Ingram, Liam J. Revell, and Jonathan B. Losos, "Exceptional Convergence on the Macroevolutionary Landscape in Island Lizard Radiations," *Science* 341, no. 6143 (2013): 292–295; D. Luke Mahler and Travis Ingram, "Phylogenetic Comparative Methods for Studying Clade-Wide Convergence," in *Modern Phylogenetic Comparative Methods and Their Application in Evolutionary Biology*, ed. László Zsolt Garamszegi (Dordrecht: Springer, 2014), 425–450.

of Order Gruiformes], gastornithiforms and dromornithids [Order Gastornithiformes], phorusrhacs [Family Phorusrhacidae of Order Cariamiformes], and the extinct Gargantuaviids [Clade Avialae]. Though once grouped in the same order [Struthioniformes] there is now evidence that they all evolved long legs, long necks, big heads, and reduced wings and keels independently.[27] Arctic diving birds have converged on the penguin-form with finned-wings and webbed feet in true penguins [Order Sphenisciformes], auks [Family Alcidae of Order Charadriiformes], mancallins [Family Mancallinae of Order Charadriiformes];[28] and scavenging birds have converged on the vulture form in Old World Vultures [Family Accipitridae of Order Accipitriformes] and New World Vultures [Family Cathartidae of Order Cathartiformes].[29] Other examples of convergent

---

[27] The exact relationships of ratite bird species are still unsettled but it does seem that the ratite form has evolved independently at least three to five times. On this see: Herculano M. F. Alvarenga and Elizabeth Höfling, "Systematic Revision of the Phorusrhacidae (Aves: Ralliformes)," *Papéis Avulsos de Zoologia* 43, no. 4 (2003): 55–91; Peter F. Murray and Patricia Vickers, *Magnificent Mihirungs: The Colossal Flightless Birds of the Australian Dreamtime* (Bloomington: Indiana University Press, 2004); John Harshman, et al., "Phylogenomic Evidence for Multiple Losses of Flight in Ratite Birds," *Proceedings of the National Academy of Sciences* 105, no. 36 (2008): 13462–13467; Matthew J. Phillips, et al., "Tinamous and Moa Flock Together: Mitochondrial Genome Sequence Analysis Reveals Independent Losses of Flight among Ratites," *Systematic Biology* 59, no. 1 (2010): 90–107; Allan J. Baker, et al., "Genomic Support for a Moa-Tinamou Clade and Adaptive Morphological Convergence in Flightless Ratites," *Molecular Biology and Evolution* 31, no. 7 (2014): 1686–1696; Kieran J. Mitchell, et al., "Ancient DNA Reveals Elephant Birds and Kiwi Are Sister Taxa and Clarifies Ratite Bird Evolution," *Science* 344, no. 6186 (2014): 898–900; Gerald Mayr, "On the Taxonomy and Osteology of the Early Eocene North American Geranoididae (Aves, Gruoidea)," *Swiss Journal of Palaeontology* 135, no. 2 (2016): 315–325; Trevor H. Worthy, et al., "The Evolution of Giant Flightless Birds and Novel Phylogenetic Relationships for Extinct Fowl (Aves, Galloanseres)," *Royal Society Open Science* 11 (2017): 170975.
[28] Truls Moum, et al., "Mitochondrial DNA Sequence Evolution and Phylogeny of the Atlantic Alcidae, including the Extinct Great Auk (Pinguinus impennis)," *Molecular Biology and Evolution* 19, no. 9 (2002): 1434–1439.
[29] Heather R. Lerner and David P. Mindell, "Phylogeny of Eagles, Old World Vultures, and other Accipitridae Based on Nuclear and Mitochondrial DNA," *Molecular Phylogenetics and Evolution* 37, no. 2 (2005): 327–346; Oksung Chung, et al., "The First Whole Genome and Transcriptome of the Cinereous Vulture Reveals Adaptation in the Gastric and Immune Defense Systems and Possible Convergent Evolution between the Old and New World Vultures," *Genome Biology* 16 (2015): 215; Erich D. Jarvis, et al., "Whole-Genome Analyses Resolve Early

evolution in birds include the ecomorphs of tiny nectar-feeding birds with long and narrow curved bills in hummingbirds [Family Trochilidae of Order Apodiformes] and sunbirds [Family Nectariniidae of Order Passeriformes];[30] of the fast-flying insectivoran swifts [Family Apodidae of Order Apodiformes] and swallows [Family Hirundinidae of Order Passeriformes] with long pointed wings and forked tails;[31] as well as of the diving form of petrels [Family Procellariidae of Order Procellariiformes] and razorbills [Family Alcidae of Order Charadriiformes].[32] There are also strong resemblances between the Australian passerine families Petroicidae, Maluridae, and Artamidae and North American robins, wrens, and magpies though they are unrelated.[33] Finally island species such as Galapagos

---

Branches in the Tree of Life of Modern Birds," *Science* 346, no. 6215 (2014): 1320–1331.

[30] David Paton and B. G. Collins, "Bills and Tongues of Nectar-Feeding Birds: A Review of Morphology, Function and Performance, with Intercontinental Comparisons," *Australian Journal of Ecology* 14, no. 4 (1989): 473–506; Roland Prinzinger, et al., "Energy Metabolism, Respiratory Quotient and Breathing Parameters in Two Convergent Small Bird Species: The Fork-Tailed Sunbird *Aethopyga christinae* (Nectariniidae) and the Chilean Hummingbird *Sephanoides sephanoides* (Trochilidae)," *Journal of Thermal Biology* 17, no. 2 (1992): 71–79; Susan W. Nicolson and Patricia A. Fleming, "Drinking Problems on a 'Simple' Diet: Physiological Convergence in Nectar-Feeding Birds," *Journal of Experimental Biology* 217 (2014): 1015–1023.

[31] Allen Keast, Laura Pearce, and Sari Saunders, "How Convergent Is the American Redstart (*Setophaga ruticilla*, Parulinae) with Flycatchers (Tyrannidae) in Morphology and Feeding Behavior?," *The Auk* 112, no. 2 (1995): 310–325; A. Landmann and N. Winding, "Guild Organisation and Morphology of High-Altitude Granivorous and Insectivorous Birds: Convergent Evolution in an Extreme Environment," *Oikos* 73, no. 2 (1995): 237–250; E. Moreno and A. Barbosa, "Convergence in Aerially Feeding Insectivorous Birds," *Netherlands Journal of Zoology* 45 (1995): 291–304; Frederick H. Sheldon, et al., "Phylogeny of Swallows (Aves: Hirundinidae) Estimated from Nuclear and Mitochondrial DNA Sequences," *Molecular Phylogenetics and Evolution* 35, no. 1 (2005): 254–270; Henri A. Thomassen et al., "Phylogenetic Relationships amongst Swifts and Swiftlets: A Multi Locus Approach," *Molecular Phylogenetics and Evolution* 37, no. 1 (2005): 264–277.

[32] Martin L. Cody, "Coexistence, Coevolution and Convergent Evolution in Seabird Communities," *Ecology* 54, no. 1 (1973): 31–44; Les Christidis and Walter Boles, *Systematics and Taxonomy of Australian Birds* (Collingwood: Csiro, 2008).

[33] Walter E. Boles, *The Robins and Flycatchers of Australia* (Sydney: Angus & Robertson, 1988); Gisela Kaplan, *Australian Magpie: Biology and Behaviour of an Unusual Songbird* (Collingwood: Csiro, 2004); Les Christidis and Walter E. Boles, *Systematics and Taxonomy of Australian Birds* (Collingwood: Csiro, 2008).

Finches and Hawaiian Honeycreepers have undergone adaptive radiation and taken on various beak-types that converge with those found in mainland birds depending upon their dietary adaptations.[34]

Mammalian Convergence

The most famous examples of convergent evolution, however, probably lie within the mammalian world.[35] We find, for example, the independent evolution of gliding arboreal forms in flying lemurs [Family Cynocephalidae of Order Dermoptera], flying squirrels [Tribe Pteromyinai of Subfamily Sciurinae of Family Sciuridae of Order Rodentia], scaly-tailed flying squirrels [Family Anomaluridae of Order Rodentia], Australian squirrel gliders and sugar gliders [Family Petauridae of Order Diprotodontia of Subclass Marsupialia], gliding eutriconodonts [Clade Volaticotherini of Order Eutriconodonta] and euharamiyids [Genus *Arboroharamiya* of Order Haramiyida] as well as the extinct eomyids [Family Eomyidae of Order Rodentia];[36] of burrowing mole forms with enlarged forelimbs for digging, elongated snouts, and reduced vision in true moles [Family Talpidae of Order Eulipotyphla], mole-rats [Family Heterocephalidae of Order Rodentia], golden moles [Family Chrysochloridae of Order Afrosoricida], marsupial

---

[34] Trevor D. Price, et al., "Recurrent Patterns of Natural Selection in a Population of Darwin's Finches," *Nature* 309, no. 5971 (1984): 787–789; Peter R. Grant, *The Ecology and Evolution of Darwin's Finches* (Princeton: Princeton University Press, 1999); Dawn M. Reding, et al., "Convergent Evolution of 'Creepers' in the Hawaiian Honeycreeper Radiation," *Royal Society Biology Letters* 51, no. 2 (2009): 221–224; Daniel J. Field, "Bird Evolution: Convergence Fits the Bill," *Current Biology* 29, no. 4 (2019): R132–R134.

[35] Ole Madsen, et al., "Parallel Adaptive Radiations in Two Major Clades of Placental Mammals," *Nature* 409, no. 6820 (February 1, 2001): 610–614; Luke Harmon, "Evolution: Contingent Predictability in Mammalian Evolution," *Current Biology* 27, no. 11 (2010): R425–R248.

[36] Mansoureh Malekian, Steven J. B. Cooper, and Susan M. Carthew, "Phylogeography of the Australian Sugar Glider (Petaurus breviceps): Evidence for a New Divergent Lineage in Eastern Australia," *Australian Journal of Zoology* 58, no. 3 (2010): 165–181; Greg Byrnes and Andrew J. Spence, "Ecological and Biomechanical Insights into the Evolution of Gliding in Mammals," *Integrative and Comparative Biology* 51, no. 6 (2011): 991–1001; Stephen M. Jackson and Richard W. Thorington, Jr., *Gliding Mammals: Taxonomy of Living and Extinct Species* (Washington: Smithsonian Scholarly Press, 2012); Jin Meng, et al., "A Mesozoic Gliding Mammal from Northeastern China," *Nature* 444 (2006): 889–893; Gang Han, et al., "A Jurassic Gliding Euharamiyidan Mammal with an Ear of Five Auditory Bones," *Nature* 551, no. 7681 (2017): 451–456 (2017).

moles [Family Notoryctidae of Order Notoryctemorphia of Infraclass Marsupialia], and fossorial epoicotherian palaeandonts [Family Epoicotheriidae of Order Pholidota], docodontids [Genus *Docofossor* of Family Docodontidae of Clade Cynodontia], and necrolestids [Family Necrolestidae of Superorder Dryolestoidea];[37] of protruding spines or quills in echidnas [Family Tachyglossidae of Order Montremata], hedgehogs [Family Erinaceidae of Order Eulipotyphla], spiny tenrecs [Subfamily Tenricinae of Family Tenrecidae of Order Afrosoricida], Old World porcupines [Family Hystricidae of Order Rodentia], and New World porcupines [Family Erethizontidae of Order Rodentia];[38] of the desert hopping rodents with large hind legs and long thin tails in true kangaroo rats [Family

---

[37] Kenneth D. Rose and Robert J. Emry, "Extraordinary Fossorial Adaptations in the Oligocene Palaeanodonts Epoicotherium and Xenocranium (Mammalia)," *Journal of Morphology* 175, no. 1 (1983): 33–56; Enrique P. Lessa, "Morphological Evolution of Subterranean Mammals: Integrating Structural, Functional, and Ecological Perspectives," *Progress in Clinical and Biological Research* 335 (1990): 211–230; Eviatar Nevo, *Mosaic Evolution of Subterranean Mammals: Regression, Progression, and Global Convergence* (Oxford: Oxford University Press, 1999); Eileen A. Lacey and James L. Patton, *Life Underground: The Biology of Subterranean Rodents* (Chicago: University of Chicago Press, 2000); Samantha S. B. Hopkins and Edward B. Davis, "Quantitative Morphological Proxies for Fossoriality in Small Mammals," *Journal of Mammalogy* 90, no. 6 (2009): 1449–1460; J. R. Ellerman, "The Subterranean Mammals of the World," *Transactions of the Royal Society of South Africa* 35, no. 1 (2010): 11–20; Michael Archer, et al., "Australia's First Fossil Marsupial Mole (Notoryctemorphia) Resolves Controversies about their Evolution and Palaeoenvironmental Origins," *Proceedings of the Royal Society of London B: Biological Sciences* 278, no. 1711 (2010): 1498–1506; Helder Gomes-Rodrigues, et al., "Life in Burrows Channelled the Morphological Evolution of the Skull in Rodents: The Case of African Mole-Rats (Bathyergidae, Rodentia)," *Journal of Mammalian Evolution* 23 (2016): 175–189; Raghavendran Partha, et al., "Subterranean Mammals Show Convergent Regression in Ocular Genes and Enhancers, along with Adaptation to Tunneling," *eLife* 6 (2017): e25884; Gabriele Sansalone, et al., "Decoupling Functional and Morphological Convergence: The Study Case of Fossorial Mammalia," *Frontiers in Earth Science* 21 (2020).

[38] Matthew J. Phillips, et al., "Molecules, Morphology, and Ecology Indicate a Recent, Amphibious Ancestry for Echidnas," *Proceedings of the National Academy of Science* 106, no. 40 (2009): 17089–17094; Nicolás R. Chimento, Federico L. Agnolin and Fernando E. Novas, "The Patagonian Fossil Mammal Necrolestes: a Neogene Survivor of Dryolestoidea," *Revista del Museo Argentino de Ciencias Naturales* 14, no. 2 (2012): 261–306; Kathryn M. Everson, et al. "Multiple Loci and Complete Taxonomic Sampling Resolve the Phylogeny and Biogeographic History of Tenrecs (Mammalia: Tenrecidae) and Reveal Higher Speciation Rates in Madagascar's Humid Forests," *Systematic Biology* 65, no. 5 (2016): 890–909.

Heteromyidae of Order Rodentia], Australian hopping mice [Genus *Notomys* of Family Muridae of Order Rodentia], jerboas [Family Dipodidae of Order Rodentia], kultarrs [Genus *Antechinomys* of Family Dasyuridae of Order Dasyuromorphia of Infraclass Marsupialia], and South American argyrolagids [Family Argyrolagidae of Order Paucituberculata of Infraclass Marsupialia];[39] and finally of insectivoran shrew forms in true shrews [Family Soridae of Order Euliptotyphla], shrew-like rats [Genus *Rhynchomys* of Family Muridae of Order Rodentia], elephant shrews [Family Macroscelididae of Order Macroscelidea], dasyurid marsupial shrews [Genus *Phascolosorex* of Family Dasyuridae of Order Dasyuromorphia of Subclass Marsupialia], and shrew opossums including the extinct form *Palaeothentes* [Clade Palaeothentinae of Order Paucituberculata of Infraclass Marsupialia] and the living shrew opossums [Family Caenolestidae of Order Paucituberculata of Infraclass Marsupialia].[40]

We have not even yet spoken of the classical examples of convergence on the carnivorous cat and dog forms in the marsupial Tasmanian devil [Genus *Sarcophilus* of Family Dasyuridae of Order Dasyuromorphia of Infraclass Marsupialia], the Tasmanian wolf [Genus *Thylacinus* of Family Thylacinidae of Order Dasyuromorphia], the placental saber-tooth tiger [Subfamily

---

[39] Michael A. Mares, "Convergent Evolution of Desert Rodents: Multivariate Analysis and Zoogeographic Implications," *Paleobiology* 2, no. 1 (1976): 39–63; Susan L. Berman, "Convergent Evolution in the Hindlimb of Bipedal Rodents," *Journal of Zoological Systematics and Evolutionary Research* 23, no. 1 (1985): 59–77; Shaoyuan Wu, et al., "The Evolution of Bipedalism in Jerboas (Rodentia: Dipoidea): Origin in Humid and Forested Environments," *Evolution* 68, no. 7 (2014): 2108–2118; Craig P. McGown and Clint E. Collins, "Why Do Mammals Hop?: Understanding the Ecology, Biomechanics and Evolution of Bipedal Hopping," *Journal of Experimental Biology* 221 (2018): 1–10; María Alejandra Abello and Adriana Magdalena Candela, "Paleobiology of Argyrolagus (Marsupialia, Argyrolagidae): An Astonishing Case of Bipedalism among South American Mammals," *Journal of Mammalian Evolution* 27 (2020).

[40] Guy G. Musser and Lawrence R. Heaney, "Philippine Rodents: Definitions of Tarsomys and Limnomys plus a Preliminary Assessment of Phylogenetic Patterns among Native Philippine Murines (Murinae, Muridae)," *Bulletin of the American Museum of Natural History* 211 (1992): 1–138; Michael J. Stanhope, et al., "Molecular Evidence for Multiple Origins of the Insectivora and for a New Order of Endemic African Mammals," *Proceedings of the National Academy of Sciences* 95, no. 17 (1998): 9967–9972; Christophe J. Douady, et al., "The Sahara as a Vicariant Agent, and the Role of Miocene Climatic Events, in the Diversification of the Mammalian Order Macroscelidea (Elephant Shrews)," *Proceedings of the National Academy of Sciences* 100, no. 14 (2003): 8325—8330; Maria A. Abello, "Analysis of Dental Homologies and Phylogeny of Paucituberculata (Mammalia: Marsupialia)," *Biological Journal of the Linnean Society* 109, no. 2 (2013): 441–465.

Machairodontinae of Family Felidae of Order Carnivora], the marsupial saber-tooth tiger [Family Thylacosmilidae of Order Sparassodonta], as well as in nimravids [Family Nimravidae of Suborder Feliformia of Order Carnivora], borhyaenids [Family Borhyaenidae of Order Sparassodonta], creodonts [Order Creodonta of Clade Ferae], and cetancodontamorphs [Genus *Andrewsarchus* of Clade Cetancodontamorpha or Order Artiodactyla].[41] One could also mention the convergence on the rhinoceros form found in the true rhinoceros [Family Rhinocerotidae of Order Perissodactyla], brontotheres [Family Brontotheriidae of Order Perissodactyla], and toxodonts [Family Toxodontidae of Order Notoungulata]; on the antelope form in pronghorns [Family Antilocapridae of Order Artiodactyla], African antelopes [Subfamily Antilopinae of Family Bovidae of Order Perissodactyla], and extinct South American litopterns [Genus *Tonatherium* of Family Proterotheriidae of Order Litopterna]; and on the tapir form in pyrotheres [Family Pyrotheriidae of Order Pyrotheria] and true tapirs [Family Tapiridae of Order Perissodactyla]. There are also the partial convergences of bipedal kangaroos [Family Macropodidae of Order Diprotodontia of Infraclass Marsupialia] and cavies [Family Caviidae of Order Rodentia]; goats [Subfamily Caprinae of Family Bovidae of Order Artiodactyla] and some litopterns [Genus *Diadiaphorus* of Family Proterotheriidae of Order

---

[41] Blaire Van Valkenburgh, "Iterative Evolution of Hypercarnivory in Canids (Mammalia: Carnivora): Evolutionary Interactions among Sympatric Predators," *Paleobiology* 17, no. 4 (1991): 340–362; L. Werdelin, "Comparison of Skull Shape in Marsupial and Placental Carnivores," *Australian Journal of Zoology* 34, no. 2 (1986): 109–117; Nick Milne and Stephen Wroe, "Convergence and Remarkably Consistent Constraint in the Evolution of Carnivore Skull Shape," *Evolution* 61, no. 5 (2007): 1251–1260; Anjali Gowsami, Nick Milne, and Stephen Wroe, "Biting through Constraints: Cranial Morphology, Disparity and Convergence across Living and Fossil Carnivorous Mammals," *Proceedings of the Royal Society B* 278, no. 1713 (2010): 1831–1839; Francisco Juan Prevosti, Guillermo Fidel Turazzini, Marcos Darío Ercoli, and Erika Hingst-Zaher, "Mandible Shape in Marsupial and Placental Carnivorous Mammals: A Morphological Comparative Study Using Geometric Morphometrics," *Zoological Journal of the Linnean Society* 164 (2012): 836–855; Carlo Meloro, Marcus Clauss, and Pasquale Raia, "Ecomorphology of Carnivora Challenges Convergent Evolution," *Organisms, Diversity, and Evolution* 15 (2015): 711–720; Paul Z. Barrett, "Taxonomic and Systematic Revisions to the North American Nimravidae (Mammalia, Carnivora)," *PeerJ* 4 (2016): e1658; Charles Y. Feigin, et al., "Genome of the Tasmanian Tiger Provides Insights into the Evolution and Demography of an Extinct Marsupial Carnivore," *Nature, Ecology, and Evolution* 2, no. 1 (2017): 182–192; Francisco J. Prevosti and Analía M. Forasiepi, *Evolution of South American Mammalian Predators During the Cenozoic: Paleobiogeographic and Paleoenvironmental Contingencies* (Dordrecht: Springer, 2018).

Litopterna]; beavers [Family Castoridae of Order Rodentia], the platypus [Family Ornithorhynchidae of Order Monotremata], and docodonts [Genera *Castrocauda* and *Haldanodon* of Family Docodontidae of Clade Cynodontia], the former of which may have had a paddle-shaped tail and the latter of which may have had a keratinized snout; and pigs [Family Suidae of Order Artiodactyla], peccaries [Family Tassyuridae of Order Artiodactyla], entelodonts [Family Entelodontidae of Order Artiodactyla], and dichobunoids [Families Cebochoeridae and Choeropotamidae of Order Artiodactyla].[42] Finally mention could be made of independently-evolved adaptations in the ant-eating or myrmecophage mammals with powerful digging forelimbs and long noses and tongues, such as with anteaters [Family Myrmecophagidae of Order Pilosa], armadillos [Family Dasypodidae of Order Cingulata], pangolins [Family Manidae of Order Philodota], aardvarks [Family Orycteropodidae of Order Tubulidentata], echidnas [Family Tachyglossidae of Order Monotremata], the fruitafossors [Genus *Fruitafossor* of Subclass Theria], and numbat [Family Myrmecobiidae of Order Dasyuromorphia of Infraclass Marsupialia];[43] and

---

[42] Christine M. Janis, Kathleen M. Scott, and Louis L. Jacobs, eds., *Terrestrial Carnivores, Ungulates, and Ungulate-like Mammals: Evolution of Tertiary Mammals of North America*, 2 vols. (Cambridge: Cambridge University Press. 1998); Kenneth D. Rose and J. David Archibald, eds., *The Rise of Placental Mammals: Origins and Relationships of the Major Extant Clades* (Baltimore: John Hopkins University Press, 2005); Qiang Ji, et al., "A Swimming Mammaliaform from the Middle Jurassic and Ecomorphological Diversification of Early Mammals," *Science* 311, no. 5764 (2006): 1123–1127; Donald R. Prothero and Scott E. Foss, *The Evolution of Artiodactyls* (Baltimore: John Hopkins University Press, 2007); Matthew C. Mihlbachler, "Species Taxonomy, Phylogeny and Biogeography of the Brontotheriidae (Mammalia, Perissodactyla)," *Bulletin of the American Museum of Natural History* 311 (2008): 5–475; Bruce D. Patterson, *Bones, Clones, and Biomes: The History and Geography of Recent Neotropical Mammals* (2012); Richard A. Fariña et al., *Megafauna: Giant Beasts of Pleistocene South America* (Indiana: Bloomington University Press, 2013); Frido Welker, et al., "Ancient Proteins Resolve the Evolutionary History of Darwin's South American Ungulates," *Nature* 522, no. 7554 (2015): 81–84; Darin A. Croft, *Horned Armadillos and Rafting Monkeys: The Fascinating Fossil Mammals of South America* (Bloomington: Indiana University Press, 2016); Emmanuel Gheerbrant, Andrea Filippo, and Arnaud Schmitt, "Convergence of Afrotherian and Laurasiatherian Ungulate-Like Mammals: First Morphological Evidence from the Paleocene of Morocco," *Plos One* 11, no. 7 (2016): e0157556.
[43] Karen Zich Reiss, "Using Phylogenies to Study Convergence: The Case of the Ant-Eating Mammals," *American Zoologist* 41, no. 3 (2001): 507–525; Zhe-Xi Luo and John R. Wible, "A Late Jurassic Digging Mammal and Early Mammalian Diversification," *Science* 308, no. 5718 (2005): 103–107.

of the dolphin form with Amazonian river dolphins [Family Iniidea of Order Artiodactyla] and South Asian river dolphins [Family Platanistidae of Order Artiodactyla].[44] Finally there is the convergent evolution of large curved horns in ramming herbivores such as the musk ox, takin, and big horn sheep [Subfamily Caprinae of Family Bovidae], cape buffalo [Subfamily Bovinae of Family Bovidae], and wildebeest [Subfamily Alcelaphinae of Family Bovidae].[45]

On the basis of such examples of convergence many biologists have suggested there is a predictability to evolution and thus the likelihood of similar evolutionary events on alien worlds. Not all are convinced, however.

Predictability and Contingency in Macroevolution

It is a great irony of history that one of the first paleontologists to devote research to large-scale patterns in evolution (macroevolution), namely Stephen J. Gould, held that evolution has no direction at all and is purely contingent; that one of the paleontologists involved in excavating the Burgess Shale fauna of incredibly diverse and unique species, namely Simon Conway Morris, argued against Gould and in favor of the predictability of evolution on the basis of evolutionary convergence; and that Conway Morris was opposed by Jonathan Losos, whose work has focused on convergent evolution in lizards. This is due in large part to the fact that in these matters scientists are not just basing their conclusions on raw scientific data but instead data interpreted in light of philosophical presuppositions, whether they recognize this or not.[46] In what follows we

---

[44] Tomas Hrbek, et al., "A New Species of River Dolphin from Brazil or: How Little Do We Know Our Biodiversity," *Plos One* 9, no. 1 (2014): e83623; Charlotte E. Page and Natalie Cooper, "Morphological Convergence in 'River Dolphin' Skulls." *PeerJ* 5 (2017): e4090.

[45] Valerius Geist, "The Evolution of Horn-Like Organs," *Behaviour* 27 (1966): 175–214; Christine Janis, "Evolution of Horns in Ungulates: Ecology and Paleoecology," *Biological Reviews* 57, no. 2 (1982): 261–318; Barbara Lundrigan, "Morphology of Horns and Fighting Behavior in the Family Bovidae," *Journal of Mammology* 77, no. 2 (1996): 462–475; George A. Bubenik and Anthony B. Bubenik, *Horns, Pronghorns, and Antler: Evolution, Morphology, Physiology, and Social Significance* (Dordrecht: Springer, 1990); Edwaerd Byrd Davis, et al., "Evolution of Ruminant Headgear: A Review," *Proceedings of the Royal Academy B: Biological Sciences* 278, no. 1720 (2011): 2857–2865.

[46] On the issue of philosophical ideas intruding into paleontology see: Stephen J. Gould, "Eternal Metaphors of Palaeontology," in *Patterns of Evolution as Illustrated by the Fossil Record*, ed. A. Hallam (Amsterdam: Elsevier, 1977): 1–26; Ronald

will seek to examine the evidence from pure science, the best scientific data
alone, and what it can tell us about whether or not evolution is predictable,
has a direction, and might lead to the existence of human-like creatures on
other planets. First though, let us briefly summarize the aforementioned
debate.

According to Gould the human mind seeks to interpret evolution
according to the categories of progress and predictability. Yet per Gould the
fossil record, particularly that of the early Cambrian Burgess shale, shows
that life started as a rapid explosion of many complex species, only a few of
which survived eventual extinction. The fact that one of these Cambrian
lineages, that descended from *Pikia* as opposed to *Anomalocaris* or
Opabinia, survived and led to human beings, or that certain Devonian lobe-
finned lungfish were able to survive when their ponds dried up whereas
other fish species died out, is a contingent happening due to "Lady Luck,"
and unlikely to repeat itself, whether on Earth or other planets. Or in the
notable words of Gould, "Wind the tape of life back to Burgess times, and
let it play again. If *Pikia* does not survive in the replay, we are wiped out of
future history—all of us, from shark to robin to orangutan."[47] So, due to the
fact that which particular life forms survive is to a great degree a luck of the
draw, "the history of any surviving set is sensible, but each leads to a world
thoroughly different from any other. If the human mind is a product of only
one such set, then we may not be randomly evolved in the sense of coin
flipping, but our origin is the product of massive historical contingency, and
we would probably never again arise even if life's tape could be replayed a
thousand times."[48]

Gould highlights two ways in which contingency operates in
macroevolution. In the first place there is a great deal of contingency
resulting from the chance extinctions of certain lineages over time, i.e.
species-sorting macroevolutionary processes. Gould additionally examines
the major evolutionary transitions—such as from single cellular to
multicellular organisms, from non-backboned to back-boned creatures,
from finned vertebrates to vertebrates with appendages for walking on
land—and argues that not only did each of these transitions occur in only
one line among many, one lineage that might not have survived the
extinction events, but in addition each transition involved an unlikely

Rainger, "Paleontology and Philosophy: A Critique," *Journal of the History of
Biology* 18, no. 2 (1985): 267–287.
[47] Stephen J. Gould, *Wonderful Life: The Burgess Shale and the Nature of History*
(New York: W. W. Norton, 1989), 323.
[48] Gould, *Wonderful Life*, 233–234, see also pp. 277–291.

rearrangement of parts originally adapted to a different end.[49] In other words evolution often reuses "features that originated by natural selection for one reason, but also manifest a capacity for subsequent recruitment (with minimal change) to substantially different and novel functions."[50] Evolution, in contemporary jargon, is a tinkerer and acts in an opportunistic manner, tweaking preexisting material to serve different purposes than originally intended. The fact that such tweaks are the result of a "quirky functional shift" or "workable happenstance," wherein certain genes or morphologies are coopted or reappropriated in evolution, inevitably suggests, though it does not prove, remarks Gould, a high degree of fortuity in what results.[51] For example, the gill arches of jawless agnathan fish were reappropriated by jawed gnathastome fish. And, had these gill arches not possessed the particular form, positioning, and developmental potential to move anteriorly and become jaws, "the gnathastome lineage would never have emerged, the agnathans might have remained a relatively minor component of marine faunas (or become extinct entirely), and terrestrial environments to this day, might have remained the domains of plants and insects . . . evolving nothing conscious to proclaim its aesthetic, extol its virtues, or to record, perhaps even to seal, its doom."[52] Similarly for Gould, if one marginal group of fishes had not evolved a peculiar fin, with a branching central element orthogonal to the body's axis with radiating rays, no support firm enough to evolve into a limb for terrestrial life might ever have emerged with the lineage of vertebrates. Consequently as humans are "Buster's [the Lungfish] legacy, and the result of a thousand other similarly happy accidents, how can we possibly view our mentality as inevitable, or even probable" when "any replay of the tape would lead evolution down a pathway radically different from the road actually taken."[53]

Far from being frightened by the randomness of human evolution, our "contingent good fortune," Gould embraces the fact that humans are a "small thing" in a "vast universe," a "wildly improbable evolutionary event," as exhilarating and a source of both freedom and consequent moral responsibility.[54] The fact that there are no predictable pathways of evolution based on general rules of anatomy or ecology and that the evolution of

---

[49] Gould, *Wonderful Life*, 292–324.

[50] Stephen J. Gould, *The Structure of Evolutionary Theory* (Cambridge: Harvard University Press, 2002), 1228.

[51] Gould, *The Structure of Evolutionary Theory*, 1160; see also 1076–1089, 1159–1161, 1224–1233, 1333–1342.

[52] Gould, *The Structure of Evolutionary Theory*, 1232

[53] Gould, *Wonderful Life*, 48 and 51.

[54] Gould, *Wonderful Life*, 291.

humans is a matter of contingency, shows us that "we must establish our own paths in this most diverse and interesting of conceivable universes—one indifferent to our suffering, and therefore offering us maximum freedom to thrive, or to fail, in our own chosen way."[55] In so asserting this Gould shows us that he is not free of interpreting scientific data in light of philosophical presuppositions. We can also see this at work in the selection of descriptive adjectives above that bear emotional connotations.

Simon Conway Morris, one of the paleontological investigators of the Burgess Shale fauna, was quick to respond to Gould's contingency thesis.

---

[55] Gould, *Wonderful Life*, 323. A number of biologists and philosophers have in large part agreed with Gould's position on the contingency and non-predictability of evolutionary processes, including: George Gaylord Simpson, who put the arguments in their clearest form in his 1964 essay "On the Nonprevalence of Humanoids," *Science* 143, no. 3608 (1964): 769–775; John H. Beatty, "The Evolutionary Contingency Thesis," in *Concepts, Theories, and Rationality in the Biological Sciences*, ed. Gereon Wolters and James G. Lennox (Pittsburgh: University of Pittsburgh Press, 1995): 45–82; Gunther J. Eble, "On the Dual Nature of Chance in Evolutionary Biology and Paleobiology," *Paleobiology* 25, no. 1 (1999): 75–87; Donald Prothero, "Inevitable Human or Hidden Agendas: A Review of Life's Solution," *Sceptic* 10, no. 3 (2003): 54–57; Michael Shermer, "The Chain of Accidents and the Rule of Law: The Role of Contingency and Necessity in Evolution," *Skeptic* 14, no. 2 (2008): 28–36; John H. Beatty, "Chance Variation and Evolutionary Contingency: Darwin, Simpson (The Simpsons), and Gould," in *The Oxford Handbook of the Philosophy of Biology*, ed. Michael Ruse (Oxford: Oxford University Press, 2008): 189–210; John H. Beatty, "Replaying Life's Tape," *Journal of Philosophy* 93 (2006): 336–362; Jerry A. Coyne, *Why Evolution is True* (New York: Penguin, 2010), 92–94; Derek D. Turner, "Gould's Replay Revisited," *Biology and Philosophy* 26, no. 1 (2011): 65–79; Derek D. Turner, "Evolutionary Contingency," and "Diversity, Disparity, and the Burgess Shale," *Paleontology: A Philosophical Introduction* (Cambridge: Cambridge University Press, 2011), 156–179, 180–196; Trevor Pearce, "Convergence and Parallelism in Evolution: A Neo-Gouldian Account," *The British Journal for the Philosophy of Science* 63, no. 2 (2012): 429–448; Thomas Lenormand, et al., "Parallel Evolution: What Does It (Not) Tell Us and Why Is It (Still) Interesting?," in *Chance in Evolution*, ed. Grant Ramsey and Charles H. Pence (Chicago: University of Chicago Press, 2016), 196–222; David Sepkoski, "'Replaying Life's Tape': Simulations, Metaphors, and Historicity in Stephen Jay Gould's View of Life," *Studies in History and Philosophy of Science Part C: Studies in History and Philosophy of Biological and Biomedical Sciences* 58 (2016): 73–81; Alison K. McConwell and Adrian Currie, "Gouldian Arguments and the Sources of Contingency," *Biology and Philosophy* 32 (2017): 243–261; T.Y. William Wong, "The Evolutionary Contingency Thesis and Evolutionary Idiosyncrasies," *Biology and Philosophy* 34, no. 2 (2019): 21–32; as well as by P.Z. Myers on his *Pharyngula* blog (https://freethoughtblogs.com/pharyngula).

He argued that Gould had failed to appreciate the phenomena of convergence in evolution wherein independent lineages evolve the same phenotype. Because of such convergences the evolution of any particular species is indeed contingent and will display a unique evolutionary pathway, but the evolution of a general body type (phenotype) is not as it often evolves more than once in response to similar environmental conditions, as we have seen. Because the history of life displays a high degree of convergent evolutionary events, sooner or later a similar body-type to the one that does not yet exist or went extinct would evolve. Or in the analogy of Conway Morris, "If Charles Walcott had not discovered the Burgess Shale, sooner or later another geologist would have done so. If I had not had the good fortune to work on the Burgess Shale, sooner or later another paleontologist would have done so."[56] Or alternatively, the fact that a particular individual becomes a biologist is highly contingent based upon all sorts of factors such as the influence of parents, teachers, friends, etc., but that there will be individuals who become biologists is a veritable certainty. So while the particular evolution of the whales as we know them today from the perspective of the Cambrian explosion is no more likely than a hundred other endpoints, the evolution of some sort of large ocean-traversing animal that sieves seawater for food is very likely and perhaps almost inevitable, and so within certain limits the outcome of evolutionary processes are quite predictable.[57]

Gould's argument then misses the point as it is based on a confusion between the unique destiny of a particular lineage versus the likelihood that a certain collection of biological features will manifest itself on account of convergent evolutionary processes. Indeed Conway Morris in a later monograph on convergent evolution argues that "the constraints of evolution and the ubiquity of convergence makes the emergence of something like ourselves [a sentient animal] a near-inevitability," though this does not mean that one exactly like us "with five fingers on each hand, a vermiform appendix, thirty-two teeth, and so on" will evolve.[58] In other

---

[56] Simon Conway Morris, *The Crucible of Creation: The Burgess Shale and the Rise of Animals* (Oxford: Oxford University Press, 1998), 201.

[57] Conway Morris, *The Crucible of Creation*, 201–202.

[58] Simon Conway Morris, *Life's Solution: Inevitable Humans in a Lonely Universe* (Cambridge: Cambridge University Press, 2003), 328 and xii. Conway Morris, indeed, argues that worlds suitable for life will be relatively rare in the cosmos on the basis of astronomical considerations. See also Simon Conway Morris, "Evolutionary Convergence," *Current Biology* 16, no. 19 (2006): R826–827 and *The Runes of Evolution: How the Universe Became Self-Aware* (West Conshohocken: Templeton Press, 2015).

words, alien planets may well harbor sentient creatures that look very little like us, perhaps resembling canines or birds or dolphins, and they may well harbor humanoid creatures that will look like us overall but differ in subtle ways as well, such as number and type of appendages or sensory apparatuses.

Taking a position in between that of Gould and Conway Morris is Jonathan Losos. Losos is well aware of convergent evolution; in fact his studies on *Anolis* island lizards are classic accounts of the commonality of convergent evolution in reptiles. And Conway Morris is congratulated by Losos for showing just how common evolutionary duplication is. Losos, however, sees limits to convergent evolutionary occurrences and to the predictability of evolution. In the first place he points out that there are evolutionary idiosyncrasies such as the Hawaiian Alula plant, the Burgess Shale creatures, chameleons, the Kiwi bird, the aye-aye, sauropod dinosaurs, *Adalatherium*, the narwhal, and the platypus.[59] Secondly, not every

---

Support for Conway Morris' defense of the general predictability of evolution can be found in: Timothy Shanahan, *The Evolution of Darwinism: Selection, Adaptation and Progress in Evolutionary Biology* (Cambridge: Cambridge University Press, 2004), 220–247; Douglas H. Erwin, "Evolutionary Contingency," *Current Biology* 16, no. 19 (2006): R825–826; Geerat J. Vermeij, "Historical Contingency and the Purported Uniqueness of Evolutionary Innovations," *Proceedings of the National Academy of Sciences* 103, no. 6 (2006): 1804–1809; Russell Powell, "Is Convergence More Than an Analogy?: Homoplasy and its Implications for Macroevolutionary Predictability," *Biology and Philosophy* 22 (2007): 565–578; Simon Conway Morris, ed., *The Deep Structure of Biology: Is Convergence Sufficiently Ubiquitous to Give a Directional Signal* (West Conshohocken: Templeton Foundation Press, 2008); Michael Rota, "Evolution, Providence, and Gouldian Contingency," *Religious Studies* 44, no. 4 (2008): 393–412; Russell Powell, "Contingency and Convergence in Macroevolution: A Reply to John Beatty," *Journal of Philosophy* 106 (2009): 390–403; Dale A. Russell, *Islands in the Cosmos: The Evolution of Life on Land* (Bloomington: Indiana University Press, 2009); Daniel W. McShea and Robert N. Brandon, *Biology's First Law: The Tendency for Diversity and Complexity to Increase in Evolutionary Systems* (Chicago: University of Chicago Press, 2010); George R. McGhee, Jr., *Convergent Evolution: Limited Forms Most Beautiful* (Cambridge: M.I.T. Press, 2011); Russell Powell, "Convergent Evolution and the Limits of Natural Selection," *European Journal for the Philosophy of Science* 2 (2012): 355–373; Russell Powell and Carlos Mariscal, "Convergent Evolution as Natural Experiment: The Tape of Life Reconsidered," *Interface Focus* 5, no. 6 (2015): 20150040; Russell Powell, *Contingency and Convergence: Toward a Cosmic Biology of Body and Mind* (Harvard: MIT Press, 2020).
[59] Jonathan B. Losos, *Improbable Destinies: Fate, Chance, and the Future of Evolution* (New York: Riverhead Books, 2017), 81–107. See also R. Brian Langerhans and Thomas J. DeWitt, "Shared and Unique Features of Evolutionary

environmental niche has the same type of creature filling it, as there is often more than one way to adapt to an environmental situation. So, for example, some underground rodents are diggers and possess exaggerated forelimbs, while others use their mouths to remove soil and so have large jaws and teeth. So too certain nectar-eating birds use long beaks and tongues to get at the nectar, such as hummingbirds, but others, such as the flowerpiercer, have a sharp hook on their bill in order to pierce the flower at its base. Again woodpeckers use their bill to dig insects out of trees but the woodpecker finch uses twigs to aid in the same process. Finally, there may be genetic limits to evolution, hereditary predispositions for evolving in certain ways, or intermediate morphological conditions between transitional states that are adaptively poor, all of which limit convergent evolution from occurring. This is perhaps why the human species evolved only once even though lemurs and other monkeys have lived in Madagascar, South America, and other areas for millions of years. Losos thus asserts "natural selection is either not as predictable or as powerful as some make it out to be. That is, even when species experience identical environments, they might not evolve in the same way,"[60] and moreover, "seemingly just as often, maybe more often, species living in similar environments don't adapt convergently."[61] Applied to extraterrestrial life this means, per Losos, that there will probably exist some parallels between terrestrial and extraterrestrial life, such as multicellularity, organisms with differentiated tissues, organs, and complex body parts including camera-like eyes, wings, and even a degree of intelligence. Still, according to Losos extraterrestrial life for the most part can be expected to be different from life as it occurs on Earth.[62] Alien creatures are likely to be mish-mashes of organisms found on Earth and so possess similar parts but have them arranged in wholly different combinations.[63] So there might be winged intelligent monkeys or duck-billed humanoids. Summing up his position Losos writes:

Diversification," *The American Naturalist* 164, no. 3 (2004): 335–349; Terry J. Ord and Thomas Summers, "Repeated Evolution and the Impact of Evolutionary History on Adaptation," *BMC Evolutionary Biology* 15 (2015): 1–12; Zachary D. Blount, Richard E. Lenski, and Jonathan B. Losos, "Contingency and Determinism in Evolution: Replaying Life's Tape," *Science* 362, no. 6415 (2018): 651–654; Jonathan B. Losos, "Adaptive Radiation, Ecological Opportunity, and Evolutionary Determinism," *The American Naturalist* 175, no. 6 (2010): 623–639; Zachary Blount, "Replaying Evolution," *Scientific American* 105, no. 3 (2017): 156–165.

[60] Losos, *Improbable Destinies*, 88.

[61] Losos, *Improbable Destinies*, 106.

[62] Losos, *Improbable Destinies*, 312–313, 318–319, 333–334.

[63] Losos, *Improbable Destinies*, 331.

At the end of the day, we know that evolution is not random or haphazard. Natural selection restricts the way that species can evolve, often constraining them to adapt in the same way when facing similar environmental circumstances. In some cases, there are single best biological solutions to problems posed by the environment, and in many cases, species repeatedly attain these optima. . . . The world of biological possibilities, however, is often a vast one, and even with biases from natural selection, genetics, and development, the set of evolutionary realizable end points may be large. As a result, evolution often goes its own way. This is particularly true when evolution begins from different starting points with different genes and developmental systems. However, even starting from the same ancestral stock and experiencing similar circumstances, the outcome can be divergent. Evolution repeats itself sometimes, but often it doesn't. So, can we predict evolution? In the short-term, yes, to some extent. But the longer the passage of time and the more different the ancestors or conditions, the less likely we are to prognosticate successfully. Dinosauroid? I don't think so. Perry the Platypusoid? Alas, no. Were we destined to be here? Hardly. . . . If any of a countless number of events had occurred differently in the past, *Homo sapiens* wouldn't have evolved. We were far from inevitable and are lucky to be here, fortunate that events happened just as they did . . . On the other hand, perhaps with a different historical sequence, humanoid doppelgangers could have evolved prolifically. Perhaps the world could have been populated by marsupial humans, as well as lemur humans, bear humans, crow humans, even lizard humans.[64]

Who is right, Gould, Conway Morris, or Losos? Is evolution contingent or readily predictable?[65] Would we expect life on extrasolar planets to be

---

[64] Losos, *Improbable Destinies*, 333–334.

[65] Here I think the fact that the fauna of the Burgess Shale has more relationships to contemporary orders of invertebrates than originally thought is not a huge threat to Gould's argument contrary to many others. It does take away some of the steam from the argument that only certain lineages survived extinction and if they had not evolution would be different. But even if we grant that more lineages than thought survived extinction Gould could still argue that the particular course that evolution took was unlikely to occur more than once. That is to say, we need other arguments against Gould's position. On this issue consult: L. Ramsköld and Hou Xianguang, "New Early Cambrian Animal and Onychophoran Affinities of Enigmatic Metazoans," *Nature* 351 (May 16, 1991): 225–228; Briggs, et al., "Morphological Disparity in the Cambrian," *Science* 256, no. 5064 (1992): 1670–1673; Mark Ridley, "Analysis of the Burgess Shale," *Paleobiology* 19 (1993): 519–521; Keynyn Brysse, "From Weird Wonders to Stem Lineages: The Second Reclassification of the Burgess Shale Fauna," *Studies in History and Philosophy of Science Part C: Studies in History and Philosophy of Biological and Biomedical Sciences* 39, no. 3 (2008): 298–313; James MacLaurin and Kim Sterelny, *What Is Biodiversity?* (Chicago: University of Chicago

similar to the forms on planet Earth? In order to get a handle on this question we need to examine evolutionary patterns involving adaptation, stagnation, novelty, multiple functional morphological solutions, convergence, and divergence, along with the timing of these events. We also need to get a handle philosophically on some of these concepts, such as the meanings of contingency and convergence. And though studies on bacterial populations or isolated island and glacial populations are instructive, in order to look at convergent evolution it is best to examine the paleontological record and evolution occurring in systems of great geographical, environmental, and temporal extent, with maximal species diversity and metabolic resources.

First, as to contingency. Gould, and even Losos at times, fails to distinguish clearly what he means by a human being. Here the work of one of the earliest Greek philosophers, Aristotle, can aid us immensely. Aristotle distinguished between substances and accidents, or those traits that are essential to something being what it is and those traits that are incidental to it being what it is.[66] While having reason is essential to being a human for Aristotle, and bipedality for Plato, wearing a particular style of clothing, or possessing a particular skin color is not. With this in mind, and going somewhat beyond Aristotle, we can ask what is essential to being a human? Here it seems being an animal that can move about and interact with the environment, being capable of rational thought and manipulation of this environment in light of one's ideas, ideals, and intentions, seem particularly essential. Yet other features of a human, such as having two arms and legs, versus four limbs, five fingers and toes, having eyes on the front of the head, even bipedality, do not seem essential. Nor is one's particular life or evolutionary history essential to being a human. Hence the fact that humans with a particular evolutionary history, such as a descent from *Pikia*, have arisen only once is in no way an argument for the contingency of evolution. Nor is even the proposal that evolution is unlikely to lead to bipedal, haired, two-armed and two-legged creatures on other planets. What matters is how evolutionarily likely are intelligent beings with a capacity to interact with, manipulate, and change their environment in ways aligning with their imagination, goals, and values (that is having some ability for motion and

Press, 2008), 42–59; Christian Baron, "A Web of Controversies: Complexity in the Burgess Shale Debate," *Journal of the History of Biology* 44 (2011): 745–780; Douglas H. Erwin, "Wonderful Life Revisited: Chance and Contingency in the Ediacaran-Cambrian Radiation," in *Chance in Evolution*, ed. Grant Ramsey and Charles H. Pence (Chicago: The University of Chicago Press, 2016), 277–298.
[66] *Categories*, 1b25-2a4. On this point see the reflections of Conway Morris above as well as Daniel Dennett, *Darwin's Dangerous Idea: Evolution and the Meanings of Life* (New York: Simon and Schuster, 1996), 56.

limbs of some sort able to manipulate objects in the environment). Whether or not these creatures resemble humans in accidental traits such as having hair versus feathers or scales, a particular type of dentition, or a particular number of limbs, is incidental. Because Gould fails to distinguish clearly essential from accidental features of humans, he exaggerates the contingency of human evolution. Losos is more willing to allow for the possibility of convergence on a human form, though he downplays this a bit by calling such beings doppelgangers, but he too is not clear enough in defining what traits are essential to being a human and what are not.

Gould is perhaps aware of this deficiency in his argumentation for the contingency of human evolution as he presents a second argument as well, i.e. that key features on the way to human beings such as bilaterality, the evolution of limbs and jaws, etc., are rare and unique occurrences involving the rearrangement of parts evolved for preexisting purposes that happened to have the right alignment or potentiality for such a change.[67] This is a better argument for human contingency if it is sound.

We can get a partial answer to this question by examining complex features that have evolved in organisms and see if they have evolved independently more than once. We need to be cautious here, however. The fact that something has evolved only once on Earth is not really relevant to human contingency. For it may be that it only needed or happened to evolve only once but that it could have evolved more than once if necessary. So the real question, and what needs examining, is how likely is it for complex features that involve the rearrangement of parts to evolve again, whether or not they evolved only once on Earth or not. And we can examine this issue via paleontological data. If we find that highly complex and rearranged systems have evolved more than once during the course of evolution then it is plausible to hold that traits that have evolved only once in Earth's history could have fairly easily evolved more than once.

Now if we examine the history of life on Earth we do find that many (though not all) complex features have convergently occurred several times throughout the course of the Earth's history. Thus the data suggests that the

---

[67] Gould, *Wonderful Life*, 309–320. See also David Jablonski and David J. Bottjer, "The Ecology of Evolutionary Innovations: The Fossil Record," in *Evolutionary Innovations*, ed. Matthew H. Nitecki (Chicago: University of Chicago Press, 1990), 253–288; John Maynard Smith and Eörs Szathmáry, *The Major Transitions in Evolution* (Oxford: W.H. Freeman and Company, 1995); Brett Calcott and Kim Sterelny, eds., *The Major Transitions in Evolution Revisited* (Cambridge: MIT Press, 2011); Neil Shubin, *Some Assembly Required: Decoding Four Billion Years of Life, from Ancient Fossils to DNA* (New York: Pantheon, 2020).

evolution of such complex and rearranged features is quite within the reach of evolution, whether on Earth or a planet similar to Earth.

For example, primitive eyes have evolved convergently in dinoflagellates, annelids, and fish, and camera-like eyes involving lenses and optic nerves have independently evolved in fish, cnidaria, and cephalopods.[68] The ability to produce silk threads has independently evolved in spiders, silk moths, and caddis flies.[69] And, as we have seen, the ability to fly has evolved in many different lineages convergently such as in butterflies, birds, pterosaurs, and bats. We can add to this the independent evolution of bioluminescence in cnidaria, fish, fireflies, and glowworms; echolocation in shrews, bats, and dolphins; needle-like poison injection systems in spiders, scorpions, snakes, and the poisonous spurs of the platypus; baleen filter-feeding mechanisms in whale sharks and true whales; and harpoon tongues in plethodontid salamanders and chameleons.[70]

Other complex features to have evolved in unrelated lines include opposable thumbs in primates, the giant panda, the red panda, koalas and opossums;[71] and prehensile tails in monkeys, squirrels, kinkajous, porcupines, opossums, ring tail possums, European harvest mice, pangolins, anteaters, as well as chameleons, skinks, and seahorses.[72] In fact some of the key traits that Gould mentions as unlikely to evolve more than once, such as vertebrate

---

[68] D.E. Nilsson and S. Pelger., "A Pessimistic Estimate of the Time Required for an Eye to Evolve," *Proceedings of the Royal Society of London B: Biological Sciences* 256, no. 1345 (1994): 53–58; M.F. Land and D.-E. Nilsson, *Animal Eyes* (Oxford: Oxford University Press, 2002); Russell D. Fernald, "Casting a Genetic Light on the Evolution of the Eye," *Science* 313, no. 5795 (2006): 1914–1918; Z. Kozmik, et al., "Assembly of the Cnidarian Camera-Type Eye from Vertebrate-Like Components," *Proceedings of the National Academy of Sciences* 105, no. 26 (2008): 8989–8993.

[69] T.D. Sutherland, et al., "Insect Silk: One Name, Many Materials," *Annual Review of Entomology* 55, no. 1 (2010): 171–188.

[70] Matthew J. Mason and Peter M. Narins, "Seismic Signal Use by Fossorial Mammals," *American Zoologist* 41, no. 5 (2001): 1171–1184; Joe Parker, et al., "Genome-Wide Signatures of Convergent Evolution in Echolocating Mammals," *Nature* 502 (2013): 228–231.

[71] Manuel J. Salesa, et al., "Evidence of a False Thumb in a Fossil Carnivore Clarifies the Evolution of Pandas," Proceedings of the National Academy of Sciences 103, no. 2 (2006): 379–382; Yibo Hu, et al. "Comparative Genomics Reveals Convergent Evolution Between the Bamboo-Eating Giant and Red Pandas," *Proceedings of the National Academy of Sciences* 114, no. 5 (2017): 1081–1086.

[72] J. M. Organ, *The Functional Anatomy of Prehensile and Nonprehensile Tails of the Platyrrhini (Primates) and Procyonidae (Carnivora)* (Baltimore: Johns Hopkins University Press, 2008); C. Neutens et al., "Grasping Convergent Evolution in Syngnathids: A Unique Tale of Tails," *Journal of Anatomy* 224, no. 6 (2014): 710–723.

limbs and jaws and notochords have analogues in invertebrates, as limbs and jaws occur in arthropods and hemichordates possess a stomochord. Indeed even though the exact origin of the notochords found in *Pikia* over 500 million years ago is still in dispute, one theory is that they evolved from midline axochords that were common in earlier invertebrates such as annelids.[73] Moreover, if we focus on the evolution of vertebrate limbs over 370 million years ago, we find examples of the convergent evolution of the limb-like fins that Gould held to be idiosyncratic and a contingent predecessor of limbs. It now seems that there was a great variety of pectoral and pelvic fin structure in Devonian fishes and that some of them converged on a limb-like structure in order to walk across the sea floor.[74] This being the case, evolution of these novel and complex structures does not seem particularly challenging and though they may have occurred only once on Earth, *in vertebrates* that is, they could well have occurred more than once and seem likely to occur in alien life forms.

If we examine some of the other major transitions that Gould discusses it is harder to know how easily such evolutionary leaps can occur on exoplanets. Though we don't know exactly how life—involving a surrounding lipid membrane, protein structures, and a replicable nucleic acid-based genetic code—arose on Earth (though we have an idea of some

---

[73] A. Hejnol and C. J. Lowe, "Animal Evolution: Stiff or Squishy Notochord Origins?," *Current Biology* 24, no. 23 (2014): R1131–R1133; Antonella Lauri et al., "Development of the Annelid Axochord: Insights into Notochord Evolution," *Science* 345, no. 6202 (2014): 1365–1368; Giovani Annona et al., "Evolution of the Notichord," *EvoDevo* 6 (2015); Thibaut Brunet, et al., "Did the Notochord Evolve from an Ancient Axial Muscle?: The Axochord Hypothesis," *BioEssays* 37, no. 8 (2015): 836–850.

[74] See Conway Morris, *Life's Solution*, 2003, 234 and 416 n. 38. Consult Zerina Johanson and Per E. Ahlberg, "Primitive Rhizodont Fish Has Limb-Like Fins," *Nature* 394 (1998): 569-573; Per E. Ahlberg and Zerina Johanson, "Osteolepiformes and the Ancestry of Tetrapods," *Nature* 395 (1998): 792–794; Brian K. Hall, *Fins into Limbs: Evolution, Development, and Transformation* (Chicago: University of Chicago Press, 2007); Thom Holmes, *March onto Land: The Silurian Period to the Middle Triassic Epoch* (New York: Chelsea House, 2008); Thomas A. Stewart, W. Leo Smith, and Michael I. Coates, "The Origins of Adipose Fins: An Analysis of Homoplasy and the Serial Homology of Vertebrate Appendages," *Proceedings of the Royal Society B: Biological Sciences* 281, no. 1781 (2014): 20133120; Jonathan E. Jeffrey, et al., "Unique Pelvic Fin in a Tetrapod-Like Fossil Fish, and the Evolution of Limb Patterning," *Proceedings of the National Academy of Sciences* 115, no. 47 (2018): 12005–12010; Borja Esteve-Altava, et al., "Evolutionary Parallelisms of Pectoral and Pelvic Network-Anatomy from Fins to Limbs," *Science Advances* 5, no. 5 (2019): eaau7459.

possible biochemical pathways),[75] life did arise fairly early on in the Earth's history, almost as soon as it was able to in fact: the Earth formed around 4.5 billion years ago and partial evidence of life dates to 4.1 to 4.2 billion years ago.[76] We also have discovered that some of the ingredients of life, such as water and complex organic molecules (methyl cyanide and cyanoacetyline), are fairly abundant in the cosmos and likely to be on certain other exoplanets.[77] Thus the origin of life seems likely to occur more than once in the universe whether through natural secondary causality or a combination of natural and supernatural secondary causality. Multicellular life is also likely quite common in the cosmos as it arose independently on Earth several times, in animals, plants, red algae, brown algae, and in a couple lines of fungi.[78] Finally, around 2.6 billion years ago cyanobacteria arose

---

[75] Julian Chela-Flores, Tobias Owen, and François Raulin, eds., *The First Steps of the Origin of Life in the Universe* (Dordrecht: Kluwer, 2001), 401–407; Nick Lane, "Life: Is It Inevitable or Just a Fluke?" *New Scientist* 2870 (June 28, 2012); Robert M. Hazen, *The Story of Earth: The First 4.5 Billion Years, from Stardust to Living Planet* (London: Penguin, 2013); Andrew H. Knoll, *Life on a Young Planet: The First Three Billion Years of Evolution on Earth* (Princeton: Princeton University Press, 2015); Bhavesh H. Patel et al., "Common Origins of RNA, Protein and Lipid Precursors in a Cyanosulfidic Protometabolism," *Nature Chemistry* 7 (2015): 301–307; Peter Ward and Joe Kirschvink, *A New History of Life: The Radical New Discoveries About the Origins and Evolution of Life on Earth* (London: Bloomsbury Press, 2015); Sidney Becker, et al., "Unified Prebiotically Plausible Synthesis of Pyrimidine and Purine RNA Ribonucleotides," *Science* 366, no. 6461 (2019): 76–82; Tamal Das, Siddharth Ghule, and Kumar Vanka, "Insights Into the Origin of Life: Did It Begin from HCN and H2O?," *ACS Central Science* 5, no. 9 (2019): 1532–1540; Callum S. Foden, at al., "Prebiotic Synthesis of Cysteine Peptides that Catalyze Peptide Ligation in Neutral Water," *Science* 370, no. 6518 (2020): 865–869.

[76] Elizabeth Bell, et al., "Potentially Biogenic Carbon Preserved in a 4.1 Billion-Year-Old Zircon," *Proceedings of the National Academy of Sciences* 112, no. 47 (2015): 14518–14521; Matthew S. Dodd, et al., "Evidence for Early Life in Earth's Oldest Hydrothermal Vent Precipitates," *Nature* 543, no. 7643 (2017): 60–64.

[77] C. M. Bradford et al., "The Water Vapor Spectrum of APM 08279+5255: X-Ray Heating and Infrared Pumping over Hundreds of Parsecs," *Astrophysical Journal Letters* 741 (2011): 1–11; Karin I. Öberg, et al., "The Comet-Like Composition of a Protoplanetary Disk as Revealed by Complex Cyanides," *Nature* 520, no. 7546 (2015): 198–201; Queenie H. S. Chan et al., "Organic Matter in Extraterrestrial Water-Bearing Salt Crystals," *Science Advances* 4 (2018): eaao3521.

[78] Joel L. Sachs, "Resolving the First Steps to Multicellularity," *Trends in Ecology and Evolution* 23, no. 5 (2008): 245–248; Andrew H. Knoll, "The Multiple Origins of Complex Multicellularity," *Annual Review of Earth and Planetary Sciences* 39 (2011): 217–239; Bettina E. Schirrmeister et al., "The Origin of Multicellularity in

that were able to develop photosynthetic systems, tap into the energy source of the Sun, and produce oxygen as an end-product, leading to an atmospheric biochemistry suitable to oxygen-breathing organisms.[79] Again, such an occurrence does not seem particularly unlikely on an exoplanet.

On the other hand, the formation of complex multi-cellular organisms, such as eukaryotic animals and plants, involving cells developing interior parts or organelles, which in part occurred when one organism incorporated another inside of its cell (endosymbiosis), and complex differentiated tissues, seems rare and not super easy to achieve. It was initially thought to have occurred only twice, with the incorporation of chloroplasts into plant cells around 1.6 billion years ago and mitochondria into animal cells around 600 million years ago in the Ediacaran period, but is now thought to have occurred on at least one other occasion about 60 million years ago.[80] Still

---

Cyanobacteria," *BMC Evolutionary Biology* 11 (2011): 45; Stuart A. West et al., "Major Evolutionary Transitions in Individuality," *Proceedings of the National Academy of Sciences* 112, no. 33 (2015): 10112–10119; William Bains and Dark Schulze-Makuch, "The Cosmic Zoo: The (Near) Inevitability of the Evolution of Complex, Macroscopic Life," *Life* 6, no. 3 (2016): 25; William Bains, "How Likely Are We?: Evolution of Organismal Complexity," in *Evolutionary Biology: Convergent Evolution, Evolution of Complex Traits, Concepts and Methods*, ed. Pierre Pontarotti (Dordrecht: Springer, 2016): 255–272; Elizabeth Pennisi, "The Momentous Transition to Multicellular Life May Not Have Been so Hard after All," *Science*, June 28, 2018, https://www.sciencemag.org/news/2018/06/momentous-transition-multicellular-life-may-not-have-been-so-hard-after-all; László Nagy and Robin Ohm, "Complex Multicellularity in Fungi," *Fungal Biology Reviews* 32, no. 4 (2018): 205–264.

[79] A. Anbar et al., "A Whiff of Oxygen before the Great Oxidation Event?," *Science* 317, no. 5846 (2007): 1903–1906; D. E. Canfield, et al., "Late-Neoproterozoic Deep-Ocean Oxygenation and the Rise of Animal Life," *Science* 315, no. 5808 (2007): 92–95; Chandler M. Ostrander et al., "Fully Oxygenated Water Columns over Continental Shelves before the Great Oxidation Event," *Nature Geoscience* 12 (2019): 186–191.

[80] Mark McMenamin, *The Garden of Ediacara: Discovering the First Complex Life* (New York: Columbia University Press, 1998); Patrick J. Keeling, "Diversity and Evolutionary History of Plastids and Their Hosts," *American Journal of Botany* 91, no. 10 (2004): 1481–1493; A.H. Knoll et al., "Eukaryotic Organisms in Proterozoic Oceans," *Philosophical Transactions of the Royal Society B: Biological Sciences* 361, no. 1470 (2006): 1023–1038; Hwan Su Yoon, et al., "Minimal Plastid Genome Evolution in the Paulinella Endosymbiont," *Current Biology* 16, no. 17 (2006): PR670–R672; Dana C. Price et al., "Cyanophora paradoxa Genome Elucidates Origin of Photosynthesis in Algae and Plants," *Science* 335, no. 6070 (2012): 843–847; S. Bengtson, et al., "Three-Dimensional Preservation of Cellular and Subcellular Structures Suggests 1.6 Billion-Year-Old Crown-Group Red Algae," *PLoS Biology*

the formation of complex cell structures and differential tissue formation took a rather long time to occur perhaps in light of the need to build up cellular and genetic precursors. So it is hard to answer the question of how easily it could have occurred again or how likely it is to occur on an alien planet. On the one hand a single occurrence may be so successful and lead to the colonization of available ecological zones that its repetition is unnecessary or unlikely. Additionally, given that it occurred on a couple of occasions, the endosymbiotic origin of organelles seems somewhat likely to occur. On the other hand, the fact that it took a long time for such acts of endosymbiosis to occur, while cyanobacteria and other prokaryotes occupied the Earth for a billion years and counting before such complex life arose, suggests their rarity. Still, not all organelles seem to have arisen through endosymbiosis so there might be other pathways of formation of similar functioning systems. Answering the question then of how likely complex multicellular life might arise involves understanding what sorts of biochemical and internal events were happening in early organic life forms, what particular events led to the formation of cell organelles, the genetic mechanisms involved, and sundry other matters, leaving the answer to the question something of a mystery.

Gould and others, of course, make much of the fact that there are periods of stagnation where nothing much seems to change, which are interrupted by explosions of life as with the Great Oxidation Event or the Cambrian Explosion. He appears to argue that such great periods of time with nothing much happening suggest that evolutionary events are fairly contingent. Yet here we cannot just look at paleontological evidence but also must have recourse to studies on living organisms. While not much may seem to be changing based on exoskeletal or hard fossil evidence much change may be occurring within the biochemistry of the organisms. Indeed we often do see changes occurring in various ways over time in different lineages even as some lineages settle into a stagnant pattern. In addition there seem to be certain precursors, such as the build-up of atmospheric oxygen, or the development of certain body forms or ecological niches, that take time before certain other evolutionary events can occur. There also seem to be

---

15, no. 3 (2017): e2000735; Ilya Bobrovskiy, et al., "Ancient Steroids Establish the Ediacaran Fossil *Dickinsonia* as One of the Earliest Animals," *Science* 361, no. 6408 (2018): 1246–1249; Rachel A. Wood, "The Rise of Animals: New Fossils and Analyses of Ancient Ocean Chemistry Reveal the Surprisingly Deep Roots of the Cambrian Explosion," *Scientific American* 320, no. 6 (2019): 24–31; Scott D. Evans, Ian V. Hughes, James G. Gehling, and Mary L. Droser, Mary L, "Discovery of the Oldest Bilaterian from the Ediacaran of South Australia," *Proceedings of the National Academy of Sciences* 117, no. 14 (2020): 7845–7850.

certain preferential convergent patterns in different forms due to a given basal morphology or metabolic system. So, for example, it seems reptiles have a predilection for taking on certain types of body shapes in evolution, such as legless ones or sauropodal ones, whereas mammals have a predilection for other types of body shapes such as ant-eating ones or squirrel-like ones. These are areas for further investigation before we can answer the question of how repeatable such events are likely to be. It may be that on alien planets there will be extended periods of stagnation as well. Yet if we have lots of different possible words and lots of time these events become much more likely and predictable. There will also likely be "living fossils" on alien worlds or organisms that have maintained the same form for a long period of time. For evolution sometimes achieves a form that successful colonizes a stable niche such as the horseshoe crabs, coelacanths, the opossum, squirrels, and elephant shrews.[81] However, this does not mean that we can't expect other life forms that undergo a high amount of adaptive radiation and converge on different ecomorphs.

Another mystery is the evolution of human consciousness. Due to humans possessing such features as free will and intentionality of mental content a purely natural evolution of consciousness does not seem likely. Then again God could have chosen to endow organisms with consciousness whenever their nervous systems reach a certain level of complexity and so in a more-or-less law-like manner, i.e. a form of supernatural secondary causality, as it were.[82] Hence it is hard to predict how common intelligent

---

[81] David Sepkoski, "Macroevolution," *The Oxford Handbook of Philosophy of Biology*, ed. Michael Ruse (Oxford: Oxford University Press, 2008), 211–237; Josef C. Uyeda, et al., "The Million-Year Wait for Macroevolutionary Bursts," *Proceedings of the National Academy of Sciences* 108, no. 38 (2011): 15908–15913; David Jablonski, "Approaches to Macroevolution: 1. General Concepts and Origin of Variation," *Evolutionary Biology* 44 (2017): 427–450; Derek D. Turner, "Paleobiology's Uneasy Relationship with the Darwinian Tradition: Stasis as Data," in *The Darwinian Tradition in Context*, ed. Richard G. Delisle (Dordrecht: Springer, 2017), 333–352; Scott Lidgard and Alan C. Love, "Rethinking Living Fossils," *BioScience*, 68, no. 10 (2018): 760–770; Derek D. Turner, "In Defense of Living Fossils," *Biology and Philosophy* 34 (2019): 21–23.

[82] In the Catholic tradition it is common to distinguish between secondary causality and divine intervention. That is to say, God typically works through laws of nature or secondary causes and does not interfere in their functioning. God only occasionally intervenes in nature through miracles, and He does so not to restore balance to a natural system or correct errant natural processes, but rather for a specific purpose, such as to reveal the divine nature, show that someone is a saint, or make known the incarnation of God. Moreover, in the Catholic tradition there is also a notion of the continuous causal operativity of God or divine concurrence, such

life will be in the cosmos even if non-intelligent life is abundant.[83] God may desire lots of planets with intelligent beings or may limit this. Here we can only speculate and are faced with the partial inscrutability of the divine will.

As we have seen, Losos' main argument for evolutionary contingency is the existence of evolutionary idiosyncrasies. And it is true that there are some unique evolutionary forms that have evolved only once and perhaps will never evolve again on Earth. For instance, the strange Burgess shale creatures *Opabinia*, *Anomalocaris*, and *Hallucigenia*, the long-necked extinct reptile *Tanystropheus*, dinosaurs such as *Stegosaurus*, *Apatosaurus*, *Pachycephalosaurus*, *Triceratops*, *Tyrannosaurus*, the temnospondyl *Gerrothorax*, the dicynodont *Placerias*, the therapsid *Cynognathus*, the giant ground sloth *Megatherium* and the giant rhino *Indricotherium*, and living forms including the hammerhead shark, angler fish, squids and octopuses, frogs, nightjar birds, the star-nosed mole, giraffes, aye-aye lemurs with their elongated fingers, and the proboscis monkey. Losos' trump card for evolutionary contingency is, however, the genus *Platypus* which he considers to be an evolutionary singleton and is an unparalleled species of aquatic mammal with a duck-like bill, webbed-feet, shielded noses and digging forelimbs, and a paddle-like tail.

Yet there are partial parallels elsewhere in the animal kingdom to even these unique creatures, such as the striped possum [Order Diprotodontia] with elongated fingers parallel to the aye-aye or the extinct apatomyids [Order Cimolesta]; *Chalicotherium* [Order Perissodactyla] which resembles the ground sloth *Megatherium* [Order Pilosa]; and the long-necked brachiosaurs [Clade Saurischia], nothosaurs, and plesiosaurs [Superorder Sauropterygia]

---

as God as the continual conserving cause of the universe, and God as continually offering grace to creatures. Hence it is possible that though the origin of life or the origin of the soul requires powers beyond those of nature, God will continually grant these powers when certain situations arise. In this way there is a form of supernatural secondary causality as well. Finally, God might intervene on select occasions in order to bestow life or souls on a planet. All of which is to say that theologically it is not always clear how common certain stages of life might be in the cosmos from the perspective of the divine will. For more on these distinctions consult Armand Maurer, "Darwin, Thomists, and Secondary Causality," *The Review of Metaphysics* 57, no. 3 (2004): 491–514; Mariano Artigas, "Causality Primary and Secondary," *Encyclopedia of Science and Religion* (Detroit: Gale, 2013), accessed July 5, 2020, http://www.enotes.com/causality-primary-secondary-reference/causality-primary-secondary.

[83] Gerhard Roth, "Convergent Evolution of Complex Brains and High Intelligence," *Transactions of the Royal Society B: Biological Sciences* 370, no. 1684 (2015): 20150049; Joseph LeDoux, *The Deep History of Ourselves: The Four-Billion-Year Story of How We Got Conscious Brains* (New York: Viking, 2019).

that resemble *Tanystropheus* [Order Prolacertiformes].[84] Furthermore there are other distinctive animal forms that have evolved more than once, such as the long-snouted swordfish [Family Xiphiidae of Order Istiophoriformes], paddle fish [Family Polyodontidae of Order Acipenseriformes], and ichthyotringids [Family Ichthyotringidae of Order Alepisauriformes]; the armored and tail-weaponed mammalian glyptodonts, which resemble the dinosaur ankylosaurs;[85] the flat and armored turtle forms of true turtles [Order Testudines] and the placodonts *Cyamodus* and *Henodus* [Order Placodontia];[86] and the sails on the backs of pelycosaurs, spinosaurids, poposauroids, and the dissorophid amphibians.[87] And regarding the platypus Losos himself admits that ducks, otters, marsupial moles, and beavers have individual parts that bear strong resemblances to the parts of the platypus.[88] Indeed a fossil of a semi-aquatic docodontan mammal that closely resembles the platypus with similar tailbones and so perhaps a flattened tail, though perhaps without the bill, was discovered and described just a few years before Losos published his book.[89] And, for that matter, the desmans [Tribe Desmanini of Family Talpidae] resemble the platypus to a great degree with enlarged, albeit horizontally flattened, tails and wide, flat, square-shaped snouts. Still Lobos is correct, and Gould as well, in holding that there are some morphologies that evolved for a peculiar situation and from a particular circumstance and are likely to be unrepeated. And there might be certain morphologies that can more readily give rise to other morphologies than others. That is, some particular starting points can

---

[84] One can peruse the volume Ross Piper, *Extraordinary Animals: An Encyclopedia of Curious and Unusual Animals* (Westport: Greenwood Press, 2007) for other examples.

[85] Victoria Arbour and Lindsay Zanno, "Tail Weaponry in Ankylosaurs and Glyptodonts: An Example of a Rare but Strongly Convergent Phenotype," *The Anatomical Record* 303, no. 4 (2019): 988–998.

[86] Olivier Rieppel and Robert R. Reisz, "The Origin and Early Evolution of Turtles, " *Annual Review of Ecology and Systematics* 30 (1999): 1–22; Rainer R. Schoch and Hans-Dieter Sues, "The Origin of the Turtle Body Plan: Evidence from Fossils and Embryos," *Palaeontology* 63, no. 3 (2020): 375–393.

[87] Richard J. Butler, et al., "The Sail-Backed Reptile Ctenosauriscus from the Latest Early Triassic of Germany and the Timing and Biogeography of the Early Archosaur Radiation," *PLoS One* 6, no. 10 (2011); e25693; M. T. Carrano, et al., "The Phylogeny of Tetanurae (Dinosauria: Therapoda)," *Journal of Systematic Palaeontology* 10, no. 2 (2012): 211–300.

[88] Losos, *Improbable Destinies*, 325–328.

[89] Qiang Ji, et al., "A Swimming Mammaliaform from the Middle Jurassic and Ecomorphological Diversification of Early Mammals," *Science* 311, no. 5764 (2006): 1123–1127.

possibly be more easily adapted to a given environment than others. So analogy can be driven by homology, i.e. some lineages with particular body plans might display a great deal of parallel evolution whereas others might not. In addition Losos (following Simpson and Wainwright) is correct in noting that different phenotypes can produce similar adaptive outcomes; in other words, there are different ways of achieving the same functional morphology (or what is called many-to-one mapping). So, for example, some rodents dig with their claws and others with their incisors.[90] In short we can anticipate that there will be life forms on other planets that will be unique and unlike anything seen on Earth, such as our horned gophers [*Ceratogaulus*], which, while not the same as the fantastical jackalope of popular imagination, come quite close. Science fiction here has been able to imagine vividly such possibilities.

That said it does seem more likely than not that evolution will repeatedly engender similar phenotypes in response to similar environmental demands.

---

[90] See Losos, *Improbable Destinies*, 101–105. See also E. P. Lessa, "Morphological Evolution of Subterranean Mammals: Integrating Structural, Functional, and Ecological Perspectives," *Progress in Clinical and Biological Research* 335 (1990): 211–230; Michael E. Alfaro, Daniel I. Bolnick, and Peter C. Wainwright, "Evolutionary Consequences of Many-to-One Mapping of Jaw Morphology to Mechanics in Labrid Fishes," *The American Naturalist* 165 (2005): e140–e154; Peter C. Wainwright et al., "Many-to-One Mapping of Form to Function: A General Principle in Organismal Design?," *Integrative and Comparative Biology* 45, no. 2 (2005): 256–262; Matthew D. McGee and Peter C. Wainwright, "Convergent Evolution as a Generator of Phenotypic Diversity in the Threespine Stickleback," *Evolution* 67, no. 4 (2013): 1204–1208; David C. Collar, et al., "Imperfect Morphological Convergence: Variable Changes in Cranial Structures Underlie Transitions to Durophagy in Moray Eels," *The American Naturalist* 183, no. 6 (2014): e168–e184; Jonathan B. Losos, "Convergence, Adaptation, and Constraint," *Evolution* 65, no. 7 (2011): 1827–1840; Daniel I. Bolnick, et al., "(Non)Parallel Evolution," *Annual Review of Ecology, Evolution, and Systematics* 49 (2018): 303–330; Cole J. Thompson et al., "Many-to-One Form-to-Function Mapping Weakens Parallel Morphological Evolution," *Evolution* 71, no. 11 (2017): 2738–2749; Sabrina Renaud, et al., "Divergent in Shape and Convergent in Function: Adaptive Evolution of the Mandible in Sub-Antarctic Mice," *Evolution* 72, no. 4 (2018): 878–892; C. Darrin Hulsey, et al., "Pleiotropic Jaw Morphology Links the Evolution of Mechanical Modularity and Functional Feeding Convergence in Lake Malawi Cichlids," *Proceedings of the Royal Society B, Biological Sciences* 286, no. 1897 (2019): 20182358; Martha M. Muñoz, "The Evolutionary Dynamics of Mechanically Complex Systems," *Integrative and Comparative Biology* 59, no. 3 (2019): 705–715; Gabriele Sansalone et al., "Decoupling Functional and Morphological Convergence: The Study Case of Fossorial Mammalia," *Frontiers in Earth Science* 21 (2020).

In light of the large amount of convergent evolution seen in the paleontological record, arguably the main thing precluding evolutionary convergence is not the starting morphology or genetic resources but the adaptive needs of the organism. The fossil record and life forms seen today even suggest that life "wants to" fill up all of the available niches and use all of the available energy resources available to it if it possibly can. Hence we find almost all of the geographical regions of the Earth colonized by life, as well as the evolution of forms that can take advantage of deficient or harsh environments such as cyanobacteria, photosynthetic organisms, carnivorous plants, vertebrate and invertebrate herbivores, vertebrate and invertebrate carnivores, carrion feeders, hematophages, and parasitic forms of life in viruses, bacteria, plants, and insects. The words Jesus says in the Bible come to mind here: "I came so that they might have life and have it more abundantly" (Jn 10:10). Though here too there are exceptions. For example, in organisms undergoing adaptive radiation on islands not every island will have the exact same morphological types; that is, a particular island may be missing an ecotype that could seemingly exploit an available niche. Niches are not always filled with organisms capable of exploiting them.[91]

It is also important to take a non-anthropocentric perspective in considering the evolution of life on Earth and its predictability or contingency. If there are lots of other potential planets on which life could evolve then there will probably be plenty of planets with environments similar to that found on Earth such as ocean, desert, rock outcrops, rivers, air, trees,[92] etc., and so similar niches to which organisms can adapt. Thus

---

[91] Science News Staff, "Lizards Take Convergent Evolution to Extreme," *Science*, March 27, 1998, https://www.sciencemag.org/news/1998/03/lizards-take-convergent-evolution-extreme; Jonathan B. Losos, *Lizards in an Evolutionary Tree: Ecology and Adaptive Radiation of Anoles* (Berkeley: University of California Press, 2011), 367–370; Darin A. Croft, et al., "Diversity and Disparity of Sparassodonts (Metatheria) Reveal Non-Analogue Nature of Ancient South American Mammalian Carnivore Guilds," *Proceedings of the Royal Society B: Biological Sciences* 285, no. 1870 (2018): 20172012.

[92] It is notable that the evolution of plants with trunk-like structures or woody stems is convergent and has happened more than once (as with club mosses [Division Lycophyta], horsetails [Class Polypodiopsida], cycads [Division Cycadophyta], and living deciduous trees and conifers), so would be likely to occur on other planets as well. On this see J. Galtier and F. M. Hueber, "How Early Ferns Became Trees," *Proceedings of the Royal Society of London B: Biological Sciences* 268 (2001): 1955–1957; McGhee, *Convergent Evolution*, 93–97; Andrew D. Hirons and Peter A. Thomas, "The Woody Skeleton: Trunk and Branches," *Applied Tree Biology* (Oxford: Wiley, 2017): 15–76.

we would expect convergence on similar ecotypes among the life forms on such planets. And if we further broaden our perspective temporally we see that evolution becomes more predictable as there are larger periods of time and lots of happenings that allow for repeatability. As the philosopher Lonergan puts it, "low probabilities are offset by large numbers of occasions, so that what is probable only once on a million occasions is to be expected a million times on a million million occasions. In like manner, the rarity of occasions is offset by long intervals of time, so that if occasions arise only once in a million years, still they arise a thousand times in a thousand million years."[93] Even the extinction events noted by Gould, when seen from a larger perspective, can be seen as not precluding the predictivity of evolution. For extinction events can reshuffle the decks of life, as it were, and allow ecological space for new species to arise, including life forms that converge on previous ones. It can take, however, several million years for such adaptive radiations or recoveries to occur as ecosystems with biologically complex and diverse organisms need to be reestablished.[94] Nonetheless even if we posit that the establishment of vertebrates on Earth was an unlikely event, as does the paleontologist Donald Prothero,[95] it may well be commonplace given the multitude of planets in the cosmos.

If we have a multitude of such events on different planets and lots of time, we have the likelihood of convergent lifeforms arising in this reshuffling. To make use of an analogy, the chances of me sequentially drawing the same card number twice in a row in a well-shuffled deck is low, around 6%, but if I repeat this process a million times I will do so around

---

[93] Bernard Lonergan, *Insight: A Study of Human Understanding* (Toronto: University of Toronto Press, 1992), 136–137.

[94] M. B. Hart, ed., *Biotic Recovery from Mass Extinction Events* (London: Geological Society of London, 1996); John Alroy, "The Fossil Record of North American Mammals: Evidence for a Paleocene Evolutionary Radiation," *Systematic Biology* 48, no. 1 (1999): 107–118; Sarda Sahney and Michael J. Benton, "Recovery from the Most Profound Mass Extinction of All Time," *Proceedings of the Royal Society B: Biological Sciences* 275, no. 1636 (2008): 759–765; Robert W. Meredith, et al., "Impacts of the Cretaceous Terrestrial Revolution and KPg Extinction on Mammal Diversification," *Science* 334, no. 6055 (2011): 521–524.

[95] Donald Prothero, "Inevitable Human or Hidden Agendas: A Review of Life's Solution," *Sceptic* 10, no. 3 (2003): 54–57. Prothero, who in this article points out how easy it is to be biased when examining these issues, somewhat ironically does not seem to have freed himself from his own unexamined biases and fails to take into account the possible convergent evolution of bilaterality, notochords, and vertebrae; the increasing complexification of life observed in the fossil record; and the commonality of convergent evolution, some cases of which his own studies have done so much to clarify.

60,000 times. So though a particular niche may not be filled in a given region, or filled with a particular form, if we have lots of time and lots of different planets there will be a multitude of colonizable zones and the odds of convergent evolutionary events happening increases dramatically. This indeed is something we can get a handle on by studying when empty niches occur and ecotypes do not develop, as Losos does. It seems overall that the general trend of life is to occupy a given niche where it can, to colonize a way of life if energy is available. Indeed there does seem to be a sort of evolutionary predilection for increasing the complexity and diversity of species over time if we look at the fossil record. That is to say, eventually new types of organisms evolve, organisms develop in complexity, open niches are filled, and resources are exploited as a general rule, but this does take time and stasis or stagnation as well as some unoccupied niches remain possible as well. Still, given the great amount of convergent evolution we have seen in the history of life, we would expect a fair amount of convergent evolutionary events to occur on alien planets and life forms similar to those found on Earth to arise, along with some novel species as well and some unfilled ecological niches.

Importantly we can test certain views of evolution's predictability or contingency by examining the history of life on this planet. We can examine, for instance, mammalian species and determine how many general adaptive forms there are and how many of them evolved just once versus more than once. If we find that most mammalian forms have evolved more than once than we have evidence that similar lineages will be likely to evolve on other planets. Of course this presumes the preevolution of a mammalian-body type, but again there might be reasons to think that this would evolve more than once in the cosmos as key mammalian traits such as endothermy, fur-coats, and mammary glands seem to work well in order to foster adaptation to changing environments.

In fact, I have done such a study and found that there are around 81 basic mammalian types, or nicotypes.[96] Of these 81 basal mammalian forms, 85% (69/81) have independently arisen more than once and so involve cases of convergent evolution. Indeed 40% (32/81) of these basic mammalian types have been converged upon four times or more. So only 15% (12/81) basic mammalian types seem to have arisen only once. Indeed, of these forms, a couple are primitive or early types of which it is hard to detect convergent events, such as with mice. The others, however, do seem to be unique evolutionary events and include such creatures as bats, burramyids,

---

[96] See elsewhere in this book my study "A Taxonomy for Alien Mammalian-Like Life Forms," pp. 198–260.

acrobatids, hippotragins, hyracodontids, the maned wolf, whales, and humans. These often involve novel traits that were very successfully evolutionary such as flight or bipedalism or filter-feeding, or unique dietary adaptations such as hematophagy or nectivory. In any case this suggests, contrary to Prothero,[97] that convergence in animals, or at least in mammalian lines, is quite common. Of course similar studies can and should be done in other animal lineages as well, such as with reptiles, birds, and invertebrates, where convergent evolution may be less common. This question, though, should be examined and answered scientifically and not based upon one's pre-existing biases.

In the end Gould, Losos, Prothero, and others, are influenced by a philosophical perspective that they bring to the interpretation of scientific data. As the Duhem-Quine thesis reminds us, all facts are theory-laden. I would like to think they were/are aware of their philosophical presuppositions but that may not be the case. Gould, as we saw, does not like any view that smacks of historical determinism and values human freedom to the extreme. So any position wherein evolutionary events are contingent is welcome for him as he thinks it allows for maximal human freedom. Hence Gould revels in the fact that the universe at large is "one indifferent to our suffering, and therefore offering us maximum freedom to thrive, or to fail, in our own chosen way."[98] Losos, as well, is convinced that evolution has no "foresight," is a "tinkerer," and so will not have an overarching directionality. Yet such a view is more philosophical than scientific; it is a conception of the ultimate nature of reality as mindless and rudderless *applied to* evolutionary theory rather than *derived from* it. Nor is there a solid scientific basis to consider the evolutionary process as completely blind as Losos seems to think. Rather such an interpretation of evolution is based upon preexisting ideas as to the ultimate nature of reality and its overall meaningfulness. Losos, in fact, ends his volume in a Gouldian manner, asserting, "We are here today, the result of billions of years of

---

[97] Prothero, "Inevitable Human or Hidden Agendas," 54–57, gives the odd argument that if convergent evolution were as common as thought than biologists would not be able to tell animals apart. But this again fails to appreciate the philosophical distinction between accidents and substances. There may well be convergences in overall morphology but also retention or development of unique features. So convergence need not occur in all features of organisms. Convergent evolution in other words may make phylogenetic systematics more difficult but it need not make it impossible. In fact his own books on mammalian evolution point out many cases of convergence and do much to help establish evolutionary relationships in spite of this convergence.

[98] Gould, *Wonderful Life*, 323.

natural selection and the flukes of history that sent life down one path and not others. Lucky? Yes. Destined, no. We should make the most of our evolutionary good fortune."[99] So here again appears a philosophical embrace of a maximal sort of human freedom as an ultimate good. A Catholic would of course respond that there are ways of mixing freedom and destiny. Though one is graced one has to cooperate with that grace. So there is not a conflict between predestination, properly understood, and freedom, and indeed a freedom without an end to which humans are called is empty. Nor would a Catholic say that if there is a directionality or predictability to evolution it need undo human freedom properly understood. Our freedom as humans may be limited but it is still a freedom and indeed perhaps can only be a freedom if limited in certain ways. Of course these are philosophical debates which we can save for a later date. But that is also the point: we need to examine the scientific data in as unbiased a manner as we can, in a manner free from underlying philosophical presuppositions, explicit or implicit, consciously brought to bear or unconsciously. Moreover, we should focus on the most concrete scientific data we have, i.e. the history of life on Earth, rather than theoretical views based upon such data. We can and should ask what the data itself and itself alone can tell us, which may of course be limited. And here Catholicism has much to offer as it instructs persons to continually examine their consciences and seek to avoid behaving in ways harmful to themselves or others including bringing their biases to bear.

Losos also seems to assume that we have a final and complete understanding of the evolutionary process. It may well be, however, that there are natural laws (i.e. forms of secondary causality) that we have yet to grasp at work here, perhaps even ones wherein there is a certain sort of feedback loop between the environment and the genome. One might imagine that certain environmental factors would trigger increased genetic diversification, fecundity, or low or high population densities, for example, or animals with genetic systems that modify themselves in light of environmental conditions such as newly available resources, abundance of resources, temperature, etc. Here again it is a matter of looking at the scientific data and determining what can account for them.

Nor is there a reason to disparage tinkering or to think that a divine being could not institute a system that involves repurposing of parts previously designed for a different end. Much of the technological progress in the perfecting of cars, televisions, cameras, cellphones, and computer programs is gradual and slow and involves a degree of tinkering or reusing of

---

[99] Losos, *Improbable Destinies*, 335.

preexisting mechanisms or working around preexisting features and limitations. Yet many important things and advances can result in this way.[100] Rather than approaching biological studies with preconceived ideas we should let nature tell us what it can and wants. In this regard methodical naturalists can be just as biased, if not more so, compared to Christian thinkers. And Catholic scientists who embrace a life of virtue and dedicate themselves to the value of uncovering truth and examining their conscience to make sure they remove biases from their investigations are well-placed to interpret nature accurately.

---

[100] Losos, *Improbable Destinies*, 95–96, 320–325, 334–335.

PART TWO:

SCIENCE FICTION, CATHOLICISM, AND EXTRATERRESTRIALS

Figure 0-2. Catholic Space Station Orbiting Alien World, Daniel Vega.

CHAPTER FOUR

FROM THE ANTIPODES TO INFINITY

ROBERT R. CHASE

It seems almost a given in various places that religious faith would collapse if the existence of intelligent extraterrestrials were proven. An Amazon blurb for Marie George's *Christianity and Extraterrestrials* reads: "Does ETI existence spell the death of Christianity? The increasingly popular answer is 'yes'." Claire Giangravè tells us that "anyone who has ever seen a sci-fi movie where aliens visit Earth knows that the general expectation is widespread panic, with religions being the first to crumble."[1]

Where does this belief come from? It seems to have been promulgated not by religious leaders, but by atheists. Thomas Paine was one of the earliest to take this tack. In *The Age of Reason* he argued that a belief in the infinite plurality of worlds "renders the Christian system of faith at once little and ridiculous and scatters it in the mind like feathers in the air." It isn't possible to affirm both simultaneously, he wrote, and "he who thinks that he believes in both has thought but little of either." Isn't it preposterous to believe God "should quit the care of all the rest" of the worlds He's created, to come and die in this one? On the other hand, "are we to suppose that every world in the boundless creation" had their own similar visitations from this God?[2] If that's true, Paine concludes, then that God would "have nothing else to do than to travel from world to world, in an endless succession of deaths, with scarcely a momentary interval of life."[3]

---

[1] Claire Giangravè, "Could Catholicism handle the discovery of extraterrestrial life?," *Crux*, February 24, 2017, https://cruxnow.com/global-church/2017/02/catholicism-handle-discovery-extraterrestrial-life/.

[2] Interestingly enough, we find a different view on just this premise in Ray Bradbury's "The Man" (1948).

[3] Quoted in Brandon Ambrosino, "If we made contact with aliens, how would religions react?," *BBC*, December 16, 2016,
https://www.bbc.com/future/article/20161215-if-we-made-contact-with-aliens-how-would-religions-react.

We see this attitude persisting to the present day. Douglas Vakoch, President of METI International, a group dedicated to researching the possibilities of extraterrestrial intelligence, cites research showing "that people who hold no religious belief are often the ones who assume people of faith would be most shaken by alien life."[4]

Catholics, however, have been speculating about the possibility of "aliens" even before it was understood that there were other worlds than our own. St. Augustine discusses records of "monsters":

> [F]or example, beings with one eye in the middle of their forehead, and others with their feet growing backwards . . . Hermaphrodites . . . others who have no mouths, breathe only through their ears, and live on air . . . others . . . called Pygmies . . . They also speak of a people who have but one leg with two feet . . . They are called Sciopodes because they lie on their backs in the summer and they keep the sun off with their feet. There are others who are neckless and with eyes on their shoulders.[5]

In the course of these considerations, Augustine seems to define as human "every mortal animal that is rational, however unusual to us may be the shape of his body, or the color of his skin, or the way his walks, or the sound of his voice, or whatever the strength, portion, or quality of his natural endowments." Admittedly, this does not apply directly to extraterrestrials since Augustine's interest is in those "descended from the first-created man." But if extraterrestrials demonstrated that they were rational, Augustine would be hard-pressed under his definition to deny them some sort of equality with humans.

Augustine cannot deal with the issue of extraterrestrials because his knowledge of astronomy does not include the possibility of other Earth-like planets. He does, however, know that the Earth is round and so, having considered monsters, he proceeds to speculate on *antipodae,* that is, "men living on the far side of the earth," if only to dismiss the likelihood. He has no reason to believe there was dry land at the antipodes and if there were, it would be too far across the sea for men to reach and populate.

---

[4] Carol Glatz, "Men in Black: Belief in aliens not so far out for some Catholics," *Angelus*, September 5, 2019, https://angelusnews.com/arts-culture/men-in-black-belief-in-aliens-not-so-far-out-for-some-catholics/.

[5] Augustine, *City of God*, trans. Marcus Dods, in *A Select Library of the Nicene and Post-Nicene Fathers of the Christian Church*, series 1, vol. 2, ed. Philip Schaff (Buffalo, NY: Christian Literature Publishing Co, 1887), Book 16, Chapter 8. The erudite reader on reading that may exclaim, "So that's where C. S. Lewis and John C. Wright got all those strange ideas!"

This is a prudential determination on Augustine's part. He may conclude that belief in *antipodae* is nonsense, but it is not contrary to the tenets of Christian faith.

With the invention of the telescope, the possible habitation of aliens moved from the antipodes to other, potentially Earth-like, worlds. Here I must stop to note that the dispute between Galileo and Pope Urban VIII was not the great confrontation between Religion and Science it is often presented to be. Michael Flynn can tell the story best, but basically it was a conflict between two proud and prickly men, one of whom had great political power and who, when publicly portrayed as a simpleton by the other, reacted in a regrettably predictable way.[6] Let me just note that all criticism by the Church of Galileo or his works ended by 1835 and in 1939, Pope Pius XII hailed Galileo as "one of the most audacious heroes of research."[7]

More recently, Pope Francis has shown himself open to speculation concerning extraterrestrial life, when he said: "Just as if, for example, tomorrow and expedition of Martians came . . . and one were to say, 'I want to be baptized!' What would happen?"[8] The former head of the Vatican Observatory, Jesuit Jose Gabriel Funes, goes a bit further in his speculations. Perhaps taking an unacknowledged hint from C. S. Lewis' *Space Trilogy*, he suggests that even if there are "other sentient life forms, they might not be in need of redemption. They could have stayed in full harmony with their Creator."[9]

These official attitudes seem to be shared by a good deal of the laity. Giangravè reports, "According to 2015 study by Joshua Ambrosius, professor at the University of Dayton, Catholics and 'nones' are the two groups most optimistic about the possibility of discovering extraterrestrials in the next 40 years."[10]

Is official sanction the only reason Catholics seem to be more open to the possibility of alien life than members of other faiths? I have no definitive

---

[6] Michael Flynn, "The Great Ptolemaic Smackdown: Trial and Error," *The TOF Spot* (blog), October 2, 2013,
http://tofspot.blogspot.com/2013/10/8-great-ptolemaic-smackdown-trial-and.html.
[7] Pius XII, "Man Ascends to God by Climbing the Ladder of the Universe," Address to the Plenary Session of the Pontifical Academy of Sciences, December 3 1939, http://www.academiadelasciencias.va/content/accademia/en/magisterium/piusxii/3 december1939.html.
[8] Tom Hoopes, "4 Catholic attitudes toward extraterrestrials," *Aleteia*, October 7, 2019, https://aleteia.org/2019/10/07/4-catholic-attitudes-toward-extraterrestrials/.
[9] Giangravè, "Could Catholicism handle?"
[10] Giangravè, "Could Catholicism handle?"

answer but allow me to speculate. Giangravè remarks, "For Catholics, enriched by Greco-Roman philosophy, the question of whether there were other worlds had a pretty early onset."[11] We see this effort to, as it were, baptize parts of pagan culture in the attempt to consider Virgil, in his Fourth Eclogue, a prophet of Christ. We see it also in the appropriation of Greco-Roman myths as well; for example, Augustine's list of "monsters" is indebted to those myths, while both Virgil and creatures from pagan myth play large parts in Dante's *Divine Comedy*. These neither add to nor subtract from the deposit of faith but they are parts of a culture at ease with the contemplation of alien beings.

Many Protestant denominations may not be so at ease. Catholicism's interest in pagan culture has often been looked on as a corruption of Christianity. And if the dispute between Galileo and Pope Urban did not signal a war between science and religion, Darwin's theory of evolution did, at least with Fundamentalist congregations. This has led to the sorry situation in which some scientists look on believers as superstitious and ignorant, and some Christians regard scientists as implacable enemies.

Furthermore, the *sola scriptura* emphasis can sometimes lead to a mindset holding that not only is the Bible inerrant but that if certain matters are not explicitly defined in the Bible they must be nonexistent. Thus, Genesis describes humanity as being created in the image and likeness of God. No other such races are described; therefore, they cannot have been created. Or if they have been created, they cannot be in God's image. This way of thinking is not mandated by *sola scriptura* nor is necessarily it restricted to Biblical fundamentalists. It is just that they are more likely to think in that manner than members of a faith which has traditionally had a wider focus.

With all of this in mind, let us see how these considerations play out in some Catholic works of science fiction. It might seem odd to start off with Mary Doria Russell's *The Sparrow*. Although raised a Catholic, Russell left the Church at the age of 15 and has since converted to Judaism. Yet it is her early formation that comes out most strongly in her story of first contact with extraterrestrials made by an expedition of Jesuit priests. The story, informed by the history of Catholic missionaries in the new world, is a cautionary tale of the dangers to the civilization being contacted and the explorers making the contact, even when that first contact is made by highly moral and intelligent men.

Michael Flynn's *Eifelheim* takes a more optimistic view. Set in a small, German hamlet during the Black Death, the story deals with marooned

---

[11] Giangravè, "Could Catholicism handle?"

aliens, who look like giant grasshoppers, and Fr. Dietrich, the town's priest. Both parties are under intense stress as the plague invades the village and the aliens face a slow death for lack of nutrition. Yet the aliens and humans come to understand (to a certain extent, at least) and sympathize with each other, in large part because of the priest's scientific curiosity and personal empathy. Flynn even gives his response to Pope Francis' hypothetical when he has some of the aliens ask for and receive baptism.

Let me finish somewhat immodestly by talking about one of my own works, *The Game of Fox and Lion*. On its face, it might seem irrelevant to the essay, since there are no aliens as such in the story. Instead there are Bestials, intelligent hybrids made from a combination of human and animal genetic material. The combination makes them much stronger to deal with the rigors of interstellar exploration. It also means that they do not have to be given the rights of human beings. The Bestials resent their mistreatment while humans become increasingly concerned at having created a race that is in many ways superior to them. After a war which both sides lose, a resolution is achieved on a basis of which Augustine would approve.

When we look at the names of American Indian tribes, we find that many of them translate as some version of "the People." Thus, for example: the Anishinaabe (original people), Aniyunwiya (principal people), Dene (the people), Dene Tha (true people), and Tsitsistas (the people). The implication of these names is that if you are not a member of the tribe, you are not a real person. Human history is our long ascent to the understanding that those who are not Greek or Chinese, European or members of the American Indigenous Peoples, are nonetheless "true people." It has been a process fraught with misunderstanding and occasional tragedy. But it is only when we are no longer alien to ourselves that we will be ready to welcome and understand aliens from another world.

CHAPTER FIVE

SCIOPODS, BLEMYAE, AND THE GREEN CHILDREN OF WOOLPIT: "ALIENS" IN THE CATHOLIC IMAGINATION, PREMODERN ERA

MICHAEL F. FLYNN

In the Middle Ages, Europe was more thoroughly Catholic than it is today, and space wasn't space as we think of it. It was more like "place," because they did not yet conceive of planets as separate worlds whirling in a void. They were just lights in the sky that went back and forth and around and around. They were features of *this* world.

That is because the English "world," like Greek κοσμος and Latin *mundus*, meant something more like "universe" than "planet." It comes from Old English *woruld*, literally "man-age" (*wer-ald*), and had originally meant "human existence," but by AD 1200, its sense had extended to mean "the universe."[1] This world was envisioned as a vast, multi-tiered structure of nested orbs in which Earth was a mere pinpoint lying in the bottom. For people of that era, the *world* was quite big enough, and somewhere in "outer place" there might be beings of unusual aspect.

So, for example, in 1357 or so, Sir John Mandeville, or someone using that name, published an *itinerarium* [travelogue] in which he set forth in search of new life and new civilizations, and encountered alien beings like blemyae, sciopods, and Muslims. Most scholars today regard the portion set in Egypt as essentially accurate, but the rest is a hodgepodge of fantasies, travelers' tales, and legends from antiquity. "Mandeville" did explain how

---

[1] *Online Etymology Dictionary*, s.v. "world," accessed October 7, 2020, https://www.etymonline.com/search?q=world.

measuring the inclination of the pole star with an astrolabe proved the Earth was round, though, and thus qualified the text as "hard science fiction."[2]

In particular he describes the blemyae as "ugly folks without heads who have eyes at each shoulder."[3] They lived on the big island of Dundeya, thought to be the Andaman Islands between India and Burma. The Franciscan friar John de Marignollis traveled to the Far East in the 1330s and, in the spirit of medieval empiricism, looked for "the monstrous races the ancients [e.g., Pliny] had spoken of." When he asked the Indians they answered, "we thought they lived where you came from."[4]

The sciopod hops swiftly on one enormous foot, rather like a kangaroo. And during the heat of the midday sun, he lies on his back and shades himself with his giant foot. This is thought to be garbled tales of Indians holding parasols to shade themselves. The cyclops, of course, is familiar to all. Pygmies were thought to exist somewhere in Africa. Medievals had no problems imagining strange people in strange places.

St. Augustine, in Book 16, Chapter 8 of *City of God*, said that he didn't know if these beings existed, but he did know that he had seen in Carthage a man who was double from the waist up and single from the waist down; in other words, he had two heads, but only two feet. The unfortunate man lived long enough for everyone to come and gawk at him for a while. If one such person can exist as a mutant, Augustine wrote, why not an entire race of them?[5]

St. Augustine took the use of language to be a sign of reason and he was not sure the dogheads had language. These were beings with the bodies of men and the heads of dogs. Medieval illustrations show them going about their daily affairs: farming, preparing their foods, and doing everything that we would expect intelligent beings to do—except they barked rather than spoke. Perhaps the barking was a language, who knows? But one of the things they did do was get baptized.

St. Christopher the Doghead, after he was baptized, took on human form, which is very interesting. Perhaps baptism makes us human. As Augustine said, however, we are not bound to believe all that we hear. We don't have to believe dogheads or blemyae exist. But if they do, then as long as they

---

[2] John Mandeville, *The Travels of Sir John Mandeville*, trans. C. W. R. D. Moseley (Harmondsworth: Penguin, 1983), 120.

[3] Mandeville, *The Travels of Sir John Mandeville,* 134.

[4] Robert Bartlett, *The Natural and the Supernatural in the Middle Ages* (Cambridge: Cambridge University Press, 2008), 106.

[5] Augustine, *City of God*, trans. Marcus Dods, in *A Select Library of the Nicene and Post-Nicene Fathers of the Christian Church*, series 1, vol. 2, ed. Philip Schaff (Buffalo, NY: Christian Literature Publishing Co, 1887).

have intellect and free will, they would be just like any other species of man.[6]

> Now Christopher was one of the dogheads, a race that had the heads of dogs and ate human flesh. He meditated much on God, but at that time he could speak only the language of the dogheads. When he saw how much the Christians suffered, he was indignant and left the city. He began to adore God and prayed. "Almighty God," he said, "give me the gift of speech, open my mouth, and make plain thy might that those who persecute thy people may be converted." An angel of God came to him and said: "God has heard your prayer." The angel raised Christopher from the ground, and struck and blew upon his mouth, and the grace of eloquence was given him as he had desired.[7]

He was baptized, and as a result gained a new appearance before getting martyred. This supposedly occurred during the reign of the emperor Decius.

According to a Welsh poem, King Arthur fought with the dogheads:

> On the mountain of Edinburgh; He fought with dog-heads; By the Hundred they fell.[8]

As for where the dogheads lived, accounts vary. One tale puts them in Scandanavia; another, beyond Ethiopia. Still a third story puts them in the mountains of India. They were effectively "extra-terrestrials"— people who lived in places beyond our reach. The existence of alien beings became popular in the medieval period. Sometimes they were used to frighten people (as we moderns do in such movies as *The Blob* or *Alien*) and sometimes they were used to illustrate virtues (e.g., *ET: The Extraterrestrial*) or vices (e.g., the Ferengi in *Star Trek: The Next Generation*).

But of a different order entirely were the Green Children of Woolpit. In 1189 a Cistercian monk, Ralph of Coggeshall, wrote in his *Chronicum Anglicanum*, of two children with green skin who climbed out of a woolpit ["wolf-pit"] one day, speaking a language no one could understand. They seemed confused by everything around them and would not eat anything except green beans, which they ate raw. After they had acclimated and learned to speak English, the young girl took the name Agnes and explained that she and her brother came from a land called St. Martin's, where

---

[6] The word "men" is thought to derive from the proto-Indo-European "*men," which means simply a rational being (cf. "mental.")

[7] J. Fraser, "The Passion of St. Christopher," *Revue Celtique* 34 (1913): 310.

[8] Rachel Bromwich, *Trioedd Ynys Prydein: The Triads of the Island of Britain* (Cardiff: University of Wales Press, 2006), 73–4.

everything was green and the sunlight perpetually dusk. They had been herding their father's cows, and the cows had wandered into a cave. When they came out of the cave, they found themselves in a strange land where not everything was green.[9]

The story is oddly prosaic, lacking in miracles or drama. They are not presented as frightening or as exemplars or cautions. They are simply puzzling. No one knew who they were or whence they came. The villagers of Woolpit took them in and raised them, and while the boy sickened and died, Agnes grew up, and went to work as a servant. She gained a reputation as being "very wanton and impudent" but eventually settled down and married a Richard de Calne, whom Ralph cited as the source of the story. Ralph lived only eight miles from Woolpit.

The temptation is strong to take the tale seriously and try to explain its various components. Over the centuries, various writers have tried to do so. The children may have suffered from some sort of dietary deficiency. They may have wandered away from a settlement of Dutch refugees—there is a St. Maarten in North Holland—but no one ever came looking for them. Or they may have been alien beings from another dimension who wandered into our continuum through a time portal, although this is not regarded as a high-probability scenario. Regardless, Agnes and her brother have become the literary ancestors of all the little green men of science fiction, who are always portrayed as small and childlike.

These stories reveal that the medieval imagination was open to tales of alien beings from unknown places, although today we imagine they are from the planets of other stars. They also tell us that these alien beings would sometimes get baptized, whether they were dogheads or little green people.[10]

---

[9] Mary Baine Campbell, "'Those two green children which Nubrigensis speaks of in his time, that fell from heaven', or the Origins of Science Fiction," in Carl Kears and James Paz, *Medieval Science Fiction* (London: King's College London, 2016), 117–132.

[10] Guy Consolmagno and Paul Mueller, *Would You Baptize an Extraterrestrial?: . . . and Other Questions from the Astronomers' In-box at the Vatican Observatory* (New York: Image, 2018), 249–286.

CHAPTER SIX

WHAT HAS OUTER SPACE
TO DO WITH CHRIST?

JOHN C. WRIGHT

1. Quid Coelus cum Christo?

Upon a time in the eighth century, Alcuin of York in vexation wrote to the Bishop of Lindisfarne about the intrusion of secular epics of the hero Ingeld being sung in church. He famously said, "Quid Hinieldus cum Christo?"— What has Ingeld to do with Christ?—for the house was narrow and could not hold both. [1]

In this generation, our bards no longer make epics about Ingeld, nor operas about Siegfried, but we do write space epics and space operas. So, the question for our generation is parallel: Quid Coelus cum Christo?—what has outer space to do with Christ? For it is commonplace today to propose that the Church is too narrow for her teachings to include the wide wonders of outer space, in particular the possibility of intelligent life on other worlds.

2. Implications of the Question

In the Christian scheme of things, the mortality of man, and his hope of immortality, spring from the specific acts of specific men; original sin springs from the fallen Adam, and redemption from the risen Christ.

Once we introduce other worlds into the Christian scheme, inhabited by rational animals like man, what becomes of the acts of Adam, or of Christ? How could a man from Mars be infected by the original sin of Adam on Earth? Adam is not his father. Absent original sin, why would a Martian be mortal? Christ is the only begotten Son of God, and no man comes to God

---

[1] "Alcuini Epistulae," in *Epistolae Karolini Aevi II*, ed. Ernst Dümmler (Berlin: Weidmann, 1895), 183 (no. 124).

save through Him. How then can salvation reach the rational creatures of Pluto or Proxima, Alpha Camelopardalis or M31 in Andromeda?

The magnitude of the cosmos renders it difficult to imagine that mankind was given dominion over all creation, and charged to subdue it. It is even more difficult to imagine that Christians could have been given the great commission to spread the good news of salvation across all the constellations in the galaxy, all the galaxies in the local group, all the clusters in our supercluster, and all the superclusters in the cosmos, of which there are ten million visible in the night sky.

One of the larger of these is the Corona Borealis Supercluster, one billion lightyears away, and three hundred million lightyears wide, three times as large as the Virgo Cluster our galaxy inhabits. Preaching the gospel to an intelligent hive-mind of methane-breathing worm things dwelling in the volcanic ocean trenches of some Ice Giant world of red star adrift in a Dwarf Galaxy amid the myriad galaxies lost in the Corona Borealis Supercluster would be a doubtful project indeed, considering the one billion year delay between any radio signal and response. That is, of course, assuming our missionaries one day learn how to harness the output of a quasar, or perhaps a galaxy full of exploding supernovas, to power a radio beam able to reach so far.

To get an idea of scale, the ray of light carrying to our eyes now the image of Corona Borealis departed its source during the Mesoproterozoic Era. This was when the first supercontinent, Rodinia, newly lifted its bald and barren stones above the waves into an oxygen-free atmosphere; and, along her shallow coastlines, a strain of red algae had recently been granted the innovation of sexual reproduction. The idea that those unfortunate worm things are condemned to hell if we do not get the message to them calls into question the justice of God.

3. Argument from Magnitude

Such is the question and its implications. But before addressing it, let us discover what kind of question it is.

3.1 Not New

Whatever this question is, first, it is not new.

In the first century BC, Cicero penned *The Dream of Scipio*, in which the Roman nobleman in a vision meets his famous ancestor, Africanus, amid the starry heavens. The lordly ghost displays the Earth underfoot as a small and dim spot. Scipio beholds that the Mediterranean—that great middle sea which Rome was so proud of entirely encircling with her conquests—is little more than that unnamed jungle pond mentioned by Herodotus where pygmies war with cranes.

The first mention in literature of occupants among the stars appears in Book III of Milton's *Paradise Lost*, published in 1667. In this scene, Lucifer is winging toward Earth, and sees the stars close at hand as he descends through them:

> *other worlds they seemed, or happy isles,*
> *Like those Hesperian gardens famed of old,*
> *Fortunate fields, and groves, and flowery vales,*
> *Thrice happy isles; but who dwelt happy there*
> *He staid not to inquire*[2]

3.2 Not Science

Second, this is not a scientific question.

Whatever theological doubt is provoked by the unimaginable size of the cosmos is not related to any change in the scientific model. As a matter of historical fact, the model of the universe proposed by Copernicus, Kepler, Hubble and Lemaitre is simply and literally smaller than that proposed by Aristotle and Ptolemy. The standard model of astronomy these days is proposing a starry universe roughly 15 billion lightyears in radius. This puts the ratio of the size of the Earth to the sphere of the universe, very roughly, at one to one sextillion. We also estimate the nearest star at four lightyears and change, which makes the ratio roughly one to one trillion. But Ptolemy in his *Almagest* said that the ratio between the size of the Earth and the sphere of the fixed stars was as a point to the heavens, or, in other words, the ratio of zero to infinity. So, the ancients, or at least some of them, thought the cosmos was larger than the current standard model does.

3.3 Not Philosophy

Nor is this a philosophical question.

If cast into a logical form, any argument expressing these astronomical doubts would betray its own absurdity at once. Bertrand Russell, for example, never cast as an argument the idea that the universe is so large that an all-powerful creator could not have created it, nor that an all-knowing creator cannot keep track of what he created in it.

---

[2] John Milton, *Paradise Lost*, Book III, ll. 567–571.

Nor did he argue that the God who made man from earth could not make a man from Mars.

What Mr. Russell did do, however, was pen a story called "The Theologian's Nightmare."[3] In this fable, a pious man in a dream about the afterlife discovers, to his chagrin, that the Milky Way, to say nothing of our solar system, is simply too small to come to the notice of Heaven. Mark Twain pulled a similar sleight of hand in his satire called "Captain Stormfield's Visit to Heaven."[4] These are stories, not arguments.

3.4 It Is a Joke

Argumentation is meant to appeal to the reason, but storytelling is meant to appeal to the imagination. "The Theologian's Nightmare" is not meant to take the idea that God created so small a creature as man and prove it to be logically absurd, but merely to take the idea and paint it as unimaginably absurd.

What kind of story is it? There are two answer to this. First, since the story is based on the wonders of science, it is a science fiction story. Second, since the story is satire, it is a joke, like knocking the top hat off a toff to make him look the fool.

3.5 But I Am Not Laughing

But the joke falls flat for anyone who actually reads the ancients. It is not because of egotism or self-satisfaction that the ancients placed the Earth at the center of the solar system, but because that was the most elegant model of the universe fitting the observations known at the time, before the invention of the telescope.

In the Ptolemaic system described by Dante in *The Divine Comedy*, Earth was at the center only because the Aristotelian view of gravity holds that all heavy and gross things are pulled to the center. In other words, Earth is where the fallen beings fall when they fall. And, in any case, mankind does not occupy the dead center of the gravity of the cosmos, Satan does. The center of the universe is not a place of honor. Far from it. For Dante, Earth is the rubbish heap of the cosmos, where all the trash is sent to burn.

---

[3] Bertrand Russell, *Fact and Fiction* (London: George Allen & Unwin Ltd.,.1961).
[4] Mark Twain, "Captain Stormfield's Visit to Heaven," *Harper's Magazine* (December 1907): 41–49.

The joke of knocking the top hat of a toff does not work if the man has already doffed his hat in reverence and already bowed his head. You cannot humiliate the humble.

I would be remiss if I did not quote G. K. Chesterton, whose sharp wit rebutted Bertrand Russell's dull joke, long before it was written. In his 1908 masterwork *Orthodoxy*, the Apostle of Common Sense quips, "It is quite futile to argue that man is small compared to the cosmos; for man was always small compared to the nearest tree."[5]

4. Argument from Mars

4.1 Augustine and the Monsters

As with the question of magnitude, the question of nonhuman rational beings is not new.

Saint Augustine, in Book 16, Chapter 8 of his *City of God*, speaks of the various monstrous races of one-eyed Arimaspians or one-foot-tall Pygmies or one-legged Sciapods Pliny and others said might dwell beyond India, or Ethiopia, or in the undiscovered regions of the Antipodes. The saint addresses the question of whether such monsters are human: "whoever is anywhere born a man, that is, a rational, mortal animal, no matter what unusual appearance he presents in color, movement, sound, nor how peculiar he is in some power, part, or quality of his nature, no Christian can doubt that he springs from that one protoplast"—the protoplast here meaning the lineage of Adam.[6] Modern science has discovered, indeed, that the genetic trace of one single male ancestor is found in the DNA of all *Homo sapiens* currently alive on Earth. St. Augustine's statement is literal and true.

But even were it not literal, it would still be true. Suppose it were discovered that the various races of man, Japhetic, or Semitic, or Hamitic, or, for that matter, Lemurian, or Lilliputian, or Cimmerian, or Hyperborean, each sprang by a Darwinian descent from different groups of ape-men. No man of Christendom would conclude that therefore men of each lineage must be ranked into different castes, enjoying unequal rights applied unequally, by virtue of having been made in the images and likenesses of various superior and inferior gods, who make different moral codes for each.

---

[5] G. K. Chesterton, *Orthodoxy* (New York: John Lane Co., 1908), 1101–111.
[6] Augustine, *City of God*, trans. Marcus Dods, in *A Select Library of the Nicene and Post-Nicene Fathers of the Christian Church*, series 1, vol. 2, ed. Philip Schaff (Grand Rapids: W. R. Eerdmans Pub. Co., 1956), 315.

Now in this passage, Saint Augustine enunciates what actually differentiates a creature made in the image and likeness of God from one who is not: namely, that he is a rational creature, regardless of "appearance in color, movement, sound, nor how peculiar he is in some power, part, or quality of his nature." Please note the doubts St. Augustine here answers are not provoked by any real scientific facts concerning the Arimaspians, Abarimone, Sciapods, Blemmyes, Cynocephalids, Sphinxes, or any other real race of real men. He is answering doubts raised by a story, and, in this case, a traveler's tale like those told by Odysseus about Cyclopes, or Gulliver about Houyhnhnms.

4.2 Saganism

In our case, the doubts we are answering spring from science fiction tales told by H. G. Wells, Arthur C. Clarke, and Robert Heinlein, but first and foremost by Carl Sagan.

I call Mr. Sagan the foremost because it is, alas, commonplace to find him and other alleged popularizers of science fact treating science fiction speculations about life on other planets in sober tones of perfect certainty. For example, Mr. Sagan, in a January 1997 *Scientific American* article, proclaims, "There can be little doubt that civilizations more advanced than the Earth's exist elsewhere in the universe." Sagan goes on to say, "From our knowledge of the processes by which life arose here on the earth we know that similar processes must be fairly common throughout the universe."[7]

In reality, Carl Sagan knows no more about the process by which life spontaneously springs from non-life than did Aristotle, who said the worms, fireflies, and other insects arise from the morning dew. He certainly does not know whether it is commonplace, or rare, or unique, or even possible at all. The unspoken idea expressed here is that since life cannot have been created by God, it must have created itself by itself under its own power.

4.3 Drake Equation

The idea that since God did not create life nor breathe a rational soul into man, therefore the stars are abundantly full of intelligent life is a heresy we can call Saganism.

---

[7] Carl Sagan and Frank Drake, "The Search for Extraterrestrial Intelligence," *Scientific American*, January 6, 1997,
https://www.scientificamerican.com/article/the-search-for-extraterre/.

As a matter of logic, Saganism is simply a non-sequitur. There is no logical contradiction to say that God commanded intelligent life to come into being by slow chemical, biochemical, and evolutionary processes. Likewise, there is no contradiction of fact or logic in the hypothesis that life arose spontaneously and godlessly by a unique process that just so happened to reach this result on this world but on no other.

Saganism is sometimes backed by a trifle of nonsense called the Drake Equation, where is it proposed that, no matter how unlikely an event, such as the spontaneous generation of intelligent life, may be, out of a given number of worlds, if we merely multiply the number of worlds under consideration by a large enough sample size, then the number of worlds where that event already took place becomes commonplace. So, if only one world in a zillion has spontaneously developed intelligent life, out of ten zillion worlds, we should find ten with intelligent life on them.

The problem with this line of reasoning can be seen when we substitute some other event in the equation. Let of suppose that the spread and triumph of the Catholic Church only happens once out of every hundred zillion worlds. Then, out of a sample of a zillion worlds, there should be one hundred space-popes eager for communion with the Holy Father on Earth.

Now, if it should be objected that a series of single, specific and unrepeated events, such as the covenant with Abraham, the epiphany to Moses, the Virgin Birth of Christ and the conversion of Constantine, were the only things that allowed Catholicism to become a major religion on Earth, and that none of these events could be repeated elsewhere, it is sufficient to reply that the spontaneous generation of life from non-life, like the conversion of Constantine, was also a single, specific and unrepeated event. If we have only one example of an event, and no idea of what caused it, no conclusion about the rate of its recurrence, or even whether it can recur, is logically permissible.

The heresy of Saganism does not depend on logic for its appeal, but on the fact that the modern mind, having shed all belief in reports of saints and angels, elves and airy phantoms our ancestors took seriously, finds itself terribly alone, and is comforted by the idea that there are people in space, who, being highly scientific, will be people just like Carl Sagan, and also will not believe in God. Saganism is a science fiction story. It is not to be answered by logic. One answers a story by telling a different story, and, or so we hope, one more truthful, virtuous, and beautiful.

4.4 A Space Odyssey

What is needed is a traveler's tale, like the *Odyssey* of Homer, but set against the backdrop of space as understood by modern astronomy—a space odyssey, in other words—or a story like the *Iliad* telling of a war amid the stars, or perhaps a tale about man's manifest destiny to subdue and fill the cosmos by means of a long trek to the stars.

What this *Space Odyssey* or *Star Wars* or *Star Trek* would be like if done by men hostile to the Christian worldview we know. It would be fundamentally untruthful. A space monolith, not the Holy Spirit, would breathe a rational soul into the first man, and the new messiah would rise again after a confusing light show, not because he died to save man from sin, but because he traveled to Jupiter. The son of the virgin would not be the promised messiah, but an evil space-knight with psychic powers. God would be a computerized fraud to be tricked by a fearless space captain into destroying itself, if not shot outright by his science officer.

Nonetheless, elements of Christian teaching, as can be sometimes found in pagan writings, still gleam bright as gold amid the brass and tin of these non-Christian space tales. But it is not true gold, and, upon close inspection, over time, it will tarnish and rust away. The stories we have of odysseys, wars, and treks are not gold. They are half-truthful. In an entertaining and sometimes moving fashion, they tell a tale of wonder. But the heart is missing.

What elements would the Christian story, when set against the backdrop of all the width of starry space, need to have, to be truthful? First, the significance of Earth, as the birthplace of the Incarnate Christ, cannot be lost, even if, like Bethlehem now, it remains a forgotten backwater in a wide world, where Christians are persecuted and driven out. The idea that many worlds have many Christs is a heresy of the Gnostics, called syncretism, and hence is popular among science fiction writers and neopagan witches alike. It is, on the other hand, standard Christian belief, affirmed by many Fathers, that Christ was active before His incarnation, such as in His appearance to Moses in the form of a burning bush, and appearances after His ascension, either on the Road to Damascus or in modern Rwanda, are faithfully attested by history. If Christ can appear to Saint John on Patmos, there is no reason He cannot visit Mars or Arcturus or Fomalhaut and appear in the flesh to Prince Malacandra the Eldil, Corpang of Threal, or D'Joan the underperson, not to mention Silk of Viron or Aenea of Hyperion.

Please note that the beings of other spheres may or may not be mortal. One might speculate that the animal life on Earth ages and dies because the beasts are under our authority and fell with us. The rational animals of other worlds may or may not also have fallen. C. S. Lewis, in his excellent yet underrated *Space Trilogy*, posits that the worlds where unfallen beings dwell are Hesperian and thrice happy. And, if they fell, their punishment may or may not be to return to the dust from which they came. If they came from dust. When the dark angels fell, they retained the immortality of their original, spiritual nature.

Also, rational creatures could be mortal without mortality being a punishment, particularly if there is easy and open fraternization between incarnate and disincarnate spirits. Both C. S. Lewis and Robert Heinlein have speculations along these lines in their rather different versions of Mars. The example of the dark angels also reminds us that, in the Christian scheme, one need not necessarily be a Son of Adam to be a fallen being.

Can a rational animal be created who is not in the image and likeness of God? For myself, I follow the answer of Saint Augustine in this. Even creatures with radically different physiognomies and psychologies to our own, if possessed of reason and therefore of a moral sense, should be treated as men, not animals.

The Ten Commandments surely apply to the degree reason and changed circumstances allow: A creature on a tide-locked world could not keep the Sabbath every seven days, because his sun never moves from noon, but set periods of rest given to his servants, and set periods of veneration set aside for the Lord are a matter of reason applying even to creatures with no need to sleep.

Creatures who reproduce asexually might have no problem with rules against adultery, since they would neither marry nor be given in marriage. But they would have customs concerning how to divide property and honors among the twin clones descended from one original, and the natural law would allow just from unjust laws and customs for handling such questions.

But what about creatures like black widow spiders? Are they allowed to commit murder, if consuming the mate during the mating act is a needed and necessary part of the sexual reproduction? That question would turn on whether this was the mating habit of their version of Adam and Eve before their fall. A father who gives his life that his children may live is as admirable as the suicide is abominable.

What of creatures possessed of odd telepathic abilities to blend or merge their minds, or to form a group mind or hive mind—how is moral responsibility shared among them? How can each covet or avoid coveting what is his neighbors' if each is one and the same as his neighbor? Christian teaching rejects the Socratic notion that the soul is composed of parts, so the question here would turn on the relation of the individual to the group mind into which he merges himself. Even among men, who have only one body apiece, we have laws and customs dealing with nations and corporations and other collective entities.

What of creatures who can raise the dead? Is it a felony for them to kill others, or only a misdemeanor, like an act of false imprisonment? Does the sea turtle of space, abandoned in the sand as an egg, have a duty to honor his father and mother?

Please note that, even if none of these questions has an obvious nor an easy answer, that outside the Christian scheme of things, it is not proper to conclude that they have no answer at all, and therefore moral laws have no divine lawgiver. Simply saying "to each his own" or "when in Rome, do as the Romans" is not an answer to any moral questions; it is merely an expression of a desire to flee from moral questions. In a universe without God, moral codes are manmade things, and therefore can be changed or abolished by man, so there is no arbiter to decide disputes, save strength alone.

There are some Saganists claiming the Christian scheme is untrue because it is impossible that there be only one Christ, who happened to be incarnated on our world. I am sure the shepherds outside Bethlehem might have said the same, had they been educated men, and therefore tempted to the folly of intellectual pride.

But whatever rational answer we Christians give as to why it pleased the Holy Spirit to visit one and only one Virgin Mary, whereas it was not the pleasure of God to create a second Mary of China, and a third Mary of the Aztecs, and so on, that same answer applies to the Mary of Mars and the Mary of Antares and the Mary Mother of God of the Greater Magellanic Cloud. And likewise, if one objects that there are millions of stars, too many for Christ to save, by the same logic, there are millions of earthlings, ergo too many for Christ to save.

Other Saganists say that there must be scientific utopias among the stars, and myriads of worlds of men, because otherwise it is an astronomical waste of space. But, if no one made it, it cannot be a waste, and if God made it, we know not His purposes.

Perhaps we are the only world, and the original plan was for prelapsarian man to have the same powers that the Risen Christ, and many of his Saints, have from time to time manifested. A glorified body, in addition to being luminous in its beauty and agility, and invulnerable to disease and death, can levitate, bilocate, walk through walls and can travel tremendous distances in a twinkling. There are historical accounts of all these miracles. Would the speed of light be an insurmountable obstacle to the Risen Christ?

The Bible says it was not God's original plan that man should never die, but that he should be fertile and multiply. If ours is the only life-bearing world, it may be that the rest of the universe was originally meant for our children. No magnitude is so large that it cannot be filled with the children of an immortal race. No magnitude is so large that it can adequately express the infinite glory or infinite abundance of God.

If ours is not the only life bearing world, and not the only fallen world, but we are the one world where the secret of salvation was first revealed, it does indeed call into question the justice of God that we, who cannot travel or communicate past the speed of light, bear the Great Commission to save all those souls.

Recall, however, that we are not discussing a scientific problem. We are discussing a science fiction story.

If the part of the story concerned with the salvation of Men of Mars and Proxima, of the Andromeda Galaxy, and the Corona Borealis Supercluster, takes place now, so soon after the First Coming, the Great Commission seems absurd and unjust. I am sure it seemed equally absurd and unjust to ask eleven men gathered in an upper room in Jerusalem to spread Christ's good news to the undiscovered hemisphere of the Antipodes. The Second Coming might be tomorrow, or it might be ten thousand times ten thousand years from now—keep in mind, ye faithful, that these may be still the days of the Early Church.

My point is that, if the part of the story concerned with the salvation of men on other worlds takes place after the Second Coming, and our glorified bodies can visit these places at the speed of thought, and speak in strange tongues, to make ourselves understood, we have a very long and time-consuming task ahead of us, and will face terrifying opposition. In other words, it would be an epic story. That is certainly a better story to tell, and more truthful, than the absurdities of Sagan and Clarke and their tales of salvation by Space Monolith or Space Utopia.

5. Conclusion

Christianity does not glorify God's merciful providence for man because of the greatness of man, but because of our smallness, meekness, and worthlessness. To the Christian, it is supposed to come as a shock that God so loved the world as to send his Son to die for us. The shock is not that man is a creature perched farther up on the great ladder of creation than expected, but that the love of God reaches farther down.

If it makes Christian teaching seem absurd because we believe Earth was the sole planet on which Christ was born, this absurdity does not spring from any discovery of science or from any speculation of science fiction. The satirist points out that Earth is not the largest nor most central planet in the solar system, much less the Milky Way or Virgo Cluster. If this is a shame embarrassing to Christians, it is a shame celebrated in all our hymns, rung from our Church steeples, spread with shed blood of missionaries and martyrs from pole to pole.

If you ask, why Milky Way? Why the Orion Arm? Why Sol? Why Earth? Then all I need do in reply is ask, why was Christ born in Judea, which was neither the largest nor most central province of the Empire? Why born among the Jews, a conquered race descended from Egyptian slaves? And Christ was not even born in the magnificent temple built by Herod the Great, amid the shining gold of lamps and vessels. He was born in the crummy little village of Bethlehem, in a stinking stable, in a cave.

The findings of science and the speculations of science fiction are not too large for the Catholic Church to fit inside her walls, precisely because the only other options, paganism, atheism, or some admixture of nihilism and materialism, are indeed much narrower. Pagan gods are frivolous, and atheist gods are mere mechanical systems of evolution and entropy without pity, point, or purpose. I place no hope in evolution: our future, without God, is one of Eloi and Morlocks. Not only is the Christian scheme a sensible frame in which the discoveries of modern science and the speculations of modern science fiction can be fitted nicely, it is the only one that makes logical sense and satisfies right reason.

In reality, the Church extends from the militant Church on Earth to the suffering in Purgatory to the triumphant in heaven. In other words, the Church is actually larger than the whole material continuum of timespace and embraces it.

CHAPTER SEVEN

SCIENCE FICTION AND RELIGION[1]

CYRIL JONES-KELLETT

I'm not sure how much to talk about my own novella, *Ad Limina*.[2] Some people look at it, and it's, you know, roughly 200 pages or something and say, "Why do you call it a novella?"

To me, primarily it's a novella because it only has one action. It only has one significant dramatic action in it. Different things happen, of course—they have to—but a novel has usually a kind of a symphony of actions, and a short story usually one, and a novella might be somewhere in between. And I think that *Ad Limina* has only one. So I'll just tell you a little bit about *Ad Limina* and then talk about science fiction and the Catholic imagination more generally, at least in the way that I understand it. Then I really do hope that we can have a little bit of conversation.

One of reasons, I think, that you don't necessarily see lots and lots of Catholic science fiction, although it's out there, is that as you write *Catholic* science fiction, you're narrowing. As you add descriptors, you're narrowing the genre. The descriptor *science fiction* is pretty narrow; *Catholic [science fiction]* is really narrow.

My little novella is about the first native bishop of Mars. It's at some time in an indeterminate future, and he's the first bishop on Mars to have been born on Mars. They've had bishops imported from Earth prior to that.

So the opportunity in that story then is—and you probably guessed this from the name *Ad Limina* because you're seminarians and you know this—an *Ad Limina* visit is a visit that every diocesan bishop makes once every five years to go to Rome, and "*ad limina*" means "to the threshold or to the doorways." And so the idea is that every diocesan bishop has to visit the tombs of Saint Peter and Saint Paul, and then they do what's called a

---

[1] This contribution is an edited transcript of a lecture that Mr. Kellett gave on March 18, 2020. Because of the COVID-19 crisis, the lecture was conducted by videoconference.
[2] Cyril Jones-Kellett, *Ad Limina: A Novella* (March 7 Media, 2013).

quinquennial visit while they're doing that, where they report to the Vatican and meet with the pope about the condition of their own diocese. So, I thought it would be kind of fun to do a story where a guy who's never even been to Earth has to make his quinquennial visit. He has to make his *ad limina* visit to go and meet the pope in Rome. He's put it off as long as he can, and now he's got to go. The pope is insisting that he goes.

In fiction, you know, there are different structures of stories. I have what I would call an enormous or a tremendous case of attention deficit, so stories that are a series of little stories within a bigger story are very attractive to me for writing. To me, [*Ad Limina* is] a picaresque. A picaresque is a Spanish story where the hero goes from place to place and has these little experiences and each little experience is a lesson. I tried to make [these] little experience[s]. He ends up going to a future fascist colony, and he ends up going to a kind of a post-human laboratory. He makes these little visits, and so it's a little picaresque; he's having these little learning experiences along the way. And, of course, the obvious idea there is that, really, it's not a book about the future, as most science fiction books are not books about the future. They're books about the present moment and the future is the context in which one is exploring moral issues, primarily, and cultural issues that have to do with the present.

I think the general commentary on *Ad Limina* is that people are very impressed with the mediocrity of my writing. They also get that this is an opportunity to have these little stories that are meant to tell or explore realities of our world today, like this idea of the bad anthropology of the post-humanists, or the kind of romance of fascism—and fascism is a kind of romanticism.

So then [the bishop] ends up on Earth, and he gets to meet the pope, and he ends up going home, and a war starts and there's the book. It's a novella, primarily because there's only one dramatic action that happens in it. The bishop is angry, because the world, the whole solar system, is being run by these kind of United Nations types who are very dismissive of a whole dimension of reality, which is the humane and religious dimension of reality. They're very dismissive of it. He's angry, but the turn that he has to make is from being angry about that to learning to love people where they are, because that's his job as a bishop. His [job] is not to be the guy who's the cultural critic, who stays aroused with anger all time, but the person who gets past that to love people where they are. He becomes a bishop who loves his people in the end. At least, that's the way that I understand it.

I think that there's always a little connection of the autobiography in these things. I can remember a time when I was becoming angry about the state of the world, when my children were in their preteen years. My wife swears she doesn't remember this conversation, but she actually said this to me one day. She said, "What's your plan? Are you planning on becoming a grumpy old man?"—which is something a wife can say to a husband. I don't even think she was thinking about it; she was just teasing me, really, and that's probably why she doesn't remember it. But to me it made an impression. You know, you only get one shot at this life, and I don't want to be a grumpy old man. That's not a good enough vocation to be, and it's not a good vocation to be a grumpy old priest, and it's not a good vocation to be a grumpy old bishop. The bishop [in *Ad Limina*] has to get over this and choose—not feel—but *choose* to love others. That's why I say it's a novella. It just has that one little thing that happens. Nothing else happens, just that one little thing: a person turns from being an angry person to being a person who loves other people. At least that's the way that I understand it.

The context of it is a world that is insane. I would like to say something about the context of our world as being insane, and I'll refer to two science fiction writers, one of whom you might be familiar with, but don't think of him as a science fiction writer, [though] you might not be familiar with him as well. The other one wrote probably the single greatest science fiction book ever written. We'll start with that second one.

In 1959, Walter Miller wrote a book called *A Canticle for Leibowitz*. I cannot see you so I can't tell by your faces if you're familiar with *A Canticle for Leibowitz*, but it is a truly great novel. It's a strange, weird, truly great novel. And the idea of Walter Miller's novel is that it's set in the far future, after a nuclear war. There's a dark age, and then there's a Renaissance, and then there's a second modern period. See, Miller is doing there what we do in science fiction, or what science fiction writers do. In a world that's different from ours, he's re-enacting the world that we actually already live in, and he's just brilliant the way he does it. It's a very, very Catholic book [and] Walter Miller was himself a Catholic. Leibowitz is an electrical engineer who becomes a monk and then becomes Saint Leibowitz, so [the book] is a song, or canticle, for Leibowitz.

The other author I want to talk about is Walker Percy. I don't know if you know Walker Percy. About the same time, maybe a couple of years after Walter Miller wrote *A Canticle for Leibowitz*, which was a huge success as a book, Percy wrote a book called *The Moviegoer*. *The Moviegoer* won the National Book Award in 1960 or 1961, something like that, and it is a great novel, and Percy is kind of famous for being Catholic and Southern. He's the Southern Catholic gentleman writer. [He's] not at all a Southern writer like Flannery O'Connor. You're probably familiar with Flannery O'Connor—probably more familiar [with her] than Walker Percy, but Percy's a different kind of Southern writer. He wrote several science fiction books that you almost don't notice are science fiction books. The very last book he wrote before he died is called *The Thanatos Syndrome*, "*thanatos*" meaning "death"—not the Thanos, by the way, for those of you who are Marvel fans, but *thanatos*—the idea of an ideology of death. And that's what he thought of our world as today, is *The Thanatos Syndrome*, that is, [as having] a love affair with death.

Percy said a lot of very pithy things that are like "Walker Percy-isms". I don't know how to describe them. One of the things he said is: when you go into the bookstore, and you see all these books about life, and on TV you see people talking about life and living life, . . . you can be sure there's a lot of death around. That's the way Percy looked at the world: modern people were kidding themselves, basically, or fooling themselves into thinking that this was a time of life and vibrancy, when what this is really is, is a time of death.

So I'll get to those two books. Those are the two that I'm going to be working towards.

Both [*A Canticle for Leibowitz* and *The Thanatos Syndrome*] are books about the insanity of the world. I feel like my little novella is written in a world that is actually insane, and I would like to speak with you for a minute about the fact—not the supposition, not the proposition—but the *fact* that the world is currently insane. I want to get to the roots of that, because if you get to the roots of why the world is insane, then you have a good grasp on, I think, what it means to be a Catholic in this moment, and you certainly have a good leaping off point to consider what's good science fiction and what's bad, because most science fiction is insane, because it's written by people who are deeply embedded in an insane world.

If I could just take a few minutes of your time, if you will tolerate it, I would like to do a brief history of the world up to this moment to talk about how we went insane. When I say that, most people think, "Ok, he's going to go back to 1967 and '68 and he's going to talk about flower power and the sexual revolution and all that, and that's what made us insane." No, that is not it. We'll have to go back 500 years. We have been working on this—or someone has been working on this—current state of insanity for 500 years. It will just take me a few minutes to give you a basic outline of how I think of those 500 years.

I would like you to think of two things. I think that Dr. Percy, who was a physician, and Walter Miller, were both people who were concerned with the fact that there's a hidden story underneath the modern story, and that's why they were great writers. I want to talk about that hidden story.

So we'll make an "x". Part of the "x" is the story of modern history that goes like this: starting in the 1400s with the Italian Renaissance and the invention of the printing press, and the discovery of the new world in America, society began an upward thrust of progress that continues to today. That's one side of the "x" and that's the story that we all know. Is that story true or is it false? Well, it's obviously true. It's obviously true because look at how we're talking to one another [i.e., via teleconferencing]. Nobody could do that 500 years ago or 5,000 years ago. Human history goes on for, I don't know, 100,000 years or something, and it's not until 500 years ago that we start to have the kind of world that ends up making things like this sort of conversation we're having now possible. So, there is this upward thrust of progress that starts during the time of the Italian Renaissance, the invention of the printing press, the discovery of America and the real flowering of Catholic universities. You have this upward thrust of progress.

All of this progress rests on Christendom. This is an important point: it all rests on Christendom. A better way to say it might be that it all grows out of the soil of Christendom; think of it more organically like that. What happened? OK, Jesus founds his Church, and his Church goes out to the whole world, like in Luke's Gospel, from Jerusalem out to the whole world. It really did go out to the whole world; we have to understand that. It didn't just go to Rome and then north into Europe. It went down into Africa: [think of] Phillip and the Ethiopian, and of the giant Catholic Church in Alexandria and Egypt and all across all of north Africa. [It went] east, into India with St. Thomas. I always like to say this just so people get a sense of how Christianity in the earliest years really went out in every direction: remember Genghis Khan, the Mongol leader Genghis Khan, the conqueror of the whole world? His mother was a Christian. This is a well-known, well-documented fact. Christianity went out from Jerusalem, just like St. Luke said, and it went to all the world.

Well, what happened was, in the seventh and eighth and ninth centuries, with the rise of Islam, Christianity—Christendom—got cut in half. North Africa was lost to the sword of Islam, and Asia was on the other side of Islam. Europeans couldn't get to [Asia]; it was on the other side of Islam. Hundreds of years later, it turned out that the Chaldeans, and other Christians—the Nestorians, and the Malabar Christians—they had stayed faithful to Christ, but they were on the other side of Islam. Think of what happens with Christendom in Europe: it gets trapped, really, in Europe and so it has to create its own world.

This is very important when we talk about colonialism and things like that. What European colonialism really is, is Christianity having [been] cut off from the rest of the world by Islam, and then, around 1400, 1500, 1600, it developed the technological means to get around Islam, to get to the rest of the world. That's why we have colonialism, not because Christianity is inherently colonial, but because Christianity got cut off from the rest of the world, and had to develop the capacities, especially technological capacities, to get around Islam. Once it got around Islam, it came in great ships and with great armies, which is not the way that Christianity normally comes. All of this is a response to Islam. The story is very Euro-centric for 1,000 years.

If you could think of this for a moment, think of our greatest public buildings. What are our greatest public buildings today? In Los Angeles, they're building one right now. They're building one of the greatest buildings ever built in the history of the world and two teams are going to play there: the Chargers and the Rams. That's what we build, sports stadiums. If you went back to the Roman Empire, you would find the exact same thing. Stadiums are the greatest buildings of the Roman period. In Medieval Europe, that is not at all the case. What are the greatest buildings of Christendom? They are cathedrals. They're these magnificent cathedrals around which cathedral towns and marketplaces develop. They are truly the center of life, these cathedrals.

If you think about it, the Catholic Church does three things. It does the same three things Jesus does: it teaches, it casts out demons, and it heals people. It teaches by creating schools, it casts out demons by creating parishes and giving people the Sacraments, and it heals people by creating hospitals. That's what Christendom is: schools, churches, hospitals. That's what it is. And that's the fertile ground out of which the modern world is born, around the 1500s.

But what happens is, right at that very moment when the modern world is being born, we have the Protestant Reformation. Liturgical Christianity—that is, people eating the Body and Blood of Jesus, people having a crucifix in their home, on their street, in the Church, people having Eucharistic processions, society being built around all that—is destroyed. And now we have the invention of a new religion, which is non-liturgical Christianity. So, in addition to this upward progress, we're going to have another side of the "x" that goes down. It's going to be from the cultural beauty of Christendom, which left the world hospitals, universities, and cathedrals, to us—it goes down and down and down. What are we going to leave to the people that follow us? We're going to leave Internet pornography and bomb craters, that's what we're going to leave. So, you see there's a moral decline, a religious and cultural decline, that happens, and the first step in that decline is the loss in the unity of liturgical Christianity.

The next step follows, and it comes this time not from northern Europe, but from southern Europe, and that is the people who are like Voltaire and Rousseau—the *philosophes*—people like Thomas Jefferson in the United

States, people who say: "Sure, we believe in God, God is good, but we don't need Jesus." Thomas Jefferson is explicitly not a Christian and he does not believe in miracles, [and] he does not believe in the Resurrection. He believes in nature and nature's God. So now we have decline. We let go of liturgical Christianity first. The second thing we let go of is Christ.

Then you get to the 19th century and you're going to suffer a third great loss. What is that third great loss? The third great loss happens after the Industrial Revolution. People move into cities, they lose contact with nature, they lose contact with farming and they're surrounded by smoke and desperation. Then new ideas are born, [through people] like Karl Marx, and even very great ideas, like those of people like Charles Darwin, and then people begin to lose God. This is the first time this happens in history. A new kind of atheism is born. And so you have Protestantism, you have Deism, and now you have agnosticism and atheism in the 19th century.

This is not the end of the losses, though. This is why we're not yet insane in the 19th century. There's still one more layer of loss to go. Between 1914 and 1945, world war, a horrible destruction [happens], and you can see this building up of an almost demonic frenzy to be able to destroy things. And you end up with the Holocaust and the destructions of Hiroshima and Nagasaki and the birth of the nuclear age. Now we're right on the cusp of that world that Walker Percy and Walter Miller are going to write about, in 1945.

In 1945, after this incredible death and destruction, for 30 years, there's not a sense of, "Wow, we kind of blew it. We need to get back to God. We need to go back to Jesus. We probably should go back to church." None of that happens, because there's an invention, that was invented in the 1930s here in California, but never got used, anywhere really, because of the Second World War, [which] took all the natural resources. In 1950, they sold 1 million of them, and there's never been fewer than 1 million of them sold since: televisions. Instead of turning to God, and repenting of what we had done by 1945, we turned on the television, we took all of our trauma, and we started watching *I Love Lucy*.

We never healed from what we had done and we enjoyed surrendering ourselves to screens, so that people began to no longer live in the real world. This is where the technological ascent meets perfectly with the moral and cultural decline. We began to lose touch with reality, so much so that, today, people honestly believe that you're being cruel if you say there's a difference between a boy and a girl. People honestly believe you're being cruel if you tell a boy that he's not a girl, or a girl that she's not a boy. This insanity is directly related to the fact that we spent more than fifty years perfecting letting go of reality. We live in unreality: that's where we're stuck.

That's the world that the science fiction writer writes in. Think of something like *Star Trek*. First of all, when you watch *Star Trek*, you are actually engaging in this unreality. That's fine. Some unreality is really important; that's an important part of our lives and I'm not criticizing that. That's where you are, then. You're in a world where images are just washing over you. Your brain activity is really low—it's not as high as if you're reading—and you're simply experiencing a different world. You're letting a different world wash over you. And what's being proposed, in *Star Trek*, is that the answer to these problems that have emerged over the last 500 years, is technological, that technology is the savior.

I would refer here to Pope Benedict, who would say, in his great encyclical *Spe Salvi*—you know, "Hope Saves"—that the horizon of our hope is contained in this world instead of the horizon of our hope being open to the next world. And when the horizon of our hope is contained in this world, we believe that things like politics, economics, ideology, and technology are salvific. This is a way in which a broken anthropology, a broken understanding of what a human being is, leads to science fiction that is very, very attractive. It's very attractive, but it won't help us, because it's lying about how you get from here to there. It's not telling the truth about what a human being is, and how you move from the situation that we are in, which is alone, without a savior, without God, without a church, and without a firm grip on reality—as a matter of fact, in many cases, no grip on reality at all. How do we recover from that? The answer is not technological. It's not economic, ideological, or political. But fiction writers continue to propose that idea. I use *Star Trek* as the example because *Star Trek* is the shining example of [addressing the question]: how did the world emerge out of this dark period that we're in? See, even *Star Trek* recognizes that this is a dark period. How did [we] emerge out of it? [We] invented warp drive and machines that could make food out of air. I don't know how they make food, but you just say, "Tea, Earl Gray," and there it is—Earl Gray tea. And that saved us.

But that doesn't save us, because, as we can see, as the technology progresses, we don't become better people. We don't become more whole. We remain the same wounded, broken creatures that we were.

So, Walker Percy, is raised as a Southern—really *Suhthen*—Stoic. The idea is that you try to . . . have this Stoic view of life, and you gain a romantic appreciation of your place in the universe—how small you are—and you just try to just live bravely out all of that. It's a very Robert E. Lee [attitude].

I don't think Robert E. Lee believed it, but that's the way people think about Robert E. Lee. It's very Southern.

[Percy] went to New York to get a medical degree and came down with tuberculosis and had to be on bed rest for a year, and something happened that he never really talked about very much: he converted to the Catholic faith. He couldn't practice medicine because of the tuberculosis, and so he became a philosopher and a novelist. As a novelist, he said, his idea was that the modern person is in a predicament. So, what he would do, instead of having a plot and all that, he would just start out with a person in a predicament: *I am lost in this unreal world.* [Percy's] south is nothing like Flannery O'Connor's South. She's the old haunted Gothic South. His South [is] full of Exxon stations and 7-Elevens and all that, and you just move through it, and it was just unreal.

The Moviegoer is about this one young boy. Every time he goes to the movies, he feels like the world is real, but he comes out of the movies, and the world seems fake. It's a genius book about this reversal. Percy's question is: how do I get out of this unreality that I'm in, back into the real world? And so he puts his characters in a predicament.

I want to talk to you just a little bit about *The Thanatos Syndrome,* a great science fiction book, that's only marginally science fiction, but it is a science fiction book. It's set in a future, and it's got technologies that we don't have, but it's only a little bit in the future. The idea is: he's got this character, Dr. Tom Moore, who has messed up his life. You can see by the name—Tom More—that he's like a broken-down version of Thomas More, and he messed up his life. He needed extra money, so he sold drug prescriptions and he went to federal prison. Now he's back out, and he comes back to his town in Louisiana, to his parish—they don't have counties there in Louisiana, they have parishes—and he comes back to this fictional parish, Feliciana, and everybody's acting strange. While he's been away in prison, something has changed and he goes on this search to try to figure out what has changed. What he finds is that these other doctors and scientists and political leaders have decided that what's wrong with people is they have too much human angst. They need to calm down. So they've put these advanced chemicals into the water supply to calm people down.

So you see, it's a technological solution to a spiritual problem, what Percy proposes for us. What results from these people doing this actually is that people are happier. They do feel happier, but they start to lose capacities. They can't relate to other people as well as they did before. They become, sexually, kind of like animals, not like people anymore. All their inhibitions start to come down. And this leads to child abuse, which leads to people being violent with one another. So it's a reduction of the human person in order to cure the human person of their humanity.

And then Percy's character, Tom, has to kind of solve this crime, but it's worse than just [solving] this crime: he has to convince people that it was a crime. All these doctors have all these spreadsheets and they say, "Look at the numbers. Crime has gone down and divorce has gone down." But Percy's character, More, is saying, "Yeah, but that where's their humanity? You rob them of their humanity. All these things are improving, but they're not human beings anymore." So the key there is that the technologists have a sick and diminished view of what a human person is. As long as you're not committing crime, as long as you're not feeling unhappy, then you're a good citizen, and everything's better.

Percy says no, and this is what Dr. More's predicament is. No, there's something more. There's a mystery here to human life. If you take that mystery away, then you've created death in life, which is why the book is called *The Thanatos Syndrome*. It also has one of the greatest pro-life priests. He's nuts, the priest in there is nuts, but he's just great, and he's funny, and wild, and he says outrageous things to people. Nobody understands what this priest is saying, because he's talking about the Gospel, and they've all forgotten about the Gospel completely. It's got Nazis in it. Great book. I highly recommend *The Thanatos Syndrome*.

But you see, the basic problem is: there's this idea that that the insanity of the world is related to the fact that we're no longer living deeply human lives. We've been cut off from our own humanity.

This brings me to what I think could fairly be claimed is among the greatest science fiction novels ever written—and I would say maybe *the* greatest science fiction novel ever written—*A Canticle for Leibowitz*, by Walter Miller.

Walter Miller was a pulp fiction writer for science fiction magazines in the 1940s and '50s. Something came over him when he wrote *A Canticle for Leibowitz*. He took three short stories that he had before he put them together into a novel and he rewrote the novel. And when he did, he created a miracle. It's just a miracle of a book. And if you have any interest at all in science fiction, and especially from a Catholic perspective, because he was a Catholic, you've got to read *A Canticle for Leibowitz*.

The basic idea [is that] the world has destroyed itself in a nuclear war. Because it was scientists who did it—and I actually think this is plausible— then the people who are left decide they're going to destroy everything that's scientific. Then they get carried away, and it becomes like the French Revolution, and now they're just burning books and destroying everything, and it's called the Great Simplification. People go back to living a very basic life.

Well, the Catholic Church is there to try to rebuild from those ashes. So in this Catholic monastery they collect written works and they keep a library and they hold to it. Then, hundreds of years later, there's a very funny scene where the secular world thinks that it's got it all figured out, and so this scientist comes to the monastery and he starts explaining electricity to the monks. The monks [respond], "No, we understand electricity," and they have much deeper questions about how electrons work than the scientist does—which I think is a very good metaphor for the way that the Church values knowledge. It really is the case that many people think that the Catholic Church is backwards. You'll find that throughout your life, [that] many people think the Church is ignorant and backwards. But it's just the opposite. The Catholic Church loves knowledge because it loves everything about the human person. [It's not] because [the Church] loves molecules and electrons, or because it thinks, "Oh, by being a scientist somehow I have elevated myself above the rest of humanity." [The Church] loves humanity, so its knowledge is deeper and thicker, and more robust and rich.

The problem that happens in *A Canticle for Leibowitz* is that over the course of about 1,000 years or something—I don't actually remember the time scale—the world comes back out of this dark age that follows the blowing up of the world, and it's a modern world again. And then, of course, at a certain point, it plunges back into nuclear war again, once they invent nuclear weapons.

The basic idea, at least the way I take what Miller is saying, is that people don't change. This is also a fundamental truth of the Catholic Church. Just because you are more technologically advanced, and even if you have the experience of having already seen humanity blow itself up before, none of that matters. You're going make the same mistakes.

You [seminarians] are all going to be hearing confessions for the rest of your lives. I'm pretty sure this is what you're going to find out, that people just keep making the same mistakes over and over and over again. That's what it is, and the Church loves them in that, and that's what Walter Miller, I think, is saying, is that he loves you. He's trying to write a love letter to humanity, to tell them to stop getting so caught up in the technological as your salvation, because it can't save you. It doesn't change you. It doesn't change the nature of who you are. It just makes you more powerful or, as C. S. Lewis used to say, it just makes you a more clever devil.

So the world destroys itself again. But this time, the pope gets on a space ship and he goes out into space to wait. The Church is off in space waiting for a rebirth.

Before I wrap up and ask you for your questions, I would like to mention one other science fiction work that is often cited as a Catholic science fiction work. It's called *The Sparrow*. I don't know how many of you are familiar with *The Sparrow*. I did not bring *The Sparrow* into this conversation, mostly because I don't understand it. It seems more like a horror story with a science fiction kind of veneer on it to me. It's very dark. It is, however, Catholic. It's about a Jesuit priest. But I'm a baby when it comes to reading books: if it's really dark, I'm going to live with that a long time. So I just [say], "No, thank you. I'm a little too impressionable, I think, or weak, or childish or whatever." But it's not fair to talk about contemporary or recent Catholic science fiction and not mention *The Sparrow* because many people say, "Well, that's the greatest Catholic science fiction [book] of all time." I think it's a horror book. I'm not sure, but it reads like a horror book to me, and I'm not interested in that.

So I will just leave you with: read Walker Percy's *The Thanatos Syndrome* and read Walter Miller's *A Canticle for Leibowitz*. As a matter of fact, read *A Canticle for Leibowitz* yesterday. If you can go back in time and read it yesterday, today will be a better day. It's just a great book. It's indescribable. It's so weird, but it's just such a great book.

That's what I wanted to present to you, but there's one other thing before I ask if there are any questions. That is: Walker Percy said that the hero of the modern world is the parish priest. The reason that Percy said that, I believe, is related to what we're talking about right now. The parish priest is devoted to helping his fellow human beings recover their humanity, [to] be healed and recover their humanity. And almost everything we do—our art, our politics, our economics—is about anything else but our humanity. We are addicted to avoiding our own humanity. The priest is the guy who's there when, in secret, the person's heart moves and says, "No, I think after all I do want to be a human being. I think after all I'm going to need Jesus to do that with me." So I agree with Walker Percy. I think that the hero of the modern world is the parish priest. I don't know if any of you are headed in that direction, but if you are, I hope that that the image of the world as a place now that has gone insane and has given up on humanity, and has circled its hopes into this reality, where what it needs to do is open its hopes up into the fullness of reality [will be helpful to you.] The parish priest really is a hero, and I hope that maybe some of that image will be helpful to you.

CHAPTER EIGHT

CATHOLIC QUESTIONS IN SCIENCE FICTION AND FANTASY

TIM POWERS

I'm a Christian—Roman Catholic variety, and a practicing one, not lapsed or "recovering"—but any readers specifically looking for Christian fiction would be disappointed to read my books.

I write science fiction and fantasy—basically supernatural adventure stories. They're not literary fiction—my stories derive from writers like Philip K. Dick, Fritz Leiber, and Theodore Sturgeon, all of whom wrote for the pulp genre magazines.

Science fiction and fantasy are predominantly atheist or agnostic fields these days, and in recent years the books published in those fields have become increasingly didactic—aggressively PC, in fact. So it might seem natural for me to write didactic Christian stories, in response.

But I hate relevance in fiction—at least deliberately contrived relevance. The characters in stories like that generally lose any appearance of autonomy or spontaneity, and become stenciled representative types, and the action is set up to convey a point about society or politics. I find such stories unconvincing, as stories. You can arrange your hand so that its shadow looks like a bird, but it's not going to seem to be a spontaneous gesture. There are exceptions, certainly—Orwell's *1984,* Steinbeck's *The Grapes of Wrath,* Lewis's *That Hideous Strength,* not to mention Dante's *Commedia.* But my work isn't meant to hold a mirror up to society—or if it does, it's just to see if society is still breathing. I do think, though, that it serves a modestly useful purpose.

I was once on a panel about vampire stories, and one panelist said, "Bram Stoker's *Dracula* is actually about the plight of 19th century women." I replied, "No—it's about a guy who lives forever by drinking other people's blood. Don't take my word for it, check it out."

The thing is, Dracula wasn't a metaphor. He was a vampire.

Somebody pointed out that what fantasy fiction does is literalize metaphors. The bloodsucking lover really is a bloodsucking lover; the long-dead ancestor who casts a shadow over his descendants really is standing between them and the Sun, on real pavement somewhere. To un-literalize them defeats the whole purpose of the genre.

If our ghosts and vampires and spaceships are metaphors for current social or political or even spiritual concerns, then they're not real ghosts and spaceships and vampires. They're useful illustrative tokens, and the story is actually about something else, outside the events and the characters. And so you'd be naïve to take the events and characters literally. If you were to say something like, "Wow, Dracula was sure a scary guy, crawling headfirst down walls and all," a scholar would rightly tell you, "Moron! He was a metaphor."

Of course a story can be both things: convincing and affecting, and, after the fact, on reflection, it can happen to work metaphorically too—probably most stories do, if you think about them in that way, with that sort of squint—but the literal story has to come first, and be vicariously experienced on its literal terms.

What you lose, if Dracula represents repression of women, if Yeats' "shape with a lion body and the head of a man" has something to do with World War I and the Irish War of Independence, and if the woman in Charlotte Perkins Gilman's "The Yellow Wallpaper" is simply insane—what you lose is the quality Rudolph Otto called the numinous, or the *mysterium tremendum.*

In his novel *The Green Man,* Kingsley Amis described a supernatural intrusion as, "something monstrous, so monstrous that the mere fact of it, its coming to pass at all, would be harder to bear than its actual menace to me personally."

And of course the intrusion of the supernatural doesn't have to be entirely scary—think of the appearance of Pan, in the chapter "The Piper at the Gates of Dawn" in *The Wind in the Willows.* When Mole and Rat see Pan on an island at dawn, Mole asks Rat if he's afraid, and Rat says, "Afraid? Afraid of Him? O, never, never! And yet—and yet—O Mole, I am afraid!"[1] It will always be a bit scary, because when it happens we're suddenly very little creatures in a world unimaginably bigger than ours, with a definite nature of its own that's vastly different from what we know.

Do you remember Edwin Abbott's book *Flatland*? It was about two-dimensional creatures who exist in a geometric plane, and of course can't comprehend "above" or "below." Our situation, when dealing with the

---

[1] Kenneth Grahme, *The Wind in the Willows* (London: Methuen, 1908).

supernatural, is like what those creatures would experience if they were trying to comprehend a ship's rigging or a Gothic cathedral. As somebody said about quantum mechanics, it's not only stranger than we know, it's stranger than we can know.

Incidentally, I'm not talking about Magic Realism stories. In Magic Realism nothing is impossible, so events we would call impossible become unremarkable. The characters are not surprised when spilled blood flows down the street to the door of a murderer, or a woman spontaneously floats away into the sky. Since none of the characters are surprised by these things, the reader isn't encouraged to believe that they really happened in a real world. A real woman didn't float away into the sky, a woman in a Dalí painting did.

Sometimes I'm asked, "Why don't you write a serious novel?" —that is, mainstream, with no supernatural stuff. It always strikes me as like asking a painter, "Why don't you do a painting without using the color blue?"

Why? People can see blue. And people can vicariously participate in supernatural stories, vicariously believe supernatural events are real, at least for the duration of a story. We even have an inclination toward believing that stuff! Even a lot of materialist atheists can't watch movies like *The Haunting* or *The Exorcist*.

The actor Lon Chaney was once asked what was the scariest thing that could happen to a person. He replied, "A knock at the door at 3 a.m., and when you open it there's a clown standing there." I know I would simply expire on the spot. It wouldn't matter if the clown had got the wrong address for a party—Powers would be dead on the threshold.

Sensible people have told me things like, "I'm not scared of ghosts, I'm scared of nuclear war and urban gangs." I nod politely, but I'm sure that if one of them were the only person in an old house at midnight, and heard something dragging downstairs, his first thought would not be, "I bet that's an urban gang member!" For at least a moment he would know precisely what it was—a reanimated mummy.

You can see people react to what they believe is a supernatural event, even when you know the mundane explanation. A while ago some people came to our door with Bibles and said they wanted to tell us about Jesus. I explained that we're Catholic and already know about Jesus, but they said that Catholicism isn't Christian, and recited some common misconceptions about the faith.

"Let me have your Bible for a minute," I said, "and I can show you why you're wrong." One of them handed over a Bible, and I flipped to, as I recall, the first page of John's gospel, and began reading. But I need a magnifying glass to read small print, and was using one, and we were outdoors, and it was a very sunny day.

And I set their Bible on fire. They fled, and I know they told all their friends, "Those Catholics just have to *touch* a Bible and it bursts into flames!"

Nearly everybody is susceptible to evidence of the supernatural, just as nearly everybody can see the color blue. So I don't limit myself to the constraints of mainstream fiction.

Mainstream fiction—for all its admittedly outweighing virtues—is like a straight-line highway between null forests. One dimensional. It's got an infinity of points, but all "possible," like the "real numbers" line in the complex plane. Fantasy is a perpendicular look, rotating the view 90 degrees to the "imaginary numbers" line, diverging at right angles from the real numbers line. It's a sudden second dimension, like a sideways look from that one-dimensional highway, down a corridor of trees to a clearing— whether it's to see a space ship or Cthulhu or a unicorn. The disorienting shift out of the familiar single-dimension is the whole point of the sort of supernatural stories I like and write. And the direction is there. The color blue is in the paintbox.

Darwin has arguably raised our foreheads and stopped us from dragging our knuckles on the ground when we walk—but the circuitry for believing in the supernatural is all still there in our heads, ready to light up.

Chesterton wrote, "Suppose somebody in a story says, 'Pluck this flower and a princess will die in a castle beyond the sea.' We do not know why something stirs in the subconsciousness, or why what is impossible seems almost inevitable. Suppose we read, 'And in the hour when the king extinguished the candle his ships were wrecked far away on the coast of Hebrides.' We do not know why the imagination has accepted that image before the reason can reject it."[2] We're ready to believe that sort of thing. A part of us *wants* to believe it!

C.S. Lewis somewhere quotes Matthew Arnold saying that being hungry doesn't prove we have bread, but—as Lewis points out—being hungry is evidence that there probably is such a thing as bread. And we are hungry— or at least eagerly receptive.

A while ago I was going to write a book about a demonic possession happening in a rural Catholic parish in San Bernardino. My wife was working at the local parish office, and it was a notably slipshod parish. For example, one year they wanted to burn all the palm fronds before Palm

---

[2] G. K. Chesterton, *The Everlasting Man* (Garden City, NY: Image Books, 1955), 107.

Sunday, to be ready for Ash Wednesday. During the rush of confessions during Lent it was proposed that the office staff could fill in and hear confessions too. Meanwhile, the ledgers showed a lot of donations to the parish from KFC because the bookkeeper never grasped that "K of C" on the donation forms was short for "Knights of Columbus." And I had a book by Malachi Martin which contained transcripts of actual exorcisms! So I had all my research lined up. But a note on the front flyleaf of the Martin book said, "The publisher and author advise reading the following prayer before and after reading each chapter."

I dropped the book and didn't write my own. It would have been too real. The supernatural is real, and fantasy fiction to some extent gets readers comfortable with the notion. A mind acclimatized to the broadened perspectives of fantasy can more easily grasp Christianity—it's done some of the warm-up exercises.

Because the claims of Christianity aren't metaphors. And it's not Magic Realism, where anything at all can happen, and there are no rules at all.

What the Christian gospels describe is real intrusions of the supernatural—another world, with its own real nature. It can be scary, and it won't be what we wish it would be. We can't choose the bits we like and discard the bits we don't like. Eve Tushnet wrote, "God doesn't promise that He'll only ask you for the sacrifices you agree with and understand."[3]

When people say, "I'm Catholic, but I don't agree with the Church about . . ."—whatever, gay marriage, abortion—it sounds like, "I have no quarrel with parts of the multiplication table—the times-two line, the times-five line—but I don't agree with the times-seven line. I think 7x8 should just be 50. It'd be so much easier on everybody."

We've got to try to adapt to it; it won't adapt to us. Aslan isn't a tame lion. The first thing angels always say, when they appear in the Bible, is, "Don't be afraid!" I don't think I'd enjoy being visited by an angel. Think of the scene in which the eldila, who are angels, visit Ransom's house, in Lewis' *That Hideous Strength!* Impressive and holy, but not relaxing.

This is a clumsy comparison, but—just as it can be tempting to reduce the scary figure of Dracula to a comfortable metaphor, it can be tempting to reduce the supernatural elements of Christianity to comfortable metaphors, to see the faith as just a helpful philosophy to make life better. It's tempting because to really admit the presence of the supernatural is to admit that we are, as I said earlier, "very little creatures in a world unimaginably bigger

---

[3] Eve Tushnet, "I'm Gay, but I'm not Switching to a Church that Supports Gay Marriage," *The Atlantic*, May 30, 2013, https://www.theatlantic.com/sexes/archive/2013/05/im-gay-but-im-not-switching-to-a-church-that-supports-gay-marriage/276383/.

than ours, with a definite nature of its own that's different from what we know."

And so, even if you're a Christian, it's tempting to disregard the claim that Christ really was dead for forty hours, and came back to life; that the bread and wine on the altar are no longer bread and wine after the priest has said the consecration prayers, but are in fact the body and blood of the Creator of the universe; and that, as Lewis again said somewhere, everybody we know will eventually be an immortal spirit so glorious that we might mistake it for God, or an immortal spirit so horrifyingly corrupted that we might mistake it for the Devil.

I've heard people say that the miracle of the loaves and fishes actually consisted of Christ persuading people who had brought food to share it with people who had not. "And," they always say, "isn't that really a greater miracle?"

Well, no. That's just the old "Stone Soup" story. The guy comes to town with an empty pot and persuades the residents to contribute various sorts of food to put in it. Comfortingly mundane, omitting any disquieting element of the supernatural. A nice story about somebody coaxing out natural virtue in people.

But of course, according to Christianity, the natural virtues in people, and all the comfortingly mundane nice things people do, or even the heroic things people do, won't save us. Even the pagans who told stories about Dionysus and Osiris and Balder knew, dimly, the shape of what we need, and it wasn't anything in our natural world or in ourselves. Being hungry doesn't prove we have bread, but it is evidence that we *need* bread.

And so I hope stories like the ones I write do their small part in keeping current moving through that primordial circuitry in our brains—not that any of the things I write about could really happen, but that that category of stuff can strike a significantly responsive chord.

And none of it is metaphorical!

CHAPTER NINE

SCIENCE FICTION AND FANTASY IN REGARD TO FACT, IMAGINATION, METAPHOR, RELIGION, AND CATHOLICISM

A DIALOGUE BETWEEN MICHAEL FLYNN, TIM POWERS, AND JOHN C. WRIGHT[1]

On Why Science Fiction Traditionally Has Not Been Very Hospitable to Religion

Tim Powers: There are just a few Christian and . . . specifically Catholic science fiction and fantasy writers. I bet I could think of five. And in fact some of those five are not currently working. I think of Gene Wolfe; R. A. Lafferty; Anthony Boucher; and Walter M. Miller, who wrote *A Canticle for Leibowitz* (1959), which might be the best Catholic science fiction novel ever written. But most science fiction and fantasy writers today you would have to categorize as atheist-agnostic. And the gap that that leaves in the mind of any mature person has, to my mind, largely been filled with a fervid devotion to contemporary controversies and issues—a more fervid devotion, that is to say, a new religious devotion, that those issues really can't support. . . . A whole lot of contemporary science fiction and also fantasy is metaphor for issues of today . . . It's as if there are ideological bases you have to touch in order to be relevant. I've never wanted to be relevant myself. In fact if I reread a rough draft of mine and find patches that do seem to be relevant I'll try to cut them out. . . . It seems to me, I think in Christian-Hebrew—I'm less acquainted with Islamic literature, but I

[1] This "dialogue" has its origins in conversations that took place during our conference on "Space in the Catholic Imagination," held on May 6, 2020. The material here was transcribed both from a public discussion between these three participants at the close of the conference and from comments made during Q&A sessions. Comments were then lightly edited and grouped into common themes.

think in all of them, and with Hesiod, and Ovid's *Metamorphoses*—throughout the ages writers with something numinous to fill that place in their mind write with more depth than writers who have had by default to fill that space in their minds with crumpled up copies of today's newspapers.

John C. Wright: At some point in the past, after the enlightened Middle Ages, it became fashionable to try to remove God from His central place in philosophy and that spilled over into art and other parts of the culture. And so the attempt was made to make a secular view of the universe, and with it a secular morality and a secular reason for civilization, a secular point to life. And those attempts spilled over into the early science fiction writers, and particularly John W. Campbell Jr.'s stable of writers—Asimov, Van Vogt, and Heinlein—and that kind of set the tone for science fiction for many-a-year. But even at that time you had writers like Cordwainer Smith who still wrote from a Christian—by which I mean a truthful—perspective. So I think it's just fashion. Christianity is not fashionable among proud people who want to have as much sex as possible with as many partners as possible. Christianity is only popular among sinners. And our peers and our elites are now sinless and perfect, and so they don't need to admit Christ anymore. But people like me still do. I speak as an ex-atheist by the way. I found out I was wrong about everything. . . . Part of the idea is that it's just not fashionable, it's just not popular, after about the 1600s to bring up God in polite conversations, because there will be Protestants and Catholics in the room and you don't want to start a fight. And part of it is, that if you are trying to sell commercial products like a science fiction story, you want to appeal to as many people as possible without offending people who might be sensitive to certain issues. And if you bring up religion you're going to offend people.

Tim Powers: I find the secular, materialist point of view contradicted at its own core, because they have no basis for believing they have free will. They pretty much are logically bound by their basic assumptions to say that every atom has to go where Newton or Niels Bohr says it will go, and therefore there really isn't any room in their philosophy for the idea that I am totally free to choose a beer or a Coke.

John C. Wright: But you are free to choose your sex.

Tim Powers. Well, yeah. And ultimately I think they would have to concede that according to their assumptions the Big Bang wrote Shakespeare's sonnets and Beethoven's symphonies. It strikes me that to maintain [an] atheist, materialist, determinist point of view requires some intellectual dishonesty.

Michael Flynn: Yeah, I would say that's about it. It's not so much intellectual dishonesty as a lack of intellectual consistency or thoroughness . . . There are certain superficial beliefs that they incorporate and they roll with it and they never look down into the fundamentals or the basis of them.

John C. Wright: It is also just a lack of education. Because whenever I have a discussion about determinism with any of my fellow amateur philosophers, I have to explain Aristotle's four causes to them over and over again, whereas back in the day, back in the so-called Middle Ages, which I call the High Ages, every educated man knew what those were, and it was just part of the cultural conversation among intellectuals. So . . . we've lost a lot of material and it's really difficult to speak clearly and precisely about things that the medievals knew backwards and forwards.

Tim Powers: These days in science fiction immortality is to be achieved by uploading your brain into a computer. I know personally at least a couple of science fiction writers who have signed up to have their heads frozen in liquid nitrogen after they die. And, of course, they hope to have people in the future defrost them and clone fresh bodies for them. . . . I always figure if they do defrost them they are only going to mount 'em on lawn mowers . . . . You'll be saying, "I'm a famous physicist," and hear back, "Shut up, you're no good at mowing the lawn." Yeah, these days it's uploading your personality into a cyborg creature or a starship control unit. And it always does strike me as if it's a token sort of immortality, as a kind of pathetic attempt to circumvent the next step. Sometimes of course they are getting uploaded into these machines just to function better as soldiers or something, and immortality isn't really even one of the considerations. But always, always the thing to be avoided at all cost, is death. And it seems to me that for a lot of the characters, and therefore probably the writers, death holds more horror than is justified by just the thought of oblivion. . . . It strikes me that [their] horror of death is a horror of something a great deal more substantial than oblivion.

On Incorporating Real-World Facts into Science Fiction and Fantasy

Tim Powers: I know I try really hard to firmly staple my story to the real world, so that, as much as possible the reader will be given the impression that this is not an alternate universe, this is where you live, this is as real as these various historical facts. What I don't want to happen is for the reader to think to themselves, "Oh, I see this is an imaginary story." I want to take every measure possible to convince the reader, no this is where you live, you haven't noticed it, but it's happening right where you live. My main goal with fiction is to trick the reader into thinking that the events and people and places are real. I want them, for the duration of reading the story, to vicariously participate and be concerned with, worried about the characters, anxious about the situation. Therefore, I like to work very hard to convince them this is happening in the real world, this is not an alternate reality, this is where you live. I mean, it may be hundreds of years ago, but it still happened in the world you are sitting in right now. And therefore I don't want to do anything that would cause to reader to say, "Oh, this didn't really happen . . . this story is violating known history." . . . At every turn I try to, as far as I know, be precisely accurate with the history. If history says this character was in this place at 10 a.m. on this particular date, I'll make sure that he is in my story. If history says six months elapsed between events, I won't, even for the convenience of the plot, shorten that six months. I'll tell myself, no, that's in ink. You can work in pencil, but you can't change anything that's in ink. So it is all for the purpose of making the reader think, "Oh yeah, good Lord, it was that way." And then I want at least part of their brain to think, "I guess this story's true." Also, in a way, it's a good luck thing. I think if I deviate from real history, if I have something happening in the wrong year, or if I have a character do something that would have been impossible for him to do, I think, "Well that's bad luck. Don't be going out of your way to step in bad luck."

Michael Flynn: I would say that for stories like *Eifelheim* (2006) that had been set in an actual historical era, I went to enormous pains to make sure that all the dates and places lined up. So that all the rulers that are mentioned, all the baronies that are mentioned, were the actual rulers and barons of that particular time and place. I consulted maps of the Schwarzwald to find a place where I could put the village without getting in the way of any actual villages that were already there. And of course it was the Black Forest, so aliens, flying grasshoppers and stuff, would not have been out of place at all.

Tim Powers: Just by accident, I was reading about Kim Philby, the British spy, and I read that he and his father both had a horror of baptism. Kilby was careful not to baptize any of his children. Not because he thought it was outmoded superstition, but clearly because he thought it really would have an effect on his children. And I thought, "Hmm, that's really interesting. That kind of points to a story." And one time I read that Thomas Edison's last breath is preserved in a test tube in a museum in Michigan— which is true, I've seen the test tube. Apparently Henry Ford was a friend of the family, and when Edison was on his death bed, Ford said to his children, "Ah here . . . kids, indulge me. Here's a test tube. When your old man breathes his last breath could you catch it in this test tube? Here's a cork. Could you catch it? For sentimental reasons I'd like to have it." So I thought, "Hmm . . . that's weird." And then unconnectedly I read that Edison's last project he was working on was a telephone with which to talk to dead people. And at that point I thought, "Okay, okay, this will work . . . we can do something with Edison." So I read several biographies of him looking for unexplained, weird, apparently irrational events, which I figured could find the explanation for; I could point out why they weren't irrational events. But yeah, history is a goldmine. [There are] things that have no reasonable excuse and [for] every one of them . . . I bet I can think of a reasonable excuse, given the supernatural.

John C. Wright: I will say that science fiction writing is like a magic trick where you're supposed to create an illusion, and part of the way you do the illusion is by means of verisimilitude of science and facts. The same way in a historical novel you create the illusion of realism by reference to real historical facts. In my *Count to a Trillion* (2012) I wanted to have the astronomical wonders of the universe be put on stage in all of their magnitude, in all of their size and glory—that's how I happened to know how far away the Supercluster Corona Borealis is—that's one of the characters in my story, the Corona Borealis Supercluster. And I took a vow not to make up anything, not to make up any astronomical wonder, because there are real astronomical wonders, in real outer space, made by the real hand of God—or if you're an atheist made by an unintelligent natural process—that I didn't need any embellishment, and I'm embarrassed if I have to embellish, even in my most outrageous space operas. I'm writing one now that I'm posting free of charge on my blog called *The Space Despot's Beautiful Daughter*. It takes place around the moons of Jupiter and I made sure the timing of the orbit of Io was correct, how long the day was, and, with the transit of Jupiter in front of the Sun, how long it would take. I looked it all up; I made sure all my facts were correct. And the only place where there's any dispute is, in my future version Pluto is still a planet because the tyrant has decreed that he is not going to have fewer planets in the solar system he rules than his ancestors did and so he declares that all fifty of the dwarf planets are planets and that the school children have to memorize all their names, because he's a tyrant. So that's in my book. But St. Christopher is in my Moth and Cobweb books and I gave him a dog's head because that's what the historical account said.

Tim Powers: Right, right, there's precedence.

John C. Wright: It's an illusion. The artist is trying to make you believe something is real that's not real; that's why it's called fiction. In order to help with the illusion, you sometimes put enough reality in it to give it a sense of starch, so that it helps maintain the illusion. But the illusion . . . it's hypnosis, but it's hypnosis with the willing cooperation of the audience. If you want to suddenly disbelieve in a story you're writing all you have to do is say there's never been a person named Scarlett O'Hara, and suddenly, poof, *Gone with the Wind* (1936) is gone. Because there never was a person named Scarlett O'Hara. Likewise, there's no such thing as warp drive. Okay, so there goes *Star Trek*. I mean you can do that to any story you like. . . . The only difference between science fiction and other types of fiction is we use more science in ours to create the illusion of reality.

Tim Powers: Yeah, I've always figured the one trick any fiction needs to do is to make the reader believe that these are real things happening to real people in real places. As soon as you've done that, you've really accomplished the trick.

John C. Wright: And you can get someone to cry over the loss of Hecuba.

Tim Powers: Yes. Yes.

Michael Flynn: What is Hecuba to you or you to Hecuba?—a heck of a thing to worry about.

On Incorporating the Imaginary and Metaphor into Science Fiction and Fantasy and How Science Fiction and Fantasy, though Escapist, Can Treat Important Philosophical Issues

Tim Powers: Fiction, of course, mimics real life, but ideally it provides all the elements real life disappoints us with. In real life, more often than not, the bad guys get away with it, the person of huge promise turns out to be nothing. Your candidate gets elected and proves to be worthless. It leaves us thinking this isn't how it's supposed to be. We have a sort of instinct that events and actions are supposed to lead toward justice. And it's in fiction that we can find it. I think fiction, good fiction, can show us how we should live, either by good examples or bad examples. And I gotta say that what I write is really escapism. If somebody asks me, "Powers, what theme do you feel you've been exploring in your work?" I always say, "Nobody wins when you play games with traffic safety." In other words, "Shut up!" What I write is supernatural adventure stories, and they are escapism. But J. R. R. Tolkien was once asked how he justifies writing what is basically escapism and he said, "Now, what is the class of people who most disapprove of escape? Jailors." So I think escapism has its own virtue. I think anything—I'm not sure I mean this—but, at the moment, anything that lifts us out of the worm's eye view that we are stuck in by default, either from daily life [or] the terrible things we read about in the news, anything that can give us a bit of distance, a bit of elevation from which we can look around and see a bigger section of our temporal landscape, is not without value.

John C. Wright: God in his mercy gave mankind the gift of speech and the devil in his envy taught us how to lie. But then God in his mercy again taught us how to use those lies to tell the truth and we call that fiction. That's what poets are for.

Tim Powers: That's very good.

John C. Wright: Thank you. That's one of the few things I didn't steal from you.

Michael Flynn: I would like to add, on that question of verisimilitude, that where science fiction most often breaks down is not in the scientific details and things of that sort but in the details of human beings and personal relationships. Because too often the characters are cardboard cutouts, stereotypes, and folks like that, who act according to the category to which they belong. So think about religion or science becoming characters in the story, reified abstractions, not real persons.

Tim Powers: Yeah, I think that often happens . . . I mean, for one thing it's bad craft; it's like making a cabinet where the door won't actually close . . . But I think it often happens because the author wants, even more than to tell a story, to make some sort of point, has some moral to advance. And would even claim that it's a metaphor. One time I was on a panel at a science fiction convention talking about vampire stories, and one of the panelists said, "Well you know *Dracula* (1897) is *actually* about the plight of nineteenth-century women." And I said, "No, it's actually about a guy who lives forever by drinking other people's blood. Don't take my word for it, check it out." The problem is that if a metaphor aspect of our fiction becomes the important point then all our space ships, time machines, and vampires, simply become sort of illustrative tokens in the service of making a point. And we lose that ability to, the freedom to get upset about the characters, to worry about them, to vicariously really experience it.

John C. Wright: I long ago vowed to make sure my stories were as pointless as possible, yet points still continue to creep in. And because I read Aristotle, I knew why this was. Art is meant to hold up a mirror to nature, even if I myself as the artist don't understand what I'm reflecting, what I'm saying—and you can tell from my conversation that I don't. If I hold a mirror to nature correctly, the same things that make your heart leap or make your heart fall in nature, are going to happen in my story. I might not myself know anything about Hecuba, but you might be moved to tears when her child is killed by this horrific Greek. And we all hate the Greeks, right? I mean that's the one thing we all agree upon. . . . Sorry, Hecuba, she means a lot to me.

Tim Powers: Yeah, I think it's true that any story is going to work metaphorically if you step back and look at it with that kind of squint. But it shouldn't be the primary aim of the author, it shouldn't be what the story was shaped to do. I always figure that if I'm holding up a mirror to society, it is mainly just to see if society is still breathing.

John C. Wright: To see if there's breath, if there's fog on the mirror.

Tim Powers: Right.

John C. Wright: If you're trying to write *Pilgrim's Progress* (1678), you're deliberately trying to use the symbols in a one-for-one, wooden, straightforward way to make your point. Now I don't have anything against *Pilgrim's Progress*, but that's not *Lord of the Rings* (1954-1955), it's not "Ode on a Grecian Urn," it's not a Shakespeare Sonnet. There are myriad levels of metaphors you can read into a sonnet, some of which the author knows, and some of which only the Muses know. So, I myself find it to be a little dubious when someone tells me what a story is really about. Because if I myself don't know what my own stories are about, I don't think someone living two hundred years after I am dead is going to be able to read my mind and figure out what the Muse is trying to say. And she's smarter than I am.

Tim Powers: I think . . . for me the big issue *is* free will. And I think science fiction and fantasy both can confront you with situations that the real world can't provide but which nevertheless raise interesting questions that could actually lead you to some valuable conclusions about the nature of free will. And certainty even the looser kind of time travel story, where you can change the past, can give you valuable moral quandaries, that again real life cannot provide. If you were to get a visit from your future self, from say twenty years in the future, and find that he is a hopelessly depraved alcoholic, you would be left with the question, "Can I change that?"—and some incentive to change it. How inevitable is that? In fact, it's Ebenezer Scrooge brushing the snow off the gravestone and asking the spirit of Christmas yet to come, "Can't these words be expunged from this stone if I change my ways?" It does give you a sort of timeless—or at least not as firmly stapled into sequential time—viewpoint, that all the mainstream fiction in the world really doesn't provide.

How to Incorporate Religion and Catholicism into Science Fiction and Fantasy

John C. Wright: It's commonplace among Communists and among those of the far left to try to use storytelling as a propaganda tool and they think a story is successful if it is subversive—their word, not mine—because it casts doubt upon the current social order and hence subverts it. Now to subvert something is to undermine it from beneath. I myself, and my wife, and one or two other like-minded crazy people, have decided to start a literary movement called the Superversive movement, where we are trying to use stories to show that there is more to life, not less, than you think there is. And not all of these superversive stories necessarily have to be Christian or Catholic but certainly there is room for that. The whole point of my talk tonight was to say: Catholicism is so large there is room for the entire universe, plus two or three more, without in any way exhausting the possibilities. If a story is supposed to or has to serve a point, which I don't think it does, the point is to glorify God. And when you do that you automatically serve a lot of other points and you sometimes give your readers things you did not even know were even in there to give. When I was younger I used foolishly to think that my job was merely to be an entertainer so I left my Christianity out of certain of my books. And I used to be an atheist too, by the way. But when one of my atheist books was criticized for being too Christian—[a book] which I wrote when I was an atheist, but the guy found out in real life I was a Christian—I decided there wasn't that much point in deciding to hide my opinions. And when I got a tear-stained letter from someone who had read one of my short stories saying it had changed her life, I said, "I'm not going to hide my light under a bushel from now on." If people are going to hate me because I'm Christian, that has nothing to do with me; it's because they don't like Him. So, at that point I decided occasionally just to have some of my characters simply be Catholics, and they would talk like Catholics and say Catholic prayers. But even if I didn't do that, I sometimes adopt what I'll call the *Beowolf* approach, which is the same approach I believe professor Tolkien used, where I merely portray the universe as it would be if you have a Catholic sense of life, a sacramental sense that not everything begins and ends with the material world. Even in science fiction you certainly don't have to believe that. And even in science fiction the number of times religious matters come up is more often than in non-science fiction secular stories. Michael the Archangel is a character in Robert Heinlein's *Stranger in a Strange Bed*, or whatever that book was called [i.e., *Stranger in a Strange Land* (1961)], and God Himself was a character in Olaf Stapledon's *Star Maker* (1937). He is the title character, the Star Maker. Now he is a gnostic god, an evil god, but he's still God. Science fiction is prone to address these real issues and the guys who actually have some of the real answers will do a disservice if we don't speak up.

Tim Powers: Yeah, in one of my novels, *Declare* (2013), Catholicism wasn't emphasized, but it clearly took place in a Catholic universe: baptism did have a real effect on a soul, prayer was efficacious. I like to think that those qualities in the book arose spontaneously, organically, from the structure of the plot, and the real historical characters I was dealing with. And I've frequently had characters who are Catholic, who, for example, will say, "Wednesday is a Holy Day of Obligation; I got to make time to make it to Mass." But I certainly try not to ever seem to be proselytizing. I don't want to interrupt the flow of the story by having the reader think, "Oh, Powers is making a Catholic speech here."

Michael Flynn: Yeah, that's the right way. You have your characters *act*; you don't put words in their mouth.

Tim Powers: I think that there are core elements of Christianity: original sin, redemption, necessity for achieving forgiveness, even ego death, in order to cross the gulf which is a gulf of our own making. In fact, one

Christian element, now that I think of it, kind of notably lacking is the idea of original sin. It strikes me in science fiction, and I think this is distinct from fantasy, in works of science fiction there is no original sin. It's always starting from a point which is lower than the point you hope to get to, but that low point in turn was higher than the previous point. It is not as if there was an initial imposed handicap. Or that some outside help is needed in order to remove that initial handicap. I don't think original sin works at all in science fiction stories. But in fantasy I think it does. In fact I think it is dramatically different from science fiction. If you look at Tolkein, of course, or H. P. Lovecraft, who wrote stories like *The Dunwich Horror* (1929) and *The Shadow over Innsmouth* (1931), not just humanity, but the whole universe, is subject to an initial error, though Lovecraft offers no equivalent of baptism. Lovecraft is a really good writer—a complete atheist—but he was haunted by nightmares. He would have very vivid, very supernatural nightmares, as if his subconscious was straining against the imposition of his atheism. And so he wrote about his nightmares and wrote some really very good, if bleak and pessimistic, supernatural stories. But yeah I think fantasy does embody, portray, present us with the idea of a fall, an initial fault, an initial sin, which all the characters, and the whole world, is trying to get out of. I don't know if they rely on beatific help in order to achieve it, but at least they do acknowledge the situation. The fact is, to my satisfaction anyway, since the supernatural is real, being aware of that, even just as background, lets me experience the events in fantasy stories without the categorical reservation that atheist readers would find themselves faced with. In fact, I pity the atheist readers.

PART THREE:

PHILOSOPHY AND THEOLOGY OF THE COSMOS AND EXTRATERRESTRIAL INTELLIGENCES

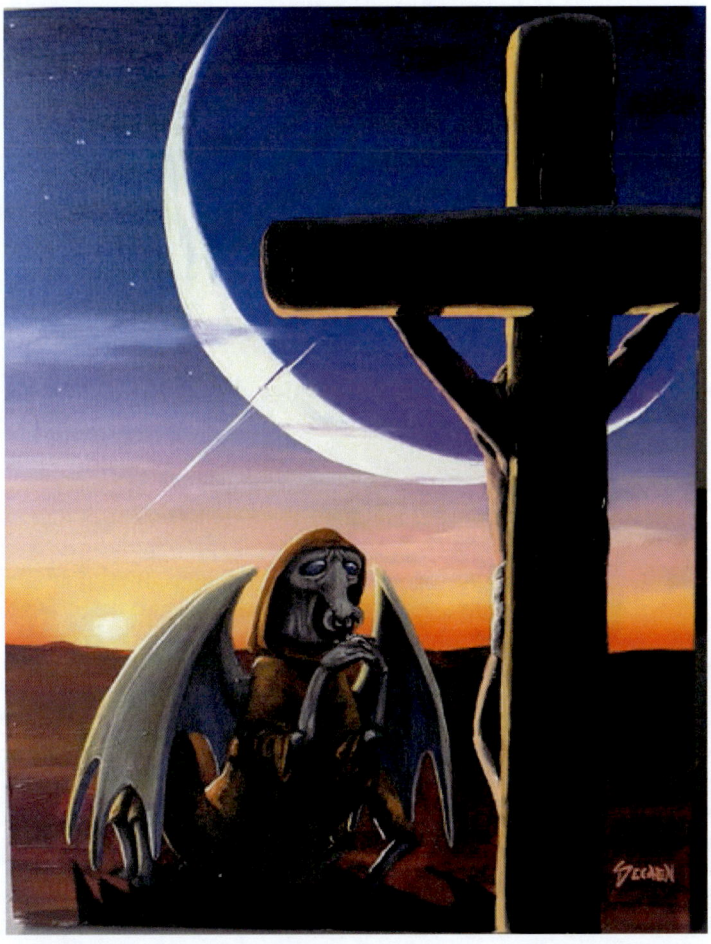

Fig. 0-3. Alien Carmelite Friar, Chris Decaen

CHAPTER TEN

HUMAN SIGNIFICANCE FOR THE MEDIEVAL MIND

ALAN VINCELETTE

If one examines many an account of the Copernican revolution in astronomy one will read about how Copernicus showed the Earth was not at the center of the universe and thus struck a blow to the inflated significance of human beings. To take an earlier example, John Draper in the nineteenth-century argued that modern astronomy launched the "progress of man from the erroneous inferences of his social infancy to the true conclusions of his maturity–from anthropocentric ideas . . . to the discovery of his true position and insignificance in the universe."[1] In the twentieth-century the geneticist Dobzhansky pointed out that with Copernicus, "Not only was the earth dethroned from its presumed centrality and preeminence, but Copernicus correctly inferred that the universe was much vaster than previously imagined."[2] More recently Dava Sobel, in her book *A More Perfect Heaven: How Copernicus Revolutionized the Cosmos* (2011), concludes that due to the heliocentrism of Copernicus "humanity lost its place at the center of the universe. . . . The earth is merely one of several planets in orbit around the Sun."[3] Even the Methodist pastor Christopher L. Fisher writes, "While the medieval worldview generally thought the earth was the center of the universe, and humans the pinnacle of creation on earth, the Copernican revolution began a process completed with Darwin of decentering humanity on the cosmic scale. The earth circles the sun, which is just a medium-size star, two-thirds of the way out from the center of a medium-size galaxy

---

[1] John Draper, *A History of the Intellectual Development of Europe* (New York: Harper Brothers, 1863), 537.
[2] Theodosius Dobzhansky, *Man's Place in the Universe: Changing Concepts*, ed. Bart J. Bok and David W. Corson (Tuscan: University of Arizona Press, 1977), 80.
[3] Dava Sobel, *A More Perfect Heaven: How Copernicus Revolutionized the Cosmos* (London: Bloomsbury, 2011), 236.

composed of billions of stars, just one among billions of other galaxies in the universe."[4] And Victor Stenger extends this into the claim that, "Since Copernicus humanity's conception of its place in the universe has steadily diminished from the biblical image that places us at the centre of the universe to one where we are but a miniscule speck in space and time."[5]

Now the implication here is that prior to Copernicus the medieval thinkers asserted that humans had pride of place in the universe, and the presupposition is that quantitative significance is tied in with qualitative significance. Both of these assertions, however, are highly questionable. In fact, the first, the view that medieval cosmology placed humans on a pedestal which the Copernican theory pulled out from under them, is a myth, one that has rooted itself insidiously in popular culture and the history of science. It makes for a nice story, but that is all it is, a fable. Of course one can still argue about the philosophical implications of the Copernican theory and advance views about heliocentrism's relation to human significance, but that is a separate matter. And if one argues from the fact that the Earth is but one planet among many orbiting stars, or is a small speck in a vast universe, to a thesis of the cosmic insignificance of humans, one engages in a particular kind of argument from quantitative size to qualitative importance.

---

[4] Christopher L. Fisher, *Human Significance in Theology and the Natural Sciences: An Ecumenical Perspective with Reference to Pannenberg, Rahner, and Zizioulas* (Eugene: Wipf and Stock, 2010), 1.

[5] Victor J. Stenger, "Atheism and the Physical Sciences," in Stephen Bullivant and Michael Ruse, eds., *The Oxford Handbook of Atheism*, Oxford: Oxford University Press, 2013), 444. Similar views are found in Chester A. Reeds, *The Earth: Our Ever-Changing Planet* (New York: University Society, 1935), 42; Marta Wankowicz, "Nicholas Copernicus," *The Catholic Digest*, 7 (1943), 27; Alexandre Koyré, *The Astronomical Revolution: Copernicus Kepler, Borelli,* trans R. E. W. Maddison (Ithaca: Cornell University Press, 1973), 17; R. N. Butler, "On the Place of Organic Life in the Universe and the Possibility of Extraterrestrial Life," *The Irish Astronomical Journal*, No. 14 (1979): 177; Jürgen Hamel, *Nicolaus Copernicus: Leben, Werk und Wirkung* (Heidelberg: Spektrum Verlag, 1994), 300; Carl Sagan and Jerome Agel, *Carl Sagan's Cosmic Connection: An Extraterrestrial Perspective* (Cambridge: Cambridge University Press, 2000), 66; William T. Vollmann, *Uncentering the Earth: Copernicus and The Revolutions of the Heavenly Spheres* (New York: Norton, 2006); Barbara A. Somerville, in her *Nicolaus Copernicus: Father of Modern Astronomy* (Minneapolis: Compass Point, 2008), 81; Friedel Weinert, *Copernicus, Darwin, and Freud: Revolutions in the History and Philosophy of Science* (Oxford: Wiley-Blackwell, 2009), 48–51; Pietro Daniel Omodeo, *Copernicus in the Cultural Debates of the Renaissance: Reception, Legacy, Transformation* (Leiden: Brill, 2014), 322–323, 382–386; and Paul M. Sutter, *Your Place in the Universe: Understanding Our Big, Messy Existence* (Amherst: Prometheus Books, 2018), 244.

Such an argument, however, is fraught with difficulty and it is easy to overreach with one's conclusions, assuming one is even aware of making an argument at all.

Patristic and Medieval Considerations of Human Size, Strength, and Abilities

Patristic and medieval authors were quite astute regarding the differences between humans and animals, and the many ways in which animals were physically superior to humans. The second and third chapters of Lactantius' *De opificio Dei* (c. 304) describe how humans are weaker and frailer [*imbecillum et fragilem, inops et infirmus*] than other animals, such as elephants. Humans, born naked and defenseless [*nudem et inermem*], are also destitute of the armaments and sources of protection given to other creatures, such as horns, talons, sharp canines, or wings. Yet for Lactantius this in no way means that humans are of less value than these other works of creation. For humans are granted the powers of perception and reason [*sensus ac ratio*] which are able to make up for their natural deficits and indeed constitute the superior gift. Lactantius hence observes that though the human being

> is possessed of a body which is not great [*non magni*], and of slight strength [*exiguarum virium*], and of infirm health [*valetudinis infirmae*], nevertheless, since he has received that which is of greater value, he is better equipped than the other animals, and more adorned. For though he is born frail and feeble [*fragilis imbecillisque*], yet he is safe from all the dumb animals, and all those which are born with greater strength, though they are able to bear patiently the inclemency of the sky, yet are unable to be safe from man. Thus it comes to pass that reason [*ratio*] bestows more on man than nature does on the dumb animals; since, in their case, neither greatness of strength nor firmness of body can prevent them from being oppressed by us, or from being made subject to our power.[6]

In fact, observes Lactantius, God created humans to stand up tall on two legs so as to be able to gaze at the heavens where their destiny lies, as opposed to being bent down towards the earth as with the animals. And God made humans with opposable thumbs in order to make use of things and craft what they need. In this way humans are unique, and "the right reason

---

[6] Translation from Alexander Roberts, James Donaldson, and A. Cleveland Coxe, eds., *The Ante-Nicene Fathers*, vol. 7, trans. William Fletcher (New York: Charles Scribner's Sons, 1905), 284.

and elevated position of man alone, and his countenance, shared with and closely resembling God his Father, bespeak his origin and Maker. His mind, nearly divine, because it has obtained the rule not only over the animals which are on the Earth, but even over his own body, being situated in the highest part, the head, as in a lofty citadel, looks out upon and observes all things."[7]

Gregory of Nyssa, in the seventh chapter of his *De opificio hominis* (379) similarly describes how lacking in natural resources humans are in comparison with other animals. Humans possess neither horns, claws, stingers, fangs with venom, wings, scaly hides, nor fleetness of foot and jumping ability, such as is found in bulls, boars, lions, tigers, leopards, bees, birds, crocodiles, hares, and deer. Yet humans possess the superior advantage of the gift of the mind wherein they are created in the image of God and have dominion over creation. For such a mind allows humans artificially to produce the weapons and defenses missing from their nature, such as swords, arrows, and iron suits of armor.[8] All the same, even in their artistic ability, humans have little to brag about in comparison with other creatures. As Augustine notes, in his *De ordine* 2.2.19 of AD 386, swallows build nests and bees hives of equal or even superior skill-level in comparison to human edifices. Though in the end, Augustine asserts that he and other humans exceed animals in possessing reason [*sed his melior, quia rationale animal sum*], or as he phrases it, not so much in making things according to measure but rather in knowing what measure is [*Non ergo numerosa faciendo, sed numeros cognoscendo melior sum*]. Hence, he remarks, "Nothing more than rationality keeps me above the brutes" [*At nihil aliud me pecori* [literally cattle] *praeponit, nisi quod rationale animal sum*].[9]

---

[7] Roberts, Donaldson, and Coxe., *The Ante-Nicene Fathers*, vol. 7, 289. Cf. Plato, *Timaeus*, 47b–c.

[8] Consult Philip Schaff and Henry Wace, eds., *Nicene and Post-Nicene Fathers: Second Series*, vol. 5, trans. H. A. Wilson (New York: Charles Scribner's Sons, 1917), 392–393.

[9] Translation from Augustine, *On Order* [*De ordine*], trans. Silvano Barruso (South Bend: St. Augustine's Press, 2007), 117. Aquinas also noted how some animals have keener external senses than humans, and so can see and smell better as with dogs, or are swifter as with birds, though humans have stronger internal senses, the most equitable temperament [*maximam aequalitatem complexionis*], and alone have a rational soul [*anima rationalis*]. And though some animals have more natural defenses such as claws and horns and tough hides, the human being with reason and arms can make arms and clothes for itself (*Summa Theologiae* I, q. 91, a. 3). This depreciation of the gifts of human beings vis-à-vis those of animals will later be found in Michel de Montaigne's *Essais* (1580) and Pierre Charron's *De la sagesse*

A fascinating text in this regard is Anselm Turmeda's comedic fantasy *Disputa de l'ase* (1417) written by a Christian friar seemingly before he had converted to Islam, a work that was to find itself placed on the Index of Forbidden Works in 1583.[10] Turmeda's *Disputa* is an imagined debate between a monk and an ass on whether humans were superior to animals and whether animals were created wholly for their benefit. In this debate, after the monk touts the senses and memory of humans, the ass points out that horses can hear better than humans, eagles see farther, cats see at night, and dogs smell better, which is why humans utilize the latter in hunting. As far as having a better memory goes, a human will often forget where his friend's house is located in a neighboring village after only one year has passed and have to ask locals for directions, but animals who migrate will return to the same spot without fail year after year. The monk next catalogs the many human achievements in the arts and crafts and governance. The ass retorts that bees, spiders, and birds build finer structures, all without tools, and insects, such as bees and ants, have equally sophisticated social structures. Nor do the songs of birds compare unfavorably to human music. Moreover, though grasshoppers and crows sometimes damage crops, rats ruin clothing, and dogs and cats steal meat, they only do so out of need, unlike humans who commit great evils and take what they do not need out of a desire of conquest.

Finally, the monk, in exasperation, pulls out the seeming trump card that humans must be superior to animals because *they eat them*; at this point the lice, fleas, and bedbugs reply that they not only dine on humans but also sleep and take dumps in their bedding, clothes, hair, and beards. And while it cannot be denied that humans alone are given an intellectual soul and made in the image of God, it is also the case that saints are represented as animals, such as St. John as an eagle, St. Mark as a lion, and St. Luke as an ox. Animals also display amazing acts of intellect such as eagles being able to distinguish their own young from those of others, birds pretending to be injured to lure predators away from their nests, or dogs and cats being careful not to harm their infants with their teeth when they carry them and eating herbs to make them throw up if they are sick to the stomach. So animals are equal to humans in most ways. The debate concludes, however,

---

(1601). Montaigne even asserts that humans are the most feeble of all creatures, dwelling in the lowest level of the universe amidst mud and dung (*Apologie de Raymond Sebond* 3.1–2).

[10] See Anselm Turmeda, *Disputation of the Donkey*, trans. Neil Kenny, in *Cambridge Translations of Renaissance Philosophical Texts, Volume 1: Moral Philosophy*, ed. Jill Kraye (Cambridge: Cambridge University Press, 1997), 3–15.

with the monk declared the victor after he points out that God chose to become incarnate in a human form and not an animal one.

The Church Fathers and later Catholic writers then clearly recognized that physical size or natural power did not equate to value or cosmic significance in any straightforward way. Humans were more valuable than other corporeal creatures even though they were much smaller in stature and physically much less imposing. And such a view has much in its favor. Is a basketball player more valuable than a gymnast on account of possessing greater height, or a defensive lineman more noble than a field goal kicker? Such a position seems foolish. Nor are men more valuable than women even though on average they are of greater height and weight. Nay something smaller in size can be of more importance and worth in the end, such as diamonds in comparison to lumps of coal. Indeed to equate physical size with importance is arguably a category error as one is linking the category of quantity (size) to that of quality (importance) in an overly simplistic manner. One would have to do much more careful and sophisticated work to show any sort of correlation between size and cosmic importance, if this could be done at all. Certainly God seems to care about things that might seem tiny or insignificant to humans, such as sparrows that are cheap to purchase or the number of hairs on a human head.[11] And humans value their babies and toy dogs as much as or more than the larger varieties. So when it comes to determining cosmic significance it is not clear that size has much of a role at all. Small or medium-sized things might indeed hold the most value.

Patristic, Medieval, and Renaissance Discussions of the Rank of Humans in the Cosmos

It is true that for the medievals humans, alone among earthly creatures, are created in the image of God (Gen 1:26) and possess reason and language. So one might presume that humans were held to be the superior beings of the universe in the Middle Ages. Yet the standard medieval view was that humans lie at a midway point in terms of cosmic excellence, situated above earthly animals, but below angels. Gregory of Nyssa, for instance, in the seventeenth chapter of his *De opificio hominis* (379) elaborates on the Scriptural view that humans "were made a little lower than angels" (Heb

---

[11] Lk 12:6–7.

2:7).[12] For fallen humans possess a body and a material mode of existence wherein they need to nourish themselves with food like the beasts. Only after the resurrection of their bodies will humans come to exist in a condition similar to that of angels, wherein their bodies will no longer be capable of being injured and there will be no need for marriage or reproduction. Gregory of Nyssa, in the following chapter, even speaks of how some may be ashamed "at the fact that our life, like that of the brutes, is sustained by food, and for this reason deems man unworthy of being supposed to have been framed in the image of God." Yet he replies that "freedom from this function will one day be bestowed upon our nature in the life we look for . . . as the resurrection holds forth to us a life equal with the angels, and with the angels there is no food, there is sufficient ground for believing that man, who will live in like fashion with the angels, will be released from such a function."[13] Hence, explains Augustine in his *De civitate Dei* 9.13, the human is mortal and miserable [*mortales ac miseros*], "a kind of mean [*medium*] between angels and beasts–the beast being an irrational and mortal animal, the angel a rational and immortal one, while man, inferior to the angel and superior to the beast [*pecoribus*], and having in common with the one mortality [*mortalitatem*], and with the other reason [*rationem*], is a rational and mortal animal [*animal rationale mortale*]."[14]

Aquinas even dedicated an article of the *Summa Theologiae* (I, q. 91, a. 1) to defending how humans, the most honorable of the lower creatures [*dignissima creaturarum inferiorum*] and the noblest of animals [*nobilissimum animalium*], and made in the image and likeness of God (Gen 1:26) with a free and rational soul and incorruptible soul, could still be made from the muck of the earth [*limo terrae*] (Gen 2:7). Aquinas answered that God bestowed perfection on all of his works, but to each in its own way and according to its capacity to receive it. God bestowed perfection on angels in the highest degree and gives them the ability to know all things in nature. Angels, therefore, absolutely speaking are more in the image of God than

---

[12] Schaff and Wace, *Nicene and Post-Nicene Fathers: Second Series*, vol. 5, 407. See also Ps 8:5 where humans are literally made a little lower than God/gods. The Septuagint, however, uses the Greek word for angels [αγγελους] as does Heb 2:7.
[13] Schaff and Wace, *Nicene and Post-Nicene Fathers: Second Series*, vol. 5, 409.
[14] Translation from Philip Schaff, ed., *Nicene and Post-Nicene Fathers: First Series*, vol. 2, trans. Marcus Dods (New York: Charles Scribner's Sons, 1907), 173. See also *De civitate Dei* 13.1 and 24. Similar views are found in the *Libri duo differentiarum*, 2.13.36–40 (c. 610) of Isidore of Seville who divides reality up into six grades of being, namely, rocks, plants, animals, humans, angels, and God, as well as in the medieval *Cosmographia* 2.10 (c. 1148) of Bernardus Silvestris, and the *De ascensu et descensu intellectus* (1305) of Raymond Lull.

humans and have a more perfect intellectual nature.[15] Still God bestowed a certain perfection on humans, albeit to a lesser degree. For humans have rational souls in likeness to angels or spiritual substances but are also composed of a material body containing the four elements, including fire and air, as well as earth and water, which, when mixed, form slime. Hence, observes Aquinas, "it was fitting that the human body was made from the four elements, so that the human would have something in common with the inferior bodies, existing as something between [*medium*] spiritual and corporeal substances."[16]

Humans then had little reason to be haughty about their standing in the universe. Indeed Lotario dei Segni, the future Pope Innocent III, wrote a treatise *De miseria humanae conditionis* (c. 1195) that expanded upon Augustine and pointed out how miserable human life really is. The first chapter of the first book describes how the human is

> formed from earth, conceived in sin, born to pain. He does depraved things that are unlawful, shameful things that are indecent, vain things that are unprofitable. He becomes fuel for the fire, food for worms, a mass of putridness. . . . Man is formed of dust, of clay, of ashes: what is more vile, from the filthiest sperm. He is conceived in the heat of desire, in the fervor of the flesh, in the stench of lust: what is worse, in the blemish of sin. He is born to labor, fear, sorrow: what is more miserable, to death.[17]

The succeeding chapters go on to trace how the human is born naked [*nuditate*], dumb [*imbecillitate*], and crying in distress, with a body created from the lowly slime of the earth rather than the nobler elements of air and fire, and leads a life that is brief [*brevitate*] and punctuated by short bouts of happiness [*brevi laetitia*] to go along with unexpected sorrows [*inopinato dolore*], diverse kinds of torments [*tormentorum*], illnesses [*aegritudinum*], and foul bodily wastes, before arriving at the many inconveniences [*incommodis*] of old age, then death, and perhaps suffering in hell. Compared to plants and trees then humans are vile creatures: "Look at the plants and the trees—they produce flowers, foliage, and fruit; you produce nits, lice, and tapeworms. They pour forth oil, wine, and balsam; you give off spit, urine, and dung. They breathe forth a sweet odor; you give off a dreadful stench."[18]

---

[15] *Summa Theologae* I, q. 93, a. 3.

[16] *Summa Theologiae* I, q. 91, a. 1, my translation. See also *Summa Theologiae* I, q. 5, a. 1; q. 93, a. 2; and q. 108, a. 5.

[17] Lotario dei Segni (Pope Innocent III), *De miseria condicionis humane*, trans. Robert E. Lewis (Athens: University of Georgia Press, 1978), 94.

[18] Dei Segni, *De miseria condicionis humane*, 12.

This led to a prolonged exchange in the Renaissance between those humanists who joined Lotario dei Segni in lamenting the misery and vileness of the human condition and those who sought to counterbalance this view by stressing the dignity and happiness of human life.[19] In the latter camp were Facio, Da Barga, Manetti, Morandi, Pico della Mirandola, Vives, Brandolini, and De Oliva. Bartolomeo Facio penned two works, *De humanae vitae felicitate* (c. 1445–1446) and *De excellentia ac praestantia hominis* (1447), detailing the many gifts of the human being, such a reason, and how happy and fulfilling human life is.[20] Made in the image of God, and possessing reason, humans are able to build cities, establish laws, observe the heavens, devise medical treatments, and write works of philosophy. Moreover, as Lactantius noted, God gave humans a body which is tall and erect so that they can look toward the heavens instead of being forced to gaze upon the ground with the animals, and the twelve apostles will be co-judgers with God at the general resurrection of humans. Hence humans, though not quite at the level of angels, occupy a rank not too far distant. Indeed not only did God assume a human form in the Incarnation, and die on the cross for humans, but he grants humans the power to change the substance of bread into the substance of the body of Christ, something not even conferred upon the angels.

Facio's second work was based upon Antonio da Barga's *Libellus de dignitate et excellentia humanae vitae* (1447) which even claimed that, to some degree, there is greater worth in being a human than an angel as God assumed a human form, not an angelic one, and humans are the only race blessed with the opportunity to receive the body and blood of Christ in the Eucharist. Furthermore, the joining of the human spirit to an earthly body allows for a unique creature, able to worship God in its own way, and to be raised up from its lowliness in order to share in God's glory. Finally, after

---

[19] The latter authors hence intended to provide the supplement that Dei Seigni promised, but was unable to deliver upon after becoming pope, on the more positive aspects of human existence. For more on these debates over whether human life is bleak or blessed see: Brian Copenhaver, "Dignity, Vile Bodies, and Nakedness: Giovanni Pico and Gionnazzo Manetti" in *Dignity: A History*, ed. Remy Debes (Oxford: Oxford University Press, 2017), 127–174; Jill Kraye, "Moral Philosophy," in *The Cambridge History of Renaissance Philosophy*, ed. Charles B. Schmitt and Quentin Skinner (Cambridge: Cambridge University Press, 2008), 301–386; Darren M. McMahon, *Happiness: A History* (New York: Grove Press, 2006); Caroline Stark, "Renaissance Anthropologies and the Conception of Man," in *New Worlds and the Italian Renaissance: Contributions to the History of European Intellectual Culture*, ed. Andrea Moudarres and Christiana Thérèse Purdy Moudarres (Leiden: Brill, 2012), 173–194.

[20] A similar work is Benedetto Morandi's *De felicitate humana* (c. 1475).

the resurrection humans will equal angels in knowledge and enjoyment.[21] A few years later Giannozzo Manetti joined in the chorus praising humans with his *De dignitate et excellentia hominis* (1452) which laid out the great beauty, resources, and privileges bestowed upon them. In the first place, the human body is a great example of the handiwork of God and indeed more beautiful than the body of other creatures with its symmetry, erect posture, and head situated at the top of the body where it can command as from a citadel. Nor do humans have any need of horns, claws, feathers, or scales, as they possess limbs able to engage in a variety of different crafts in order to provide for their needs. In this way the human body, proclaims Manetti, is "the most handsome, clever, judicious, noble and finally the most capable of all . . . in it we perceive a kind of divine resemblance showing itself and shining forth . . . What framing of limbs, what symmetry of lines, what shape, what looks . . . can be more beautiful than the human?"[22] The human body is also gifted with a tongue able to speak and is even give immortality. So though the human body is made from the slime of the earth, it is nobler than those of other material bodies, such as those of the stars, fishes, and birds, since it is immortal and well-suited for acting, speaking, and understanding creation. In the second place, the human is also given an indestructible soul created in the likeness of God, and so possessing reason, memory, and freedom: "God created a soul for man to surpass and master all other animals, equipping it with reason and immortality, with intelligence and memory and will."[23] This intellectual soul, when combined with the body, allows humans to craft such magnificent works as ships, pyramids, buildings, paintings, sculptures, languages, poems, and to look up into the sky and contemplate God. Indeed, as Lactantius noted, God fashioned the world and the creatures in it for the sake of humans and even grants each human a guardian angel in heaven; and God became incarnate in a human versus an angelic form. Regarding the view that human life is full of misery, and the human frail and subject to illnesses and numerous disturbances—pointed out by Job, Cicero, Seneca, Pliny, and Lotario dei Segni among others—Manetti replies that the afflictions of the body are not from nature but from original sin, and so would not occur had Adam and Eve not sinned. And though life on occasion brings pain, anguish, and distress, "more kinds of pleasure than distress rule this ordinary, everyday life of ours,"[24] and

---

[21] These texts are found in Giannozzo Manetti, *On Human Worth and Excellence*, trans. Brian P. Copenhaver (Cambridge: Harvard University Press, 2018), 257–267 and 269–295.

[22] Manetti, *On Human Worth*, 129.

[23] Manetti, *On Human Worth*, 85.

[24] Manetti, *On Human Worth*, 203.

there are various remedies that humans can use to counter the discomforts of cold, heat, toil, pain, and disease. Indeed life is full of simple pleasures, such as seeing beautiful bodies, hearing pleasant songs, smelling flowers, tasting gourmet dishes and fine wines, touching soft things, warming up, cooling down, lying down for a rest, or having sex. Finally, by leading holy lives humans can return to their natural state of original justice, and in this way acquire a modicum of felicity in this life and the even fuller joy of the beatific vision in heaven. In short, though the human being is created a little lower than the angel to whom is given a place of prominence in heaven, the human lot is one of excellence, full of cheer in this life and eternal joy in the life to come, for those who do God's will.

Perhaps the most famous work in this vein is Pico della Mirandola's *De hominis dignitate* (1496). He too extols the preeminence of human beings who are therein worthy of unbound admiration. The endowments of humans, who are favored with an intellect in a body able to meditate upon the grandeur of creation as well as the freedom of choice to spurn earthly things and aspire to heavenly ones, are the envy not just of animals but even of angels. Moreover, by making use of their gifts, humans can rise almost to the level of angels: "As the sacred mysteries tell us, the Seraphim, Cherubim and Thrones occupy the first places; but, unable to yield to them, and impatient of any second place, let us emulate their dignity and glory. And, if we will it, we shall be inferior to them in nothing [*nihilo inferiores*]" (nn. 52–53).[25] Still, in the end, humans are not quite at the level of angels for Pico della Mirandola. Humans sit squarely in the middle [*in mundi positum meditullio*] of creation and a little lower than the angels [*ab angelis . . . paulo deminutum*] (n. 18), and so dwell between the heights of the celestial regions and the "fermenting dung-heap of the inferior world [*excrementarias ac foeculentas inferioris mundi*]" (n. 10).[26] Hence, as he elaborates,

> We have given you, O Adam, no visage proper to yourself, nor endowment properly your own, in order that whatever place, whatever form, whatever gifts you may, with premeditation, select, these same you may have and possess through your own judgement and decision. The nature of all other creatures is defined and restricted within laws which We have laid down; you, by contrast, impeded by no such restrictions, may, by your own free will, to whose custody We have assigned you, trace for yourself the

[25] Giovanni Pico della Mirandola, *Oration on the Dignity of Man*, trans. A. Robert Caponigri (Washington: Gateway, 1956), 12–13.
[26] For the Latin text see Pico della Mirandola, *Opera omnia* (Basileae: Heinricum Petri, 1557), 314 and 316.

lineaments of your own nature. I have placed you at the very center of the
world, so that from that vantage point you may with greater ease glance
round about you on all that the world contains. We have made you a creature
neither of heaven nor of earth, neither mortal nor immortal, in order that you
may, as the free and proud shaper of your own being, fashion yourself in the
form you may prefer. It will be in your power to descend to the lower, brutish
forms of life; you will be able, through your own decision, to rise again to
the superior orders whose life is divine.[27]

Charles de Bovelles, in his *Liber de sapiente* 26 (1509) even notes that
if we had to picture the location of humans in the cosmos it would be at the
center as they are the mirrors of nature and able to relate to and know all
things in the cosmos.[28]

Later optimistic works regarding the lot of humans on Earth include the
Fabula de homines (1518) of Juan Luis Vives, as well as the *De humanae
vitae conditione* (1543) of Aurelio Brandolini, and the *Dialogo de la
dignidad del hombre* (1543) of Fernán Pérez de Oliva. Vives' fable involves
the enactment of a pagan-inspired play wherein the gods, impressed by the
beauty of the human form; the craftwork of human towns, houses, and metal
objects; the wisdom, prudence, and memory of humans; their ability to act
out diverse roles in a play; and their invention of language and medicine,
allow humans to be seated next to them at the table.[29] In De Oliva's dialogue
the character Aurelio presents the negative view that humans are of little
worth. Aurelio points out that humans are located in the dregs of the world,
where everything is in flux and in darkness; they are confined to a tiny spot
in comparison to the rest of the universe, and even restricted to that portion
of the planet Earth which is not too cold or too hot to dwell upon.
Furthermore, on said planet humans are born naked, without scales, shells,
wings, horns, or sharp teeth, and with fragile skin and bones that are easily
injured, almost as if nature gave humans a place to dwell against her own

---

[27] Pico della Mirandola, *Opera omnia*, 7–8. So though Pico della Mirandola points
out that humans are situated at the center of the universe this is not on account of
their cosmic significance but rather to allow them more conveniently to look around
and see the glory of creation.
[28] Charles de Bovelles, The Book on the Sage: Translation of Chapters 1–8 and 22–
26, trans. Matthias Riedl, 20–22, accessed July 4, 2020,
https://www.academia.edu/7040927/Charles_de_Bovelles_The_Book_on_the_Sag
e_--_Translation_of_chapters_1-8_and_22-26.
[29] See Fernán Pérez de Oliva, *Dialogue on the Dignity of Man*, trans. Eleazar
Gutwirth, in *Cambridge Translations of Renaissance Philosophical Texts, Volume
1: Moral Philosophy*, ed. Jill Kraye (Cambridge: Cambridge University Press,
1997), 38–43.

wishes. Indeed, in many ways, humans would seem to be the least of the animals as bulls are stronger, tigers are swifter, lions are more dexterous, crows live longer, and humans have to toil endlessly to survive. In reply the character Antonio observes that humans are created with a highly ordered and proportionate body unlike other animals, and made to stand erect in order to gaze upon the heavens; they possess a beautiful face with round prominent eyes that can express emotions and a tongue that can express thoughts and beautiful lyrics; and finally humans have hands with which they can forge iron weapons, clothes, houses, roads, and ships. Indeed humans are given reason with which they can not only contemplate the heavens, but also subjugate elephants, lions, bulls, and horses, and a free will by which they can choose how they wish to adorn themselves or what they wish to eat.

There were then some Renaissance thinkers who placed humans closer to the level of angels than that of animals. Yet, in many ways, angels, not humans, were still the pinnacle of creation. They were created before humans. They were given a position close to God from the get go, unlike fallen humans who have to wait for the resurrection to join God in heaven. Nor was the human position in the cosmos linked in any way with their location at the center of the universe. In addition, there were various Renaissance thinkers who stressed the dreary side of human existence such as Bracciolini, Beroaldo, and Gerson. Poggio Bracciolini defended the fickleness and misery of human life in his *De varietate fortunae* (1447) and *De miseria humanae conditionis* (1455). In these works Bracciolini argued that seeking fame, fortune, power, physical beauty, marriage or children, as opposed to virtue, leads to much suffering, whether out of envy of others, endless labor, sleepless nights, or the squalls of fortune turning wealth to poverty, and power to enslavement. Human life then involves "disease, poverty, exile, the death of those dear to us, defects of the body and soul, and all the other drawbacks of human frailty. The course our lives take is uncertain too, and made more so by the arbitrary whims of fortune, so that no one can bank on any period of security in his life".[30] Continuing these motifs were Filippo Beroaldo with his *De felicitate opusculum* (1499) and Jean Gerson (not as was previously thought Giovanni Garzoni) with his *De miseria humana* (1505).

---

[30] Poggio Bracciolini, *On the Misery of the Human Condition*, trans. Martin Davies, in *Cambridge Translations of Renaissance Philosophical Texts, Volume 1: Moral Philosophy*, ed. Jill Kraye (Cambridge: Cambridge University Press, 1997), 25.

Marsilio Ficino, in his *Theologia Platonica* 3.2 (1482), mediates between these two positions on the misery and happiness of human existence.[31] For Ficino the human soul is located at the center of the hierarchy, in a "third and middle essence," situated below God but above body and matter, indeed placed as a bridge between the two orders. Hence the human being shares things in common with both the order above and the order below it. Human beings can use their heavenly gift of reason to learn about and govern material creation, but at the same time they are subject to the passions and limitations of the flesh which curb their search for knowledge and their ability to lead a virtuous life. Thus the human possesses great dignity but at the same time lives a wretched life and is often sunk into the mire of the material dimension.

One will thus be hard-pressed to find a work of the Church Fathers, medieval Scholastics, or Renaissance humanists asserting that human are the most important creatures in existence, to say nothing of the view that this importance is related to their dwelling on a planetary body lying at the center of the universe.[32]

Medieval and Renaissance Notions of the Centrality of the Earth in the Cosmos

To be sure medieval thinkers who wrote on astronomy defended an Aristotelian or Ptolemaic cosmology wherein the other planets rotate around the Earth, a view that went back to Aristotle and various Greek mathematicians.[33] Isidore of Seville, in his *Etymologiae* 3.32 (AD 625), for instance, describes how the celestial sphere surrounds the Earth, which is at its center, equidistantly on all sides.[34] Such defenses of geocentrism become

---

[31] *Theologia Platonica* 3.2. See Marsilio Ficino, *Platonic Theology*, vol. 1, ed. James Hanks (Cambridge: Harvard University Press, 2001), 231–292.

[32] See Arthur O. Lovejoy, *The Great Chain of Being* (Cambridge: Harvard University Press, 1976), 101–102. Lovejoy correctly notes that for the medieval "the centre of the world was not a position of honor; it was rather the place farthest removed from the Empyrean, the bottom of the creation, to which its dregs and baser elements sank." So, as Lovejoy asserts, if anything, "the geocentric cosmography served rather for man's humiliation rather than his exaltation, and that Copernicanism was opposed partly on the ground that it assigned too dignified and lofty a position to his dwelling–place" (102).

[33] Aristotle, *De caelo* 2.13–14.

[34] Geocentrism is also found in Bede's *De natura rerum* 5 (AD 703) and Johannes de Sacrobosco's *De sphaera mundi* 1 (c. AD 1240). For example Sacrobosco writes that "All, too, are mobile except earth, which, as the center of the world, by its weight

especially prominent in the later Middle Ages when many commentaries were written on Aristotle's *De caelo* 2.13–14, a book in which it was debated whether the center or periphery is the more precious place and whether the Sun or Earth is located at the center of the world. In these commentaries the medieval thinkers were one with Aristotle in holding that the earth was at the center of the universe and that the stars and planets rotated around it. Aquinas, for instance, in his *De caelo* 2.20 (c. 1273), agrees with Aristotle that the Earth lies at the center of the universe because heavy bodies by nature move towards the middle of the cosmos and the element earth is the heaviest and least noble [*maxime materialis et ignobilissima corporum*] of the four elements whereas the lightest and noblest elements are located at the outer spheres [*maxime formalis et nobilissima*].[35] Peter of Auvergne, in his *Quaestiones de caelo* 2.40 (1271–1274), similarly remarks that all heavy things by nature move to the center of the Earth which is heavy and so the Earth lies at the center of the universe.[36] Yet there is nothing here about humans being of central importance in the cosmos. In fact, if anything things are quite to the contrary.

Jean Buridan, in his *Quaestiones de caelo et mundo*, 2.22 (c. 1330), explicitly discusses the argument for geocentrism based upon the idea that the most noble spot is found in the middle, which is why a kingdom is located at the center of an empire, and so the Earth must remain at rest in the center of the universe.[37] He replies that a kingdom is so located in the

---

in every direction equally avoiding the great motion of the extremes, as a round body occupies the middle of the sphere" (Lynn Thorndyke, *The Sphere of Sacrobosco and Its Commentators* [Chicago: University of Chicago Press, 1949], 119). The Renaissance astronomer Georg von Peuerbach defended Ptolemaic astronomy in his *Theoricae novae planetarum* (c. 1450).

[35] Corpus Thomisticum, Sancti Thomae de Aquino, *In libros Aristotelis De caelo et mundo exposition*, liber II, ed. Roberto Busa, accessed July 4, 2020, https://www.corpusthomisticum.org/ccm2.html. See also Albert the Great, *De caelo et mundo* (c. 1255), 2.4.7–8; and the Conimbricenses' *Commentarii, Collegii, Conimbricenses, Societatis, Jesu in quattuor, libros, physicorum, Aristotelis de coelo* (Coimbra, 1592), 14.3.

[36] Peter of Auvergne, *Questions on Aristotle's De Caelo: A Critical Edition with an Interpretative Essay*, ed. Griet Galle (Leuven: Leuven University Press, 2003), 280–282.

[37] See Benoît Patar, ed., *Ioannis Buridani Expositio et Quaestiones in Aristotelis De Caelo* (Louvain: Peeters, 1996), 500–508. See also, Buridan's *Expositio in Aristotelis De Caelo* 2.3.3, ibid., 151–154. Buridan even notes that our subjective experience alone cannot tell us that the Earth is at rest as someone on a moving ship

center of an empire due to presence of enemies at the border, but no such thing occurs in the natural universe. So with natural bodies the center is not necessarily more noble. Nor is it necessarily more noble for something to lie at rest than to move. In fact, says Buridan, it is not clear that the Earth has the exact same center of magnitude and center of gravity as certain portions of the Earth may be more compacted than others, and so while the Earth may be in the center of the world according to its gravity, this need not coincide with its center of magnitude. Hence the heavens are more noble than the Earth even though they move around the Earth and are located at the periphery.

Nicholas Oresme's *Le livre du ciel et du monde* 2.25 (c. 1377) goes so far as to argue that reason can neither prove nor disprove that the Earth is at rest.[38] He points out that Scriptural passages that seem to suggest the Earth lies at rest and the Sun moves around the Earth are not conclusive as they can be interpreted in a figurative manner.[39] And though Oresme does hold that rest is nobler than motion, contrary to Averroes, as God has no movement and rest is the purpose of motion, and so "to rest or to be moved less is a better and nobler condition than to be moved or to be moved farther and farther from rest,"[40] he uses this premise to hypothesize that the heavens might lie at rest and the Earth, which is comprised of the vilest element, might be in motion. Moreover, if the Earth is moving this would offer a simpler explanation of our stellar observations than if the heavens were moving, and in addition the heavens would not have to move at such an extraordinary speed. Indeed a moving Earth would render God's miracle even easier in the time of Joshua as it would allow God to lengthen the day by stopping the movement of the Earth which is very small and a mere dot in comparison to the heavens. Still in the end Oresme does proclaim that the Sun and stars rotate around the Earth as "God hath established the world which shall not be moved, in spite of contrary reasons because they are clearly not conclusive persuasions . . . [And], at first sight, this seems as much against natural reason as, or more against natural reason, than all or many of the articles of our faith."[41]

---

who thinks it is at rest in the ocean may think that another ship that is passed by is moving even though it is actually at rest.

[38] Consult Nicholas Oresme, *Le livre du ciel et du monde*, ed. A. D. Menut and A. J. Denomy (Madison: University of Wisconsin Press, 1968) and *Questiones super De caelo*, ed. C. Kren (Madison: University of Wisconsin Press, 1965).

[39] Namely, Eccles 1:5–6; Jos 10:12–14; Is 38:7–8; 2 Kings 20:11; Ps 92:1.

[40] Nicholas Oresme, *Le livre du ciel et du monde*, ed. A. D. Menut and A. J. Denomy (Madison: University of Wisconsin Press, 1968), 2.25, 533.

[41] Oresme, *Le livre du ciel et du monde*, 2.25, 537–539.

Albert of Saxony, in his own *Quaestiones de caelo* 2.25–26 (c. 1359), also distinguishes whether something is the center of gravity or the center of magnitude and points out that these may not coincide with the Earth as some parts feature the heavier element of earth more prominently and others the lighter element of water. So we can only say the Earth is the middle of the world in terms of its center of its gravity not its center of magnitude. Albert of Saxony also argues that the Earth is situated at the middle of the world on account of the fact it is heavier than the other elements. Again none of the arguments for the Earth's centrality have to do with the Earth being more noble. Indeed Albert of Saxony, similar to Jean Buridan, challenges the view that the center of natural bodies is the most noble location. He argues that though the heart is in the center of the human body this is because it is so positioned to regulate its energy and heat and not because the center is the noblest place. In fact, the heavens, which are more noble than the Earth, are placed at the circumference rather than the center of the universe (2.25 ad. 1). As to the argument that it is better to be at rest than in motion and so the heavenly bodies must be at rest, Albert of Saxony replies that this applies to things moving to their natural place where they come to rest, but for things already in their natural place it is better to be in motion than at rest and so the heavens move and the Earth is at rest (2.26 ad. 3).[42]

Similar arguments are found in Renaissance commentaries on Aristotle's *De caelo*. John of Jandun, in his *In libros Aristotelis De coelo et mundo* 2.16 (1552), grants that it is true that the heavenly sphere, and so the circumference, is nobler than the Earth which rests at the center of the world. Yet he also points out that "in the middle" can be said in different ways, either as a central location or as a center of influence. The former applies to the Earth, the latter to the heavens.[43] Hence John of Jandun disassociates centrality of location from centrality of influence, again showing how astute the medieval and Renaissance thinkers were on this issue. Christopher Clavius, in his *In sphaerum Iohannis de Sacro Bosco* (1581), sharply rejects the nobility of the Earth writing, "And assuredly it appears that nature has quite rightly placed the earth in the middle of the universe as such a worthless and crude body ought to be uniformly separated from all parts of the heavens, which is a body of the highest excellence."[44] Cesare

---

[42] Alberti de Saxonia, *Quaestiones in Aristotelis De caelo*, ed. Benoît Patar (Louvain: Peeters, 2008), 415–428.

[43] Ioannis de Ianduno, *In libros Aristotelis de coelo et mundo* (Venetiis: Iuntas, 1552), fol. 31–32.

[44] Christopher Clavius, *In sphaerum Iohannis de Sacro Bosco* (Romae: Dominici Basae, 1581), 143.

Cremonini's *Disputatio de coelo* 3.1–2 (1613) takes the opposite side of John of Jandun. He similarly argues that center can be understood in terms of center of magnitude or center of power, but concludes that while the Earth is the center of magnitude of the universe, the heavens are the center of power and ultimately more noble.[45]

There were even a few Renaissance works defending geocentrism with the very words *homo* and *centris* in the title which might be thought to suggest that humans were of central importance in the cosmos. They include the *De homocentricis* (1531) of Gasparo Contarini and the *Homocentrica sive de stellis* (1538) of Girolamo Fracastoro (1483–1553).[46] Yet these were merely works of natural philosophy and mathematics and discussed the various theories about how to account for the movement of the stars, defending the earlier Aristotelian and Eudoxian theory of simple circular spheres as more befitting of the divine order than the later Ptolemaic theory involving more complex epicycles. They nowhere explicitly appealed to arguments from human importance or the central location being the most noble.

We additionally find that the most vigorous opponents of Copernican heliocentrism do not anywhere appeal to the argument from human importance, but rather invoke passages of Scripture depicting the Earth at rest or the heavens in motion (Gn 1:14; Jo 10:12–14; Ps 18:6–7; Is 38:7–8; Eccl 1·4–6, etc.), or otherwise appeal to the location of hell at the center of the Earth,[47] tradition, Aristotelian natural philosophy, the methods and limits of knowing, basic sense observations, and other physical and mathematical arguments. Such is the case with the unpublished work of Giovanni Maria Tolosani, *De coelo supremo immobili et terra infima stabili*

---

[45] Caesaris Cremonini, *Disputatio de caelo* (Venetiis: Thomam Balionum, 1613), 279–280. See also Bartholomew Amicus, *In Aristotelis libros De caelo et mundo* tr. 5, q. 6, d. 2, a. 2, n. 10–14 and tr. 8, q. 4, d. 6, aa. 1–3, nn. 1–25 and d. 7 (Neapoli: Secundium Roncaliolum, 1626), 290–291, 597–604.

[46] *Gasparis Contareni Cardinalis Opera*, ed. D. Hugonis (Paris: Sebastianum Niuellium, 1571), 238–252. See also the use of the terms *homocentricus* or *homocentricis* in John Fernel, *Cosmotheoria* (Parisiis: Simonis Colinaei, 1528) 1.3, fol. 7, and Giovanni Battista Amico, *De motibus corporum coelestium iuxta principia peripatetica sine eccentricis et epicyclis* (Parisiis: Iacobi Keruer, 1540), c. 4, in order to contrast the Aristotelian homocentric view with the Ptolemaic eccentric view. Consult also the article Noel Swerdlow, "Aristotelian Planetary Theory in the Renaissance: Giovanni Battista Amico's Homocentric Spheres," *Journal for the History of Astronomy* 3 (1972): 36–48.

[47] Thomas Campanella, in his *Apologia pro Galilaeo* (Francofurti: Godefridi Tampachii, 1622), ad 3, pp. 35–40, refutes the idea that hell has to be located at the center of the Earth.

(1546),[48] Philipp Melanchthon's *Initia Doctrinae Physicae* (1550),[49] Francesco Ingoli's letter to Galileo of January 1616, and Georgio Polacco's *Anticopernicus catholicus* (Venitiis: Guerilios, 1644). To the extent they do talk about the location and value of the Earth it is in terms of the traditional view that the Earth is of lower nobility than the heavens. For example, Ludovico delle Colombe, in his unpublished work *Contra il moto della terra* (1611), asserts that reason teaches us that the most impure and vile things [*impure e vili*] are located in the lowest places and the most eminent and supreme in the highest places, and therefore the Earth, the lowest and smallest of the bodies, lies at the center of the world rather than the Sun which is the beauty and life of nature [*bellezza e vita della natura*].[50] Libert Froidmond, in his *Anti-Aristarchus sive orbis terrae immobilis* (Antverpiae: Plantiniana et Balthasaris Moreti, 1631), argues that being at rest is more noble than being in motion only with supernatural entities, but for natural bodies, which move for an end, it is more noble that they observe the laws of motion than lie at rest. Hence the Earth lies at the rest in the center of the universe and the Sun moves.[51]

Nor do the early Renaissance proponents of heliocentrism worry that their theory would call into question the importance of humans, and indeed they share the view that the Earth is the least noble of the worldly spheres. Copernicus himself points out, in his *De revolutionibus orbium coelestium* 1.8 (1543), that motion is better suited to the Earth than the heavenly spheres as immobility is nobler and more divine than motion and befits the stars more than the Earth. Thomas Digges' *A Perfit Description of the Caelestial Orbes* (1576) likewise appeals to the fact that "the condition of immobilitie is more noble and divine than that of change, alteration, or instabilitie," and thus "more agreeable to Heaven than to this Earth, where all things are subject to continual mutability," to support the Copernican view that the Earth is not the center of the universe but instead the heavenly orbs.[52] Paolo Antonio Foscarini, in his *Letter on the Pythagorean and Copernican Opinion of the Earth's Motion and Sun's Rest* (1615), argues in support of

---

[48] The text can be found in Michel Pierre Lerner, "Aux origines de la polémique anticopernicienne I," *Revue des Sciences Philosophiques et Théologiques* 86 (2001): 693–719.

[49] See his *Initia doctrinae physicae* (Wittebergae: Johannem Lusst), 1, 39–43.

[50] This critique of delle Colombe with a response by Galileo can be find in Galileo Galilei, *Le opere*, ed. Antonio Garbasso (Firenze: G. Barbèra, 1930), 3.1, 276–277.

[51] Ch. 13, ad. 7, 77–78. He also invoked the argument that hell lies in the interior of the Earth (Galilei, *Le opere*, ch. 12, 73).

[52] See Marie Boas Hall, ed., *Nature and Nature's Laws: Documents of the Scientific Revolution* (London: Palgrave Macmillan, 1970), 33.

Copernicanism that the center is the nobler and worthier place, as with the heart of animals, the pith or kernel of vegetables which contains the seeds. But he uses this premise to advance the view that God is the center of spiritual things, the sun of corporeal things, and Christ of those mixed of both.[53]

So none of the Patristic or medieval or Renaissance thinkers argued that human existence is significant due to the centrality of the Earth in the known cosmos. In this they were more astute than many moderns who seem to conflate geographical centrality with being a center of value, or displacement from the geographical center with a reduction in importance, i.e. the claims we saw earlier that human life is insignificant on a cosmic level as the Earth is like other planets in rotating around the Sun and indeed a tiny planet among a sextillion of others. Yet such an equivalence of

---

[53] Text in Thomas Salusbury, *Mathematical Collections and Translations* (London: William Laybourne, 1667), vol. 1, 522–523. See also Thomas Burnet, *The Theory of the Earth* (London: Walter Kettilby, 1681), 2.11, 219–221. For more on medieval views of the cosmos consult: John Gmeiner, *Mediæval and Modern Cosmology* (Milwaukee: Hoffmann Brothers, 1891); Mary A. Evershed (Orr), *Dante and the Early Astronomers* (London: Gall and Inglis, 1913); Clive S. Lewis, *The Discarded Image: An Introduction to Medieval and Renaissance Literature* (Cambridge: Cambridge University Press, 1964); Francis S. Benjamin, Jr., and G. R. Toomer, *Campanus of Novara and Medieval Planetary Theory: Theorica Planetarum* (Madison: University of Wisconsin Press, 1971); Edward Grant, *Physical Science in the Middle Ages* (Cambridge: Cambridge University Press, 1978), 60–82; David C. Linberg, ed., *Science in the Middle Ages* (Chicago: University of Chicago Press, 1980), 265–337; James A. Weisheipl and William E. Carroll, eds., *Nature and Motion in the Middle Ages* (Washington: Catholic University of America Press, 1985); Pierre Duhem, *Medieval Cosmology: Theories of Infinity, Place, Time, Void, and the Plurality of Worlds*, trans. Roger Ariew (Chicago: University of Chicago Press, 1987); J. D. North, *Stars, Mind, and Fate: Essays in Ancient and Mediaeval Cosmology* (London: Continuum, 1989); Edward Grant, *Planets, Stars, and Orbs: The Medieval Cosmos, 1200–1687* (Cambridge: Cambridge University Press, 1996); Edward Grant, "The Medieval Cosmos: Its Structure and Operation," *Journal for the History of Astronomy* 28 (1997): 146–167; Stephen C. McCluskey, *Astronomies and Cultures in Early Medieval Europe* (Cambridge: Cambridge University Press, 2000); Evelyn Edson and Emilie Savage-Smith, *Medieval Views of the Cosmos: Picturing the Universe in the Christian and Islamic Middle Ages* (Oxford: Oxford University Press, 2004); Andrew J. Hicks, *Composing the World: Harmony in the Medieval Platonic Cosmos* (Oxford: Oxford University Press, 2016); Eric M. Ramírez-Weaver, *A Saving Science: Capturing the Heavens in Carolingian Manuscripts* (State College: Pennsylvania State University Press, 2016); Bruce S. Eastwood, *The Revival of Planetary Astronomy in Carolingian and Post-Carolingian Europe* (London: Routledge, 2017).

quantitative size with qualitive importance is again highly problematic and the medievals grasped this. You do not find them advancing the view, for instance, that beings located at the equator are more valuable than those located near the poles. If the medievals do discuss what is of central importance in the universe they speak not of humans, but of God or Christ. Take, for instance, the Renaissance witness of Nicholas of Cusa. Nicholas of Cusa was one of the first theologians to speculate on the motion of the celestial bodies and broached the real possibility of life on other celestial bodies in the universe. In his *De docta ignorancia* 2.11–12 (1440) Nicholas of Cusa advances various arguments to show that it is not humans but God who is the center of the universe. In the first place the Earth cannot be the center of the world, since the world, not having its own beginning or end in itself, lacks boundaries and so does not have a fixed center or a fixed circumference. Or to put it differently the universe is unbounded and infinite and so has neither a natural center nor circumference. Moreover, the very idea of a center is relative.[54] A center is a point equidistant from the circumference but no such thing exists as there cannot exist a sphere so true that a truer one could not be posited and hence a truer center. Therefore, concludes Nicholas of Cusa, "God alone is Infinite Equality . . . the center of the world . . . also the center of the earth, of all spheres, and of all things in the world. Likewise, He is the infinite circumference of all things."[55] Nicholas of Cusa also writes of the complexities of relating size to importance. He notes that just because the Earth is smaller than the Sun and influenced by it, this does not mean it is more lowly than the Sun. For the entire region of the Earth, which extends out into space, may be quite large, even larger than the entire region of the Sun, and in any case the Earth is larger than the moon and the planet Mars, and even perhaps larger than other stars. And though the Earth is influenced by the Sun it may also influence the Sun in turn. Hence we cannot know on the basis of size whether the Earth exists in a less noble or less perfect state than other celestial bodies. Indeed each thing has its own form of perfection and so the Earth has its

---

[54] Similar ideas occur in Giordano Bruno in his *De l'infinito universo et mondi* (1584) which argues that in light of Copernicus the Earth and the heavy elements do not lie at the center of the universe. Indeed space is infinite and there are as many centers as there are individuals, globes, spheres, and worlds, within which centers and circumferences coincide. Indeed each celestial body is animated by its own eternal intellectual spirit. See Giordano Bruno, *On the Infinite, the Universe and the Worlds: Five Cosmological Dialogues*, trans. Scott Gosnell (Port Townsend: Huginn, Muninn, and Company, 2014), 194.

[55] Nicholas of Cusa, *On Learned Ignorance*, trans. Jasper Hopkins (Minneapolis: Arthur J. Banning Press, 1990), 91.

own worthy type of light, heat, and influence that are different than that of the other stars. Similarly Nicholas of Cusa suggests that the whole idea of comparing one intellectual creature to another in terms of importance is misguided, for each is good in its own way. Therefore he avers:

> [We cannot rightly claim to know] that our portion of the world is the habitation of men and animals and vegetables which are proportionally less noble [than] the inhabitants in the region of the sun and of the other stars. For although God is the center and circumference of all stellar regions and although natures of different nobility proceed from Him and inhabit each region (lest so many places in the heavens and on the stars be empty and lest only the earth—presumably among the lesser things—be inhabited), nevertheless with regard to the intellectual natures a nobler and more perfect nature cannot, it seems, be given (even if there are inhabitants of another kind on other stars) than the intellectual nature which dwells both here on earth and in its own region. For man does not desire a different nature but only to be perfected in his own nature. Therefore, the inhabitants of other stars—of whatever sort these inhabitants might be—bear no comparative relationship to the inhabitants of the earth. . . . We surmise that in the solar region there are inhabitants which are more solar, brilliant, illustrious, and intellectual—being even more spiritlike than [those] on the moon, where [the inhabitants] are more moonlike, and than [those] on the earth, [where they are] more material and more solidified. Thus, [we surmise], these intellectual solar natures are mostly in a state of actuality and scarcely in a state of potentiality; but the terrestrial [natures] are mostly in potentiality and scarcely in actuality; lunar [natures] fluctuate between [solar and terrestrial natures].[56]

So in the end Nicholas of Cusa maintains that because of our ignorance we cannot know the relative importance of humans in comparison to other intellectual creatures in the universe. Indeed in many ways such a query is misguided as God creates each thing with a perfection of its own, so weighing the relative perfection of one thing to another is a mistake. Neither did any of the supporters of Copernicanism or heliocentrism discuss this view affecting human importance one way or another.[57]

---

[56] Nicholas of Cusa, *On Learned Ignorance*, 95–97.

[57] Tommaso Campanella, in his *Apologia pro Galileo* 4 (1622), notes that whether the Earth is in the center of the universe [*centro mundi*] or not does not affect the dogma of the faith one way or the other, noting that several Church Fathers did not place the Earth but hell in the center of the universe (Francofurti: Goedfridi Tampachii, 1622), 35–36. For more on Renaissance and Modern Astronomy see: Dorothy Stimson, *The Gradual Acceptance of the Copernican Theory of the Universe* (New York: Columbia University Press, 1917); Francis R. Johnson,

Astronomical Thought in Renaissance England: A Study of the English Scientific Writings from 1500 to 1645 (Baltimore: Johns Hopkins University Press, 1937); Lynn Thorndike, *A History of Magic and Experimental Science, Volume 8: The Seventeenth Century* (New York: Columbia University Press, 1958); Martin Kugler, *Astronomy in Elizabethan England, 1558 to 1585: John Dee, Thomas Digges, and Giordano Bruno* (Montpellier: Université Paul Valéry, 1982); Edward Grant, *In Defense of The Earth's Centrality and Immobility: Scholastic Reaction to Copernicanism in the Seventeenth Century* (Philadelphia: American Philosophical Society, 1984); A.J. Kinder, "The Progress of Astronomy in England: Earliest Times to 1558," *Journal of the British Astronomical Association* 100, no. 4 (1990): 182–190; James M. Lattis, *Between Copernicus and Galileo: Christoph Clavius and the Collapse of Ptolemaic Cosmology* (Chicago: University of Chicago Press, 1994); Edward Rosen, ed., *Copernicus and his Successors* (London: Hambledon Press, 1995); Edgar Laird, "Heaven and the Sphaera Mundi in the Middle Ages," *Culture and Cosmos* 4, no. 1 (2000): 10–35; Michael-Pierre Lerner, "Aux origines de la polémique Anticopernicienne," *Revue des Sciences Philosophiques et Théologiques* 86 (2001), 681–721; 90 (2006), 409–452; Edward Grant, "The Partial Transformation of Medieval Cosmology by Jesuits in the Sixteenth and Seventeenth Centuries," in *Jesuit Science and the Republic of Letters*, ed. Mordechai Feingold (Cambridge: MIT Press, 2003), 127–155; Hanne Andersen, Peter Barker, and Xiang Chen, *The Cognitive Structure of Scientific Revolutions* (Cambridge: Cambridge University Press, 2006), 130–163; Dennis Danielson, *The First Copernican: Georg Joachim Rheticus and the Rise of the Copernican Revolution* (New York: Walker & Company, 2006); Maurice A. Finocchiaro, *Defending Copernicus and Galileo: Critical Reasoning in the Two Affairs* (Dordrecht: Springer, 2010); André Goddu, *Copernicus and the Aristotelian Tradition: Education, Reading, and Philosophy in Copernicus's Path to Heliocentrism* (Leiden: Brill, 2010); Patrick Bonner, *Change and Continuity in Early Modern Cosmology* (Dordrecht: Springer, 2011); Robert Westman, *The Copernican Question: Prognostication, Skepticism, and Celestial Order* (Berkeley: University of California Press, 2011); Sabetai Unguru, ed., *Physics, Cosmology and Astronomy, 1300–1700: Tension and Accommodation* (Dordrecht: Springer, 2012); William A. Wallace, *Prelude to Galileo: Essays on Medieval and Sixteenth-Century Sources of Galileo's Thought* (Dordrecht: Springer, 2012); Christopher M. Graney, *Setting Aside All Authority: Giovanni Battista Riccioli and the Science Against Copernicus in the Age of Galileo* (Notre Dame: University of Notre Dame Press, 2015); Miguel Á. Granada, Patrick J. Boner, and Dario Tessicini, *Unifying Heaven and Earth. Essays in the History of Early Modern Cosmology* (Barcelona: Edicions Universitat Barcelona, 2016); Pietro Daniel Omodeo, "Heliocentrism, Plurality of Worlds and Ethics: Anton Francesco Doni and Giordano Bruno," in *Literature in the Age of Celestial Discovery: From Copernicus to Flamsteed*, ed. Judy A. Hayden (Houndmills: Palgrave Macmillan, 2016): 23–44; Rivka Feldhay, and F. Jamil Ragep, *Before Copernicus: The Cultures and Contexts of Scientific Learning in the Fifteenth Century* (Montreal: McGill-Queen's University Press, 2017).

The Rise of the Modern Conception of the Insignificance of Humans in the Cosmos

Now how did the modern view that ties size and location to human cosmic importance arise? It appears to have done so quite gradually, coming to the fore in the mid-seventeenth-century.[58] As we have seen, some of the medieval and Renaissance thinkers began pointing out the small size of the Earth in comparison to that of the cosmos. We noted that Nicholas Oresme, in his *Le livre du ciel et du monde* 2.25 (c. 1377), argued that it would be easier to conceive of God stopping the movement of the Earth rather than the heavens in order to lengthen the day in the miracle found in Joshua (10:12–14) as the Earth is a mere dot in comparison to the heavens. We have also seen the character Aurelio remark, in the *Dialogo de la dignidad del hombre* (1543) of Fernán Pérez de Oliva, that humans are confined to a "space so small that it seems a mere point when compared to the whole universe."[59] Robert Recorde's *The Castle of Knowledge* 1 (1556) similarly records that the "earthe in comparison to the whole world beareth no greater vewe, then a mustarde corne on Malborne hylles, or a droppe of water in the Ocean sea, for of all the partes of the worlde, the earthe is the leaste," but he does not relate this to human significance.[60] This set the stage for a linking of human size to cosmic significance in the Modern Period, such as we find, for instance in Blaise Pascal. Pascal, in his *Pensées* (1670), famously asserted how the eternal silence of the infinite spaces frightened him. For the Earth being a pinpoint in comparison to the Sun and stars, dwelling in a forgotten outpost of nature. It is a small space swallowed upon in the infinite immensity of space. And so the human is "a nothingness compared to the infinite, everything compared to a nothingness, a mid-point between nothing and everything."[61]

---

[58] For more on this topic consult Paolo Rossi, "Nobility of Man and Plurality of Worlds," in *Science, Medicine, and Society in the Renaissance*, ed. Allen G. Debus (London: Heinemann, 1972), vol. 2, 131–162; Wolfgang Neuber, Thomas Rahn, and Claus Zittel, eds., *The Making of Copernicus: Early Modern Transformations of a Scientist and his Science* (Leiden: Brill, 2014).

[59] See Fernán Pérez de Oliva, *Dialogue on the Dignity of Man*, trans. Eleazar Gutwirth, in *Cambridge Translations of Renaissance Philosophical Texts, Volume 1: Moral Philosophy*, ed. Jill Kraye (Cambridge: Cambridge University Press, 1997), 38.

[60] Robert Recorde, *The Castle of Knowledge*, treatise 1 (London: Reginalde Wolfe, 1556), 5; see also treatise 4, 164–165.

[61] Blaise Pascal, *Pensées and Other Writings*, trans. Honor Levi (Oxford: Oxford University Press, 1995), 26, 66–67, 73, nn. 102 [205], 230 [72], 233 [206]. See also

We also observed that several Renaissance thinkers tried to supplement Innocent III with a volume on the dignity of the human being. In so doing, some, such as Pico Della Mirandola greatly stressed the greatness of humans and placed them almost on a level equal to the angels. And Charles de Bovelles made humans the center of creation, though he stressed not so much their significance as their ability to be a mirror of all things and know creation. This again set the stage for the view we find in the middle of the seventeenth-century among a few Modern geocentrists who defended the Earth's location at the center of the universe as it is the location of humans, the noblest of material beings. And there were modern heliocentrists who argued in favor of displacing the Earth from the center of the universe as it was a celestial body of great nobility and so should be situated at the periphery rather than in the center of the universe. Galileo Galilei hints at this view in his *Dialogo sopra i due massimi sistemi del mondo* 1 (1632) when he has the character Sagredo assert against the view that the Earth is the dregs of the universe and sink of uncleanliness that it possesses great ornamentation and perfection:

> I cannot without great astonishment—I might say without great insult to my intelligence—hear it attributed as a prime perfection and nobility of the natural and integral bodies of the universe that they are invariant, immutable, inalterable, etc., while on the other hand it is called a great imperfection to be alterable, generable, mutable, etc. For my part I consider the earth very noble and admirable precisely because of the diverse alterations, changes, generations, etc. that occur in it incessantly. If, not being subject to any changes, it were a vast desert of sand or a mountain of jasper, or if at the time of the flood the waters which covered it had frozen, and it had remained an enormous globe of ice where nothing was ever born or ever altered or changed, I should deem it a useless lump in the universe, devoid of activity and, in a word, superfluous and essentially nonexistent. . . . The deeper I go in considering the vanities of popular reasoning, the lighter and more foolish I find them. What greater stupidity can be imagined than that of calling jewels, silver, and gold "precious," and earth and soil "base"? People who do this ought to remember that if there were as great a scarcity of soil as of jewels or precious metals, there would not be a prince who would not spend a bushel of diamonds and rubies and a cartload of gold just to have enough

the astronomer Christiaan Huygens, *Cosmotheoros* 1 (Hagae: Adrianum Moetjens, 1698), who speaks of the Earth as a small speck of dirt (*The Celestial Worlds Discover'd* (London: Timothy Childe, 1698), 10 and François Fénelon, *Demonstration de l'existence de Dieu tirée de la connoissance de la nature* 10 and 18 (Paris: Jacques Etienne, 1713) (translated as *The Existence of God*, trans. Henry Morley [London: Cassell, 1894], 20–21, 38–41). These latter two authors, however, do not see this as diminishing human significance.

earth to plant a jasmine in a little pot, or to sow an orange seed and watch it sprout, grow, and produce its handsome leaves, its fragrant flowers, and fine fruit. It is scarcity and plenty that make the vulgar take things to be precious or worthless; they call a diamond very beautiful because it is like pure water, and then would not exchange one for ten barrels of water.[62]

The heliocentrist John Wilkins, in his *Discourse concerning a New Planet* 6–7 (1640), also begins to bring out the possible nobility of the planet Earth. He rejects the anti-Copernican argument stemming from "the vileness of our Earth, because it consists of a more sordid and base Matter than any other part of the World, and therefore it must be situated at the Centre, which is the worst place."[63] He argues that this assumes that bodies must be as far distant from the center in place as in nobility, that the Earth has more ignoble matter than the other planets, and that the center is the worst place, but these things need not be true. Wilkins tends to argue that there are grounds for both views, for though the best part of humans lies in the center with the heart, this may or may not apply to the heavenly spheres.[64] Thus Wilkins broaches the possibility that the Earth may be among the more noble of the cosmic bodies and that is another plank in favor of Copernicanism. That same year the geocentrist Alexander Ross, in his *The New Planet, No Planet, or the Earth No Wandering Star* 6.3, 8.5, and 9.7 (1640), went one step further. After noting that the Earth is made of the basest matter and occupies the lowest material place in the world, clarifies his position by stating, "That the center is the worst place, is not held by us; for though we say the earth to be the ignoblest and basest element, in respect of its matter, and therefore the lowest; yet as it is the

[62] Galileo Galilei, *Dialogue Concerning the Two Chief World Systems, Ptolemaic and Copernican*, trans. Stillman Drake (New York: Modern Library, 2001), 67–68. Galileo also notes the common view that all things in the world are made for the benefit of humans and proceeds to challenge it (62–63). In any case such a view is only partially true of the medievals as they recognized that part of God's motivation for creation is to manifest the greater glory of God. (See for instance Augustine who famously noted, in response to the question of why God created heaven and earth, "because He wanted to" [*De Genesi* 1.2.4; Aquinas, *Summa Theologiae* I, q. 47 a. 1 and q. 65, a. 2; and II-II, q. 25, a. 3].) Even if Aquinas did not think animals would join humans in the resurrection (*Summa Theologiae*, Supplement q. 91 a. 5).
[63] John Wilkins, *A Discourse concerning a New Planet* (London: John Maynard, 1640), 80.
[64] Wilkins, *A Discourse concerning a New Planet*, 102–103.

center and habitation of the noblest creature, it is placed in the middle, as being the noblest place."[65] He goes on to explain,

> if the middle or center were always the fittest place for a luminous body, God would have commanded Moses to set the candlesticke with the lamps in the midst of the tabernacle, and not in the side of it: our eyes had beene placed in our navels, not in our heads. . . . But you give us a profound reason why in living creatures the chiefest part is not always placed in the midst, because they are not of an orbicular forme as the world is; then it seems that the outward figure is the cause why the best part is not placed in the midst. What thinke you of a Hedge hog when he wraps himselfe up in his prickles as round as a bowle, is the best part then more in the middle of his body then it was before? Or hath the earth which is of a round forme better things in the center then in the superficies?[66]

And he concludes that it is not less noble to be at rest than to move, for "Man is a more noble creature then a rocke, yet man moveth, and the rocke is immoveable. The heart in our bodies is more noble then the guts, yet that moveth, they move not. Is the body of man lesse excellent when it is moved by the soule, then when it is at rest putrifying in the grave?"[67] Giovanni Battista Riccioli, in his *Almagestum novum* 9.4.8 and 9.4.33 (1651) similarly proclaims that in the natural domain the center rather than the periphery is the most noble part of a sphere, and so the Earth is more noble than the Sun and is the site of rational animals, but in the supernatural domain the periphery is more noble as this is where heaven lies and hell lies in the middle.[68]

It was left to Cyrano de Bergerac to connect the dots in his novel *Les états et empire de la lune* (1656) having one of the characters state,

> As he who Sails along a Shore thinks the Ship immoveable, and the Land in motion; even so Men turning with the Earth round the Sun have thought that it was the Sun that moved about them. To this may be added the unsupportable Pride of Mankind, who perswade themselves that Nature hath only been made for them; as if it were likely that the Sun, a vast Body Four

---

[65] Alexander Ross, *The New Planet, No Planet, Or the Earth No Wandering Star* (London: I. Young, 1640), 60.

[66] Ross, *The New Planet, No Planet, Or the Earth No Wandering Star*, 72–73.

[67] Ross, *The New Planet, No Planet, Or the Earth No Wandering Star*, 109.

[68] Giovanni Battista Riccioli, *Almagestum novum* (Bononiae: Haeredis Victorii Benatii, 1651), 330–331 and 469–471.

hundred and thirty four times bigger than the earth, had only been kindled to ripen their Medlars and plumpen their Cabbage.[69]

This view was echoed a year later by Bernard de Fontenelle, in his dialogue *Entretiens sur la pluralité des mondes* (1657), who wrote that humans once foolishly thought that the vast frame of nature was created to serve themselves, but Copernicus had "humbled the Vanity of Mankind, who had usurp'd the first and best Situation in the Universe," for there is a natural tendency for a natural philosopher to "place himself in the Centre of the World."[70] Interestingly the character of the Marchioness immediately objects that she esteems herself not one whit the less after finding out the Earth rotates around the Sun rather than vice versa. Though later in the dialogue after the Marchioness emotes that she feels lost and terrified in grasping the small size of the solar system in comparison to so vast a universe, to which the main character responds that the universe seems more magnificent to him due to its great extent and prodigiousness.[71] Much the same Voltaire, in his *Zadig ou la destinée: Histoire orientale* 9 (1747), proclaims that the Earth appears to the cupidity of humans as something noble and grand even though it is in reality but an imperceptible point in the vast universe.[72]

By the start of the nineteenth-century this view had become fairly standard. The physicist Pierre-Simon de LaPlace ends his *Exposition du système du monde* 5.6 (1796) with the words:

> Astronomy, from the dignity of the subject, and the perfection of its theories, is the most beautiful monument of the human mind—the noblest record its intelligence. Seduced by the illusion of the senses, and of self-love, man considered himself, for a long time, as the centre about which the celestial

---

[69] Cyrano de Bergerac, *A Voyage to the Moon*, trans. Curtis H. Page (New York: Doubleday and McClure, 1899), 29–30.

[70] Bernard de Fontenelle, *The Theory or System of Several New Inhabited Worlds*, trans. Aphra Behn (London: Sam Briscoe, 1700), 16–17.

[71] De Fontenelle, *The Theory or System of Several New Inhabited Worlds*, 95–96. In response to such view Richard Bentley, in a sermon of 1692, declared, "We are far from such arrogance, as to pretend to the highest dignity, and be the chief of the whole Creation; we believe in an invisible World and a Scale of Spiritual Beings all nobler than our selves" (*A Confutation of Atheism from the Origin and Frame of the World, a Sermon* [London: Henry Mortlock, 1692], 29). And indeed Bentley argues that the soul of a virtuous man is of more worth than the vastly larger sun and cosmos of stars.

[72] See Voltaire, *Zadig and L'Ingenu* 9, trans. John Butt (London: Penguin Classics, 1978), 52.

bodies revolved, and his pride was justly punished by the vain terrors they inspired. The labour of many ages has at length withdrawn the veil which covered the system. And man now appears, upon a small planet, almost imperceptible in the vast extent of the solar system, itself only an insensible point in the immensity of space. The sublime results to which this discovery has led, may console him for the limited place assigned to the Earth, by showing him his proper magnitude, in the extreme smallness of the base which he made use of to measure the heavens. [73]

Another physicist Joseph-Jérôme de Lalande, in his introduction to the works of Fontenelle, brings out the view of the cosmic insignificance of humans by quoting the geologist Horace Bénédict de Saussure's reflections on traveling through the Alps: "if, during his meditations, the thought of the insignificant beings that move on the face of the earth offers itself to his mind, if he compares their duration with the grand epochs of nature, how great will be his astonishment that man, occupying so small a space, existing so short a time, can ever imagine that his being is the only end for which the universe was created." [74]

---

[73] Pierre-Simon de LaPlace, *The System of the World*, trans. Henry H. Harte (Dublin: Longman, Rees, Orme, Brown, and Green, 1830), vol. 2, 341–342. The original French version can be found in Pierre-Simon de LaPlace, *Exposition du système du monde* (Paris: Cercle-Social, 1796), vol. 2, 310–311. Such a view also appears in some early nineteenth-century German thinkers such as Johann Wolfgang Goethe, "Materialien zur Geschichte der Farbenlehre" (c. 1810), in *Goethes Werke*, ed. Erich Trunz (Hamburger: Christian Wegner Verlag, 1960), vol. 14, 81; Ernst Haeckel, *Natürliche Schöpfungsgeschichte: Gemeinverständliche wissenschaftliche Vorträge über die Entwickelungslehre* 2 (Berlin: Reimer, 1874), vol. I, 35. Translated as *The History of Creation*, trans. E. Ray Lankester (New York: D. Appleton, 1880), 38–39. In France a similar view occurs in Émil du Bois-Reymond, "Darwin and Copernicus," *The Popular Science Monthly* 23 (1883): 249.
[74] Joseph-Jérôme de Lalande, "Critical Account of the Life and Writings of Fontenelle," in Bernard de Fontenelle, *Conversations on the Plurality of Worlds*, trans. Elizabeth Gunning (London: J. Cundee, 1803), viii. Saussure's account appears in his "Discours préliminaire," *Voyages dans les Alpes* (Neuchâtel: Louis Fauche-Borel, 1803), vol. 1, ix–x. See again the work of John Draper, *A History of the Intellectual Development of Europe* (New York: Harper Brothers, 1863), 537. Thomas Chalmers' *A Series of Discourses on the Christian Revelation, Viewed in Connection with the Modern Astronomy* (Edinburgh: John Smith and Son, 1817), William Whewell' *Of the Plurality of Worlds* (London: J. W. Parker and Son, 1855), and David Brewster, *More Worlds than One: The Creed of the Philosopher and the Hope of the Christian* 7 (New York: Robert Carter and Brothers, 1856), 131–161 seek to show the imagined freethinker that even though the Earth is one among the planets that revolve around the Earth and perhaps the Sun itself one among the stars with planets and living creatures, this does not make the world too insignificant for

This view became the norm by the early twentieth-century. Sigmund Freud argued that science caused a great blow to humanity's love of itself when Copernicus showed the Earth was not the center of the universe but one of several tiny planets orbiting the Sun.[75] Edwin Burtt ironically asserted, after noting that it is all too easy to accept unquestionably the assumptions of one's own age, that, "For the Middle Ages man was in every sense the centre of the universe. The whole world of nature was believed to be teleologically subordinate to him and his eternal destiny."[76] Then with the discovery in 1925 by Edwin Hubble that the Milky Way is just one among many galaxies new impetus was given to this position. Bertrand Russell proclaimed:

> In the visible world, the Milky Way is a tiny fragment; within this fragment, the solar system is an infinitesimal speck, and of this speck our planet is a microscopic dot. . . . In the days before Copernicus there was no need of philosophic subtlety to maintain the anthropocentric view of the world. The heavens visibly revolved about earth, and on the earth man had dominion over the beasts of the field. But when the earth lost its central position, man,

God to have a personal love for its inhabitants and to send His Son to ransom them. And indeed they point out that the view that Christianity is for our world alone is a presupposition of the opponents of Christianity and not necessarily of Christians themselves. On the other hand Samuel Miller, *The Bible and Nature Versus Copernicus: A Series of Lectures in Defense of Sacred Truths Discredited by Modern Science* (New York: Abbey Press, 1903), 177–179, rejects the idea the Earth is just a speck in the vast universe and with it Copernican theories; and Alfred Russell Wallace, *Man's Place in the Universe: A Study of the Results of Scientific Research in Relation to the Unity or Plurality of Worlds* (London: Chapman, 1904), 318–325 presents the rare earth argument to show that human life is significant on a cosmic level. As we have seen, for the medievals size has little or nothing to do with importance. For similar anthropocentric views in medieval Judaism, such as in Saadia Gaon, see Norman Lamm, "Man's Position in the Universe. A Comparative Study of the Views of Saadia Gaon and Maimonides," *The Jewish Quarterly Review* 55, no. 3 (1964): 208–234 and Rémi Brague, "Geocentrism as a Humiliation for Man," *Medieval Encounters* 3, no. 3 (1997), 193–194.

[75] Sigmund Freud, *Vorlesungen zur Einführung in die Psychoanalyse* (Leipzig: Internationaler Psychoanalytischer Verlag, 1920), 323–324, translated by G. Stanley Hall as *A General Introduction to Psychoanalysis* (New York: Horace Liveright, 1920), 246–247.

[76] Edwin Arthur Burtt, *The Metaphysical Foundations of Modern Physical Science* (London: Kegan, Paul, Trench, and Trübner, 1923), 4.

too, was deposed from his eminence, and it became necessary to invent a metaphysic to correct the 'crudities' of science.[77]

Alexandre Koyré, in spite of the fact that he was aware of diverse Renaissance views, wrote that "I need not insist on the overwhelming scientific and philosophical importance of Copernican astronomy, which, by removing the earth from the center of the world and placing it among the planets, undermined the very foundations of the traditional cosmic world-order with its hierarchical structure and qualitative opposition of the celestial realm of immutable being to the terrestrial or sublunar region of change and decay."[78] And though Thomas Kuhn justly pointed out that the Copernican view raised a whole bunch of thorny theological issues that needed to be examined regarding the nature of the earth and heavens, the location of heaven and hell, potential rational life elsewhere in the cosmos and its salvation, etc., he went too far in claiming, "More than a picture of the universe and more than a few lines of Scripture were at stake. The drama of Christian life and the morality that had been made dependent upon it would not readily adapt to a universe in which the earth was just one of a number of planets. . . . and the frequency with which the charge of atheism was hurled at the Copernicans is evidence of the threat to the established order posed to many observers by the concept of a planetary earth."[79]

In spite of the fact that such views had been challenged on philosophical and historical grounds,[80] they became even more commonplace at the end

---

[77] Bertrand Russell, *Sceptical Essays* (London: George Allen and Unwin, 1924), 31 and 33.

[78] Alexandre Koyré, *From the Closed World to the Infinite Universe* (Baltimore: John Hopkins University Press, 1957), 29. See Jean-François Stoffel, "Alexandre Koyré and the Traditional Interpretation of the Anthropological Consequences of the Copernican Revolution," in Raffaele Pisno, Joseph Agassi, and Daria Drozdova, eds., *Hypotheses and Perspectives in the History and Philosophy of Science: Homage to Alexandre Koyré 1892–1964* (Dordrecht: Springer, 2018), 421–452.

[79] Thomas S. Kuhn, *The Copernican Revolution: Planetary Astronomy in the Development of Western Thought* (Cambridge: Harvard University Press, 1957), 192–193.

[80] Various scientists and historians of science have detailed how mistaken it is to attribute the view that humans were of central importance in the universe to the medievals: Ernest Cassirer, *Individuum und Kosmos in der Philosophie der Renaissance* (Leipzig: B. G. Teubner, 1927), translated as *The Individual and the Cosmos in Renaissance Philosophy*, trans. Mario Domandi (Chicago: University of Chicago Press, 1963); Claude Savary, "La révolution copernicienne: Freud et le géocentrisme medieval," *Dialogue* 8, no. 3 (1969): 417–432; Raymond Montpetit, "Freud, Copernic et la méprise," *Dialogue* 9, no. 1 (1970): 88–92; Hans Blumemberg, *Die Genesis der kopernikanischen Welt* (Frankfurt: Suhrkamp, 1975), translated as

of the twentieth-century and into the beginning of the twenty-first. Carl Sagan, in his *Pale Blue Dot: A Vision of the Human Future in Space*, famously waxed, "The Earth is a very small stage in a vast cosmic arena. . . . Our posturings, our imagined self-importance, the delusion that we have some privileged position in the Universe, are challenged by this point of pale light. Our planet is a lonely speck in the great enveloping cosmic dark. In our obscurity, in all this vastness, there is no hint that help will come from elsewhere to save us from ourselves."[81] Stuart Ross Taylor pronounced that

---

The Genesis of the Copernican World, trans. Robert M. Wallace (Cambridge: MIT Press, 1987), 169–208; Karsten Harries, "Copernican Reflections," *Inquiry* 23, no. 2 (1980): 253–269; Fernand Hallyn, *La structure poétique du monde: Copernic, Kepler* (Paris: Seuil, 1987), translated as *The Poetic Structure of the World*, trans. Donald M. Leslie (New York: Zone Books, 1990); Rémi Brague, "Le géocentrisme comme humiliation de l'homme," in *Herméneutique et ontologie: Hommage à Pierre Aubenque*, ed. Rémi Brague and Jean-François Courtine (Paris: Presses Universitaires de France, 1990), 203–223, translated as Rémi Brague, "Geocentrism as a Humiliation for Man," *Medieval Encounters* 3, no. 3 (1997), 187–210; Jean-François Stoffel, "La révolution copernicienne et la place de l'homme dans l'Univers: Étude programmatique," *Revue Philosophique de Louvain* 96, no. 1 (1998): 7–50; Dennis R. Danielson, "The Great Copernican Cliché," *American Journal of Physics* 69 (2001): 1029–1035; Jean-François Stoffel, "Géocentrisme, héliocentrisme, anthropocentrisme: Quelles interactions," *Scientiarum Historia* 27, no. 2 (2001): 77–92; Rémi Brague, *La Sagesse du monde: Histoire de l'expérience humaine de l'Univers* (Paris: Librairie Arthème Fayard, 2002); Mano Singham, "The Copernican Myths," *Physics Today* 60, no. 12 (2007): 47–52; Dennis R. Danielson, "That Copernicanism Demoted Humans from the Center of the Cosmos," in *Galileo Goes to Jail and Other Myths about Science and Religion*, ed. Ronald L. Numbers (Cambridge: Harvard University Press, 2009), 50–58; Christopher M. Graney, "The Work of the Best and Greatest Artist: A Forgotten Story of Religion, Science, and Stars in the Copernican Revolution," *Logos* 15, no. 4 (2012): 97–124; Jean-François Stoffel, "Origine et constitution d'un mythe historiographique: L'interprétation traditionnelle de la révolution copernicienne, sa phase de structuration (1835–1925)," *Philosophica* 41–42 (2012): 95–132; Jim Slagle, "The Myth of Mortification: The Cosmic Insignificance of Humanity and the Rhetoric of 'Copernican Revolutions'," *Theology and Science* 11, no. 3 (2013): 289–303; Dennis Danielson, *Paradise lost and the Cosmological Revolution* (Cambridge: Cambridge University Press, 2014); Dennis Danielson and Christopher M. Graney, "The Case against Copernicus," *Scientific American* 310, no. 1 (January 2014): 72–77; Ian Hesketh, "From Copernicus to Darwin to You: History and the Meaning(s) of Evolution," in *Rethinking History, Science, and Religion: An Exploration of Conflict and the Complexity Principle*, ed. Bernard Lightman (Pittsburgh: University of Pittsburgh Press, 2019), 191–205.

[81] Carl Sagan, *Pale Blue Dot: A Vision of the Human Future in Space* (New York: Random House, 1994), 8–9. Similar views occur in Michael Ruse, *Taking Darwin*

revival of learning in the sixteenth-century and with it the Copernican worldview led to a blow to the human ego with its comfortable idea that the idea is at the center of the universe.[82] Stephen Hawking announced, "We are just a somewhat advanced breed of monkeys on a minor planet orbiting a very average star. But we can understand the universe and that makes us something very special."[83]

Such a view of the cosmic insignificance of humans based on quantitative considerations has even crept into popular culture. For instance, in 2011 the Planetary Society testified before the United States House of Representatives Subcommittee on Space and Aeronautics that the Copernican theory that the Earth revolved around the Sun like any other planet was a seminal moment in human history influencing changes in religion, philosophy, and politics and quoted Goethe to the effect that the Earth had to waive the privilege of being the center of the cosmos.[84] And a *Scientific American* Blog on Cocktail Party Physics similarly asserted, using the same quote of Goethe, that "Accepting Copernicus meant removing man from his place at the top of the cosmological food chain."[85] And in 2016 a blog advertised the display on Medieval Cosmology at the Getty Museum in Los Angeles by asserting that "The geocentric system of the world, with the Earth at the center of the Universe, was as long lasting as it was flawed.

Seriously: A Naturalistic Approach to Philosophy (Buffalo: Prometheus Books, 1986), 274; Martin Rees, *Before the Beginning: Our Universe and Others* (New York: Basic Books, 1998), 100; Ronald Dworkin, *Sovereign Virtue* (Cambridge: Harvard University Press, 2000), 246; Steve Stewart-Williams, *Darwin, God and the Meaning of Life: How Evolutionary Theory Undermines Everything You Knew* (Cambridge: Cambridge University Press, 2010), 162–189; Susan Wolf, "The Meaning of Lives," in *The Variety of Values: Essays On Morality, Meaning, And Love* (Oxford: Oxford University Press, 2014), 99–105.

[82] Stuart Taylor Ross, *Destiny or Chance: Our Solar System and Its Place in the Cosmos* (Cambridge: Cambridge University Press, 1998), 2.

[83] "Wir sind nur eine etwas fortgeschrittene Brut von Affen auf einem kleinen Planeten, der um einen höchst durchschnittlichen Stern kreist. Aber wir können das Universum verstehen, und das macht aus uns etwas sehr Besonderes" in Klaus Franke and Henry Glass, "Wir alle wollen wissen, woher wir kommen," *Der Spiegel* 42 (October 17, 1988), 270.

[84] Charlene Anderson, "Planetary Society Statement Entered into Testimony for House Hearing on Future of Planetary Science," *Planetary Society* (November 15, 2011). Accessed March 18, 2020, at https://www.planetary.org/blogs/guest-blogs/charlene-anderson/3263.html.

[85] Jennifer Ouelette, "In Praise of Insignificance," *Scientific American* (November 22, 2011). Accessed March 18, 2020, at https://blogs.scientificamerican.com/cocktail-party-physics/in-praise-of-insignificance/.

Formulated in ancient Greece as a debatable theory, it was turned into a dogma by the church. Making the Earth the center of the Universe, the geocentric system had probably hampered the idea of space flight for 18 centuries."[86]

Again philosophically it is quite complicated to relate quantitative size with qualitative importance. There are lots of human beings on Earth but we don't think that makes any single one of them less important or valuable. And in environmental ethics though there are many species of animals this does not make any single species somehow less valuable. This is why conservation efforts tend to be very broad. There are also different ways to look at the significance of numerosity and diversity. Aquinas, in fact, argued that because God's goodness "cannot be adequately represented by a single creature, He produced multiple and diverse creatures."[87] Bernard Lonergan built upon this Thomistic view when he argued that God creates via "schemers of recurrence" where probabilistic events occur regularly due to large amounts of numbers and times leading to novelty and diversity.[88] And though I wouldn't follow them in this, others have argued that the Earth's importance stands out as we see how rare life-bearing planets are.[89] In any case the point is that linking size to value is quite complex.[90]

---

[86] Header before article by Brian C. Keene, Getty, "Medieval Cosmology: A Tour with Images in Illuminated Manuscripts," *Brewminate* (November 25, 2016). Accessed on March 18, 2020, at https://brewminate.com/medieval-cosmology-a-tour-with-images-in-illuminated-manuscripts/.

[87] Aquinas, *Summa Theologiae* I, q. 47, a. 1.

[88] Lonergan, *Insight* 4.2 (Toronto: University of Toronto Press, 1992), 140-157.

[89] Guillermo Gonzalez and Jay W. Richards, *The Privileged Planet: How Our Place in the Cosmos is Designed for Discovery* (Washington: Regnery, 2004); Simon Conway Morris, *Life's Solution: Inevitable Humans in a Lonely Universe* (Cambridge: Cambridge University Press, 2004); Hugh Ross, *Improbable Planet: How Earth Became Humanity's Home* (Grand Rapids: Baker Books, 2016).

[90] Other astronomers and philosophers, however, have quite rightly pointed out that determining human significance on the basis of scientific theories of cosmic scale is fraught with difficulties. See, for example, Thomas Nagel, "The Absurd," *Journal of Philosophy* 68, no. 2 (1971): 717; Joel R. Primack and Nancy Ellen Abrams, *The View From the Center of the Universe: Discovering Our Extraordinary Place in the Cosmos* (London: Penguin, 2007); Guy Kahane, "Our Cosmic Insignificance," *Noûs* 48:4 (2014): 745–772; Caleb Scharf, *The Copernicus Complex: Our Cosmic Significance in a Universe of Planets and Probabilities* (New York: Farrar, Straus and Giroux, 2014); Olli-Pekka Vainio, *Cosmology in Theological Perspective: Understanding Our Place in the Universe* (Grand Rapids: Baker Academic, 2018); Todd Timberlake and Paul Wallace, *Finding Our Place in the Solar System: The Scientific Story of the Copernican Revolution* (Cambridge: Cambridge University Press, 2019).

In conclusion neither did the medievals have an over-inflated view of humans nor does the size of something directly tie in with its value. This is one more attempt to set the record straight. Whether it will have any effect on society at large is debatable. Perhaps not. Just last month in Seattle at an American Association for the Advancement of Science annual meeting session on exoplanets, a talk opened by quoting Carl Sagan on the pale blue dot that Earth is when seen from space and the various implications of this. Now portions of what Sagan says there are moving and show how fragile much of what we care about is, but mixed in with his remarks are a bit of self-aggrandizement of the modern scientific worldview and a critique of the medieval worldview. It is hoped that slowly and inexorably an accurate understanding of medieval cosmology will prevail just as in actuality there was a slow and inexorable progression of medieval and Renaissance views that led to the position of Copernicus in the first place.

CHAPTER ELEVEN

CHRISTIANITY AND INTELLIGENT EXTRATERRESTRIALS?

MARIE I. GEORGE

It might seem that a consideration of the relationship between Christianity and intelligent extraterrestrials (ETIs) amounts to frivolous speculation, given we have no evidence of their existence. There are two reasons to reject this view. First, examining the relationship between the two serves an apologetic purpose. Michael Crowe, author of *The Extraterrestrial Life Debate 1750–1900*, documents ten cases of individuals who gave up their Christian faith upon becoming convinced that the existence of intelligent extraterrestrial life was beyond doubt.[1] I myself was contacted by someone who was struggling with his faith for the same reason. A second reason in favor of considering the relationship between Christianity and intelligent extraterrestrials is that it provides an opportunity to reflect on the role that Jesus Christ plays in the cosmos, as well as to reflect on the place that we humans have in the cosmos.

Pope Francis said in a homily: "If—for example—tomorrow an expedition of Martians came, and some of them came to us, here . . . Martians, right? Green, with that long nose and big ears, just like children paint them . . . And one says, 'But I want to be baptized!' What would happen? . . . Who are we to close doors?"[2] To baptize ETs, however, depends upon there being

---

[1] Michael J. Crowe, *The Extraterrestrial Life Debate 1750–1900: The Idea of a Plurality of Worlds from Kant to Lowell* (New York: Cambridge University Press, 1986).

[2] Pope Francis, "Homily for May 12, 2014," quoted by Abby Ohlheiser in "Pope Francis Says He Would Definitely Baptize Aliens If They Asked Him To," *The Atlantic*, May 12, 2014,
https://www.theatlantic.com/international/archive/2014/05/pope-francis-says-he-would-definitely-baptize-aliens-if-they-wanted-it/362106/.

ETs to baptize.[3] I am going to consider the question of whether ETs exist from a theological perspective.[4] The two questions I will address are, first: Is Christianity compatible with the existence of ETs or would it be exposed as a false religion if they proved to exist? And secondly, if the two are not mutually exclusive, does Christianity render ET existence likely or unlikely?

The Apparent Incompatibility of ET Existence with Christian Belief

The political philosopher Thomas Paine (1737–1809) is perhaps the best-known proponent of the view that ET existence is incompatible with Christian belief. He was adamant that "the two beliefs cannot be held together in the same mind; and he who thinks that he believes in both has thought but little of either."[5]

More recently it has become increasingly popular to oppose a belief in Christianity to a belief in ET existence. For instance, physicist Paul Davies maintains that "it is hard to see how the world's great religions could continue in anything like their present form should an alien message be received."[6] And philosopher Willem B. Drees maintains that extraterrestrials need not "be conformed to traditional theological schemes; Bethlehem does not have to be the center of the universe."[7]

The reason why some see Christian belief as incompatible with ET existence is articulated by Thomas Paine:

> Though it is not a direct article of the Christian system that this world that we inhabit is the whole of the habitable creation, yet it is so worked up therewith from what is called the Mosaic account of the Creation, the story of Eve and the apple, and the counterpart of that story—the death of the Son

---

[3] "ET" is typically understood to include non-intelligent and intelligent extraterrestrials (ETIs). However, in this essay "ET" will refer only to intelligent extraterrestrials.

[4] According to Crowe, in the fifteenth-century Guillame de Vaurouillon was the "first author who raised the question whether the idea of a plurality of worlds is compatible with the central Christian notions of a divine incarnation and redemption" (*The Extraterrestrial Life Debate*, 149). Crowe's book is one of two that cover the history of the ETI-Christian debate. The other is Steven J. Dick, *Life on Other Worlds: The 20th-Century Extraterrestrial Life Debate* (Cambridge: Cambridge University Press, 1998).

[5] Thomas Paine, *The Age of Reason* (Buffalo, NY: Prometheus Books, 1984), 52.

[6] Paul Davies, *Are We Alone?* (New York: Basic Books, 1995), 54.

[7] Willem B. Drees, "Bethlehem: Center of the Universe?" in *God for the 21st Century*, ed. Russell Stannard (Philadelphia: Templeton Foundation Press, 2000), 69.

of God, that to believe otherwise, that is, to believe that God created a plurality of worlds at least as numerous as what we call stars, renders the Christian system of faith at once a little ridiculous.[8]

William Whewell expresses a similar view:

The earth . . . can not, in the eyes of any one who accepts this Christian faith, be regarded as being on a level with any other domiciles. It is the Stage of the great Drama of God's Mercy and Man's Salvation. . . . This being the character which has thus been conferred upon it, how can we assent to the assertion of Astronomers, when they tell us that it is only one among millions of similar habitations?[9]

The Apparent Compatibility of ET Existence with Christian Belief

Of course, many disagree that the existence of ETs is opposed to the Christian message. They typically justify their view by noting that God is all–powerful and the universe is an immense place, from which they infer that there would be nothing surprising about God populating other planets. The problem with this approach is that it passes over the specific theological difficulties in reconciling the two beliefs, difficulties which led Paine and others to conclude that the two were incompatible.

Some will maintain that the scriptural point that Paine raises really poses no difficulty to ET existence on the grounds that the Bible was written for the purpose of human salvation and consequently does not say anything that has bearing on the existence of other intelligent beings in the universe; thus, Scripture cannot rule out ET existence.

Now, it is true that Scripture was written for our salvation. Nevertheless, Scripture does tell us about intelligent beings other than humans, namely, the angels and devils; e.g., Rv 12:7–9 recounts the battle between Michael the Archangel and Satan. God is certainly free to reveal to us how humankind's savior Jesus Christ relates to all created beings, purported ETs included. God, if he so chooses, can also reveal to us how the redemption wrought by Christ fits into his plan for the entire universe. Thus, there is no reason to reject in advance the possibility that Scripture says something that has bearing on the ET question.

---

[8] Paine, *The Age of Reason*, 52.
[9] William Whewell, *Of the Plurality of Worlds*, ed. Michael Ruse (Chicago: The University of Chicago Press, 2001), 44–45.

Scripture Passages that Bear on the Question of ET Existence

To deal with the sort of objections that Paine and others make, we need to turn to Scripture.

There are a number of passages in Scripture that support the notion that the central event in the universe's history was the Incarnation, death, and Resurrection of Christ. Again, one could claim that this story is a story of importance only to us on Earth. A number of Scripture passages, however, indicate that it is the heart of the plan for the entire cosmos:

> He has let us know the mystery of his purpose, the hidden plan he so kindly made in Christ from the beginning to act upon when the times had run their course to the end: that he would bring everything together under Christ, as head, everything in the heavens and everything on earth. (Eph 1:8–10 [JB])

> I, who am less than the least of all the saints, have been entrusted with this special grace, not only of proclaiming to the pagans the infinite treasure of Christ, but also of explaining how the mystery is to be dispensed. Through all the ages, this has been kept hidden in God, the creator of everything. Why? So that the Sovereignties and Powers should learn only now, through the Church, how comprehensive God's wisdom really is, exactly according to the plan which he had from all Eternity in Christ Jesus our Lord. (Eph 3:9–12 [JB])

Accordingly, the Catholic Church understands God's plan for creation to center on Christ:

> Creation is the foundation of "all God's saving plans," the "beginning of the history of salvation" that culminates in Christ. Conversely, the mystery of Christ casts conclusive light on the mystery of creation and reveals the end for which "in the beginning God created the heavens and the earth": from the beginning, God envisaged the glory of the new creation in Christ.[10]

One might try to say that God's plan for creation centers on Divine Word and not on the God-man, Jesus Christ. However, there are passages in Scripture, in addition to those from Ephesians quoted above, that indicate that Christ as man, and not just as God, is the central figure in the Cosmos:

---

[10] *Catechism of the Catholic Church*, 2nd ed. (Washington, DC: United States Catholic Conference, 2000), §280.

His state was divine, yet he did not cling to his equality with God, but emptied himself to assume the condition of a slave, and became as men are; and being as all men are, he was humbler yet, even to accepting death, death on a cross. But God raised him high and gave him the name which is above all other names, so that all beings in the heavens, on the earth and in the underworld, should bend at the name of Jesus and that every tongue should acclaim Jesus Christ as Lord, to the glory of God the Father. (Phil 2:6–11 [JB])

"You have put him in command of everything." Well then, if he has "put him in command of everything," he [God] has left nothing which is not under his command. At present it is true, we are not able to see that "everything has been put under his command," but we do see in Jesus one who was "for a short while made lower than the angels and is now crowned with glory and splendor" because he submitted to death. (Heb 2:8, 9 [JB])

He [God] has put all things under his [Christ's] feet, and made him, as ruler of everything, the head of the Church; which is his body, the fullness of him who fills the whole creation. (Eph 1:22 [JB])

Paine appears to be quite correct when he says Christianity teaches that the central story of the cosmos is Christ's redemption of fallen man by his death on the cross. It does not, however, follow immediately from this that there is no room for any other sort of intelligent being in this story. Again, Christians believe that there are other such beings, the angels and devils. Just as Jesus Christ is Lord and head of the angels, he could in principle be Lord and head of other intelligent beings as well. Paine however raises the following objection against this being the case:

Are we to suppose that every world in the boundless creation had an Eve, and apple, and serpent, and a redeemer? In this case, the person who is irreverently called the Son of God, and sometimes God himself, would have nothing else to do than to travel from world to world, in an endless succession of deaths, with scarcely a momentary interval of life.[11]

---

[11] Paine, *The Age of Reason*, 59, 60. Mark Twain, who read *The Age of Reason* three times, adopts Paine's thesis: "How insignificant we are . . . an atom glinting with uncounted myriads of other atom worlds . . . & yet prating complacently of our speck as the Great World & other specks as pretty trifles made to steer our schooners. . . . Did Christ live 33 years in each of the millions and millions of worlds . . . ? Or was *our* small globe the favored one of all?" (quoted in Crowe, *The Extraterrestrial Life Debate*, 448).

It is undoubtedly true the Word of God could have become incarnate multiple times. Uniting his person to human nature certainly did not exhaust his infinite power, and so he can become incarnate over and over again. In addition, Paine's assumption that God would not leave fallen races unredeemed seems eminently reasonable in light of God's goodness and mercy. Nevertheless, Paine's multiple incarnations and redemptions are not the only way the redemption of fallen races could come about. For Christ's sacrifice on the cross is infinite in its saving power, and thus could have made satisfaction for any number of fallen races. And in fact Colossians 1:18–20 indicates that Christ is the savior of all of the fallen:

> As he is the Beginning, he was first to be born from the dead, so that he should be first in every way; because God wanted all perfection to dwell in him and all things to be reconciled through him and for him, everything in heaven and everything on earth when he made peace by his death [literally "blood"] on the cross. (Col 1:18–20 [JB])

The same is indicated by Christ's words: "When I am lifted up from the earth, I will draw all things to myself" (Jn 12:32).

Scripture Passages that Speak Against the Existence of Fallen ETs

Simply acknowledging that Christ's sacrifice on Calvary could in principle save other fallen beings says nothing one way or the other about whether such beings exist. Further scrutiny of Scripture turns up a passage that speaks against ET existence:

> As it was his purpose to bring a great many of his sons into glory, it was appropriate that God, for whom everything exists and through whom everything exists, should make perfect, through suffering, the leader who would take them to their salvation. For the one who sanctifies, and the ones who are sanctified are of the same stock; that is why he openly calls them brothers. . . . Since all the children share the same blood and flesh, he too shared equally in it, so that by his death he could take away all the power of the devil, who had power over death, and set free all those who had been held in slavery all their lives by the fear of death. For it was not the angels that he took to himself; he took to himself descent from Abraham. (Heb 2:10–17 [JB])

One might be inclined to take the line about the one sanctifying and ones who are sanctified being of the same stock to establish that there are no fallen ETs. But the phrase "are of the same stock" could also be translated as "are all from one" (*ex uno omnes*) and indeed Thomas Aquinas interprets this sentence to say that Christ and humans are from the same Father—which certainly could be said of ETs.

The next lines are more telling, however. They affirm that the Word took on the same blood and flesh as humanity *since* the children were all of the same blood and flesh, so that by his death he could set free all those who had been held in slavery. Clearly Paul means to extend what was promised to the descendants of Abraham to all human beings. But how could such a claim be extended to include nonhuman beings? It does not make any sense to say that the Word shared in human nature in order to free ETs and humans from the slavery of sin and death *because* the children share the same blood and flesh, when, presumably, ETs do not share our blood and flesh.

Romans 5:15–19 supports this reading of Hebrews 2:14 insofar as it speaks of the correlation between sin coming into the world through one man (Adam) and salvation coming into the world through another man (Christ).

Another problem is that Christ as ET savior does not offer a solution to the "divine dilemma" that the ET fall would pose.[12] The "divine dilemma" generated by original sin is this: God in his mercy did not want the human race to be lost on account of original sin. Although God in his graciousness could simply have remitted the sin, mankind would not have fulfilled what justice demands by way of satisfaction. At the same time, no human being could ever make adequate satisfaction for an offense against the infinite God. It is only the God-man, Jesus Christ, who is capable of making infinite satisfaction for this human debt. Similarly, only the God-ET could solve the divine dilemma posed by fallen ETs.

Yet another problem is that Christ as ET savior would not serve as the best model for ET behavior:

> It was essential that he should in this way become completely like his brothers so that he could be a compassionate and trustworthy high priest of God's religion, able to atone for human sins. That is, because he himself has been through temptation he is able to help others who are tempted (Heb 2:17–18 [JB]).

---

[12] St. Athanasius poses the "divine dilemma" in *On the Incarnation of the Word*, c. 3. St. Thomas Aquinas speaks about it in *Summa contra Gentiles,* Bk. IV, c. 54.

Is Paine Right in Maintaining that ET Existence Is Incompatible with Christian Belief?

Is Paine right to oppose ET existence with Christian belief? There are two reasons to answer in the negative. First, the interpretations of Scripture, and particularly of Heb 2:10–17 as to the Savior wanting to be of the same blood as the saved, are my interpretations and are not official Church teachings. Secondly, even if the Church was to adopt the views I articulate, they exclude the existence of fallen ETs, but not unfallen ones.

Does Christian Belief Render ET Existence Unlikely?

Thus far we have seen that Christian belief does not eliminate the possibility of ET existence. Now we will consider whether it renders ET existence unlikely. I am going to focus on unfallen ETs, as in light of the Scripture passages quoted above, their existence as more likely than the fallen. Note, though, that some of the problems I will mention in regard to unfallen ETs are also applicable to the fallen.

There are a number of reasons that weigh against the existence of unfallen ETs. First, given that some of the angels fell, despite their greater perfection than material beings, it would be surprising if no member of an intelligent material race fell. Secondly, the simple fact that ETs are of a fallible nature, makes it highly unlikely that no member belonging to an ET species would ever fall. Thirdly, looking at the case of both angels and humans, the reality of free will stands out better when there are good and bad individuals, and it seems that God desires this. Lastly, one wonders what kind of relationship they could have with Christ.

On the other hand, a reason to think that unfallen ETs do exist is that they add richness to the universe; they would be an intelligent material species that reflects God in a different way than humans do. Fr. José Funes, S.J., former director of the Vatican Observatory, suggests that:

> We borrow the gospel image of the lost sheep. The pastor leaves the 99 in the herd for go look for the one that is lost. We think that in this universe there can be 100 sheep, corresponding to diverse forms of creatures. We that belong to the human race could be precisely the lost sheep, sinners who have need of a pastor. God was made man in Jesus to save us. In this way, if other intelligent beings existed, it is not said that they would have need of redemption. They could remain in full friendship with their Creator.[13]

---

[13] José Funes, S.J., "The Extraterrestrial is my Brother," *L'Osservatore Romano* (May 14, 2008).

The question remains, however, what kind of relationship could unfallen ETs have with Christ? Christ could be their Lord and Head, as he is in the case of the Angels. And they could know about Christ through revelation directly from God or through an angel or ET prophet (or maybe even through us). Matters would become complicated, however, if the Word became incarnate as one of them. Which Incarnation would be central to the universe's story? The body of which Incarnation of the Word (or other Divine Person) would be seated at God's right hand?

Would ET Existence Undermine the Christian Understanding of Human Specialness?

Another contention of those who hold that there is an opposition between Christian belief and ET existence is that ET existence would undermine biblical teachings concerning the special place that humans hold in the cosmos. Physicist Paul Davies articulates this view:

Four hundred years ago, the Roman Catholic church burned Giordano Bruno at the stake for heresy. Among other things, he proposed the existence of an infinite number of inhabited worlds. Since this ran counter to the doctrine of man as God's supreme and special creation, Bruno was undermining a key tenet of the Christian faith at that time.[14]

Before I give a theological response to this, it is worth noting that a certain number of people, instead evaluating reasons for and against the possibility and likelihood of ET existence, engage in the fallacy of personal attack. For example, Kenneth Delano says:

With the jealousy of a spoiled only child, the human race is upset by the suggestion that it may have to share its cosmic domicile with others. To make their instinctive reaction seem less like childish resentment, many think of themselves as being "Defenders of the Faith" in denying the possibility of intelligent beings existing on other worlds.[15]

---

[14] Paul Davies quoted on the back cover of Steven Dick, ed., *Many Worlds: The New Universe, Extraterrestrial Life & the Theological Implications* (Philadelphia: Templeton Foundation Press, 2000).
[15] Kenneth J. Delano, *Many Worlds, One God* (Hicksville, New York: New York Exposition Press, 1977), 8.

The fallacy of personal attack consists in writing off arguments that a person presents because of some purported flaw in his or her character when, of course, what needs to be done is to address the arguments.

What are Christian beliefs in regard to human specialness? First, we are created in the image of God (we have an immortal soul endowed with the immaterial faculties of intellect and free will). Secondly, all non-rational creatures are ordered to us. Thirdly, our souls are specially created by God. Fourthly, God exercises special providence over us. Fifthly, the universe achieves it completion through us: first and foremost because of Christ; secondarily insofar as we respond to Christ's grace. ET existence would change none of these things.

God showed us special favor by uniting our nature to one of the Divine Persons. This was something extraordinary and unexpected: "For it was not the angels that he took to himself; he took to himself descent from Abraham" (Heb 3:16 [JB]). That this favor was special in the sense of extraordinary would be true even if it was not special in the sense of something that only occurred in the case of human nature.

The Incompatibility Thesis and the Likelihood Thesis

Thus far we have seen that there is a theological response to the thesis that Christian belief and ET existence are incompatible. At the basis of the response is the assumption that the universe exists for the sake of Christ's incarnation, death, and resurrection. As for the existence of fallen ETs, Christ's sacrifice is infinite in its saving power and thus Christ could be the redeemer of fallen ETs. As for the existence of unfallen ETs, the story of Christ could be revealed to unfallen ETs. He would be their Lord as he is Lord of the Angels.

While Christian belief does not render ET existence impossible, it does give reason for reservations when it comes to the likelihood of ET existence.

The beliefs that Christ reconciled all things through his sacrifice on the cross (Col. 1:20), while wanting to be of the same blood of those he redeemed (Heb. 2:14–17) speak against the likelihood of the existence of fallen ETs.

As for the existence of an unfallen ET race, it is unlikely because is implausible that every member of a fallible race would avoid falling, especially given that some of the angels, who are of a far more perfect nature, fell. Also, although unfallen ETs can be fit into the story of Christ which is *the* story of the universe, they do not readily fit as an integral part of it.

Should ETs Be Baptized?

If they are fallen, yes. It is reasonable to think that the ever-merciful God would want to redeem them. Scripture proclaims Christ to be the universal savior. Nothing impedes Christ's sacrifice, which is infinite in its saving power, from being applied to ETs for their salvation. It seems reasonable to presume that Christ's salvific grace would be applied to them through baptism.

Baptizing fallen ETs, however, supposes they exist. For the reasons given above, it seems more likely than not that we are the only material rational being. This view fits with the vision of the universe articulated by Pope John Paul II:

> This varied scenario of celebrations of the Eucharist has given me a powerful experience of its universal and, so to speak, cosmic character. Yes, cosmic! Because even when it is celebrated on the humble altar of a country church, the Eucharist is always in some way celebrated on the altar of the world. It unites heaven and earth. It embraces and permeates all creation. The Son of God became man in order to restore all creation, in one supreme act of praise, to the One who made it from nothing. He, the Eternal High Priest who by the blood of his Cross entered the eternal sanctuary, thus gives back to the Creator and Father all creation redeemed. He does so through the priestly ministry of the Church, to the glory of the Most Holy Trinity. Truly this is the *mysterium fidei* which is accomplished in the Eucharist: the world which came forth from the hands of God the Creator now returns to him redeemed by Christ.[16]

Divine Extravagance

Some people find it hard to believe that this whole universe filled with countless stars exists just for us. However, this is in keeping with God's nature as Love.

---

[16] Pope John Paul II, *Ecclesia De Eucharistia,* encyclical latter, Vatican website, April 17, 2003, http://www.vatican.va/content/john-paul-ii/en/encyclicals/documents/ hf_jp-ii_enc_20030417_eccl-de-euch.html, §8. Christ, in his real presence, has even been in outer space. Astronaut Mike Hopkins was allowed to take consecrated hosts with him for his stay on the International Space Shuttle: see ChurchPop Editor, "How This Astronaut & Convert to Catholicism Took the Eucharist to Space", *ChurchPOP*, April 17, 2016,
https://churchpop.com/2016/04/17/how-this-astronaut-convert-to-catholicism-took-the-eucharist-to-space/.

In the natural order there are many other instances of extravagance beside the immense number of stars, e.g., the number of spores that are produced in order that one mushroom grow. In the supernatural order, Cardinal Ratzinger points to two of Christ's miracles: the seven baskets left over after he feeds 4000 men and the approximately 130–190 gallons of wine produced at the marriage feast of Cana. Ratzinger continues:

> [Those two miracles] . . . both point back . . . to the structural law of creation, in which life squanders a million seeds in order to save one living one; in which a whole universe is squandered in order to prepare at one point a place for spirit, for man. Excess is God's trademark in creation. . . . At the same time excess is also the real foundation and form of salvation history, which in the last analysis is nothing other than the breathtaking fact that God, in an incredible outpouring of himself, expends not only a universe but his own self in order to lead man, a speck of dust, to salvation. So excess or superfluity—let us repeat—is the real definition or mark of the history of salvation. The purely calculating mind will always find it absurd that for man God himself should be expended. Only the lover can understand the folly of a love to which prodigality is a law and excess alone is sufficient.[17]

The Incarnation and Paschal Mystery are gratuitous and lavish acts of love that God has bestowed upon us. It is fitting, then, for material creation to mirror this immense love by its extravagant size.

Why Are We Fascinated with ETs?

People are often disappointed when I provide reasons to think that ET existence is unlikely. Why is this? As a friend of mine quipped: are they lonely?

There are a variety of reasons for people's hopeful speculations about ET existence. For one, now that we know there are other planets, it is natural to wonder whether they are inhabited. Scientists working in several different areas would revel in the opportunity to study another type of rational being, for example, those seeking to discover the origin of life, those studying human physiology, linguists, and so forth.

Another reason people hope that ETs exist, is that they think that ETs, being more intelligent than ourselves, would bring solutions to problems such as war and world hunger. When it comes to war, ETs could reasonably be expected to help alleviate certain sources of tension between peoples

---

[17] Joseph Ratzinger, *Introduction to Christianity* (San Francisco: Communio, 2004), 262.

(e.g., problems with water allocation) due to their superior scientific knowledge. However, when it comes to moral aspects of war (e.g., the injustice that is at the root of it), it is a mistake to assume that they will be of help. We see already in the case of our species that those of greater intelligence sometimes employ it for doing evil. This theme is explored in sci-fi literature in which aliens are just as likely to be malevolent as benevolent.

Yet another reason why people hope that ETs exist is rooted in distaste for Christianity or for religion in general. The latter seems to be the case of astronomer Jill Tarter: "At a minimum, this inferred result [namely, ETI longevity] is likely to have a great deal to say about religions throughout the universe. In my opinion, it will mean that the detected, long-lived extraterrestrials either never had, or have outgrown, organized religion."[18] William Drees also reveals a willingness to discard religion, specifically the Christian faith, when he affirms: "Bethlehem does not have to be the center of the universe."[19]

Whether or not we are hopeful that ETs exist, a common reason for our fascination with them is that they afford a more or less surreptitious way of reflecting on ourselves. In the words of Alfred Karcher: "This is what I believe to be the root of our fondness for aliens. It is not that they tell us what *they* are, it is that they tell *us* that we are human."[20] David Wilkinson, a Christian theologian, concurs:

> We want to find out about aliens because we want to find out about ourselves. Humans do that fundamentally in relationship. Science fiction has used this device on many occasions. Star Trek . . . explored themes such as racism through encounters with "aliens."[21]

Whether or Not ETs Exist, We Are Not Alone

As mentioned earlier, some people hope that ETs will bring us salvation of a sort. Deep down many of us, perhaps all of us, feel a need for redemption. We, as Christians, believe that there is One "who came down from heaven" (Jn 3:13 [JB]) to provide just that. He didn't land on Earth in a space ship; he arrived in a stable, born of a woman. His physical appearance didn't

---

[18] Jill Tarter, "SETI and the Religions of the Universe," in Dick, *Many Worlds*, 145.
[19] Drees, "Bethlehem: Center of the Universe?", 69.
[20] Alfred Karcher of Iowa State University, talk given September 2000 at the Center for Theology and the Natural Sciences conference held at Iowa State University:
[21] David Wilkinson, *Alone in the Universe* (Crowborough, East Sussex, Great Britain: Monarch Publications, 1997), 143.

attract the attention that an alien physiognomy would. The people of his hometown, Nazareth, saw nothing special about him: "This is the carpenter, surely, the son of Mary, the brother of James and Joset" (Mk 6:3 [JB]). He showed himself to have powers, though: "Even the sea and winds obey him" (Mt 8:27 [JB]). "He healed every kind of disease and illness" (Mt 4:23 [JB]). Indeed he had powers greater than any ET could have: "Courage my child, your sins are forgiven" (Mt 9:2 [JB]). And his power was matched by his boundless love: "While we were still sinners, Christ died for us" (Rom 5:8 [JB]). No mere ET could ever redeem us. Christ's supreme act of love on the Cross is able to save us because Christ was God, as well as being human. So indeed we should look to heaven "where Christ is, seated at God's right hand" (Col 3:1 [JB]), confident that he who calls us his friends, so long as we obey his commandments (cf. Jn 15:15), will be with us "until the end of time" (Mt 28:20 [JB]). We are not alone.

CHAPTER TWELVE

ARE EXTRATERRESTRIALS SAVED?

JANICE DAURIO

Raised at the recent conference on Space in the Catholic Imagination at St. John's Seminary in Camarillo, California, was the question of how many saviors or saving acts or appearances of Jesus there might be. A related question is whether extraterrestrials are saved?

What follows is a defense of a "yes" answer, as a formal rather than a substantive claim. In a substantive defense, each group is identified and described as having certain qualities, on the basis of which, the argument concludes, the group is included in salvation. In a formal defense, the goal is to establish that like groups, whatever they are, should be thought of alike. What is true of human persons or terrestrials (hereafter Ts) is also true of non-human, non-Earth-dwelling persons or extraterrestrials (hereafter ETs).

PART I: The No-Relevant Difference Argument[1]

The No-Relevant Difference Argument, First Version

Premise 1. If ETs are persons, then there is no ontologically-relevant difference between Ts and ETs.

Premise 2. If there is no ontologically-relevant difference between Ts and ETs, then there is no soteriologically-relevant difference between Ts and ETs.

Premise 3: ETs are persons.

Conclusion: There is no soteriologically-relevant difference between Ts and ETs.

---

[1] The inspiration for this argument comes from Eric Schwitzgebel and Mara Garza, "A Defense of the Rights of Artificial Intelligences," *Midwest Studies in Philosophy* 39, no. 1 (2015): 98–119. Their No-Relevant Difference Argument was used for AIs and ethics.

The argument is valid; the conclusion follows from the premises. If all three premises are true, then the argument is sound and we must accept the conclusion. Establishing Premise 3 requires both a description of what a person is and as yet unavailable empirical data on ETs. For this reason we will call the first version the substantive argument.

The No-Relevant Difference Argument, Second Version

Premise 1. If ETs are persons, then there is no ontologically-relevant difference between Ts and ETs.

Premise 2. If there is no ontologically-relevant difference between Ts and ETs, then there is no soteriologically-relevant difference between Ts and ETs.

Conclusion: If ETs are persons, then there is no soteriologically-relevant difference between Ts and ETs.

This version of the argument is valid; the conclusion follows from the premises. If both premises are true, then the argument is sound and we must accept the conclusion. The task for this hypothetical syllogism is much easier than the first version, requiring only that that likes be treated alike, without the need to say what the likeness is.

PART II: Some Terms

Salvation

Among the senses of the word "salvation" is deliverance and the offer of the means of being delivered.[2] The life, death and resurrection of Jesus Christ effected that deliverance in some way or ways that it is the task of theologians and biblical scholars to elucidate. The term "salvation" is more neutral than "redemption" because redemption implies certain ways in which salvation is brought about, usually involving punishment or ransom. No soteriological theory (e.g., penal substitution, ransom, etc.) is assumed here. No claim is being made in what follows about how salvation is offered, whether it is accepted, or what the conditions of acceptance are, if any.

An author well-known to Christian apologists is C. S. Lewis. Lewis wrote *Perelandra*, the second book in his so-called space trilogy, in which

---

[2] John Hardon, *Modern Catholic Dictionary* (Bardstown, Ky.: Eternal Life Publications, 1999), http://www.therealpresence.org/dictionary/sdict.htm.

he imagines a world in which the inhabitants have committed no sin.[3] Do they need redemption? The best theology gives a "yes" answer to this question. It is not (or not only) in virtue of our status as sinners that we require salvation, but it is in virtue of our status as contingent, dependent, mortal creatures that we require salvation. We should avoid diminishing the notion of salvation to a moral category. Sinless persons on other planets, should there be any, require salvation, too.

Universal Salvation

There are several ways to understand universal salvation.

(1) Salvation is universal in the "no child of God left behind" sense: All persons are saved, i.e., apokatastasis. The extension of "all" is persons. All persons can be or are saved. If ETs are persons, then ETs are saved.

(2) Salvation is universal in the sense that everything—not just persons—is saved. The world to come is a "new and improved" version or continuation of this world. The theologian Scott Hahn favors this view, noting that Jesus said, "I will make all things new," not "I will make all new things." Since ETs are part of this universe as much as Ts are, there is no need to inquire further whether they can be saved; the thinking problem would shift to what renewal could be, not what or who it includes. If universal salvation includes everything, then necessarily it includes ETs.

(3) Salvation is universal in the "one Savior" sense. There are not many saviors; there is just one, Jesus Christ, the Son of God. The one Savior may or may not have made more than one appearance in the world. If where the one Savior appears matters for salvation, then although all Ts can be saved, it is not known if ETs can be, unless or until it is known whether the one Savior appeared somewhere else besides this planet. Even if Ts are saved, ETs might not be.

(4) Salvation is universal in the "one-saving event" sense. Those who are or can be saved are drawn from anywhere in the universe or any time in its history. Contrary to what those in the real estate business say, location isn't everything. In fact, it is nothing with respect to the connection between those saved and the saving event. Jesus lived, died, and rose from the dead, once and for all time and all places. Since that one saving moment in history made T salvation possible, that one saving moment in history made ET salvation possible.

Like rings of water going out from where a rock was thrown into a pool, the grace of the saving life, death, and resurrection of Jesus goes out from

---

[3] C. S. Lewis, *Perelandra*, (New York: HarperCollins Publishers, 2012).

Mt. Calvary in both space and time. Like quantum entanglement, the quanta of Jesus's body reconfigure other quanta instantly in other parts of the universe. Distance from Mt. Calvary doesn't matter. Distance in time (past or future) does not matter.

The Mt. Calvary event is unique, unprecedented and unrepeatable. There is a good theological reason in support of this position: it places no limits on the power of that event. It gives infinite value to that event. There is no good theological reason to think that distance from Earth, as in some far-off planet or galaxy, matters. If Ts are saved, so are ETs, even if they existed before the first century A.D. on Earth.

If the No-Relevant Difference Argument is sound then salvation is universal in the first sense above: if all ETs are persons, then ETs are saved. It may be that salvation is universal in the more expansive second sense: if ETs are part of "everything," as they doubtless are, if there are any, then salvation is universal in the second sense. Although Christian doctrine requires that salvation is universal in the third sense—there is just one Savior—the work of exploring the third sense is left to the theologians. Although I consider the fourth sense—just one saving act for all time and space—to be sound theology, again that task of analysis will be left to theologians.

Ontology

Ontology here refers to the question of what entities exist in the universe and the imagined task of making a complete list of those entities.[4]

These entities could then be arranged by categories. If Tom, Dick, and Harry are persons living on Earth, and Manny, Mo, and Jack are persons living on Planet X, then all six appear in the "person" place on our inventory. No qualities of either Ts or ETs matter other than those qualities that make up what it is to be a person.

Whatever it means to be a person, if ETs are persons, that is enough for Premise 1 to be true, because the claim is formal: we should classify like individuals together and unlike individuals separately. If personhood is the ontologically-relevant property of some beings, then it is the ontologically-relevant property for all beings. We must, under pain of contradiction, recognize any other group as such, no matter how apparently different or distant or disinclined we are to do so.

---

[4] Achille C. Varzi, "On Doing Ontology without Metaphysics," *Philosophical Perspectives* 25 (2011): 407–423.

Metaphysics, on the other hand, is substantive and explanatory. It is the task of metaphysicians to figure out what it means to be a person, to figure out what the nature of a person is. Although the metaphysical task does not affect the second version of the No-Relevant Differences Argument, what follows are a few brief remarks about what that task might look like.

PART III: The No-Relevant Difference Argument, First Version

Because of the presence of Premise 3, those interested in the first version will have to consider the metaphysics of personhood—of what a person is.

Some metaphysicians take a teleological approach: whatever is the *telos* for human persons is the *telos* for non-human persons, if there are any. Those who describe persons as essentially rational animals will have to tolerate ET persons, no matter how odd they seem. This task has three parts: (1) teasing out what being an animal is, (2) what being rational is, and (3) what the relationship is between being rational and being animal. If ETs are persons, then they are animals in the same way, rational in the same way, and animality and rationality are related in the same way as in Ts.

Whether the *type* of body matters for the ontological status of a species as persons depends on what the relationship is between embodiment and personhood. Embodiment is a necessary part of personhood for residents of the universe. (Although bodiless, angels are not residents of the universe.) In anticipating a visit from ETs, we are waiting not for another variation of humans but for another—doubtless very different-looking—person, a non-human.[5]

In more contemporary terms, a human person is an embodied consciousness. Opinions vary widely regarding the relationship of embodiment to consciousness. Some cleave to the "embodied" part and accept some form of materialism, narrowly (reductionist materialism) or broadly (non-reductionist materialism) conceived. Others border on a kind of angelism, minimizing the place of the body in personhood. Still others are Cartesian dualists, allowing not only distinctness but equal importance to and separation of body and soul or mind.

Being a person usually includes self-consciousness or having a first-person point of view. It includes the ability to reason; discovery of ETs might expand our understanding of rationality beyond currently recognized

---

[5] With a nod to Alasdair McIntyre for the syntax here. See Alasdair MacIntyre, *After Virtue* (South Bend: Univ. of Notre Dame Press, 1981, 1984), 263.

borders. Whatever personhood is, it's plausible to suppose that it includes the ability to have social relationships and to communicate as self-conscious, though, in the case of ETs, in ways we probably cannot imagine now.

What makes something a person might depend on either internal or external factors.

Descartes's *cogito* is the clearest example of the internal type. Whether the "I" is a T or an ET, I know by internal inspection that I am a thinking thing, so I can know that I am a person, though internal inspection would not let me know if I am a T person or an ET person. ETs in the future, like slaves and women in the past, and human fetuses in the present, can be misclassified as non-persons. Given the dismal history of abuse by some Ts of other Ts, abuse of ETs by Ts seems all but inevitable.

According to behaviorist, externalist theories, Ts can know the mental states of ETs because those mental states are their behaviors or dispositions to behave. Mental states are not "in the head"; they consist in my relationship to my environment. Ts know as well as ETs that they are persons because their being such relies on what's accessible to both Ts and ETs. ETs have no privileged access to their own mental states and therefore no infallibility with respect to what kind of being they are. The Turing test might work with ETs. If it turns out that externalism is true, then correctly identifying ETs becomes a bit easier. Ts can use empirical data to judge ETs as persons.

If God or angels are persons, then the ontological work becomes much harder, but this seems like work for theologians. Some philosophers think that there are non-human persons on this planet: dolphins, for example. We can ignore these complicating features because Premise 1 is modest; the only comparison is between Ts and ETs. If other things besides Ts and ETs are persons, Premise 1 is not affected.

Speciesism

Since our own case is the clearest to us with respect to personhood, we run the risk of species-ism—of missing the way in which person-making features appear in ETs. Thus the likelihood of misclassification in the case of ETs is much greater than that in the case of slaves or women, so we should not be surprised if ET persons are misclassified as non-persons.

The metaphysical task of adequately describing personhood is ongoing, substantive, and unresolved. Whatever it is, if it fits T persons, it will have to fit ET persons.

Favoring Ts over ETs for no reason other than they are Ts like us is a form of prejudice: speciesism. If personhood is not a matter of degrees, (even if there are borderline cases), then whatever dignity some persons have is the dignity that all persons have. An intellectually-handicapped or physically-handicapped person is fully a person. Being a person is not a matter of passing a test, whether the "test" has one or more items. If ETs are persons, they have the full dignity of personhood, even if the abilities they have are, by our standards, inferior or underdeveloped.

Consider the possibility that ETs just visit, rather than assimilate among us, or that they visit and assimilate but do not join the Church. ETs are sometimes referred to as "aliens." That the same word is used for Samaritans in the Bible and migrant workers who are either legal or illegal immigrants today. Just as Samaritans and illegal migrant workers can be saved, so can those other aliens: ETs.

Of course there may not be any life at all other than on Earth. That would eliminate the problem of trying to find out if ETs are persons. Then Premise 3 is false, but the first two premises can be true even if there are no ETs, since the first two premises are hypothetical claims.

If there is extraterrestrial life, it might not be intelligent life; if so, then there are no ETs, at least in the sense that we are using that term here. Or ETs might be persons but because of space/time and length-of-life limitations, they are not able to communicate.

There might be several different species of ETs, each presenting its own identification problem. But it is individuals we meet, not species. We would rely on inductive reasoning to form a claim about one or more species of ETs. The more ETs we encounter, the more likely is the truth of the conclusion of our inductive argument.

Determining whether ETs are persons, we encounter the problem of vagueness. The category of persons has borderline cases. For example, say that rationality is a necessary condition for personhood. Even Ts exhibit rationality in varying degrees. ETs might be rational in ways sufficiently inferior to Ts that we would misidentify them. The other extreme is possible—that we misidentify ETs because they are superior to us. And, of course, they might misidentify us as non-persons if they are vastly superior to us as persons. ETs might be so superior to Ts that we would misidentify them (and, of course, they might misidentify us).

Ultimately, we have to wait for a close encounter with ETs before we can seriously attend to the business of deciding if Premise 3 is true or false. We can even now, however, think about the rest of the No-Relevant-Difference Argument.

Here is a good place for a reminder of the principle, "Better Safe than Sorry." If there are ETs, then, with respect to what they are, there are two possibilities: ETs are persons or they are not. But with respect to what we know, there are three possibilities: We know that they are, we know that they are not, or we don't know. How we should treat ETs, if such there are and we encounter them, is a moral consideration. If likes should be treated alike and unlikes treated unlike, then it is clear that ETs must be treated in the same way as Ts. But if we don't know, should we treat them as persons or not? It's merely inconvenient to treat beings who don't merit special consideration as if they do. But it's immoral to treat beings who do deserve special consideration as if they do not. The moral answer seems clear: treat ETs as persons until or if we know otherwise—rather than treat ETs as if they are not persons until we find out otherwise.

Similarly, it's better to think of ETs as able to be saved, if and until we know otherwise. With respect to soteriology, how to think of them, in the interim between knowing and not knowing, has theological significance, propelled by what we think God is like.

ETs as Persons

"ETs are persons" is an empirical claim and awaits some communication or visit from beyond the borders of planet Earth.

If ETs are persons, then there exist ETs. Right now (where "now" is to be appropriately understood in keeping with Einstein's theory of relativity) in the universe, either there are ETs or there are not. We don't know if there are, but that doesn't settle the matter of whether there are. Premise 3 is a claim about reality, not knowledge. Knowing submits to reality, not vice versa.

What ETs are made of doesn't matter for salvation if what persons are made of doesn't matter. What ETs are made of might matter for what psychological and social properties they have. At a minimum, it's typical to think of persons as rational, conscious, embedded in their environment, and capable of caring for others. *A priori*, all these qualities are open to ETs, too.

The Problem of Psychological Difference

ETs might be so different from Ts that there is no point at which there could be even remotely detectable similarity; that is a possibility, unless some form of externalism regarding personhood is the case. Consciousness must be a minimum requirement for personhood, but consciousness is not sufficient. If ETs are conscious but not persons, then Premise 3 is false, but even so we draw no conclusion concerning their soteriological status.

ETs might be conscious but lack self-consciousness; if so, will they be persons? There is a tradition within Christianity that persons can be saved even if they lack robust, libertarian free will. If so, then personhood status does not depend on free will. The reader is invited to untie this philosophical and theological Gordian knot. The truth of Premise 3 depends and only depends on the ontological status of ETs as persons, whatever that is. Personhood status, not libertarianism, is the relevant category for soteriology.

Some philosophers think that having a soul, immortal or otherwise, is necessary (and perhaps also sufficient) for being a person. Others, such as nonreductive materialists, think not. This debate need not concern us here because all we need to insist on is that what is said of Ts as persons—whatever that is—also be said of ETs as persons. If having a soul (immortal soul, rational soul, etc.) is what makes Ts persons, then having a soul (immortal soul, rational soul, etc.) is what makes ETs persons, too. If having some other property—p—is what makes Ts persons, then having p is what makes ETs persons.

The same will be claimed with respect to moral obligation. Just as what our moral obligations are to fetuses depends on their personhood status, so, too, our moral obligations to ETs depends on their personhood status, whatever that is. Just as with fetuses, or future generations, even if they are not persons, we have duties to ETs. To treat beings as capable or deserving of salvation is one such mark of respect.

If Ts need not be explicit members of some religious community in order to be saved, then neither do ETs. If Ts can be "anonymous Christians," then ETs can, too.[6] A theological reason in favor of the view that explicit Christian membership does not matter is that it makes God's decision more important than the decisions of either Ts or ETs.

Moral Considerations

Ontology and metaphysics are binary—everything is either a person or a non-person. Epistemology is not binary: (1) we might know that ET are persons; or (2) we might know that ETs are not persons, or (3) we might not know if ETs are persons or non-persons. If we don't know, then treating them as if they are persons (until and if we find out otherwise) is preferable

---

[6] Anonymous Christian is the controversial notion introduced by the Jesuit theologian Karl Rahner (1904–1984) according to which people who have never heard the Christian Gospel might be saved through Christ. Non-Christians could have "in [their] basic orientation and fundamental decision, accepted the salvific grace of God, through Christ, although [they] may never have heard of the Christian revelation" (Gavin D'Costa, "Karl Rahner's Anonymous Christian—A Reappraisal," *Modern Theology* 1, No. 2 [January 1985]: 132).

on moral grounds: better to mistakenly treat non-persons as persons than to treat persons as non-persons.

It would be a mistake to think that persons have to look like us. Look at an image of a one-day or even one-week or one-month old human being *in vitro*; if even very young T persons don't look like other T persons, then it also doesn't matter if ET persons don't look like us. In the minds of racists and sexists, looking "like us" is very narrow: these others have to look a lot like us. The tendency of any group of Ts to consider other groups of Ts to be something other than persons is verified by anthropologists. Incorrectly excluding ETs would stem from a similar kind of narrowness.

Recall the instructive true story of John Carey Merrick (1862-1890), exhibited at a freak show as the Elephant Man, so severely distorted that his abusers treated him as not human.[7] They may have sincerely believed that he was not a human person; *mutatis mutandis*, Ts, potential abusers, might sincerely believe that ETs are not persons. Would they be morally culpable for mistreating ETs? Or can the abusers justifiably plead excusable ignorance? Caution is the right approach: treat ETs as persons until or if you find out otherwise.

The moral task follows from the ontological one. Persons have some exalted or special status requiring more from us with respect to how we should treat them. From their nature we derive their rights and our duties. If there are ETs and if they are persons, however "person" is defined, then we must think of them in the same way that we think of human persons and treat them accordingly.

If there are ETs and if they are persons, but we don't see that they are, then we will mistreat them and not realize that we are unjustified in doing so. Ignorance is no excuse. Moral responsibility is twofold: cognitive and active—correctly identifying entities—and acting accordingly.

ETs might meet the standard for persons but we will, at least at first, be ill-equipped to recognize them as such. If we are careful and use slow thinking, we could be cautiously optimistic that we can successful, always leaving open the possibility that we might be mistaken. Slow thinking avoids putting too much faith in intuition and hunches. It avoids emotional responses that prejudice rational judgement.[8]

The No-Relevant-Difference Argument is anthropocentric in that it takes human beings to be the standard of personhood and ETs are judged accordingly. (Nathalie Cabrol of the SETI Institute wrote in a 2016

[7] "Joseph Merrick," Wikipedia, accessed August 19, 2020, https://en.wikipedia.org/wiki/Joseph_Merrick.
[8] Daniel Kahneman, *Thinking, Fast and Slow* (New York: Farrar, Straus and Giroux, 2011).

Astrobiology paper, "So far, in our quest to find ET, we have only been searching for other versions of ourselves.") [9]

It's instructive and humbling to notice that ETs might return the favor by making themselves the standard of personhood and judge *us* accordingly. They may judge us "ET-centrically" or "ET-morphically." The moral caution follows in their case, too. We should hope that ETs will treat us as worthy of the rights and privileges they accord to themselves. Ts and ETs can converse. Neither Ts nor ETs can be treated as food or be used instrumentally in any other way, if Ts and ETs are persons.

Note that for Premise 1 to be true, status as persons is sufficient, but not necessary, for either soteriological or moral consideration.

PART III: Premise 2

Premise 2 states this: If there is no ontologically-relevant difference between Ts and ETs, then there is no soteriologically-relevant difference between Ts and ETs.

It is as a human being and therefore as a T that God appeared in the world in the person of Jesus Christ. His one personhood includes two natures, human nature and divine nature. But that need not mean that his saving act is limited to human persons. For one thing, Jesus was a Jew, but being saved is not limited to Jews. For another, Jesus was a male person, but being saved is not limited to men. Similarly, the Son of God, Jesus, appeared as a human being, but that doesn't mean that salvation is limited to human persons. It's personhood as such, not being a T-person, that matters.

In Catholic theology, Jesus Himself is not a human person but a divine person: "Christ's humanity has no other subject than the divine person of the Son of God . . . The Church thus confesses that Jesus is inseparably true God and true man."[10]

Soteriology

To say that Jesus's life, death, and resurrection brought salvation for Ts but not for ETs (if such there be) puts limits on the efficacy of his death and

---

[9] Quoted in Wade Roush, "Life as We Don't Know it," *Scientific American Blog Network*, April 7, 2020, https://blogs.scientificamerican.com/observations/life-as-we-dont-know-it/.

[10] *Catechism of the Catholic Church*, 2nd ed. (Washington, DC: United States Catholic Conference, 2000), §469, §466.

resurrection, and that is just quite straightforwardly bad theology—whether or not ETs are persons. If ETs are persons, it is all the more plausible (or perhaps undeniable) that the life, death and resurrection of Jesus accomplished for them what it accomplished for us.

It might be objected that something other than ontological status as persons matters for soteriological status. But what could that be? Maybe the reason that ontological status as persons does not matter for ETs is that ontological status does not matter at all for salvation, because all God's creatures enjoy salvation-ready status. Maybe universalism in one of the senses described at the beginning of this essay is the case: the inclusion of all creation in salvation. Every part of creation will be made new, will become the new heavens and the new earth—i.e., renewed universe. Here ontological status doesn't matter because salvation is wider than personhood. (Ontological status might matter for how one experiences the life of the world to come, but it doesn't matter for whether one can experience the life of the world to come.) Let's say that this is true: that ontological status as persons does not matter for salvation because ontological status does not matter at all; salvation is wider than persons. This is hardly bad news, so the objection is harmless. Ts and ETs are saved, whether because all things (including persons) are saved or because all persons (only) are saved. Keep in mind that salvation extends to all persons, with or without a history of sinfulness. Limiting salvation to a moral category implies that only part of what we are needs saving: the sinful part. But again it is bad theology to put limits on the saving life, death, and resurrection of Jesus. It is as what we are metaphysically that we are saved, not just what we are morally.

Or an objection might come from the opposite direction. Status as persons is not enough because not all persons, Ts or ETs, are saved. Some Ts are saved and some Ts are not; some ETs are saved and some ETs are not. This objection also fails to threaten the No-Relevant-Difference Argument, because the some-but-not-all claim does not fall along the lines of all-Ts-but-only-some-ETs. If some but not all Ts are saved, then similarly some but not all ETs are saved, too. Another reason why this objection does not pertain to the No-Differences Argument is that salvation is described above as salvation-ready, not (or not necessarily) salvation-secure.

Predestination

W: Salvation depends on God's will only.

At first glance, W might seem to threaten Premise 2; the ontological status of ETs as persons doesn't figure in salvation. The nature nor the will of Ts matter for salvation, so neither the nature nor the will of ETs matter for salvation. But a closer look at W reveals that W does not threaten Premise 2. W is just a variation of the some-but-not all assertion. If God saves only some Ts—those Ts whom God has predestined to be saved—then God saves only some ETs—those Ts whom God has predestined to be saved.

If we say that all Ts are saved, then Premise 2 is threatened if and only if we add that no or only some ETs are saved. But in that case we have reintroduced the irrelevant criterion of spatial (temporal/spatial) distance from Mt. Calvary. But distance in either time or space from Mt. Calvary must be irrelevant to salvation. Even if W is true, Premise 2 is still true.

Keep in mind that Premise 2 is not epistemological; it might be that we just cannot know who is saved and who isn't. Perhaps we cannot know whether some or all ETs are saved, but the same applies to Ts, too. We do not know who among Ts are saved. So again a parallel holds between an analysis of Ts and an analysis of ETs—even if our project were epistemological.

ETs, if they can be saved, can be saved even if we determine incorrectly that they are not persons, or if we correctly discern that they are not persons but being persons is not necessary for being saved. Salvation depends on facts, not knowledge of the facts: we affirm metaphysical realism.

PART IV: Conclusion

Both versions of the No-Relevant-Difference argument are sound. Whether the first version of the argument is sound depends as always on the premises. We can think about the truth or falsity of the first two premises now. The truth or falsity of Premise 3 will have to wait.

As to whether there is more than one saving irruption by God into the cosmos, the best soteriology is on the one, unique Mt. Calvary event; it is impossible to sufficiently appreciate the significance of that event, and there is no good theological reason for another.

APPENDIX

A TAXONOMY FOR ALIEN MAMMALIAN-LIKE LIFE FORMS

ALAN VINCELETTE

If life is present on other planets (and this is a big if), and if it takes similar forms to those found on Earth (another very big if), then what sort of classification scheme is best suited for such life forms?[1] This is what will be explored in the following paper. I will argue that though phylogenetic systems based on evolutionary descent are worthwhile given that alien life forms will have a highly divergent tree than that found on Earth, a schema based on generalized convergent body plans or *nicotypes* will also be as or even more useful. I go on to present such a schema for mammalian-like life forms.

A Brief History of Taxonomy

The earliest detailed classification scheme for animals that we know of belongs to Aristotle with his *Historia Animalium* 1.1-6, 2.15, and 4.1.[2]

---

[1] For answers to these questions see my earlier paper in this collection, "The Likelihood of Complex Multicellular Life on Earth-Like Exoplanets," pp. 42–81. I wish to thank all my former colleagues in the geology division of the San Bernardino County Museum.

[2] Aristotle, *Historia animalium*, trans. D'Arcy Wentworth Thompson (Oxford: Clarendon Press, 1910), 486a15-491a26, 505b25-506b23, 523a30-523b21. On Aristotle's system of classification consult: David M. Balme, "Aristotle's Use of Differentiae in Zoology," *Aristote e les problèmes de méthode*, ed. Suzanne Mansion (Louvain: Publications Universitaires de Louvain, 1961), 195–212; G. E. R. Lloyd, "The Development of Aristotle's Theory of the Classification of Animals," *Phronesis* 6, no. 1 (1961): 59–81; James G. Lennox, "Aristotle on Genera, Species, and 'The More and the Less'," *Journal of the History of Biology* 13, no. 2 (1980): 321–346; Pierre Pellegrin, *Aristotle's Classification of Animals: Biology and the Conceptual Unity of the Aristotelian Corpus*, trans. Anthony Preus (Berkeley: University of

Aristotle distinguished "genera" of animals based upon such factors as whether they had red blood or not, whether or not they had wings, legs, or fins, or were legless, what type of foot they had, what kind of integument or outer protective layer they had, and whether they were oviparous or viviparous, among other things. His basic classification system for the animals with red blood, or what roughly corresponds to the subphylum Vertebrata, breaks animals up into four main groups based upon adaptations to primary form of locomotion (i.e. flying with wings, swimming with fins, walking with legs, and legless undulation).

Taxonomy of Aristotle (350 B.C.)

Red-Blooded and Motile Organisms [i.e. Subphylum Vertebrata]

I. Winged and Lunged (Airborne; Viviparous)
   A. Feathered, Feathered-Winged, and Bipedal Legged: birds [i.e. Class Aves]
      i. Talon-footed (Nocturnal and Diurnal): owls; falcons; kites, hawks, eagles, buzzards, and vultures
         i.e. Orders Strigiformes; Falconiformes; Accipitriformes
      ii. Web-footed [Palmate] or Lobe-footed [Lobate; Fissipalmate] (Aquatic): duck, shelduck, goose, swan; coots; grebes; cormorants; gulls, sandpipers, plovers, calidrises, and auks
         i.e. Orders Anseriformes; Gruiformes; Podicipediformes; Suliformes; Charadriiformes
      iii. Semi-web-footed [Semipalmate] (Waterside): pelicans, herons, spoonbills; storks
         i.e. Orders Pelecaniformes; Ciconiiformes
      iv. Large-footed and Weak-flying [Ground-dwelling]: ostriches; bustards; partridges, quails, chickens
         i.e. Orders Struthioniformes; Otidiformes; Galliformes
      v. Small standard four-toed (Air, Marsh, River, or Tree Dwelling): pigeons and doves; kingfishers; woodpeckers; treecreepers, buntings, dippers, thrushes, warblers, swallows, titmice, sparrows, finches, linnets, batises, robins, wrens, pipits, tanagers, crows, ravens, rooks, nightingales
         i.e. Orders Columbiformes; Coraciiformes; Piciformes; Passeriformes

---

California Press, 1986); J. J. Hall, "The Classification of Birds, in Aristotle and Early Modern Naturalists," *History of Science* 29, no. 2-3 (1991): 111–151, 223–243; Richard A. Lockshin, "Aristotle's and Linnaeus' Classifications of Living Creatures," *The Joy of Science: An Examination of How Scientists Ask and Answer Questions Using the Story of Evolution as a Paradigm* (Dordrecht: Springer, 2007), 55–68; Alexander Fürst von Lieven and Marcel Humar, "A Cladistic Analysis of Aristotle's Animal Groups in the Historia animalium," *History and Philosophy of the Life Sciences* 30, no. 2 (2008): 227–262.

B. Haired, Leathery-Winged, and Bipedal Legged: bats and flying foxes
i.e. Order Chiroptera of Class Mammalia

II. Finned (Aquatic)
A. Scaled and Gilled (Oviparous and Viviparous; Bony or Cartilaginous): shark/sheatfish, pipefish, capelin, carp, eel/bony fish
i.e. Superorder Selachimorpha of Class Chondrichthyes; Class Actinopterygii; Class Osteichthyes
B. Smooth and Lunged: dolphins and whales/seals (Viviparous)
i.e. Infraorder Cetacea of Order Artiodactyla of Class Mammalia; i.e. Clade Pinnipediformes of Order Carnivora of Class Mammalia

III. Legged (without Wings) (Land-Dwelling)
A. Smooth and Lunged Quadripeds (Oviparous): newts/frogs
i.e. Orders Urodela and Anura of Class Amphibia
B. Scaled and Lunged Quadripeds (Oviparous): lizards/crocodiles/turtles
i.e. Suborder Lacertilia of Order Squamata of Class Reptilia; Orders Crocodilia and Testudines of Class Reptilia
C. Haired and Lunged Quadripeds (Viviparous)
i. Small Herbivores: shrews, moles, and hedgehogs; mice, beavers, and porcupines; hares
i.e. Orders Eulipotyphla, Rodentia, and Lagomorpha of Class Mammalia
ii. Carnivores [i.e. Order Carnivora]: weasels and otters; civets; lions; hyaenas; wolves and foxes; bears; and the legendary manticore
i.e. Families Mustelidae, Viverridae, Felidae, Hyaenidae, Canidae, and Ursidae of Order Carnivora of Class Mammalia
iii. Large Herbivores and Omnivores
a. Solid-Footed: elephants; horses and donkeys
i.e. Order Proboscidea of Class Mammalia; Family Equidae of Order Perissodactyla of Class Mammalia
b. Cloven-Footed (often Horned) [i.e. Order Artiodactyla]: camels; hippopotamus; cows, sheep, goats; antelope and oryx; deer; pigs
i.e. Families Camelidae, Hippopotamidae, Bovidae, Cervidae, and Suidae of Order Artiodactyla of Class Mammalia
c. Large Arboreal Mammals: monkeys and apes
i.e. Order Primates of Class Mammalia
D. Haired and Lunged Bipeds (Viviparous): humans
i.e. Genus *Homo* of Order Primates of Class Mammalia

IV. Legless and Finless (without Wings)
A. Scaled and Gilled (Oviparous and Viviparous): rays and guitarfish/muraena eels
i.e. Superorder Batoidea of Class Chondrichtyes; Family Muraenidae of Order Anguilliformes of Class Actinopterygii
B. Scaled and Lunged (Oviparous and Viviparous): snakes
i.e. Suborder Serpentes of Order Squamata of Class Reptilia

Carl Linnaeus in his *Systema naturae* (1735) recognized that there were issues with Aristotle's system[3]—namely, by prioritizing adaptations for major environmental zones (oceans, air, land, etc.) and locomotion (flying, swimming, walking, undulation), Aristotle failed to combine groups of organisms that shared basic morphologies and internal anatomies. For example, bats share many similarities with deer, such as possessing hair, mammary glands, and being viviparous, rather than the birds with whom Aristotle grouped them. The same goes for whales who were grouped with the fish by Aristotle but came to be grouped with mammals by Linneaus with the 10th edition of the *Systema naturae* (1758). Hence Linnaeus grouped vertebrates into a hierarchical system of classes and orders based upon basic body types such as integument, heart-structure, limb structure,

---

[33] In the sixteenth and seventeenth centuries Aristotelian taxonomy was revivlfIéd with Pierre Belon, *L'histoire naturelle des éstranges poissons marins* (Parisiorum: Regnaud Chaudiere, 1551) and *L'histoire de la nature des oyseaux* (Parisiorum: B. Prevost, 1555); Conrad Gessner, *Historia animalium*, 5 vols. (Zürich: C. Froschauer, 1551-1587); Edward Wotton, *De differentiis animalium* (Parisiorum: Vasconsanum, 1552); Ulisse Aldrovandi, *Ornithologiae hoc est de avibus historiae* (Bononiae: Baptistam Bellagambam, 1599-1603), *De piscibus et de cetis* (Bononiae: Baptistam Bellagambam, 1613), *Quadrupedum omnium bisulcorum historia* (Bononiae: Sebastianum Bonhommium 1621), *Serpentum et draconum* (Bononiae: C. Ferronium, 1640); Claude Perrault, *Mémoires pour servir à l'histoire naturelle des animaux* (Paris: Imprimerie Royale, 1676); Francis Willughby and John Ray, *Ornithologiae* (London: John Martyn, 1676) and *Historia Piscium* (Oxford: Theatro Sheldoniano, 1686). See also Johann Baptist von Spix, *Geschichte und Beurtheilung aller Systeme in der Zoologie nach ihrer Entwicklungsfolge von Aristoteles bis auf die gegenwärtige Zeit* (Nürnberg: Schrag, 1810); Mary P. Winsor, "Non-Essentialist Methods in Pre-Darwinian Taxonomy," *Biology and Philosophy* 18 (2003): 387–400 and "The Creation of the Essentialism Story: An Exercise in Metahistory," *History and Philosophy of the Life Sciences* 28 (2006): 149–174; Anita Guerrini, "Perrault, Buffon and the Natural History of Animals," *Notes and Records* 66, no. 4 (2012): 393–409 and *The Courtiers' Anatomists: Animals and Humans in Louis XIV's Paris* (Chicago: University of Chicago Press, 2015); Peter Sahlins, *1668: The Year of the Animal in France* (Boston: MIT Press, 2017).

and dentition.[4] His classification of vertebrates in the 10th edition of 1758-1759 is as follows:[5]

Classification of Linnaeus (1758-1759)

Kingdom Animalia

Class Mammalia [four-chambered heart; lungs; warm-blooded, viviparous, four legs, hair, mammary glands, land or ocean dwelling]:
    Order Bestiae [many side foreteeth and extra canine, elongated snout, diggers]: opossums; moles, shrews, hedgehogs; armadillos, and pigs
        i.e. Order Didelphimorphia of Infraclass Marsupalia; Order Eulipotyphla; Order Cingulata; Family Suidae of Order Artiodactyla
    Order Glires [two cutting foreteeth, claws, gnawers, root and vegetable eaters]: mice; squirrels; beavers; porcupines; rabbits; and rhinoceroses
        i.e. Families Muridae, Sciuridae, Castoridae, and Hystricidae of Order Rodentia; Order Lagomorpha; Family Rhinocerotidae of Order Perissodactyla
    Order Ferae [molars with conic projections, six conic fore-teeth, sharp canines, subulate claws, carnivores]: weasels; mongooses; civets; cats; hyaenas; dogs; bears; seals
        i.e. Families Mustelidae, Herpestidae, Viverridae, Felidae, Hyaenidae, Canidae, Ursidae of Order Carnivora; Clade Pinnipediformes or Order Carnivora
    Order Pecora [no upper fore-teeth, reduced lower fore-teeth, hoofed and cloven feet, four stomachs, chewers of cud, herbaceous plant eaters]: camels; giraffes; musk deer; antelope, goats, sheep, cows

---

[4] For more on Linneaus see William T. Stearn, "The Background of Linnaeus's Contributions to the Nomenclature and Methods of Systematic Biology," *Systematic Zoology* 8, no. 1 (1959): 4–22; Marc Ereshefsky, "Some Problems with the Linnaean Hierarchy," *Philosophy of Science* 61, no. 2 (1994): 186–205, "The Evolution of the Linnaean Hierarchy," *Biology and Philosophy* 12, no. 4 (1997): 493–519, and *The Poverty of the Linnaean Hierarchy: A Philosophical Study of Biological Taxonomy* (Cambridge: Cambridge University Press, 2000); Tore Frängsmyr and Sten Lindroth, *Linnæus, the Man and His Work* (Canton: Science History Publications, 1994); Don E. Wilson and DeeAnn M. Reeder, "Class Mammalia Linnaeus, 1758," *Zootaxa* 3148 (2011): 56–60.

[5] Carolus Linnæus, *Systema naturæ per regna tria naturæ, secundum classes, ordines, genera, species, cum characteribus, differentiis, synonymis, locis*, 3 vols. (Holmiae: Salvius, 1758-1759), translated as *A General System of Nature: Through the Three Grand Kingdoms of Animals, Vegetables, and Minerals, Systematically Divided into Their Several Classes, Orders, Genera, Species, and Varieties with Their Habitations, Manners, Economy, Structure, and Peculiarities*, 5 vols. (London: Lackington, Allen, and Company, 1802).

i.e. Families Camelidae, Giraffidae, Moschidae, Cervidae, and Bovidae of
Order Artiodactyla

Order Belluae [obtuse fore-teeth, large hoofed feet, herbivores]: horses;
hippopotamuses

i.e. Families Equidae and Hippopotamidae of Order Perissodactyla

Order Bruta [tusks with no fore-teeth, large hoofs with strong nails; herbivores]:
elephants; manatees; sloths; anteaters; and pangolins

i.e. Orders Proboscidea Sirenia and Pholidota; Suborders Folivora and
Vermilingua of Order Pilosa

Order Cete [aquatic, cartilaginous or bony teeth, lungs, breathing hold in head,
fins, flat tails]: narwhals, rorquals or baleen whales, sperm whales, dolphins and
porpoises

i.e. Families Monodontidae, Balaenopteridae, and Physeteridae of
Infraorder Cetacea of Order Artiodactyla; Superfamily Delphinoidea of
Infraorder Cetacea of Order Artiodactyla

Order Primates [four cutting fore-teeth, two canines, two pectoral teats, two arms
and two feet, flat oval nails; fruit eaters and omnivores]: bats; colugos; lemurs;
macaques, monkeys, and apes; humans

i.e. Orders Chiroptera and Dermoptera; Infraorder Lemuriformes of Order
Primates; Family Cercopithecidae of Order Primates; Parvorder Catarrhini
and Family Hominidae of Infraorder Simiiformes of Order Primates

Class Aves [four-chambered heart; lungs; warm-blooded, oviparous, winged, two
legs, feathers, beaks]:

Order Accipitres: condors; vultures, condors, falcons, eagles; owls, shrikes

i.e. Orders Cathartiformes, Accipitriformes, Strigiformes; Family Laniidae
of Order Passeriformes

Order Picae: parrots; toucans; wrynecks and woodpeckers; hornbills; anis,
cuckoos, and hoopoes; rollers; crows and ravens; bee-eaters, and kingfishers;
orioles; mynas; birds-of-paradise; nuthatches; treecreepers; hummingbirds

i.e. Orders Psittaciformes, Bucerotiformes, Cuculiformes, Coraciiformes;
Families Ramphastidae and Picidae of Order Piciformes; Family Corvidae,
Icteridae, Sturnidae, Paradisaeidae, Sittidae, and Certhioidea of Order
Passeriformes; Family Trochilidae of Order Apodiformes

Order Anseres: ducks, geese, swans, mergansers, gulls, terns, skimmers; auks
and puffins; petrols and albatrosses; penguins; pelicans; tropicbirds; grebes;
loons

i.e. Orders Anseriformes, Procellariiformes, Sphenisciformes, Phaethontiformes,
Podicipediformes, and Order Gaviiformes; Family Laridae of Order
Charadriiformes; Family Pelecanidae of Order Pelecaniformes

Order Grallae: flamingoes; storks; cranes, coots, rails, trumpeters; herons;
spoonbills, ibises; godwits, phalaropes, sandpipers; plovers; avocets; oystercatchers;
bustards; ostriches

i.e. Orders Phoenicopteriformes, Ciconiiformes, Gruiformes, Otidiformes,
Struthionifores; Families Ardeidae and Threskiornithidae of Order

Pelecaniformes; Families Scolopacidae, Charadriidae, Recurvirostridae, and Haematopodidae of Order Charadriiformes

Order Gallinae: peafowl, turkeys, curassows, pheasants, chickens, grouse

i.e. Order Galliformes

Order Passeres: pigeons, doves; larks, pipits, starlings, thrushes, cardinals, bullfinches, buntings, finches, wagtails, tits, chickadees, swallows; swifts; nightjars

i.e. Orders Columbiformes, Passeriformes, Caprimulgiformes; Family Apodidae of Order Apodiformes

Class Amphibia [two-chambered heart, cold-blooded, lungs, lobate liver, bony terrestrial or cartilaginous aquatic; oviparous]:

Order Reptiles: turtles and tortoises; lizards and gliding lizards; crocodilians; newts and salamanders; crocodilians; frogs and toads

i.e. Orders Testudines and Crocodilia of Class Reptilia; Suborder Lacertilia of Order Squamata of Class Reptilia; Orders Urodela and Anura of Class Amphibia

Order Serpentes [legless reptiles and amphibians]: snakes and worm snakes; slowworms; worm lizards; caecilians

i.e. Suborder Serpentes, Clade Aguioidea, and Clade Amphisbaenia of Order Squamata of Class Reptilia; Order Gymnophiona of Class Amphibia

Order Nantes [cartilaginous fish]: lampreys; rays; sharks; ratfishes; anglerfishes; sturgeons

i.e. Order Petromyzontiformes of Class Hyperoartia; Superorders Batoidea and Selachimorpha and Order Chimaeriformes of Class Chondrichthyes; Orders Lophiiformes and Acipenseriformes of Class Actinopterygii

Class Pisces [one-chambered heart, cold-blooded, gills, radiate fins, aquatic, scales, bony skeleton]:

Order Apodes: eels; electric knifefishes; cutlassfishes, wolffishes; sand eels; butterfishes; swordfishes

i.e. Orders Anguilliformes, Gymnotiformes, and Istiophoriformes of Class Actinopterygii; Family Trichiuridae of Order Perciformes of Class Actinopterygii; Family Ammodytidae of Order Trachiniformes of Class Actinopterygii; Family Stromateidae of Order Scombriformes of Class Actinopterygii

Order Jugulares: dragonets; stargazers; weevers; cod; cusk-eels; blennies

i.e. Orders Callionymiformes, Gadiformes, Ophidiiformes, and Blenniiformes of Class Actinopterygii; Families Uranoscopidae and Trachinidae of Order Trachiniformes of Class Actinopterygii

Order Thoracici: lumpfishes, sculpins, scorpionfishes, sea robins; remoras, dolphinfishes; gobies; john dories; flatfishes; butterflyfishes; beams; snappers; perch; goatfishes; wrasses; sticklebacks; mackerel and tuna

i.e. Orders Scorpaeniformes, Carangiformes, Gobiiformes, Zeiformes, Pleuronectiformes, Labriformes, and Gasterosteiformes of Class Actinopterygii; Families Chaetodontidae, Sparidae, Lutjanidae, Percidae, and Mullidae of

Order Perciformes of Class Actinopterygii; Family Scombridae of Order
Scombriformes of Class Actinopterygii
Order Abdominales: loaches, carp; catfishes; salmon and trout; cornetfishes;
pike; herring; smelts; silversides; mullets; flying fishes; threadfins
    i.e. Orders Cypriniformes, Siluriformes, Salmoniformes, Esociformes,
    Clupeiformes,   Osmeriformes,   Atheriniformes,   Mugiliformes,   and
    Beloniformes of Class Actinopterygii; Family Fistulariidae of Order
    Syngnathiformes of Class Actinopterygii; Family Polynemidae of Order
    Perciformes of Class Actinopterygii
Order Branchiostegi: elephantfishes; triggerfishes, boxfishes, pufferfishes,
porcupinefishes; snipefishes, pipefishes, seahorses, seamoths
    i.e. Orders Osteoglossiformes and Tetraodontiformes of Class
    Actinopterygii; Suborder Syngnathoidei of Order Syngnathiformes of Class
    Actinopterygii

A competing taxonomy was that of Étienne Geoffroy Saint-Hilaire,
Georges Cuvier, and John Edward Gray, based primarily on limb structure
rather than dentition. The mammals were classified as follows in their
system:

St.-Hilaire-Cuvier-Gray Taxonomy (1827)[6]

---

[6] See Georges Cuvier, *Le règne animal distribué d'après son organisation pour
servir de base à l'histoire naturelle des animaux et d'introduction à l'anatomie
compare* (Paris: Deterville, 1817), vol. 1, translated as *Cuvier's Animal Kingdom:
Arranged According to Its Organization*, trans. Edward Blyth and Robert Mudie
(London :W.S. Orr and Company, 1840); John Edward Gray, "On the Natural
Arrangement of Vertebrose Animals," *London Medical Repository* 15 (1821): 296–
310, "An Outline of an Attempt at the Disposition of the Mammalia into Tribes and
Families with a List of the Genera Apparently Appertaining to Each Tribe," *Annals
of Philosophy* 10 (1825): 337–344, and "Synopsis of the Species of the Class
Mammalia," in *The Animal Kingdom Arranged in Conformity with its Organization
by the Baron Cuvier with Additional Descriptions*, ed. Edward Griffith (London:
George B. Whittaker: 1827), vol. 1-55; and Étienne Geoffroy Saint-Hilaire and
Georges Cuvier, *Histoire naturelle des mammifères* (Paris: A. Belin, 1824). Gray,
Saint-Hilaire, and Cuvier built upon earlier work by such taxonomists as: Mathurin-
Jacques Brisson, *Regnum animale in classes IX distributum sive Synopsis methodica*
(Lugduni Batavorum: Theodorum Haak, 1762); Johann Karl Wilhelm Illiger,
Prodromus systematis mammalium et avium (Berolini: C. Salfeld, 1811); Gotthelf
Fischer von Waldheim, *Zoognosia tabulis synopticis illustrata* (Mosquae: Nicolai S.
Vsevolozsky, 1813); Constantine Samuel Rafinesque, *Analyse de la nature ou,
Tableau de l'univers et des corps organisés* (Palermo: C. S. Rafinesque, 1815). On
the history of post-Linnean taxonomy see: Edward, Griffith, ed., *The Animal
Kingdom Arranged in Conformity with its Organization by the Baron Cuvier with
Additional Descriptions* (London: George B. Whittaker: 1827), xiii–lxxx; Edward

Class Mammalia
    Order Bimana [bipedal, digits, thumb, incisors, canines, molars]: humans

    Order Quadrumana [quadrupedal, digits, thumb, incisors, canines, molars]:
    monkeys and apes

    Order Carnassiers [quadrupedal, digits, no thumbs, incisors, canines, molars]:
        Family Cheiroptera: bats
        Family Insectivora: hedgehogs, shrews, moles
        Family Carnivora: badgers, weasels, cats, dogs, bears, civets, hyaenas, seals
        Family Marsupiata: opossums, kangaroos, wombats

    Order Rodenta [quadrupedal, digits, no thumbs, two large incisors, molars]:
    beavers, rats, squirrels, porcupines

    Order Edentata [quadrupedal, no incisors, large nails]: sloths, armadillos,
    anteaters, platypus

    Order Pachydermata [quadrupedal, hooves, non-ruminate]:
        Family Proboscidiana: elephants
        Family Pachydermata: hippopotamus, pigs, rhinoceros, tapir, hyrax
        Family Solipedes: horses

    Order Ruminantia [quadrupedal, bifurcated hooves, ruminate]: camels, sheep,
    deer, cows, antelopes

    Order Cetacea [aquatic]: dolphins, whales

    When the idea of evolution gained ground in the later 1800s with the
influence of Buffon, Lamarck, Darwin, and Wallace—along with further
studies in paleontology by Cope, Marsh, Osborn, Merriam, and others; and
in embryology and morphology by Cuvier, De Blainville, Oken, Von Spix,
Blumenbach, MacLeay, Griffith, Struthers, Owens, Haeckel, and others[7]—

D. Cope, "Synopsis of the Families of Vertebrata," *The American Naturalist* 23
(1889): 1–29; William King Gregory, "The Orders of Mammals," *American
Museum of National History Bulletin* 27 (1910): 469–475; Malcolm C. McKenna
and Susan K. Bell, *Classification of Mammals Above the Species Level* (New York:
Columbia University Press, 1997), 11–34; Theodore W. Pietsch, *Trees of Life: A
Visual History of Evolution* (Baltimore: John Hopkins University Press, 2013);
Frank E. Zachos and Robert J. Asher, eds., *Mammalian Evolution, Diversity and
Systematics* (Berlin: Walter de Gruyter, 2018), 39–58.
[7] Such as the works by Lorenz Oken, *Grundriss der Naturphilosophie* (Frankfurt:
Eichenberg, 1802 1802); Richard Owens, *On the Archetype and Homologies of the
Vertebrate Skeleton* (London: John Van Voorst, 1848) and *Anatomy of Vertebrates*

it was recognized that Linnaeus and his followers still gave preference to certain traits that were tied too closely to diet and habitat rather than evolutionary relationships. Hence biologists began more carefully to classify animal species, including mammals, based on homologies or synapomorphies, that is shared structural features inherited from a nearest common ancestor. The goal became to avoid paraphyletic groups, or groups that did not share a nearest common ancestor and so to classify organisms on the basis of their evolutionary relationships, or a phylogeny.

With regard to the mammals the key classification schemes of the higher taxa in the later nineteenth and early-twentieth centuries are those by Grant, Gill, King, and Simpson. They greatly expanded the number of mammalian orders, in effect doubling them, and expanded the number of sub-categories in order to show evolutionary relationships. An early effort in this regard was that of Robert Edmund Grant.

Taxonomy of Grant (1861)[8]

Class Mammalia:
    Subclass Unguiculata
        Order Bimana: humans
        Order Quadrumana
            Suborder Catarrhina: old world monkeys
            Suborder Platyrrhina: new world monkeys
            Suborder Strepsirhina: lemurs
        Order Chiroptera
            Suborder Pteropodida: megabats
            Suborder Noctilionida: common bats
            Suborder Vespertilionida: vesper bats
            Suborder Phyllostomida: vampire bats
            Suborder Rhinolophida: horseshoe bats
        Order Insectivora
            Suborder Brachycauloda: hedgehogs
            Suborder Macrocauloda: shrews and moles
        Order Carnivora
            Suborder Plantigrada: bears and badgers
            Suborder Digitigrada: cats and weasels
            Suborder: Palmigrada: dogs and otters
        Order Pinnipedia
            Suborder Phocida: seals

(London: Longmans, Green, and Company, 1866); Ernst Haeckel, *Generelle Morphologie der Organismen* (Berlin: Georg Reimer, 1866).
[8] Robert Edmund Grant, *Tabular View of the Primary Divisions of the Animal Kingdom* (London: Walton and Maberly, 1861).

        Suborder Trichechida: manatees
    Order Rodentia
        Suborder Claviculata: beavers
        Suborder Subclaviculata: mice, squirrels
    Order Edentata
        Suborder Brachyrhyncha: armadillos
        Suborder Macrorhyncha: sloths
        Suborder Anodonta: anteaters
Subclass Ungulata
    Order Ruminantia
        Suborder Tubicornia: sheep and cows
        Suborder Plenicornia: giraffes
        Suborder Ecornia: camels and deer
    Order Solidungula: horses
    Order Multungula: tapirs, hippopotamus
    Order Proboscidia: elephants
Subclass Bipinnata:
    Order Sirenia: manatees
    Order Cetacea: dolphins and whales
Subclass Dimetroa:
    Order Marsupialia: opossums and kangaroos
        Suborder Sarcophaga: Tasmanian devil
        Suborder Entomophaga: opossums
        Suborder Phytophaga: kangaroos
    Order Monotrema
        Suborder Stenorhyncha: echidna
        Suborder Platyrhyncha: platypus

Something approaching the modern view is finally found in the
taxonomy of Theodore Gill of the Smithsonian Museum.

Taxonomy of Gill (1872)[9]

Class Mammalia
    Subclass Placentalia
    Supeorder Educabilia
        Order Primates
            Suborder Anthropoidea: humans, monkeys, apes
            Suborder Prosimiae: lemurs

---

[9] Theodore Gill, *Arrangement of the Families of Mammals* (Washington:
Smithsonian Institution, 1872). See also Max Weber, *Die Saugetiere: Einfuhrung in
die Anatomie und Systematik der recenten und fossilen Mammalia* (Jena, Gustav
Fischer, 1904). See also William King Gregory, "The Orders of Mammals,"
American Museum of National History Bulletin 27 (1910): 1–524.

Order Ferae
    Suborder Fissipedia: cats, dogs, hyaenas, weasels, bears
    Suborder Pinnipedia: seals
Order Ungulata
    Suborder Artiodactyli: camels, giraffes, cows, pigs, hippopotamus
    Suborder Perissodactyli: horses, tapirs, rhinoceros
Order †Toxodontia:[10] toxodonts
Order Hyracoidea: hyraxes
Order Proboscidea: elephants
Order Sirenia: manatees
Order Cete
    Suborder †Zeuglodontia: basilosaurids
    Suborder Denticete: dolphins
    Suborder Mysticete: whales
Superorder Ineducabilia
Order Chiroptera
    Suborder Animalivora: bats
    Suborder Frugivora: megabats
Order Insectivora
    Suborder Dermoptera: colugos
    Suborder Insectivora: shrews, moles
Order Glires
    Suborder Simplicidentoti: mice, beavers, squirrels
    Suborder Duplicidentati: rabbits
Order Bruta
    Suborder Vermilinguia: anteaters
    Suborder Squamata: pangolin
    Suborder Fodientia: aardvark
    Suborder Tardigrada: sloth
    Suborder Loricata: armadillos
Subclass Didelphia
Order Marsupialia
    Suborder Rhizophaga: wombats
    Suborder Syndactyli: kangaroos
    Suborder Dasyuromorphia: Tasmanian devils
    Suborder Didelphimorphia: opossums
Subclass Ornithodelphia
Order Monotremata
    Suborder Tachyglossa: echidna
    Suborder Platypoda: platypus

---

[10] The symbol † is used to indicate an extinct taxon.

However, George Gaylord Simpson is usually credited with coming up with the modern classification scheme for mammals. His taxonomy is as follows:

Taxonomy of Simpson (1945)[11]

Class Mammalia
    Subclass Prototheria
        Order Monotremata: echidna, platypus
    Subclass Allotheria
        Order †Multituberculata: multituberculates
    Subclass Theria
    Infraclass Pantotheria
        Order †Pantotheria: pantotheres
        Order †Symmetrodonta: symmetrodonts
    Infraclass Metatheria
        Order Marsupialia
            Superfamilies Didelphoidea: opossums; †Borhyaenoidea: sparassodonts; Dasyuroidea: Tasmanian devil; Perameloidea: bandicoots; Caenolestoidea: shrew opossums; Phalangeroidea: kangaroos
    Infraclass Eutheria
    Cohort Unguiculata
        Order Insectivora
            Superfamilies †Deltatheridioidea: deltatheridioids; Tenrecoidea: African shrews; Chrysochloroidea: golden moles; Erinaceoidea: hedgehogs; Macroscelidoidea: elephant shrews; Soricoidea: shrews and moles; †Pantolestoidea: pantolestoids; †Mixodectoidea: mixodectoids
        Order Dermoptera: colugos
        Order Chiroptera
            Suborder Megachiroptera: megabats
            Suborder Microchiroptera
                Superfamilies Emballonuroidea: sac-winged bats; Rhinolophoidea: horseshoe and leaf-nosed bats; Phyllostomatoidea: vampire bats; Vespertilionoidea: vesper bats
        Order Primates
            Suborder Prosimii

---

[11] George Gaylord Simpson, "The Principles of Classification and a Classification of Mammals," *American Museum of National History Bulletin* 85 (1945): 1–350. See also George Gaylord Simpson, "A New Classification of Mammals," *Bulletin of the American Museum of Natural History* 59 (1933): 259–293; Herluf Winge, *The Interrelationships of the Mammalian Genera*, trans. E. Deichman and G. M. Allen, 3 vols. (Kobenhavn: C. A. Reitzel, 1941).

Infraorder Lemuriformes
    Superfamilies Tupaioidea: tree shrews; Lemuroidea: lemurs; Daubentonioidea: aye-ayes
Infraorder Lorisiformes: galagos and lorises
Infraorder Tarsiiformes: tarsiers
Suborder Anthropoidea
    Superfamilies Ceboidea: new world monkeys; Cercopithecoidea: old world monkeys; Hominoidea: apes and humans
Order †Tillodontia: tillodont
Order †Taeniodonta: taeniodontss
Order Edentata
    Suborder †Palaeanodonta: palaeanodonts
    Suborder Xenarthra
    Infraorder Pilosa
        Superfamilies †Megalonychoidea: giant sloths; Myrmecophagoidea: anteaters; Bradypodoidea: sloths;
    Infraorder Cingulata
        Superfamilies Dasypodoidea: armadillos; and †Glyptodontoidea: glyptodonts
Order Pholidota: pangolins
Cohort Glires
Order Lagomorpha: rabbits
Order Rodentia
    Suborder Sciuromorpha
        Superfamilies Aplodontoidea: aplodontids; Sciuroidea: squirrels; Geomyoidea: kangaroo mice; Castoroidea: beavers; Anomaluroidea: scaly-tailed squirrels
    Suborder Myomorpha
        Superfamilies Muroidea: mice; Gliroidea: dormice; Dipodoidea: jumping mice
    Suborder Hystricomorpha
        Superfamilies Hystricoidea: old world porcupines; Erethizontoidea: new world porcupines; Cavioidea: cavies; Chinchilloidea: chinchillas; Octodontoidea: octodontids; Bathyergoidea: mole-rats; Ctenodactyloidea: gundis
Cohort Mutica
Order Cetacea
    Suborder †Archaeoceti: primitive cetaceans
    Suborder Odontoceti
        Superfamilies †Squalodontoidea: shark-tooth dolphins; Platanistoidea: river dolphins; Physeteroidea: sperm whales; Delphinoidea: dolphins and killer whales
    Suborder Mysticeti: baleen whales
Cohort Ferungulata

Superorder Ferae
    Order Carnivora
        Suborder †Creodonta
            Superfamilies †Arctocyonoidea: arctocyonids; †Mesonychoidea: mesonychids; †Oxyaenoidea: oxyaenids
        Suborder Fissipeda
            Superfamilies †Miacoidea: miacids; Canoidea: bears, dogs, racoons, weasels, badgers; Feloidea: cats, hyaenas, civets
        Suborder Pinnipedia: seals
Superorder Protungulata
    Order †Condylarthra: condylarths
    Order †Litopterna: litopterns
    Order †Notoungulata
        Suborder †Notioprogonia: notioprogons
        Suborder †Toxodonta: toxodonts
        Suborder †Typotheria: typotheres
        Suborder †Hegetotheria: hegototheres
    Order †Astrapotheria
        Suborder †Trigonostylopoidea: trigonostylopids
        Suborder †Astrapotherioidea: astrapotherids
    Order Tubulidentata: aardvarks
Superorder Paenungulata
    Order †Pantodonta: pantodonts
    Order †Dinocerata: dinocerats
    Order †Pyrotheria: pyrotheres
    Order Proboscidea
        Suborder †Moeritherioidea: moeritheres
        Suborder Elephantoidea: elephants
        Suborder †Deinotherioidea: deinotheres
        Suborder †Barytherioidea: barytheres
    Order †Embrithopoda: embrithopods
    Order Hyracoidea: hyraxes
    Order Sirenia
        Suborder Trichechiformes: manatees
        Suborder †Desmostyliformes: demostylids
Superorder Mesaxonia
    Order Perissodactyla
        Suborder Hippomorpha
            Superfamilies Equoidea: horses; †Brontotherioidea: brontotheres; †Chalicotherioidea: chalicotheres
        Suborder Ceratomorpha
            Superfamilies Tapiroidea: tapirs; Rhinocerotoidea: rhinoceroses
Superorder Paraxonia
    Order Artiodactyla
        Suborder Suiformes
        Infraorder †Palaeodonta

Superfamilies †Dichobunoidea; †Entelodontoidea
Infraorder Suina
    Superfamily Suoidea: pigs
Infraorder Ancodonta
    Superfamilies †Anthracotherioidea: anthracotherids; †Cainotherioidea: cainotherids
Infraorder Oreodonta
    Superfamily †Merycoidodontoidea: merycoidodontids
Suborder Tylopoda: camels
Suborder Ruminantia
Infraorder Tragulina
    Superfamilies †Amphimerycoidea: amphimerycids; †Hypertraguloidea: hypertragulids; Traguloidea: chevrotains
Infraorder Pecora
    Superfamilies Cervoidea: deers; Giraffoidea: giraffes; Bovoidea: cows

The most recent systems of mammalian classification are similar to that of Simpson, with there being about 30 orders and 150 families of living mammals,[12] though there is still much dispute about the exact evolutionary relationships of some of the groupings and whether they are paraphyletic or not, such as with the insectivores and rodents. Other problems are whether or not some of the taxa are still based too much on adaptations to environment instead of evolutionary relationships and whether or not the subgroupings should reflect similar degrees of morphological difference and thus be commensurate with other subgroupings. Regarding the first issue, the insectivores have been grouped together primarily based on tooth structure but such structures may have arisen independently from each other. Regarding the second issue, there is much more morphological diversity in the Orders of Carnivora and Artiodactyla than in other orders and this is often not represented in the higher-level taxa.

One much-utilized recent system of mammalian classification is that of McKenna and Bell, and it is the only one to include extinct taxa, even if at times it settles too much for non-objective pragmatic criteria, is too closely tied to a cladistics framework, and has an abundance of categories.

---

[12] Sydney Anderson and J. Knox Jones, Jr., eds., *Orders and Families of Recent Mammals of the World* (Oxford: Wiley, 1984); Benton, Michael J., ed., *The Phylogeny and Classification of the Tetrapods, vol. 2: Mammals* (Oxford: Clarendon Press, 1988); G. B. Corbet and J. E. Hill, *A World List of Mammalian Species* (New York: Facts on File, 1991); N. N. Kalandadze and A. S. Rautian, *Phylogenetics of Mammals* (Moscow: Moscow State University Press, 1992).

McKenna and Bell Taxonomy (1997)[13]

Class Mammalia
    Subclass Prototheria: monotremes
        Order Platypoda
            Family Ornithorhynchidae: platypuses
        Order Tachyglossa
            Family Tachyglossidae: echidnas
    Subclass Theriiformes
        Infraclass †Allotheria
        Order †Multituberculata
            Families   †Plagiaulacidae;   †Bolodontidae   †Hahnodontidae;
            †Albionbaataridae; †Arginbaataridae; †Kogaionidae;
            Suborder †Cimolodonta
            Family †Sloanbaataridae
            Superfamily †Ptilodontoidea
            Families †Cimolodontidae; †Ptilodontidae
            Superfamily †Taeniolabidoidea
            Families †Cimolomyidae; †Eucosmodontidae; †Taeniolabididae
            Suborder †Gondwanatheria
            Families †Ferugliotheriidae; †Sudamericidae
        Infraclass †Triconodonta
            Families   †Austrotriconodontidae;   †Amphilestidae;
            †Triconodontidae
        Infraclass Holotheria
            Family †Chronoperatidae
        Superlegion †Kuehneotheria
            Families †Kuehneotheriidae; †Woutersiidae
        Superlegion Trechnotheria
            Legion †Symmetrodonta
            Family †Shuotheriidae
        Order †Amphidontoidea
            Family †Amphidontidae
        Order †Spalacotherioidea
            Families †Tinodontidae; †Spalacotheriidae; †Barbereniidae
            Legion Cladotheria
            Sublegion †Dryolestoidea
        Order †Dryolestida
            Families   †Dryolestidae;   †Paurodontidae;   †Donodontidae;
            †Mesungulatidae; †Reigitheriidae; †Brandoniidae
        Order †Amphitheriida
            Family †Amphitheriidae
            Sublegion Zatheria

---

[13] Malcolm C. McKenna and Susan K. Bell, *Classification of Mammals Above the Species Level* (New York: Columbia University Press, 1997).

Families †Arguitheriidae; †Arguimuridae; †Vincelestidae
Infralegion †Peramura
Family †Peramuridae
Infralegion Tribosphenida
Family †Necrolestidae
Supercohort †Aegialodontia
Family †Aegialodontidae
Supercohort Theria
Families †Pappotheriidae; †Holoclemensiidae; †Kermackiidae; †Endotheriidae; †Picopsidae; †Potamotelsidae; †Plicatodontidae
Order †Deltatheroida
Families †Deltatheridiidae; †Deltatheroididae
Order †Asiadelphia
Family †Asiatheriidae
Cohort Marsupialia: marsupials
Family †Yingabalanaridae
Suborder †Archimetatheria
Families †Stagodontidae; †Pediomyidae
Magnorder Australidelphia
Superorder Microbiotheria
Family Microbiotheriidae: monito del monte
Superorder Eometatheria
Order †Yalkaparidontia
Family †Yalkaparidontidae
Order Notoryctemorphia
Family Notoryctidae: marsupial moles
Grandorder Dasyuromorphia
Families †Thylacinidae: Tasmanian tiger; Dasyuridae: Tasmanian devil, quolls, numbats
Grandorder Syndactyli
Order Peramelia: bandicoots
Families Peramelidae: bandicoots; Peroryctidae: spiny bandicoots
Order Diprotodontia
Families †Palorchestidae; †Wynardiidae; †Thylacoleonidae; Tarsipedidae: honey possums
Superfamily Vombatoidea
Families †Ilariidae; †Diprotodontidae; Vombatidae: wombats
Superfamily Phalangeroidea
Families Phalangeridae: phalangers; Burramyidae: pygmy possums; Macropodidae: kangaroos and wallabies; Petauridae: marsupial gliders; †Ektopodontidae; Phascolarctidae: koala bears; †Pilkipildridae; †Miralinidae; Acrobatidae: phalangers
Magnorder Ameridelphia
Order Didelphimorphia
Families Didelphidae: opossums; †Sparassocynidae
Order Paucituberculata

Superfamily Caenolestoidea
Families †Sternbergiidae; Caenolestidae: shrew opossums; †Paleothentidae; †Abderitidae
Superfamily †Polydolopoidea
Families †Sillustaniidae; †Polydolopidae; †Prepidolopidae; †Bonapartheriidae
Superfamily †Argyrolagoidea
Families †Argyrolagidae; †Patagoniidae; †Groeberiidae
Superfamily †Caroloameghinioidea
Families †Glasbiidae; †Caroloameghiniidae
Order †Sparassodonta
Families †Mayulestidae; †Hondadelphidae; †Borhyaenidae
Cohort Placentalia: placentals
Order †Bibymalagasia
Magnorder Xenarthra
Order Cingulata
Family †Protobradidae
Superfamily Dasypodoidea
Families Dasypodidae: armadillos; †Peltephilidae
Superfamily †Glyptodontoidea
Families †Pampatheriidae; †Palaeopeltidae; †Glyptodontidae: glyptodonts
Order Pilosa
Family †Entelopidae
Suborder Vermilingua
Families Myrmecophagidae: giant anteaters; Cyclopedidae: pygmy anteaters
Suborder Phyllophaga
Family †Rathymotheriidae
Infraorder †Mylodonta
Superfamily †Mylodontoidea
Families †Scelidotheriidae; †Mylodontidae
Superfamily †Orophodontoidea
Family †Orophodontidae
Infraorder Megatheria
Superfamily Megatherioidea
Families †Megatheriidae: ground sloths; Megalonychidae: two-toed sloths
Superfamily Bradypodoidea
Family Bradypodidae: three-toed sloths
Magnorder Epitheria: epitheres
Superorder †Leptictida
Families †Gypsonictopidae; †Kulbeckiidae; †Didymoconidae; †Leptictidae
Superorder Preptotheria

Grandorder Anagalida
    Families †Zambdalestidae; †Anagalidae; †Pseudictopidae
Mirorder Macroscelidea
    Family Macroscelididae: elephant shrews
Mirorder Duplicidentata
Order †Mimotonida
    Family †Mimotonidae
Order Lagomorpha
    Families Ochotonidae: pikas; Leporidae: rabbits
  Mirorder Simplicidentata
Order †Mixodontia
    Family †Eurymylidae
Order Rodentia: rodents
    Families †Alagomyidae; †Laredomyidae
  Suborder Sciuromorpha
  Superfamily †Ischyromyoidea
    Family †Ischyromyidae
  Superfamily Aplodontoidea
    Families   †Allomyidae;   Aplodontiidae: mountain   beavers;
    †Mylagaulidae
  Infraorder †Theridomyomorpha
    Family †Theridomyidae
  Infraorder Sciurida
    Families †Reithroparamyidae; Sciuridae: squirrels
  Infraorder Castorimorpha
        Families †Eutypomyidae; Castoridae: beavers; †Rhizospalacidae
  Suborder Myomorpha
      Family †Protoptychidae
  Infraorder Myodonta
  Superfamily Dipodoidea
    Families †Armintomyidae; Dipodidae: jumping mice and jerboas
  Superfamily Muroidea
    Families †Simimyidae; Muridae: rats and mice
  Infraorder Glirimorpha
    Family Myoxidae: dormice
  Infraorder Geomorpha
  Superfamily †Eomyoidea
    Family †Eomyidae
  Superfamily Geomyoidea
    Families †Florentiamyidae; Geomyidae: pocket gophers, pocket
    mice, and kangaroo rats
  Suborder Anomaluromorpha
  Superfamily Pedetoidea
    Families †Parapedetidae; Pedetidae: springhaas
  Superfamily Anomaluroidea
        Families †Zegdoumyidae; Anomaluridae: scaly-tailed squirrels

Suborder Sciuravida
    Families †Ivanantoniidae; †Sciuravidae; †Chapattimyidae; †Cylindrodontidae; Ctenodactylidae: gundis
Suborder Hystricognatha
    Family †Tsaganomyidae
Infraorder Hystricognathi
    Families Hystricidae: Old World porcupines; Erethizontidae: New World porcupines; †Myophiomyidae; †Diamantomyidae; †Phiomyidae; †Kenyamyidae; Petromuridae: rock rats; Thryonomyidae: cane rats
Parvorder Bathyergomorphi
    Families Bathyergidae: mole-rats; †Bathyergoididae
Parvorder Caviida
    Superfamily Cavioidea
        Families Agoutidae: agoutis and pacas; †Eocardiidae; Dinomyidae: pacaranas; Caviidae: cavies; Hydrochoeridae: capybaras
    Superfamily Octodontoidea
        Families Octodontidae: degus, tuco-tucos; Echimyidae: spiny rats, nutria; Capromyidae: hutias; †Heptaxodontidae
    Superfamily Chinchilloidea
        Families Chinchillidae: chinchillas; †Neoepiblemidae; Abrocomidae: rat chinchillas
Grandorder Ferae
Order Cimolesta
    Family †Palaeoryctidae
Suborder †Didelphodonta
    Family †Cimolestidae
Suborder †Apatotheria
    Family †Apatemyidae
Suborder †Taeniodonta
    Family †Stylinodontidae
Suborder †Tillodonta
    Family †Tillotheriidae
Suborder †Pantodonta
    Family †Wangliidae
    Superfamily †Bemalambdoidea
        Families †Harpyodidae; †Bemalambdidae
    Superfamily †Pantolambdoidea
        Families †Pastoralodontidae; †Titanoideidae; †Pantolambdidae; †Barylambdidae; †Cyriacotheriidae; †Pantolambdodontidae
    Superfamily †Coryphodontoidea
        Family †Coryphodontidae
Suborder †Pantolesta
    Families †Pantolestidae; †Paroxyclaenidae; †Ptolemaiidae
Suborder Pholidota

Families   †Epoicotheriidae;   †Metacheiromyidae;   Manidae: pangolins
  Suborder †Ernanodonta
    Family †Ernanodontidae
Order †Creodonta: creodonts
    Families †Hyaenodontidae; †Oxyaenidae
Order Carnivora: carnivores
  Suborder Feliformia
    Families †Viverravidae; †Nimravidae; Felidae: cats; Viverridae: civets, Asiatic palm civets; Herpestidae: mongooses; Hyaenidae: hyaenas, aardwolf; Nandiniidae: African palm civets
  Suborder Caniformia
    Family †Miacidae
  Infraorder Cynoidea
    Family Canidae: dogs
  Infraorder Arctoidea
Parvorder Ursida
  Superfamily †Amphicyonoidea
    Family †Amphicyonidae
  Superfamily Ursoidea
    Families Ursidae: bears; †Hemicyonidae
  Superfamily Phocoidea
    Families Otariidae: eared seals; Phocidae: walruses
Parvorder Mustelida
    Families Mustelidae: weasels and skunks; Procyonidae; ringtails, olingos, kinkajous, raccoons, coatis, red pandas
Grandorder Lipotyphla
    Family †Adapisoriculidae
Order Chrysochloridea
    Family Chrysochloridae: golden moles
Order Erinaceomorpha
    Families   †Sespedectidae;   †Amphilemuridae;   †Adapisoricidae; †Creotarsidae
  Superfamily Erinaceoidea
    Family Erinaceidae: hedgehogs and relatives
  Superfamily Talpoidea
    Families †Proscalopidae; Talpidae: moles; †Dimylidae
Order Soricomorpha
    Families †Otlestidae; †Geolabididae
  Superfamily Soricoidea
    Family †Nesophontidae: west Indian shrews; †Micropternodontidae; †Apternodontidae; Solenodontidae: solenodons; †Plesiosoricidae; †Nyctitheriidae; Soricidae: shrews
  Superfamily Tenrecoidea
    Family Tenrecidae: tenrecs

Grandorder Archonta
Order Chiroptera: bats
    Suborder Megachiroptera
        Family Pteropodidae: flying foxes
    Suborder Microchiroptera
        Families †Archaeonycteridae; †Paleochiropterygidae; †Hassianycterididae; Emballonuridae: sac-winged bats
    Infraorder Yinochiroptera
    Superfamily Rhinopomatoidea
        Families Rhinopomatidae: mouse-tailed bats; Craseonycteridae: bumblebee bats
    Superfamily Rhinolophoidea
        Families Megadermatidae: false vampire bats; Nycteridae: hispid bats; Rhinolophidae: horseshoe and Old World leaf-nosed bats
    Infraorder Yangochiroptera
        Family Mystacinidae: New Zealand short-tailed bats
    Superfamily Noctilionoidea
        Families Noctilionidae: fishing bats; Mormoopidae: spectacled bats; Phyllostomidae: New World leaf-nosed and vampire bats
    Superfamily Vespertilionoidea
        Families †Philisidae; Molossidae: free-tailed bats; Natalidae: funnel-eared bats; Furipteridae: smoky bats; Thyropteridae: New World sucker-footed bats; Myzopodidae: Old World sucker-footed bats; Vespertilionidae: common bats
Order Primates: primates
        Families †Purgatoriidae; †Microsyopidae; †Micromomyidae; †Picromomyidae; †Plesiadapidae; †Palaechthonidae; †Picrodontidae
    Suborder Dermoptera
        Families †Paramomyidae; †Plagiomenidae; †Mixodectidae; Galeopithecidae: colugos
    Suborder Euprimates
    Infraorder Strepsirrhini
        Family †Plesiopithecidae
    Superfamily Daubentonioidea
        Family Daubentoniidae: aye-ayes
    Superfamily Lemuroidea
        Families †Adapidae; Lemuridae: lemurs
    Superfamily Loroidea
        Families Lorisidae: lorises and galagos; Cheirogaleidae: dwarf lemurs
    Superfamily Indroidea
        Families †Archaeolemuridae; †Palaeopropithecidae; Indriidae: indris and sifakas
    Infraorder Haplorhini

Parvorder Tarsiiformes
    Superfamily †Carpolestoidea
        Family †Carpolestidae
    Superfamily Tarsioidea
        Families †Omomyidae; †Microchoeridae; †Afrotarsiidae; Tarsiidae: tarsiers
Parvorder Anthropoidea
        Families †Eosimiidae; †Parapithecidae
    Superfamily Cercopithecoidea
        Families †Pliopithecidae; Cercopithecidae: Old World monkeys and colobuses; Hominidae: humans and apes
    Superfamily Callitrichoidea
        Families Callitrichidae: marmosets; Atelidae: New World monkeys
Order Scandentia
        Family Tupaiidae: tree shrews
Grandorder Ungulata: ungulates
Order Tubulidentata
        Family Orycteropodidae: aardvarks
Order †Dinocerata
        Family †Uintatheriidae
Mirorder Eparctocyona
Order †Procreodi
        Families †Oxyclaenidae; †Arctocyonidae
Order †Condylarthra
        Families †Hyopsodontidae; †Mioclaenidae; †Phenacodontidae; †Periptychidae; †Pellgrotheriidae; †Didolodontidae
Order †Arctostylopida
        Family †Arctostylopidae
Order Cete: whales and relatives
    Suborder †Acreodi
        Families †Triisodontidae; †Mesonychidae: mesonychids; †Hapalodectidae
    Suborder Cetacea
    Infraorder †Archaeoceti
        Families †Basilosauridae; †Protocetidae; †Remingtonocetidae
    Infraorder Autoceta
        Family †Agorophiidae
    Superfamily †Squalodontoidea
        Families †Squalodontidae; †Rhabdosteidae
Parvorder Mysticeti
        Families †Aetiocetidae; †Mammalodontidae; †Cetotheriidae; Balaenopteridae: rorquals and grey whales; Balaenidae: right and bowhead whales
Parvorder Odontoceti
    Superfamily Physeteroidea
        Family Physeteridae: sperm whales

Superfamily Hyperoodontoidea
    Family Hyperoodontidae: beaked whales
Superfamily Platanistoidea
    Family Platanistidae: river dolphins
Superfamily Delphinoidea
    Families Delphinidae: dolphins; Pontoporiidae: La Plata River
    dolphins; Lipotidae: baiijis; Iniidae: Amazon River dolphins;
    †Kentridontidae;   Monodontidae: beluga   and   narwhal;
    †Odobenocetopsidae; †Dalpiazinidae; †Acrodelphinidae; Phocoenidae:
    porpoises; †Albireonidae; †Hemisyntrachelidae
Order Artiodactyla: even-toed ungulates
    Suborder Suiformes
        Families †Raoellidae; †Choeropotamidae
    Superfamily Suoidea
        Families Suidae: pigs; Tayassuidae: peccaries; †Santheriidae;
        Hippopotamidae: hippopotamus
    Superfamily †Dichobunoidea
        Families   †Dichobunidae;   †Cebochoeridae;   †Mixtotheriidae;
        †Helohyidae
    Superfamily †Anthracotherioidea
        Families †Haplobunodontidae; †Anthracotheriidae
    Superfamily †Anoplotherioidea
        Families †Dacrytheriidae; †Anoplotheriidae; †Cainotheriidae
    Superfamily †Oreodontoidea
        Families †Agriochoeridae; †Oreodontidae
    Superfamily †Entelodontoidea
        Family †Entelodontidae
    Suborder Tylopoda
        Family †Xiphodontidae
    Superfamily Cameloidea
        Families Camelidae: camels and llamas; †Oromerycidae
    Superfamily †Protoceratoidea
        Family †Protoceratidae
    Suborder Ruminantia
        Families †Amphimerycidae; †Hypertragulidae; Tragulidae: mouse
        deer;   †Leptomerycidae;   †Bachitheriidae;   †Lophiomerycidae;
        †Gelocidae
    Superfamily Cervoidea
        Families Moschidae: musk deer; Antilocapridae: pronghorn
        antelopes; †Palaeomerycidae; †Hoplitomerycidae; Cervidae: deer
    Superfamily Giraffoidea
        Families †Climacoceratidae; Giraffidae: giraffes and okapis
    Superfamily Bovoidea
        Family Bovidae: cows and antelope
Mirorder †Meridiungulata
        Families †Perutheriidae; †Amilnedwardsiidae

Order †Litopterna
    Family †Protolipternidae
    Superfamily †Macrauchenioidea
        Families †Macraucheniidae; †Notonychopidae; †Adianthidae
    Superfamily †Proterotherioidea
        Family †Proterotheriidae
Order †Notoungulata: notoungulates
    Suborder †Notioprogonia
        Families †Henricosborniidae; †Notostylopidae
    Suborder †Toxodontia
        Families   †Isotemnidae;   †Leontiniidae;   †Notohippidae; †Toxodontidae; and †Homalodotheriidae
    Suborder †Typotheria
        Families †Archaeopithecidae; †Oldfieldthomasiidae; †Interatheriidae; †Campanorcidae; †Mesotheriidae
    Suborder †Hegetotheria
        Families †Archaeohyracidae; †Hegetotheriidae
Order †Astrapotheria
        Families   †Eoastrapostylopidae;   †Trigonostylopidae; †Astrapotheriidae
Order †Xenungulata
    Family †Carodniidae
Order †Pyrotheria
    Family †Pyrotheriidae
Mirorder Altungulata
Order Perissodactyla: odd-toed ungulates
    Suborder Hippomorpha
        Families Equidae: horses; †Palaeotheriidae
    Suborder Ceratomorpha
    Infraorder †Selenida
    Superfamily †Brontotherioidea
        Families †Brontotheriidae; †Anchilophidae
    Superfamily †Chalicotherioidea
        Families †Eomoropidae; †Chalicotheriidae
    Infraorder Tapiromorpha
    Superfamily Rhinocerotoidea
        Families †Hyracodontidae; Rhinocerotidae: rhinoceroses
    Superfamily Tapiroidea
        Families   †Helaletidae;   †Isectolophidae;   †Lophiodontidae; †Deperetellidae; †Lophialetidae; Tapiridae: tapirs
Order Uranotheria
    Suborder Hyracoidea
        Families †Pliohyracidae; Procaviidae: hyraxes
    Suborder †Embrithopoda
        Families †Phenacolophidae; †Arsinoitheriidae
    Suborder Tethytheria

Infraorder Sirenia
Families †Prorastomidae; Dugongidae: dugongs; Trichechidae: manatees
Infraorder Behemota
Parvorder †Desmostylia
Family †Desmostylidae
Parvorder Proboscidea
Families †Anthracobunidae; †Moeritheriidae; †Numidotheriidae; †Barytheriidae; †Deinotheriidae; †Palaeomastodontidae; †Phiomiidae; †Hemimastodontidae
Superfamily ‡Mammutoidea
Family †Mammutidae: mastodons
Superfamily Elephantoidea
Families †Gomphotheriidae: gomphotheres; Elephantidae: elephants

More recently data have suggested other evolutionary relationships that are not reflected in McKenna-Bell, some at a higher superorder level, and others involving lower-level relations of insectivores, marsupials, rodents, and primates.[14] Such studies have led to the classification of extant

---

[14] Early genetic studies of mammalian phylogeny include: Mark S. Springer, et al., "Endemic African Mammals Shake the Phylogenetic Tree," *Nature* 388, no. 6637 (1997): 61–64; Michael J. Stanhope, et al., "Molecular Evidence for Multiple Origins of the Insectivora and for a New Order of Endemic African Mammals," *Proceedings of the National Academy of Sciences* 95, no. 17 (1998): 9967–9972; John Gatesy, Patrick O'Grady, and Richard H. Baker, "Corroboration among Data Sets in Simultaneous Analysis: Hidden Support for Phylogenetic Relationships among Higher Level Artiodactyl Taxa," *Cladistics* 15 (1999): 271–313; William J. Murphy, et al., "Molecular Phylogenetics and the Origins of Placental Mammals," *Nature* 409, no. 6820 (2001): 614–618; C. J. Douady, et al., "Molecular Phylogenetic Evidence Confirming the Eulipotyphla Concept and in Support of Hedgehogs as the Sister Group to Shrews," *Molecular Phylogenetics and Evolution* 25, no. 1 (2002): 200–209; Mark S. Springer, et al., "Molecules Consolidate the Placental Mammal Tree," *Trends in Ecology and Evolution* 19, no. 8 (2004): 430–438. Recent studies have led to the proposal of four to six placental mammalian (Eutherian) clades or superorders in addition to the Monotreme and Marsupial clades: Xenarthra [Pilosa (anteaters and sloths) and Cingulata (armadillos)]; Euarchontoglires or Glires [Lagomorpha (rabbits), Primates (monkeys), and Rodentia (rodents)]; Laurasiatheria or Therictoidea or Boreotheria [Carnivora (dogs and cats), Chiroptera (bats), Insectivora (shrews), Pholidota (pangolins), and Scandentia (tree shrews)]; Ungulata [Artiodactyla, Cetacea, and Perissodactyla]; Afrotheria or Paenungulata [(Hyracoidea (hyraxes), Proboscidea (elephants), Sirenia (manatees), Tubulidentata (aardvark), Macroscelidea (elephant shrews), and Afrosoricida (tenrecs)]. See, for instance: Hidenori Nishihara, et al., "Retroposon

mammals proposed by Wilson and Reeder in 2005 and Burgin, Colella, Kahn, and Upham in 2018. The newer systems, in part on account of their focus on living mammals, have also reduced the number of subcategories that tended to proliferate in McKenna and Bell's system. There are some unique features of each, such as Burgin's system grouping whales under the Order Artiodactyla instead of a separate Order Cetacea. The influential mammalian classification schema of Wilson and Reeder (2005) and Burgin, Colella, Kahn, and Upham (2018) are as follows:

Taxonomy of Wilson and Reeder (2005)[15]

Class Mammalia
 Order Monotremata
  Families Tachyglossidae: echidnas; Ornithorhynchidae: platypus
 Order Didelphimorphia
  Family Didelphidae: opossums
 Order Paucituberculata
  Family Caenolestidae: shrew opposums
 Order Microbiotheria
  Family Microbiotheriidae: monito del monte
 Order Notorcytemorphia
  Family Notoryctidae: marsupial moles
 Order Dasyuromorphia
  Families Thylacinidae: Tasmanian wolf; Myrmecobiidae: numbats; Dasyuridae: marsupial shrews, Tasmanian Devil

---

Analysis and Recent Geological Data Suggest Near-Simultaneous Divergence of the Three Superorders of Mammals," *Proceedings of the National Academy of Sciences* 106, no. 13 (2009): 5235–5240; Nicole M. Foley, Mark S. Springer, and Emma C. Teeling, "Mammal Madness: Is the Mammal Tree of Life not yet Resolved?" *Philosophical Transactions of the Royal Society of London B: Biological Sciences* 371, no. 1699 (2016): 20150140; Gillian C. Gibb, et al., "Shotgun Mitogenomics Provides a Reference Phylogenetic Framework and Timescale for Living Xenarthrans," *Molecular Biology and Evolution* 33, no. 3 (2016): 621–642.

[15] Don E. Wilson and DeeAnn M. Reeder, *Mammal Species of the World: A Taxonomic and Geographic Reference*, 2 vols. (Baltimore: John Hopkins University Press, 2005). See also Ronald M. Nowak, *Walker's Mammals of the World* (Baltimore: Johns Hopkins University Press, 1999); Robert Martin, Ronald Pine, and Anthony F. DeBlase, *A Manual of Mammalogy with Keys to Families of the World* (Dubuque: William C. Brown, 2000); Don E. Wilson and Russell Mittermeier, eds., *Handbook of the Mammals of the World*, 9 vols. (Barcelona: Lynx Edicions, 2009-2019); Frank E. Zachos and Robert J. Asher, eds., *Mammalian Evolution, Diversity and Systematics* (Berlin: Walter de Gruyter, 2018).

Order Peramelemorphia
     Families Thylacomyidae: bilbies; Chaeropodidae: pig-footed bandicoot;
     Peramelidae: bandicoots
Order Diprotodontia
   Suborder Vombatiformes
     Families Phascolarctidae: koalas; Vombatidae: wombats
   Suborder Phalangeriformes
   Superfamily Phalangeroidea
     Families Burramyidae: pigmy possums; Phalangeridae: cuscuses
   Superfamily Petauroidea
     Families Pseudocheiridae: ringtailed possums; Petauridae: gliding
     possums; Tarsipedidae: honey possum; Acrobatidae: feather-tailed
     possums
   Suborder Macropodiformes
     Families Hypsiprymnodontidae: rat kangarooos; Potoroidae: bettongs;
     Macropodidae: kangaroos
Order Tubulidentata
     Family Orycteropodidae: aardvarks
Order Sirenia
     Families Dugongidae: dugong; Trichechidae: manatees
Order Afrosoricida
   Suborder Tenrecomorpha
     Family Tenrecidae: tenrecs
   Suborder Chrysochloridea
     Family Chrysochloridae: golden moles
Order Macroscelidea
     Family Macroscelididae: elephant shrews
Order Hyracoidea
     Family Procaviidae; hyraxes
Order Proboscidea
     Family Elephantidae: elephants
Order Cingulata
     Family Dasypodidae: armadillos
Order Pilosa
   Suborder Folivora
     Families Bradypodidae: three-toed sloths; Megalonychidae: two-toed
     sloths
   Suborder Vermilingua
     Families Cyclopedidae: silky anteaters; Myrmecophagidae: anteaters
Order Scandentia
     Families Tupaiidae: tree shrews; Ptilocercidae: pen-tailed tree shrews
Order Dermoptera
     Family Cynocephalidae: colugos
Order Primates
   Suborder Strepsirrhini
   Infraorder Lemuriformes

Superfamily Cheirogaleoidea
    Family Cheirogaleidae: mouse lemurs
Superfamily Lemuroidea
    Families Lemuridae: lemurs; Lepilemuridae: sportive lemurs; Indridae:
    indris
Infraorder Chiromyiformes
    Family Daubentoniidae: aye-ayes
Infraorder Lorisiformes
    Families Lorisidae: lorisids; Galagidae: galagos
Suborder Haplorrhini
Infraorder Tarsiiformes
    Family Tarsiidae: tarsiers
Infraorder Simiiformes
    Families Cebidae: capuchins; Aotidae: night monkeys; Pitheciidae: titis;
    Atelidae: spider monkeys
Superfamily Cercopithecoidea
    Family Cercopithecidae: macaques
Superfamily Hominoidea
    Families Hylobatidae: gibbons; Hominidae: apes
Order Rodentia
Suborder Sciuromorpha
    Families Aplodontiidae: mountain beavers; Sciuridae: squirrels;
    Gliridae: dormice
Suborder Castorimorpha
    Families Castoridae: beavers; Heteromyidae: kangaroo rats; Geomyidae:
    gophers
Suborder Myomorpha
Superfamily Dipodoidea
    Family Dipodidae: jerboas
Superfamily Muroidea
    Families Platacanthomyidae: spiny dormice; Spalacidae: mole-rats;
    Calomyscidae: mouse-like hamsters; Nesomyidae: African rock mice;
    Cricetidae: hamsters, voles, lemmings; Muridae: mice
Suborder Anomaluromorpha
    Families Anomaluridae: scaly-tailed squirrels; Pedetidae: springhares
Suborder Hystricomorpha
Infraorder Ctenodactylomorphi
    Family Ctenodactylidae: gundis
Infraorder Hystricognathi
    Families Bathyergidae: mole-rats; Hystricidae: Old World porcupines;
    Petromuridae: dassie rats; Thryonomyidae: cane rats; Erethizontidae:
    New World porcupines; Chinchillidae: chinchillas; Dinomyidae:
    pacaranas; Caviidae: cavies and guinea pigs; Dasyproctidae: agoutis;
    Cuniculidae: pacas; Ctenomyidae: tuco-tucos; Octodontidae: degus;
    Abrocomidae: chinchilla rats; Echimyidae: spiny rats; Myocastoridae:
    nutrias; Capromyidae: hutias; Heptaxodontidae: giant hutias

Order Lagomorpha
　　Families Ochotonidae: pikas; Prolagidae: prolagids; Leporidae: rabbits
Order Ereinaceomorpha
　　Family Erinaceidae: hedgehogs
Order Soricomorpha
　　Families Nesophontidae: West Indian shrews; Solenodontidae: solenodons; Soricidae: shrews; Talpidae: moles
Order Chiroptera
　　Families Pteropodidae: megabats; Rhinolophidae: horseshoe bats; Hipposideridae: Old World leaf-nosed bats; Megadermatidae: false vampire bats; Rhinopomatidae: mouse-tailed bats; Craseonycteridae: hog-nosed bats; Emballonuridae: sac-winged bats; Nycteridae: slit-faced bats; Myzopodidae: myzopods; Mystacinidae: short-tailed bats; Phyllostomidae: New World leaf-nosed bats; Mormoopidae: ghost-faced bats; Noctilionidae: bulldog bats; Furipteridae: smoky bats; Thyropteridae: disc-winged bats; Natalidae: funnel-eared bats; Molossidae: free-tailed bats; Vespertilionidae: vesper bats
Order Pholidota
　　Family Manidae: pangolins
Order Carnivora
　Suborder Feliformia
　　Families Felidae: cats; Viverridae: civets; Eupleridae: Malagasy carnivores; Nandiniidae: palm civet; Herpestidae: mongoose; Hyaenidae: hyaenas
　Suborder Caniformia
　　Families Canidae: dogs; Ursidae: bears; Otariidae: eared seals; Odobenidae: walrus; Phocidae: earless seals; Mustelidae: weasels and badgers; Mephitidae: skunks; Procyonidae: racoons; Ailuridae: red pandas
Order Perissodactyla
　　Families Equidae: horses; Tapiridae: tapirs; Rhinocerotidae: rhinoceroses
Order Artiodactyla
　　Families Suidae: pigs; Tayassuidae: peccaries; Hippopotamidae: hippopotamus; Camelidae: camels; Tragulidae: chevrotains; Moschidae: musk deers; Cervidae: deers Antilocapridae: antelope; Giraffidae: giraffes; Bovidae: cows, goats, sheep
Order Cetacea
　Suborder Mysticeti
　　Families Balaenidae: right whales; Balaenopteridae: rorquals; Eschrichtiidae: gray whales Neobalaenidae: pygmy right whale
　Suborder Odontoceti
　　Families Delphinidae: oceanic dolphins; Monodontidae: narwhal; Phocoenidae: porpoises; Physeteridae: sperm whales; Platanistidae: river dolphins; Iniidae: South American river dolphins; Ziphiidae: beaked whales

Taxonomy of Burgin, Colella, Kahn, and Upham (2018)[16]

Class Mammalia
    Subclass Prototheria
        Order Monotremata
            Families Ornithorhynchidae: platypus; Tachyglossidae: echidnas
    Subclass Theria
    Infraclass Marsupialia
        Order Didelphimorphia
            Family Didelphidae: opossums
        Order Paucituberculata
            Family Caenolestidae: shrew opossum
        Order Microbiotheria
            Family Microbiotheriidae: monito del monte
        Order Notoryctemorphia
            Family Notoryctidae: marsupial moles
        Order Dasyuromorpha
            Families Dasyuridae: Tasmanian devil; Myrmecobiidae: numbats; †Thylacinidae
        Order Peramelemorphia
            Families †Chaeropodidae; Peramelidae: bandicoots; Thylacomyidae: bilbies
        Order Diprotodontia
            Families Acrobatidae: feather-tailed possums; Burramyidae: pygmy possums; Hypsiprymnodontidae: rat kangaroos; Petauridae: wrist-winged gliding possums; Phalangeridae: cuscusses; Phascolarctidae: koalas; Potoroidae: bettongs; Vombatidae: wombats
    Infraclass Placentalia
    Superorder Afrotheria
        Order Tubulidentata
            Family Orycteropodidae: aardvarks
        Order Afrosoricida
            Families Chrysochloridae: golden moles; Potamogalidae: otter shrews; Tenrecidae: tenrecs
        Order Macroscelidea
            Family Macroscelididae: elephant shrews
        Order Hyracoidea
            Family Procaviidae: hyraxes
        Order Proboscidea
            Family Elephantidae: elephants
        Order Sirenia
            Families Dugongidae: dugongs; Trichechidae: manitees

---

[16] Connor J. Burgin, Jocelyn P. Colella, Philip L. Kahn, and Nathan S. Upham, "How Many Species of Mammals Are There?," *Journal of Mammalogy* 99, no. 1 (2018): 1–14.

Superorder Xenarthra
    Order Cingulata
        Families Chlamyphoridae: South-American armadillos; Dasypodidae: armadillos
    Order Pilosa
        Families Bradypodidae: three-toed sloth; Cyclopedidae: silky anteater; Megalonychidae: two-toed sloths; Myrmecophagidae: anteaters
Superorder Euarchontoglires
    Order Scandentia
        Families Ptilocercidae: pen-tailed tree shrew; Tupaiidae: tree shrews
    Order Dermoptera
        Family Cynocephalidae: colugos
    Order Primates
        Families †Archaeolemuridae; Atelidae: spider monkeys; Cebidae: capuchin monkeys; Cercopithecidae: macaques and baboons; Cheirogaleidae: dwarf lemurs; Daubentoniidae: aye-ayes; Galagidae: galagos; Hominidae: ape; Hylobatidae: gibbons; Indriidae: indriid lemurs; Lemuridae: lemurs; Lepilemuridae: sportive lemurs; Lorisidae: lorisis; †Megaladapidae; †Palaeopropithecida; Pitheciidae: titis; Tarsiidae: tarsiers
    Order Lagomorpha
        Families Leporidae: rabbits; Ochotonidae: pikas; †Prolagidae
    Order Rodentia
        Families Abrocomidae: chinchilla rats; Anomaluridae: scaly-tailed squirrels; Aplodontiidae: mountain beavers; Bathyergidae: blesmols; Calomyscidae: mouse-like hamster; Capromyidae: hutias; Castoridae: beavers; Caviidae: cavies; Chinchillidae: chinchillas; Cricetidae: hamsters, voles, lemmings; Ctenodactylidae: gundis; Ctenomyidae: tuco-tucos; Cuniculidae: pacas; Dasyproctidae: agoutis; Diatomyidae: Laotian rock rat; Dinomyidae: pacaranas; Dipodidae: dipodids; Echimyidae: spiny rats ; Erethizontidae: New World porcupines; Geomyidae: gophers; Gliridae: dormice; Heterocephalidae: naked mole-rats; Heteromyidae: kangaroo rats; Hystricidae: Old World porcupines; Muridae: mice; Nesomyidae: Malagasy giant rats; Octodontidae: viscacha rats; Pedetidae: springhares; Petromuridae: dassie rats; Platacanthomyidae: spiny dormice; Sciuridae: squirrels; Sminthidae: birch mouse; Spalacidae: spalacids; Thryonomyidae: cane rats; Zapodidae: jumping mice; Zenkerellidae: Cameroon scaly-tail rat
Superorder Laurasiatheria
    Order Eulipotyphla
        Families Erinaceidae: hedgehogs; †Nesophontidae; Solenodontidae: selonodons; Soricidae: shrews; Talpidae: moles
    Order Chiroptera
        Families Cistugidae: cistugos; Craseonycteridae: Kitti's hog-nosed bat; Emballonuridae: sac-winged bats; Furipteridae: smoky and thumbless bats; Hipposideridae: Old World leaf-nosed bats; Megadermatidae: false

vampire bats; Miniopteridae: bent-winged bats; Molossidae: free-tailed bats; Mormoopidae: ghost-faced bats; Mystacinidae: New Zealand short-tailed bats; Myzopodidae: sucker-footed bat; Natalidae: funnel-eared bats; Noctilionidae: bulldog bats; Nycteridae: hollow-faced bats; Phyllostomidae: New World leaf-nosed bats, vampire bats; Pteropodidae: megabats; Rhinolophidae: horseshoe bats; Rhinonycteridae: nose-leafed bats; Rhinopomatidae: mouse-tailed bats; Thyropteridae: disk-winged bats; Vespertilionidae: simple-nosed bats

Order Carnivora

Families Ailuridae: red panda; Canidae: dogs; Eupleridae: Malagasy mongoose; Felidae: cats; Herpestidae: mongoose; Hyaenidae: hyaenas; Mephitidae: skunks; Mustelidae: weasels, badgers, otters; Nandiniidae: African palm civet; Odobenidae: walrus; Otariidae: eared seals; Phocidae: earless seals; Prionodontidae: linsangs; Procyonidae: racoons; Ursidae: bears; Viverridae: civets

Order Pholidota

Family Manidae: pangolins

Order Perissodactyla

Families Equidae: horses; Rhinocerotidae: rhinoceros; Tapiridae: tapirs

Order Artiodactyla

Families Antilocapridae: antelopes; Balaenidae: baleen whales; Balaenopteridae: rorquals; Bovidae: cows, sheep, and goats; Camelidae: camels; Cervidae: deer; Delphinidae: dolphins; Eschrichtiidae: gray whales; Giraffidae: giraffe; Hippopotamidae: hippopotamus; Iniidae: South American river dolphins; Kogiidae: sperm whales; Lipotidae: river dolphins; Monodontidae: narwhals and beluga whales; Moschidae: musk deer; Neobalaenidae: baleen whales; Phocoenidae: porpoises; Physeteridae: sperm whales; Platanistidae: Asian river dolphins; Pontoporiidae: La Plata dolphin; Suidae: pigs; Tayassuidae: peccaries; Tragulidae: chevrotains; Ziphiidae: beaked whales

Philosophical Debates about Systematics

Philosophical debates about the best approach to systematics continued throughout this period. In the 1960s and 1970s the phenetic school (also called numerical taxonomy, taximetrics, or the Neo-Adansonian movement) gained traction, especially in regard to the classification of insects, bacteria, angiosperm plants, and the use of molecular genetics in classification. The phenetic approach argued that the best way to uncover the phylogentic or evolutionary relationships in nature is to use computer algorithms to group or cluster organisms together on the basis of overall similarity. That is, in order to avoid biases, one should use as many character traits as possible and give each of them equal weight in classifying; each is assigned a numerical degree (say 1 to 5) or discrete numerical state (0 or 1). So classification should be polythetic, or based on a large amount of equally-weighted character traits, rather than monothetic, or based upon just a few prioritized character traits. There are several problems, however, with the phenetic approach. One is that there are certain character traits, such as possession of mammary glands or pouches that seem highly indicative of phylogeny and thus should be given preference. Indeed, weighing character traits equally can result in classifications that do not reflect phylogeny due to convergent evolution or adaptive radiation. That is, different groups of organisms may independently evolve similar characteristics and closely-related groups may diverge to a great morphological degree over time. So the phenetic method has a hard time distinguishing between apomorphies or traits that evolve independently in separate lineages and plesiomorphies or traits inherited from a common ancestor. As the philosopher Quine has also warned, data are usually theory-laden so supposedly unbiased collection and multivariate analysis of data can be driven by biased investigative choices. Indeed there is an assumption made here that grouping together the most similar taxa in light of a multitude of characters will produce the best phylogenetic classification, i.e. will accord with evolutionary descent. But this is a questionable assumption and likely to fail at times.[17]

---

[17] On phenetics, or numerical taxonomy under the Neo-Adansonian school, i.e. the use of a multitude of unweighted characteristics and multivariate statistical analysis to classify organisms, see: Sergius G. Kiriakoff, "On the Neo-Adansonian School," *Systematic Zoology* 11, no. 4 (1962): 180–185; Joseph H. Camin and Robert R. Sokal, "A Method for Deducing Branching Sequences in Phylogeny," *Evolution* 19, no. 3 (1965): 311–326; Sergius G. Kiriakoff, "Some Remarks on Sokal and Sneath's Principles of Numerical Taxonomy," *Systematic Zoology* 14, no. 1 (1965): 61–64; Ernst Mayr, "Numerical Phenetics and Taxonomic Theory," *Systematic Zoology* 14 (1965): 73–97; Robert R. Sokal and Joseph H. Camin, "The Two Taxonomies: Areas of Agreement and Conflict," *Systematic Zoolology* 1 (1965): 176–195; Nicholas Jardine and Robert Sibson, *Mathematical Taxonomy* (London: John Wiley and Sons, 1971); Robert R. Sokal and Peter H. A. Sneath, *Principles of Numerical Taxonomy* (San Francisco: W. H. Freeman, 1973); Harold T. Clifford and William Stephenson, *An Introduction to Numerical Classification* (New York: Academic Press, 1975); James S. Ferris, "On the Phenetic Approach to Vertebrate Classification," in in *Major Patterns in Vertebrate Evolution*, ed. Max K. Hecht, Peter C. Goody, and Bessie M. Hecht (New York: Plenum Press, 1977), 823–850; Peter H. A. Sneath, "Thirty Years of Numerical Taxonomy," *Systematic Biology* 44, no. 3 (1995): 281–298. The system of phenetics, however, has problems in that though unweighted characters can be useful in resolving taxonomy, some characteristics are wholly indifferent to the process, and others are quite revelatory of evolutionary descent, such as Marsupial pouches, and should be given prominence.

Prior to phenetics in the 1950s the approach called cladistics became popular, and in fact is a major methodology still in use. Cladistics dedicated itself to classifying according to evolutionary relationships or clades above all else and so potentially multiplying taxa indefinitely and focusing on morphological or genetic traits that reflect common lines of descent. Cladists hence work on identifying and classifying on the basis of character traits that reflect evolutionary relationships and are synapomorphies (homologies) or traits unique to a lineage of descendants rather than symplesiomorphies or traits shared with more primitive ancestors of a clade and perhaps with members not in one's clade, or homoplasies or traits that have evolved independently. The cladist thus wants to make sure that all taxonomic designations represent monophyletic groups, groups with a nearest common ancestor, and avoid both polyphletic taxa, or taxa that do not share a nearest common ancestor and instead represent independent evolutionary lineages, and even paraphyletic taxa or groups descending from a common ancestor but not including all descendent groups. As a result systematic ranks of the same level (i.e. Class, Order, Family, etc.) are not necessarily equivalent and may exhibit greater or lesser degrees of intrinsic diversity. So, for example, cladists will tend to place the birds within the reptilian class (or therapod clade) and so Aves, with all of its diversity, becomes equivalent to an Order.[18]

---

[18] On cladistics see: Willi Hennig, *Phylogenetic Systematics* (Urbana: University of Illinois Press, 1966); L. A. S. Johnson, "Rainbow's End: The Quest for an Optimal Taxonomy," *Systematic Zoology* 19 (1970): 203–239; Gareth J. Nelson, "Cladism as a Philosophy of Classification," *Systematic Zoology* 20 (1971): 373–376; Ernst Mayr, "Cladistic Analysis or Cladistic Classification?" *Journal of Zoological Systematics and Evolutionary Research* 12, no. 1 (1974): 94–128; Gareth J. Nelson, "Darwin-Henning Classification: A Reply to Ernst Mayr," *Systematic Zoology* 23 (1974): 452–458; Søren Løvtrup, "Phylogetics: Some Comments on Cladistic Theory and Method," in *Major Patterns in Vertebrate Evolution*, ed. Max K. Hecht, Peter C. Goody, and Bessie M. Hecht (New York: Plenum Press, 1977), 805–822; Willi Hennig, "Cladistic Analysis or Cladistic Classification?: A Reply to Ernst Mayr," *Systematic Zoology* 24 (1975): 244–256; Robert R. Sokal, "Mayr on Cladism and His Critics," *Systematic Zoology* 24 (1975): 257–262; Niles Eldredge and Joel Cracraft, *Phylogenetic Patterns and the Evolutionary Process: Method and Theory in Comparative Biology* (New York: Colombia University Press, 1985); Mark Ridley, *Evolution and Classification: The Reformation of Cladism* (London: Longman, 1986); E. O. Wiley et al., *The Compleat Cladist* (Kansas: University of Kansas Press, 1991); R. K. Brummitt, "Taxonomy versus Cladonomy: A Fundamental Controversy in Biological Systematics," *Taxon* 46, no. 4 (1997): 723–734; Quentin Wheeler, *Species Concepts and Phylogenetic Theory: A Debate* (New York: Columbia University Press, 2000); Michel Laurin, "The Advantages of Phylogenetic

Indeed on the basis of preference for cladistic classification some systematicians have proposed abandoning Linnaean hierarchical taxa altogether and instead grouping things in terms of a phylocode where the levels of the clades need not share any similarities. In other words they propose a radical phylogentic system that would be rankless in contrast to the rank-based Linnaean one, which takes rank and overall similarity within ranks into account (gradistics). This has led to recent systematic debates about whether all taxa should be monophyletic or whether descendent groups that share strong similarities can be grouped separately (i.e. paraphyletic groups), whether taxa of the same rank should be roughly equal in age or morphological diversity, about how many ranks there should be, if any at all, and about whether or not traditional names should be given a priority. A major problem with contemporary classification in my eyes is that a cladistic focus can result in rankings at the same level that do not share the same level of diversity. For example, the Family Mustelidae contains otters, weasels, badgers, skunks, and wolverines, or a very diverse groups in terms of morphology, dwelling-place, and diet, whereas the Family Giraffidae containing giraffes and okapis is much more uniform.[19] Though

Nomenclature over Linnean Nomenclature," in *Animal Names*, ed. Alessandro Minelli, Gherardo Ortalli, and Glauco Sanga (Venice: Instituto Veneto di Scienze, Lettere ed Arti, 2005), 67–97; Paul C. Sereno, "The Logical Basis of Phylogenetic Taxonomy," *Systematic Biology* 54, no. 4 (2005): 595–619; Michel Laurin, "The Splendid Isolation of Biological Nomenclature," *Zoologica Scripta* 37, no. 2 (2008): 223–233; David Williams, Michael Schmitt, Quentin Wheeler, eds., *The Future of Phylogenetic Systematics: The Legacy of Willi Hennig* (Cambridge: Cambridge University Press, 2016); David M. Williams and Malte C. Ebach, *Cladistics: A Guide to Biological Classification* (Cambridge: Cambridge University Press, 2020).
[19] On debates over the methodology of biological classification consult: George Gaylord Simpson, *Principles of Animal Taxonomy* (New York: Columbia University Press, 1961); Walter J. Bock, "Evolution and Phylogeny in Morphologically Uniform Groups," *The American Naturalist* 97 (1963): 265–285; Ernst Mayr, *Principles of Systematic Zoology* (New York: McGraw-Hill, 1969); Walter J. Bock, "Philosophical Foundations of Classical Evolutionary Classification," *Systematic Zoology* 11 (1974): 375–392; Herbert H. Ross, *Biological Systematics* (Reading: Addison Wesley, 1974); E. O. Wiley "Karl R. Popper, Systematics, and Classification: A Reply to Walter Bock and Other Evolutionary Taxonomists," *Systematic Zoology* 24 (1975): 233–243; Ernst Mayr, "Biological Classification: Toward a Synthesis of Opposing Methodologies," *Science* 214, no. 4520 (1981): 510–516; Susan Jones and Anne Gray, *Classification: A Beginner's Guide to Some of the Systems of Biological Classification in Use Today* (London: British Museum of Natural History, 1983); Scott Atran, *The Phenomenal Foundations of Biological Classification: An Anthropological Inquiry into the Scope and Limits of Common Sense* (New York: Columbia University Press, 1984); Ernest Small, "Systematics of Biological

as a tool for making clear the evolutionary relationships of animal lineages cladistics is invaluable.

Such reflections give rise to the idea that yet another system of classification is warranted. Moreover, if we consider the possibility of life on other planets, such a system becomes one of the preferred choices. Such a system involves classifying organisms on the basis of body forms that have evolved again and again, or convergent body plans.

Convergent Evolution in Mammals

A major reason that convergence occurs in evolution is that animals evolve particular traits to adapt to their environments and there are a limited

---

Systematics (Or, Taxonomy of Taxonomy)," *Taxon* 38, no. 3 (1989): 335–356; Kevin de Queiroz, "Phylogenetic Definitions and Taxonomic Philosophy," *Biology and Philosophy* 7 (1992): 295–313; Alec L. Panchen, *Classification, Evolution, and the Nature of Biology* (Cambridge: Cambridge University Press, 1992); Harold N. Bryant, "Comments on the Phylogenetic Definition of Taxon Names and Conventions Regarding the Naming of Crown Clades," *Systematic Biology* 43 (1994): 124–129; Ernst Mayr, "Systems of Ordering Data," *Biology and Philosophy* 10 (1995): 419–434; Benoît Dayrat, et al., "Species Names in the PhyloCode: The Approach Adopted by the International Society for Phylogenetic Nomenclature," *Systematic Biology* 57 (2008): 507–514; Michael J. Benton, "Stems, Nodes, Crown Clades, and Rank-Free Lists: Is Linnaeus Dead?," *Biological Reviews* 75, no. 4 (2000): 633–648; Philip D. Cantino, "Phylogenetic Nomenclature: Addressing Some Concerns," *Taxon* 49, no. 1 (2000): 85–93; Randall Schuh, *Biological Systematics* (New York: Cornell University Press, 2000); Harold N. Bryant and Philip D. Cantino, "A Review of Criticisms of Phylogenetic Nomenclature: Is Taxonomic Freedom the Fundamental Issue?," *Biological Reviews* 77, no. 1 (2002): 39–55; Inger Nordal and Brita Stedje, "Paraphyletic Taxa Should Be Accepted," *Taxon* 54, no. 1 (2005): 5–8; Matjaž Kuntner and Ingi Agnarsson, "Are the Linnean and Phylogenetic Nomenclatural Systems Combinable?: Recommendations for Biological Nomenclature," *Systematic Biology* 55, no. 5 (2006): 774–784; John C. Avise and Jin-Xian Liu, "On the Temporal Inconsistencies of Linnean Taxonomic Ranks," *Biological Journal of the Linnean Society* 102 (2011): 707– 714; Frank E. Zachos, "Linnean Ranks, Temporal Banding, and Time-Clipping: Why Not Slaughter the Sacred Cow?," *Biological Journal of the Linnean Society* 103, no. 3 (2011): 732–734; Miguel Vences, Juan M. Guayasamin, Aurélien Miralles, Ignacio De La Riva, "To Name or Not to Name: Criteria to Promote Economy of Change in Supraspecific Linnean Classification Schemes," *Zootaxa* 3636, no. 2 (2013): 201–244; Cody E. Hinchliff, et al., "Synthesis of Phylogeny and Taxonomy into a Comprehensive Tree of Life," *Proceedings of the National Academy of Sciences* 112 (2015): 12764–12769; Richard A. Richards, *Biological Classification: A Philosophical Introduction* (Cambridge: Cambridge University Press, 2016).

number of environments, mediums of transportation, dietary adaptations, and motile adaptations.[20]

In terms of environment ecologists have recognized different life zones or biomes, which in turn are based upon levels of altitude, temperature, and precipitation. Typically seven to nine major biomes are recognized, and even up to thirty at times. For the purposes of mammalian classification on alien planets we will recognize thirteen biomes: freshwater [river, lake, creek], marine [benthic; ocean], desert [xeric shrubland], savannah [tropical grassland], tropical rainforest [hydric forest; rain forest], swamp [marsh; wetland; estuary], evergreen broadleaf woodland, temperate forest [deciduous forest; mesic forest], boreal forest [taiga; coniferous forest], temperate grassland [plain; prairie], scrub [steppe; high plateau], tundra, high rocky slopes and meadows [scree; rock outcrops].[21]

Such ecozones naturally lead to different types of adaptations in animals, i.e. animals that live underground (fossorial), live in trees (arboreal, scansorial), fly or glide, run on the plains (cursorial), hop in deserts (saltatorial or ricochetal), live in lakes or streams (semiaquatic), or are fully aquatic and live in freshwater or in the open sea (pelagic) or deep sea (benthic).

It is also important to note different types of diet, dentition, locomotion, limbs, and defensive systems in mammals. In terms of diet we can distinguish animals that are herbivores and either graze or browse or gnaw or eat fruit (frugivores), seeds (granivores), leaves (folivores), wood (xylovores), sap (gummivores), or nectar (nectarivores); those that are carnivores and eat game or fish (piscivores), insects (insectivores), molluscs (molluscivores), or plankton (planktivore or filter feeders); and omnivores (hypocarnivores) that eat both animals and plants.

---

[20] Again see my other paper in this volume for more information, pp. 42–81.

[21] See C. L. Rodgers and R. E. Kerstetter, *The Ecosphere, Organisms, Habitats, and Disturbances* (New York: Harper and Row, 1974); Robert A. Whittaker, *Communities and Ecosystems* (New York: Macmillan, 1975); R. G. Bailey, "Explanatory Supplement to Ecoregions Map of the Continents," *Environmental Conservation* 16 (1989): 307–309; D. W. Goodall, ed., *Ecosystems of the World*, 36 vols. (Amsterdam: Elsevier, 1974-2005); David M. Olson., "Terrestrial Ecoregions of the World: A New Map of Life on Earth," *Bioscience* 51 (2001): 933–938; Jürgen Schultz, *The Ecozones of the World: The Ecological Divisions of the Geosphere* (Berlin: Springer, 2005).

Classification Scheme for Mammalian-Like Forms
on Earth and on Exoplanets

With this in mind we can come up with a classification of mammalian-like creatures that could be expected or have a good chance of evolving on alien planets based upon general mammalian adaptive body plans. Such basic plans I call *nicotypes*, but they can also be considered general "ecomorphs" with the term *ecomorphs* reserved for even more specific groupings.[22]

Here are the basic mammalian nicotypes that have existed on Earth and that one might expect to encounter on alien worlds. In many ways these are archetypes as not all specimens fit in each category perfectly, and it stands in need of future refinements, including more detailed descriptions, fine-tuning of the organisms included in each grouping, development of smaller categories (ecomorphs), and inclusion of other non-vertebrate, vertebrate, and plant lines.[23]

I. Grade Mammalianus [Mammalian-Like Forms]

A. Sortal Insectivorum [Insect-Eating Forms]

1. Nicotype Soricis [Terrestrial insectivorous shrew-like forms]: Tiny terrestrial mammal, primarily insectivorous and partly carnivorous (on amphibians), with long tail, four short limbs with plantigrade feet, multiple

---

[22] The word ecomorph goes back to Ernest E. Williams, "Evolution of Lizard Congeners in a Complex Island Fauna: A Trial Analysis," in *Evolutionary Biology*, ed. Theodosius Dobzhansky et al. (Dordrecht: Springer, 1972), 72, and has frequently been made use of by Jonathan Losos, as in his "Contingency and Determinism in Replicated Adaptive Radiations of Island Lizards," *Science* 279, no. 5359 (1998): 2115–2118. See also Eric W. Schaad and Steven Poe, "Patterns of Ecomorphological Convergence among Mainland and Island Anolis Lizards," *Biological Journal of the Linnean Society* 101, no. 4 (2010): 852–859 and Steven Poe and Christopher G. Anderson, "The Existence and Evolution of Morphotypes in Mainland and Island Environments," *PeerJ* 6 (2019): e6040. The term ecomorph is used to refer to species that were not phyletically related but occupied a similar habit and had a similar morphology and behavior. Hence it can be associated with somewhat minor differences in body plan, such as changes in teeth alone, vs. easily distinguishable basic body forms. Hence I prefer the term nicotype.

[23] Utilizing the Classification Scheme of Wilson and Reeder (2005) for living families of mammals and of McKenna and Bell (1997) for extinct mammalian families. I make use of the Latin third-declension genitive singular noun suffix -is for names of nicotypes (i.e. of Nicotype X) and the Latin second-declension nominative singular noun suffix -us or -um for higher level categories.

digits, and short claws, elongated skull with narrowed and elongated snout, reduced eyes, and enlarged ears, teeth with enlarged (often bicuspid) procumbent pincer-like incisors, small but sharp unicuspid peg-like canines and premolars, and triangular dilambdodont to quadrate molars

[Family Caenolestidae of Order Paucituberculata, Genera *Lestodelphys* and *Monodelphis* of Family Didelphidae of Order Didelphimorpha, Genera *Antechinus, Dasycercus. Dasykatula, Murexia, Myoictis, Neophascogale, Ningaui, Parantechius, Phascolosorex, Planigale, Pseudoantechinus,* and *Sminthopsis,* of Family Dasyuridae of Order Dasyuromorphia, and Family Peramelidae of Order Peramelemorphia, of Infraclass Marsupialia; Family Soricidae and Subfamily Uropsilinae of Family Talpidae of Order Euliptotyphla; Genus *Geogale* and *Microgale* of Family Tenrecidae of Order Afrosoricida; Genus †*Palaeothentes* of Clade †Palaeothentinae of Order Paucituberculata of Infraclass Marsupialia; Genera †*Eozostrodon* and *Morganucodon* of Family †Morganucodontidae and Genera *Sinoconodon* and †*Hadrocodium,* and Genus †*Megazostrodon* of Family †Megazostrodontidae, of Clade †Cynodontia; Genus †*Kuehneotherium* of Family †Kuehneotheriidae of Clade Holotheria; Genus †Batodonoides of Families †Geolabididae and †Apternodontidae of Order Euliptotyphla]

2. Nicotype Talpicis [Fossorial insectivorous mole-like forms]: Very small fossorial mammals that are insectivorous with reduced eyes and ears, with large procumbent (often bicuspid) incisors and unicuspid peg-like canines and premolars and tribosphenic to dilambdodont to zalambdodont molars, four short limbs with enlarged forelimbs and spade-like clawed hands for digging, and medium-long tails

[Family Talpidae of Order Eulipotyphla; Family Chrysochloridae of Order Afrosoricida; Genus *Anourosorex* of Family Soricidae of Order Euliptotyphla; Genus *Oryzoryctes* of Family Tenrecidae of Order Afrosoricida; Family Notoryctidae of Order Notoryctemorphia of Infraclass Marsupialia; Family †Epoicotheriidae of Order Pholidota; Genus †*Docofossor* of Family †Docodontidae of Clade †Cynodontia; Family †Necrolestidae of Superorder †Dryolestoidea; Genus †*Hyopsodus* of Family †Hyopsodontidae of Order Perissodactyla]

3. Nicotype Macroscelicis [Cursorial to semi-ricochetal (often xeric) elephant shrew-like insectivorous forms]: Very small cursorial to semi-ricochetal animals with lengthened limbs for plantigrade walking and digitigrade running or occasional hopping (often in a desert environment), large eyes and ears, long pointed snouts, long tails, enlarged incisors, long

sharp unicuspid canines (often) and premolars and triangular dilambdodont to zalambdodont molars

[Genera *Antechinomys* and *Dasyuroides* of Family Dasyuridae of Order Dasyuromorpha of Infraclass Marsupialia; Family Macroscelididae of Order Macroscelidea; Family Solenodontidae, Subfamily Galericinae of Family Erinaceidae, and Genus *Notiosorex* of Family Soricidae, of Order Euliptotyphla; Genera *Melasmothrix* and *Paucidentomys* of Family Muridae of Order Rodentia; Family †Nesophontidae of Order Euliptotyphla; Family †Zalambdolestidae of Infraclass Eutheria; Family †Megazostrodontidae of Clade †Morganucodonta; Genus †*Leptictidium* of Family †Pseudorhyncocyonidae of Order †Leptictida]

4. Nicotype Scandenticis [Arboreal insectivorous forms]: Small insectivorous and partly carnivorous mammals with large eyes and ears, four limbs with enlarged digits and claws for walking in trees, long pointed snouts with enlarged procumbent incisors (and sometimes canines), and unicuspid peg-like premolars, and triangular dilambdodont molars, and long (occasionally semi-prehensile) thick bushy tails

[Families Tupaiidae and Ptilocercidae of Order Scandentia; Genera *Glironia*, *Marmosa,* and *Metachirus* of Family Didelphidae of Order Didelphimorpha and Genus *Phascogale* of Family Dasyuridae of Order Dasyuromorpha, and Family Hypsiprymnodontidae of Order Diprotodontia, of Infraclass Marsupialia; Genus *Dromiciops* of Family Microbiotheriidae; Genus †*Juramaia* and Order †Asioryctitheria of Infraclass Eutheria; Family †Cimolestidae of †Order Cimolesta; Genus †*Agilodocodon* of Clade Cynodontia†; Genus †*Henkelotherium* of Family †Paurodontidae of Order †Dryolestida]

5. Nicotype Petauricis [Arboreal gliding insectivores]: Very small arboreal animals with large eyes, enlarged gnawing incisors, triangular dilambidodont molars, four limbs, busy tails, and membrane between legs for gliding

[Family Petauridae of Order Diprotodontia of Infraclass Marsupialia; Genus †*Volaticotherium* of Order †Volaticotheria]

6. Nicotype Daubentonicis [Arboreal woodpicking forms]: Medium-sized arboreal mammals with large eyes, greatly enlarged gnawing incisors, partial to full diastema, and long tongue, four limbs, busy tails, lengthened front digits including one extra-long fore digit to dig insects out of trees

[Family Daubentoniidae of Order Primates; Genus *Dactylopsila* of Family Petauridae of Order Diprotodontia of Infraclass Marsupialia; Family †Apatemyidae of Order †Cimolesta]

7. Nicotype Microgalicis [Semi-aquatic insectivorous forms]: Small semi-aquatic insectivorous and partly carnivorous (on arthropods or fish) with long pointed snouts, enlarged procumbent incisors, peg-like premolars, and partially webbed feet
[Species *Sorex palustris*, Genera *Chimarrogale*, *Nectogale,* and *Neomys* of Family Soricidae of Order Euliptotyphla; Species *Microgale mergulus* and Genera *Limnogale* of Family Tenrecidae and Genus *Micropotamogale* of Family Potamogalidae, of Order Afrosoricida]

8. Nicotype Desmanicis [Aquatic insectivorous platypus-like forms]: Medium-small aquatic mammals that are macroinvertebravorous or piscivorous or durophagous with fully webbed feet, an enlarged and flattened tail (sometimes dorsoventrally, other times laterally), and a long, wide, and often billed snout
[Tribe Desmanini of Family Talpidae of Order Eulipotyphla; Family Ornithorhynchidae of Order Monotremata; Genus †*Dimylus* of Family Dimylidae†; Genera †*Castorocauda* and †*Haldanodon* of Family †Docodontidae of Clade †Cynodontia]

9. Nicotype Erinacis [Spiked medium-small insectivorous hedgehog-like forms]: Medium-small insectivores and partly carnivorous (on amphibians) with protruding spines or spiky hair, with long pointed snout, procumbent extended incisors, peg-like premolars, zalambdodont molars, rounded body, large ears and eyes, digitigrade posture, reduced tail
[Family Erinaceidae of Order Eulipotyphla; Subfamily Tenricinae of Family Tenrecidae of Order Afrosoricida]

10. Nicotype Myrmecis [Medium-sized terrestrial to arboreal myrmecophagic aardvark-like forms]: Medium-sized mammals with extremely long rostra and vermiform tongues used to eat social insects living in colonies, loss of anterior teeth or completely edentate condition with small peg-like cheek teeth, with powerful forelimbs and long thick claws used for digging, and often body-armor, with four medium-long limbs, a plantigrade gait, and a long (and sometimes prehensile) tail
[Families Cyclopedidae and Myrmecophagidae of Order Pilosa; Family Dasypodidae of Order Cingulata; Families Manidae and †Eomanidae of Order Philodota; Family Orycteropodidae of Order Tubulidentata;

Family Tachyglossidae of Order Monotremata; Genus †*Fruitafossor* of Subclass Theria; Genus †*Spinolestes* of Family †Gobiconodontidae of Order †Eutriconodonta; Subfamily †Glyptodontinae of Family Chlamyphoridae of Order Cingulata]

11. Nicotype Protelicis [Medium to large myrmecophagic aardwolf-like forms]: Large long-legged forms cursorial with somewhat elongated nose and large ears but partly adapted for burrowing and myrmecophagy
[Genus *Proteles* of Family Hyaenidae of Order Carnivora; Family Myrmecobiidae of Order Dasyuromorphia of Infraclass Marsupialia]

12. Nicotype Chiropticis [Small aerial insectivorous bat-like forms]: Small flying insectivorous to carnivorous mammalian forms with large ears, enlarged nose often forming snout, long forelimb bones with membrane between them forming wing, clawed short hind limbs, short tail, large canines, sharp premolars and triangular dilambdodont to zalambdodont molars
[Subfamilies Phyllostominae and Brachyphyllinae of Family Phyllostomidae, Families Mormoopidae, Noctilionidae, Furipteridae, Thyropteridae, Natalidae, Molossidae, Vespertilionidae, Cistugidae, Miniopteridae, Rhinolophidae, Hipposideridae, Megadermatidae, Rhinopomatidae, Craseonycteridae, Rhynonycteridae, Emballonuridae, Mystacinidae Nycteridae, Myzopodidae, of Order Chiroptera]

B. Sortal Nectivorum [Nectar-Eating Forms]

13. Nicotype Tarsipicis [Small arboreal nectivores]: Small primary nectivores and secondary insectivores, arboreal forms with sharp hooked claws, four limbs, large snout and long tongue for feeding on nectar and pollen, large procumbent incisors, reduction of premolar number and size forming partial diastema, reduction of molar size with sometimes plagiaulacoid cheek teeth, long tail that is often prehensile, and sometimes a gliding membrane between front and hind limbs
[Families Burramyidae and Tarsipedidae of Order Diprotodontia]

14. Nicotype Acrobaticis [Small gliding nectivores]: Small primary nectivores and secondary insectivores, arboreal forms with sharp hooked claws, four limbs, and long tongue for feeding on nectar and pollen, large procumbent incisors, reduction of premolar number and size forming partial diastema, reduction of molar size, long tail that is often prehensile and may

be feathered to aid in gliding, and a gliding membrane between front and hind limbs
[Family Acrobatidae of Order Diprotodontia]

15. Nicotype Glossophagicis [Small aerial nectivorous bat-like forms]: Small flying nectivorous mammalian forms with large ears, enlarged nose often forming snout, long forelimb bones with membrane between them forming wing, clawed short hind limbs, short tail, large canines, sharp premolars and molars
[Subfamily Glossophaginae of Family Phyllostomidae of Order Chiroptera]

C. Sortal Frugivorum [Fruit-Eating Forms]

16. Nicotype Glossophagicis [Small aerial frugivorous bat-like forms]: Small flying frugivoroius mammalian forms with large ears, enlarged nose often forming snout, long forelimb bones with membrane between them forming wing, clawed short hind limbs, short tail, large canines, sharp premolars and molars
[Subfamilies Carolliinae and Stenodermatinae of Family Phyllostomidae, and Family Pteropodidae of Order Chiroptera]

D. Sortal Granivorum

17. Nicotype Muricis [Terrestrial granivorous mouse-like forms]: Very small terrestrial animals, plantigrade with four limbs with digits and short claws, primary granivorous but occasionally herbivorous and insectivorous, with long arc-shaped, sharp, chisel-edged incisors, toothless diastema behind incisors, loss of canines and most premolars, and lophodont to bunodont molars, plantigrade with short limbs ending in digits with short claws, long ears, pointed snouts, and long tails
[Subfamilies Heteromyinae and Perognathinae of Family Heteromyidae, Subfamily Neotominae of Family Cricetidae, Subfamily Sicistinae of Family Dipodidae, Genus *Desmodilliscus* of Subfamily Gerbillinae of Family Muridae, Families Calomyscidae and Muridae, and Genus *Myomimus* of Family Gliridae, of Order Rodentia]

18. Nicotype Ratticis [Terrestrial granivorous to omnivorous rat-like forms]: Small terrestrial to partially arboreal to semi-aquatic animals with long tails that are omnivorous, and so granivorous, herbivorous, frugivorous, and partly insectivorous to carnivorous, plantigrade with four

limbs with digits and short claws, pointed snout with long arced incisors, diastema behind chisel-like incisors, bunodont to lophodont to plagiaulacoid cheek teeth

[Genus *Bettongia* of Family Potoroidea of Order Diprotodontia of Infraclass Marsupialia; Genera *Ichthyomys*, *Nectomys*, *Neotoma*, *Scapteromys*, and *Tylomys* of Family Cricetidae and Genera *Hydromys*, *Leptomys*, *Mallomys*, *Paraleptomys*, and *Rattus* of Family Muridae, and Families Echimyidae and Nesomyidae, of Order Rodentia; Genus †*Cimexomys* and Suborders †Plagiaulacida and †Cimolodonta of Order †Multituberculata; Genus †*Paracricetodon* of Order Rodentia; Genus †*Oligokyphus* of Family †Tritylodontidae of Clade †Cynodontia]

19. Nicotype Bathyercis [Highly fossorial granivorous mole rat-like forms]: Small fossorial mammals that are granivorous or root eaters with reduced eyes and ears, flat races, large noses, with large procumbent (often bicuspid) incisors with diastema separating incisors from flat-crowned lophodont molars, plump body, four short limbs with enlarged forelimbs and enlarged hands and claws, short to absent tails

[Families Bathyergidae, Heterocephalidae, and Spalacidae, Genera *Celaenomys*, *Melasmothrix*, and *Rhynchomys* of Family Muridae, Genus *Blarinomys* of Family Cricetidae, of Order Rodentia; Subfamily Chlamyphorinae of Family Chlamyphoridae of Order Cingulata]

20. Nicotype Arvicolicis: [Small burrowing vole-like forms]: Rodent-like forms that are tiny with compact and stout rounded bodies, round heads and noses, short faces, small ears and eyes, four short legs, slightly enlarged feet with short claws though the claws may be slightly flattened, short tails, and large incisors, diastema, and high-crowned molars with angular cusps, that are herbivores and root eaters to granivores

[Genera *Notiomys* and *Reithrodon* of Subfamily Sigmodontinae and Subfamily Arvicolinae of Family Cricetidae, Genus *Parotomys* of Subfamily Murinae of Family Muridae, Genera *Brachytarsomys* and *Barchyuromys* of subfamily Nesomyinae of Family Nesomyinae, and Genera *Clyomys*, *Carterodon*, and *Eurzygomatomys* of Family Echimyidae, of Order Rodentia]

21. Nicotype Geomycis [Small burrowing granivorous and herbivorous gopher-like forms]: Small rodents adopted to burrowing with short legs, plump round bodies and heads, with short necks, short eats, short tails, large

incisors with diastema separating them from bunodont to lophodont molars, and large forelimbs with large claws for digging

[Families Abrocomidae, Aplodontidae, Ctenomyidae, Geomyidae, and Octodontidae, and Genera *Euryzygomatomys*, *Clyomys*, and *Carterodon* of Family Echimyidae, Genera *Nesokia* and *Tachyoryctes* of Family Muridae, Genus *Kunsia* of Family Cricetidae, and Genus *Rhizomys* of Family Spelacidae, of Order Rodentia; Genus *Cynomys* of Family Sciuridae of Order Marmota; Genus †*Platychoerops* of Family †Plesiadapidae of Order †Plesiadapiformes]

22. Nicotype Marmoticis [Medium-sized burrowing marmot-like forms]: Plump granivores and herbivores with large flat head and snout, small ears, short to absent tails, short but thick legs, enlarged claws for digging, enlarged incisors and diastema between incisors and bunodont to lophodont molars

[Genus *Marmota* of Family Sciuridae, Genus *Myoprocta* of Family Dasyproctidae, and Family Cuniculidae of Order Rodentia; Family Vombatidae of Order Diprotodontia of Infraclass Marsupialia; Genus †*Paleocastor* of Family Castoridae, and Genus †*Ceratogaulus* of Family †Mylagaulidae, of Order Rodentia; Suborder †Taeniodonta of Order †Cimolesta]

23. Nicotype Cavicis [Medium-small thick-bodied terrestrial (often) tailless granivorous to herbivorous guinea pig-like forms]: Terrestrial rodents often with short tails, thick bodies, plantigrade, with large legs, large heads, large eyes, plantigrade with long hind feet and sharp claws, and granivorous to herbivorous, with large incisors, diastema, and lophodont molars

[Families Caviidae, Capromyidae, Genus *Otomys* of Family Muridae, of Order Rodentia; Family †Eocardiidae of Order Rodentia]

24. Nicotype Hydricis [Medium-sized herbivorous to granivorous capybara-like terrestrial forms]: Very large rodent-like forms that are primary terrestrial with large bodies and long legs, short tails, flattened muzzles, large incisors with diastema separating them from lophodont molars

[Families Agoutidae, Dasyproctidae Dinomyidae, Hydrochaeridae, and Thryonomyidae, and Genera *Dolichotis* and *Hydrochoerus* of Family Caviidae, of Order Rodentia; Genera †*Meniscotherium* of Family †Phenacodontidae of Order Perissodactyla; Genus *Carsioptychus* of Family †Periptychidae of Order †Condylarthra; Genus †*Taeniolabis* of

Family †Taeniolabididae of Order †Multituberculata; Family
†Pantolambdidae of Order †Cimolesta; Genus †*Phoberomys* of Family
†Neoepiblemidae of Order Rodentia; Family †Pliohyracidae of Order
Hyracoidea]

25. Nicotype Dipodicis [Small kangaroo rat-like forms]: Desert-adapted
small ricochetal terrestrial animals with long hind legs adapted for leaping,
long thin tails, narrow heads, enlarged ears, pointed snout, large incisors and
diastema with bunodont to plagiaulacoid cheek teeth for eating seeds and
vegetation
[Genera *Lorentzimys* and *Notomys* of Subfamily Murinae and Subfamily
Gerbillinae of Family Muridae, Subfamily Dipodomyinae of Family
Heteromyidae, Genus *Eligmodontia* of Family Cricetidae, and Family
Dipodidae of Order Rodentia; Genus *Antechinomys* of Family
Dasyuridae of Order Dasyuromorphia and Genus *Aepyprymus* of Family
Potoroidae of Order Diprotodontia of Infraclass Marsupialia; Family
†Chaeropodidae of Order Peramelemorphia of Infraclass Marsupialia;
Family †Argyrolagidae of Order †Polydolopimorphia; †Genus
Platypittamys of Family Octodontoidae and Genus †*Pseudoltinomys* of
Family †Theridomyidae of Order Rodentia; Genus †*Leptictidium* of
Family †Pseudorhyncocyonidae of Order †Leptictida; Genera
†*Nemegtbaatar* and †*Catopsbaatar* of Order †Multituberculata]

26. Nicotype Leporicis [Rabbit-like hopping forms]: Medium-small
terrestrial, often burrowing, hopping animals with (normally) very short
tails, very large ears, large hind limbs for hopping, herbivorous to
granivorous to partly insectivorous, with (usually) flattened snout, large
peg-like incisors for gnawing with diastema between bilophodont molars
and incisors
[Families Leporidae and Pedetidae, Genus *Hypogeomys* of Family
Nesomyidae, Genera *Lagidium* and *Lagostomus* of Family Chinchillidae,
of Order Rodentia; Genera *Lagorchestes*, *Lagostrophus*, and *Setonix* of
Family Macropodidae and Genus *Caloprymnus* of Family Potoroidae of
Order Infraclass, and Genus *Macrotis* of Family Thylacomyidae of
Order Peramelemorphia, of Infraclass Marsupialia; Genus †*Cainotherium*
of Family †Cainotheridae and Genus †*Sespia* of Family
†Merycoidodontidae of Order Artiodactyla; Genus †*Protypotherium*
of Family †Interatheriidae, Genus †*Pachyrukhos* of Family
†Hegetotheriidae, and Family †Notostylopidae, of Order †Notoungulata;
Genus †*Arctostylops* of Family †Arctostylopidae of Order Arctostylopida]

27. Nicotype Hydromycis [Web-footed semi-aquatic rat forms]: Small four-legged rat-like forms with webbed hind feet, long bodies, and semi-aquatic habitat, large incisors, large diastema, herbivorous to carnivorous, and sometimes with a laterally flattened tail
[Genus *Hydromys* of Family Muridae, Genus *Myocastor* of Family Echimyidae, Genera *Anotomys, Arvicola, Daptomys, Holochilus*, *Ichtyomys*, *Neofiber*, *Neusticomys*, *Ondatra, Rheomys,* and *Scapteromys* of Family Cricetidae of Order Rodentia]

28. Nicotype Petromycis [Pika-like granivorous to herbivorous forms that live in and among rocky outcrops]: Rodent-like forms with large round head, rounded bodies, large eyes and large flat ears, (often) short but thick and sometimes bushy tails, short front limbs and thick digits and sharp claws with somewhat enlarged hindlimbs, large incisors and diastema and bunodont molars, granivorous to herbivorous
[Genera *Myotomys* and *Zyzomus* of Family Muridae, Genus *Laonastes* of Family Diatomyidae, Families Chinchillidae, Ctenodactylidae, Petromuridae, Subfamily Petromyscinae of Family Nesomyidae, Genus *Kerodon* of Family Caviidae, and Genus *Octodon* of Family Octodontidae, of Order Rodentia; Family Procaviidae of Order Hyracoidea; Family Ochotonidae of Order Lagomorpha; Family †Archaeohyracidae of Order †Notoungulata]

29. Nicotype Gliricis [Small arboreal dormouse/chipmunk-like forms]: Tiny rodents with partially bushy (or naked prehensile) tail, four plantigrade limbs, long digits, short sharp curved claws for climbing trees, large incisors with diastema and bunodont molars, and granivorous to herbivorous (and frugivorous and insectivorous) in diet
[Families Gliridae and Platacanthomyidae, Subfamily Dendromurinae and Genera *Eliurus* and *Macrotarsomys* of Subfamily Nesomyinae of Family Nesomyidae, Genera *Chiropodomys*, *Micromys*, and *Thallomys* of Subfamily Murinae of Family Muridae, Genera *Eutamias* and *Tamias* of Family Sciuridae, of Order Rodentia]

30. Nicotype Sciuricis [Arboreal squirrel-like forms]: Small arboreal mammals (often) with long bushy tail, four limbs with plantigrade feet, long and occasionally opposable digits, with long narrow sharp nails, scansorial, pointed muzzle, large ears, long incisors, diastema, bunodont molars, herbivorous to insectivorous, and sometimes with cheek pouches
[Genus *Glis* of Family Gliridae, Genera *Anomalurus* and *Zenkerella* of Family Anomaluridae, Genera *Dactylomys, Diplomys, Echimys,*

Kannabateomys, Lonchothrix, and Mesomys of Family Echimyidae, and Family Sciuridae of Order Rodentia; Genera *Pseudocheirus* and *Wyulda* of Family Phalangeridae and Family Pseudocheiridae of Order Diprotodontia of Infraclass Marsupialia; Genus †*Shensou* of Order †Haramiyida; Genus †*Paramys* of Family Ischyromidae of Order Rodentia; Genus †*Ptilodus* of Family †Ptilodontidae of Order †Multituberculata; Family †Plesiadapidae of Order †Plesiadapiformes; Genus †*Kopidodon* of Family †Paroxyclaenidae of Order †Cimolesta]

31. Nicotype Pteromycis [Arboreal flying squirrel-like forms]: Small herbivore and folivore forms with large incisors and diastema with bunodont molars, four legs, large ears, pointed snout, long bushy tails, long digits with sharp curved claws, scansorial, membrane between limbs for gliding
   [Tribe Pteromyinai of Subfamily Sciurinae of Family Sciuridae, and Family Anomaluridae of Order Rodentia; Family Cynocephalidae of Order Dermoptera; Genus *Petauroides* of Family Pseudocheiridae of Order Diprotodontia or Infraclass Marsupialia; Order †Volaticotheria; Family †Eleutherodontidae of Order †Haramiyida; Genus †*Eomys* of Family †Eomyidae of Order Rodentia]

32. Nicotype Hysticis [Spined arboreal porcupine-like forms]: Medium-sized animals with longer legs, spines on body, large head, flattened muzzle, prehensile tails, sharp claws, shortened tails
   [Families Hystricidae and Erethizontidae, Subfamily Lophiomyinae of Family Muridae, of Order Rodentia]

33. Nicotype Criceticis [Pouched hamster-like rodents]: Terrestrial and burrowing pouched rodents with short tails, stout body with short legs, incisors and diastema and bunodont molars, and scansorial nature, herbivorous to insectovirous.
   [Subfamily Cricetinae of Family Cricetidae and Subfamily Cricetomyinae of Family Nesomyidae of Order Rodentia]

E. Sortal Herbivorum

34. Nicotype Castoricis [Aquatic beaver-like forms]: Aquatic forms with webbed feet and tail flattened into paddle shape, herbivorous in the main, large incisors, diastema, lophodont cheek teeth
   [Family Castoridae of Order Rodentia; Genera †*Kimbetopsalis* and †*Taeniolabis* of Family †Taeniolabididae of Order †Multituberculata]

35. Nicotype Macropodicis [Large kangaroo-like forms]: large hopping animals with large hind legs for hopping, small forelimbs, bipedal posture, long tail, large ears, with large incisors and large diastema and bilophodont molars

[Family Macropodidae of Order Diprotodontida of Infraclass Marsupialia; Order †Leptictida]

36. Nicotype Hippicis [Large semi-aquatic herbivorous hippo-like forms]: Large rounded bodies, large head with small ears and mouth, short limbs and tail, large sharp incisors and canines, flat selenodont molars, unguligrade

[Family Hippopotamidae of Order Artiodactyla; Genus †*Promerycochoerus* of Family †Merycoidodontidae of Order Artiodactyla; Genus †*Metamynodon* of Family †Amynodontidae and Genus †*Aktautitan* of Family †Brontotheriidae of Order Perissodactyla; Family †Moeritheriidae of Order Proboscidea; Subfamily †Zygomaturinae of Family †Diprotodontidae of Order Diprotodontia of Infraclass Marsupialia; Genus †*Desmostylus* of Family †Desmostylidae of Order Desmostylia; Genus †*Prorastomus* of Family †Prorastomidae of Order Sirenia]

37. Nicotype Grafficis [Very large and tall and long-necked giraffe-like herbivores]: Very long-legged, long-necked animals with pointed snout, sloped back, and tall herbivores with hooved feet, eating twigs of trees and shrubs, sharp lower incisors, diastema, flat rectangular selenodont molars and long tongue, unguligrade, high browsking

[Family Giraffidae of Order Artiodactyla; Genus †*Aepycamelus* of Family Camelidae of Order Artiodactyla; Genus †*Macrauchenia* of Family †Macraucheniidae of Order †Lipoterna]

38. Nicotype Camelicis [Large long-necked and humped camel-like herbivores]: Very long-legged, long-necked animals with pointed snout, often humps, and hooved feet, eating twigs of trees and shrubs and grass, sharp incisors, diastema, flat rectangular selenodont molars and long tongue, unguligrade, high browsing

[Family Camelidae; Genus †*Theosodon* of Family †Macraucheniidae of Order †Litopterna; Genus †*Palaeotherium* of Family †Palaeotheriidae of Order Perissodactyla]

39. Nicotype Okapicis [Large okapi-like mammals with long legs sloped back and medium-length necks]: Large form with long legs, selenodont to lophodont molars, medium-long neck, sloping back, large head, unguligrade, high browsing

[Genera *Okapia*, †*Helladotherium*, †*Palaeotragus*, †*Giraffokeryx*, †*Climacoceras*, and †*Sivatherium* of Family Giraffidae; Genus †*Tylocephalonyx* of Family †Chalicotheriidae of Order Perissodactyla]

40. Nicotype Alcis [Large browsing moose-like forms]: Large browsing herbivores with large prominent vertical (often spiral) horns or antler racks, large body, thin legs, unguligrade cloven hoofs, large ears, pointed face, square mouth, selenodont cheek teeth

[Genera *Alces* and *Rangifer* of Family Cervidae, and Genera *Boselaphus*, *Tragelaphus,* and *Taurotragus* of Family Bovidae, of Order Artiodactyla; Genera †*Prolibytherium* and †*Sivatherium* of Family Giraffidae of Order Artiodactyla]

41. Nicotype Bovicis [Large grazing cow-like forms]: Thick-bodied and thick-legged grazing forms with horizontally-extended horns with curved tips and thick middle section for sparring, cloven hooves, reduced or absent canines and premolars, selenodont molars, unguligrade

[Subfamily Bovinae, Genus *Connochaetes* of Subfamily Alcelaphinae, and Genera *Ovibos* and *Oreamnos* of Subfamily Caprinae, of Family Bovidae, of Order Artiodactyla]

42. Nicotype Hippotragicis [Medium-large grazing addax-like forms]: Medium-large forms with long legs, solid body, thick muscular neck, selenodont molars, cloven hooves, often with long vertical horns and furry tails, grazing

[Subfamily Hippotraginae of Family Bovidae of Order Artiodactyla]

43. Nicotype Caprinicis [Medium-sized goat to sheep-like rock-dwelling browsing to grazing forms]: Medium-sized browsing forms with medium-sized thick legs, medium-thick bodies, often furry body, cloven hoofs, often large curved horns, selenodont molars, unguligrade

[Subfamily Caprinae of Family Bovidae of Order Artiodactyla; Family †Periptychidae of Order †Condylarthra; Genus †*Adinotherium* of Family †Toxodontidae of Order †Notoungulata]

44. Nicotype Cervicis [Medium-sized browsing deer- and antelope-like forms]: Medium-sized browsing herbivores usually with horns or antlers and sometimes with canine tusks, long necks, short tail, thin legs, cloven hooves, selenodont cheek teeth, cursorial, unguligrade
[Families Moschidae, Antilocapridae, and Cervidae, and Subfamily Antiloprinae and Genera *Boselaphus* and *Tragelaphus* of Family Bovidae, of Order Artiodactyla; Family †Protoceratidae of Order Artiodactyla; Genus †*Thoatherium* of Family †Proterotheriidae of Order †Litopterna]

45. Nicotype Tragulicis [Medium-small sized browsing herbivorous duiker- or chevrotain-like forms]: Medium-sized with thin legs, long face, pointed ears, short tail, often with short horns and sometimes with long canine tusks, cursorial and ungulate with cloven hooves, selenodont molars, digitigrade to unguligrade
[Genera *Pudu*, *Muntiacus*, *Elaphodus*, and *Hydropotes* of Family Cervidae, Genera *Sylvicapra, Cephalophus, Pelea, Madoqua, Neotragus, Oreotragus, Raphicerus, Ourebia*, and *Dorcatragus* of Family Bovidae, and Family Tragulidae of Order Artiodactyla; Family †Dichobunidae and Genus †*Archaeomeryx* of Family †Archaeomerycidae of Order Artiodactyla]

46. Nicotype Bradypodicis [Medium-sized arboreal sloth-like herbivores]: Medium-sized arboreal forms with large nose and ears, often opposable digits, short tail, large paws with long claws, short tail, slow moving, folivores with peg-shaped cheek teeth
[Families Bradypodidae and Megalonychidae of Order Pilosa; Family Phascolarctidae of Order Diprotodontia of Infraclass Marsupialia; Genus *Nycticebus* of Family Lorisidae and Genus †*Megaladapis* of Family †Megaladapidae, of Order Primates]

47. Nicotype Phenacis [Medium-sized cursorial herbivores]: Medium-length legs, browsing to grazing herbivores, with large seleno-lophodont cheek teeth, legs ending in multiple digits with claws, digitigrade posture
[Genus †*Phenacodus* of Family †Phenacodontidae and Family †Hyrachidae of Order Perssidactyla; Genus †*Hyracotherium* of Family †Palaeotheriidae, Genus †*Eotitanops* of Family †Brontotheriidae, and Genera †*Eohippus* and †*Mesohippus* of Family Equidae of Order Perissodactyla; Genera †*Elomeryx* and †*Aepinacodon* of Family †Anthracotheriidae and Family †Agriochoeridae of Order Artiodactyla; Genus †*Ngapakaldia* of Family †Diprotodontidae of Order

Diprotodontia of Infraclass Marsupialia; Family †Didolodontidae of Order †Meridiungulata]

48. Nicotype Equicis [Large cursorial horse-like forms]: Large long-legged grazing herbivores with short tail, unguligrade, long ears, thick body, thick neck, long face and snout, with hooves, with wide incisors, diastema, hypsodont and lophodont molars, occasional horns
[Family Equidae of Order Perissodactyla; Genus *Hyracodon* of Family †Hyracodontidae of Order Perissodactyla; Family †Notohippidae of Order †Notoungulata; Family †Proterotheriidae of Order †Litopterna; Genus *Protomoropus* of Family †Chalicotheroidea of Order Perissodactyla]

49. Nicotype Tapicis [Medium-large semi-aquatic tapir-like forms]: Medium-large medium-legged browsers, with longer forelimbs, hooved toes, unguligrade, long necks, large proboscis, chisel-shaped incisors, diastema, brachyodont and pi-shaped lophodont molars, short tail
[Family Tapiridae of Order Perissodactyla; Family †Phiomiidae of Order Proboscidea; Family †Coryphodontidae of Order †Cimolesta; Family †Astrapotheriidae of Order †Astrapotheria; Genus †*Brachycrus* of Family †Merycoidodontidae of Order Artiodactyla; Genus *Cadurcodon* of Family Amynodontidae, Genus *Palaeosyops* of Family Brontotheriidae, and Family †Palaeotheriidae of Order Perissodactyla; Family †Carodniidae of Order †Xenungulata]

50. Nicotype Rhinocericis [Large terrestrial grazing or browsing rhino-like forms]: Large short legged grazing or browsing forms with large ears, thick bodies, flattened snout, often with horns, hooved toes, unguligrade, pi-shaped lophodont molars
[Family Rhinocerotidae of Order Perissodactyla; Family †Brontotheriidae of Order Perissodactyla; Family †Arsinoitheriidae of Order †Embrithopoda; Family †Toxodontidae of Order †Notoungulata; Family †Uintatheriidae of Order †Dinocerata]

51. Nicotype Elephicis [Very large herbivorous elephant-like forms]: Very large high browsing terrestrial forms with trunk, extended nose, often tusks, large body and legs with hoofs, unguligrade, large ears, reduced or absent canines and incisors, loxodont molars
[Families Eliphantidae and †Gomphotheriidae of Order Proboscidea; Family †Pyrotheriidae of Order †Pyrotheria; Genus †*Astrapotherium* of Family †Astrapotheriidae of Order †Astrapotheria]

52. Nicotype Indricothicis [Huge terrestrial herbivores]: Huge terrestrial high-browsing herbivores with long neck, long legs, lophodont molars, hoofed feet, unguligrade
[Subfamily †Indricotheriinae of Family †Hyracodontidae of Order Perissodactyla]

53. Nicotype Nothropicis [Very large terrestrial ground sloth-like herbivores]: Very large and thick-limbed animals with long trunk, neck, and tail, long forelimbs with shorter hind limbs and very long claws, reduction in incisors and often canines and hypsodont V-shaped cheek teeth for high browsing on tree vegetation
[Families †Megatheriidae, †Mylodontidae, and †Nothrotheriidae of Order Pilosa; Family †Homalodotheriidae of Order †Notoungulata; Family †Chalicotheriidae of Order Perissodactyla; Family †Barylambdidae of Order †Cimolesta; Family †Palorchestidae of Order Diprotodontia of Infraclass Marsupialia]

54. Nicotype Diprotodonticis [Large terrestrial herbivorous bear or diprotodont-like forms]: Very large body and limbs with long claws, forelimbs and hindlimbs nearly of equal proportions, large canines, lophodont molars, herbivorous and folivorous
[Genus *Ailuropoda* of Family Ursidae of Order Carnivora; Genus †*Trogosus* of Family †Esthonychidae and Families †Coryphodontidae, and †Titanoideidae of Suborder †Pantodonta of Order †Cimolesta; Family †Diprotodontidae of Order Diprotodontia of Infraclass Marsupialia; Genus †*Scarrittia* of Family †Leontiniidae of Order †Notoungulata; Genus †*Megalohyrax* of Family †Pliohyracidae of Order Hyracoidea]

55. Nicotype Trichecis [Large aquatic herbivorous flippered manatee-like forms]: Large aquatic mammals with flattened lips and snout, reduced or absent incisors and canines, and flat but high-crowned molars, streamlined fusiform body shape, reduced or absent ears, reduced eyes, large fore flippers, reduced or absent hind-flippers, and reduced tail, sometimes forming a paddle
[Familie Dugongidae and Trichechidae of Order Sirenia; Family †Paleoparadoxiidae of Order †Desmostylia]

F. Sortal Omnivorum

56. Nicotype Didelphicis [Small omnivorous scansorial opossum-like forms]: Small, arboreal, large eyes and ears, opposable digits, very long prehensile tails, pointed nose, reduced incisors, large canines, many tribosphenic premolars and molars, eat insects, fruits, amphibians, plants, and grains

[Subfamilies Caluromyinae and Didelphinae of Family Didelphidae of Order Didelphimorphia of Infraclass Marsupialia; Genus *Crossarchus* of Family Herpestidae of Order Carnivora; Family †Alphadontidae; Genus †*Eomaia* of Clade Tribosphenida; Genus †*Sinodelphys* and Genus *Wynardia* of Clade Marsupialiformes; Family †Paurodontidae of Order †Dryolestida; Genus †*Deinogalerix* of Family Erinaceidae of Order Eulipotyphla; Family †Jeholodentidae of Order †Eutriconodonta; Family †Zhangheotheriidae of Order †Symmetrodonta; Family †Vincelestidae of Clade Cladotheria]

57. Nicotype Tarsicis [Small arboreal leaping omnivorous tarsier-like forms]: Small arboreal herbivores with rounded heads, large ears, large forward-facing eyes, large incisors and canines, bunodont cheek teeth, long tails, long digits ending in large finger pads with nails, sometimes with opposable thumb, plantigrade, omnivores, insectivorous to frugivorous and gummivorous

[Families Tarsiidae, Cheirogaleidae, and Galigidae of Order Primates; Families †Omomyidae and †Eosimiidae of Order Primates; Family †Carpolestidae of Order †Plesiadapiformes]

58. Nicotype Lemuricis [Medium-sized arboreal omnivorous lemur-like forms]: Medium-sized arboreal herbivores and frugivores, gummivores, and insectivores with small founded heads, medium-sized often rounded ears, flat to pointed snout, large incisors and canines, bunodont cheek teeth, medium-sized arms with long fingers often ending in finger pads or sometimes curved and sharp foreclaws for grasping branches, usually with an opposable thumb, plantigrade, large forward-facing eyes, large nose, long (often) furry and sometimes prehensile tail

[Families Lemuridae, Lepilemuridae, Lorisidae, and Aotidae, of Order Primates; Genus *Pseudocheirus* of Family Pseudocheiridae, and Genera *Ailurops*, *Phalanger*, *Spilocuscus*, and *Strigocuscus* of Family Phalangeridae, of Order Diprotodontia of Infraclass Marsupialia; Genera *Potos* and *Bassaricyon* of Family Procyonidae of Order Carnivora; Family

†Plesiadapidae of Order †Plesiadapiformes; Families †Adapidae and †Notharctidae of Order Primates]

59. Nicotype Cebicis [Medium-sized arboreal omnivorous forms with very long arms and (sometimes prehensile) tails, long digits ending in short claws or nails, usually opposable thumb, plantigrade, large incisors and canines, bunodont cheek teeth, small rounded faces and muzzles with large noses and ears, frugivorous to folivorous to gummivorous to insectivorous
[Families Hylobatidae, Indriidae, Callitrichidae, Cebidae, Pitheciidae, and Atelidae, and Subfamily Colobinae of Family Cercopithecinae of Order Primates; Families †Notharctidae and †Propliopithecidae of Order Primates]

60. Nicotype Cercopicis [Large semi-arboreal to terrestrial baboon and chimpanzee-like forms]: Semi-arboreal to terrestrial omnivores, shortened tails, stocky build, plantigrade gait, very large canines, bunodont cheek teeth, gregarious often forming social groups
[Subfamily Cercopithecinae of Family Cercopithecinae, Genus *Pan* of Subfamily Homininae of Family Hominidae, of Order Primates]

61. Nicotype Hylobatiicis [Large arboreal brachiating gibbon-like forms]: Large arboreal forms with long arms, reduced or absent tail, forward-facing eyes, large snout, brachiating motion in trees, large canines, bunodont cheek teeth, omnivorous, folivorous to frugivorous to insectivorous
[Family Hylobatidae, and Subfamily Ponginae of Family Hominidae, of Order Primates]

62. Nicotype Gorillicis [Very large terrestrial gorilla-like forms]: Large terrestrial ape form with long arms, reduced tail, large snout, large canines, bunodont cheek teeth, omnivorous, folivorous
[Genus *Gorilla* of Tribe Gorillini of Subfamily Homininae of Family Hominidae; Genus †*Gigantopithecus* of Tribe †Sivapithecini of Family Hominidae]

63. Nicotype Hominicis [Medium-sized bipedal omnivorous human-like forms]: Medium-sized bipedal omnivores with reduced canines, bunodont molars, omnivorous, with long digits ending in nails, large head and ears, forward-facing eyes, capable of advanced tool-use and communication and culture
[Species *Homo sapiens* of Subfamily Homininae of Family Hominidae]

64. Nicotype Procyonicis [Omnivorous to carnivorous to folivorous semi-arboreal racoon-like forms]: Medium-sized, omnivorous animals with pointed snout, small incisors, large and sharp canines and premolars and widened molars, rounded body, stout hind quarters, compact legs with wide digits and sharp pointed claws, plantigrade in gait but scansorial, partly arboreal, with thick (often striped) tails
[Families Eupleridae, Procyonidae, Viverridae, and Ailuridae, and Genus *Nyctereutes* of Family Canidae of Order Carnivora; Genera *Dasyurus* and *Satanellus* of Family Dasyuridae of Order Dasyuromorphia and Genus *Trichosurus* of Family Phalangeridae, and Genus *Dendrolagus* of Family Macropodidae, of Order Diprotodontia of Infraclass Marsupialia; Genera †*Chriacus* and *Loxylophus* of Family †Arctocyonidae of Order †Arctocyonia; Genus †*Deinogalerix* of Family Erinaceidae of Order Eulipotyphla; Genus †*Hesperocyon* of Family Canidae and Genus †*Plesictis* of Family Mustelidae of Order Carnivora]

65. Nicotype Melinicis [Squat fossorial omnivorous badger-like forms]: Fossorial omnivorous to carnivorous forms with shorter limbs and thick squat bodies, enlarged feet and thick claws for digging, secodont cheek teeth with carnassial pair, pointed nose, short tail, often a stink gland
[Subfamilies Melinae, Mellivorinae, and Taxideinae of Family Mustelidae, and Families Mephitidae and Nandiniidae, of Order Carnivora; Genus *Scarcophilus* of Family Dasyuridae of Order Dasyuromorphia of Infraclass Marsupialia; Genus †*Repenomamus* of Family †Gobiconodontidae of Order †Gobiconodonta; Genus †*Psittacotherium* of Family †Stylinodontidae of Order †Cimolesta]

66. Nicotype Gulonicis [Medium-sized omnivorous wolverine-like forms]: Terrestrial medium-sized omnivore with large canines, carnassial pair, thick body, thick hind quarters, medium-sized legs, and long claws
[Subfamily Guloninae of Family Mustelidae of Order Carnivora; Genera *Civettictis* and *Arctictis* of Family Viverridae, of Order Carnivora; Genus †*Oxyaena* of Family †Oxyaenidae of Order †Creodonta; Genera †*Megalictis* of Family Mustelidae and Genus †*Chapoalmalania* of Family Procyonidae of Order Carnivora]

67. Nicotype Chrysicis [Thin long-legged omnivorous maned wolf-like form]: Cursorial with digitigrade posture, long legs, long tail, thin body, and pointed snout, large canines with carnassial pair, omnivore to frugivore
[Genus *Chrysocyon* of Family Canidae of Order Carnivora]

68. Nicotype Suicis [Medium-sized to large snouted pig-like forms]: Medium-sized omnivore with large head, short flattened snout, round bodies, short limbs ending with cloven hoofs, small ears, short tail, sometimes with horns, large procumbent incisors and canines and bunodont molars

[Families Suidae and Tayassuidae of Order Artiodactyla; Family †Stylinodontidae of Order †Cimolesta; Genus †*Thomashuxleya* of Family †Isotemnidae of Order †Notoungulata; Families †Entelodontidae and †Merycoidodontidae of Order Artiodactyla; Genus †*Eoconodon* of Family †Triisodontidae of Order †Mesonychia]

69. Nicotype Ursicis [Large omnivorous bear-like form]: Very large forms with thick bodies, medium-sized snouts, and medium-long thick legs with very long and sharp claws, semi-arboreal to arboreal, sometimes with opposable digits, dentition with small incisors, large canines, carnassial pair, plantigrade, bunodont molars, omnivorous to herbivorous

[Family Ursidae of Order Carnivora; Family †Amphicyonidae and Genus †*Chapalmalania* of Family Procyonidae of Order Carnivora; Family †Arctocyonidae of Order †Arctocyonia; Genus †*Ankalagon* of Family †Mesonychidae of Order †Mesonychia; Family †Titanoideidae of Order †Cimolesta; Genus †*Sarkastodon* of Family †Oxyaenidae of Order †Creodonta]

G. Sortal Carnivorum

70. Nicotype Felicis [Large carnivorous tiger-like form]: Medium to large carnivores with large to very large (sometimes huge sabre-like) canine teeth, secodont cheek teeth with a carnassial pair for shearing, compact snout, long tails, fairly long legs with broad paws with sharp (often) retractable claws, flexible spine, typically digitigrade, cursorial to arboreal thin elongated midsection

[Family Felidae and Genus *Cryptoprocta* of Family Eupleridae of Order Carnivora; Genus †*Thylacoleo* of Family †Thylacoleonidae of Order Diprotodontia, of Infraclass Marsupialia; Family †Thylacosmilidae of Order †Sparassodonta; Subfamily †Machaeroidinae of Family †Oxyaenidae of Order †Creodonta; Family †Nimravidae and Subfamily †Machairodontinae of Family Felidae, of Order Carnivora; Genus †*Paroodectes* of Clade Carnivoraformes]

71. Nicotype Lynxicis [Small carnivorous lynx-like forms]: Small carnivores with large canine teeth, secondont cheek teeth with carnassial pair, compact snout, long tails, fairly long legs with broad paws with sharp often rectractable claws, flexible spine, typically digitigrade, cursorial to arboreal

[Genera *Caracal*, *Felis*, and *Lynx* of Family Felidae of Order Carnivora; Genera †*Oxyaena* and †*Tytthaena* of Family †Oxyaenidae of Order †Creodonta; Genus †*Dinictis* of Family †Nimravidae of Order Carnivora; Genus †*Miacis* of Family †Miacidae of Order Carnivora]

72. Nicotype Canicis [Carnivorous dog-like forms]: Large carnivorous animals with long legs, digitigrade posture, short incisors, sharp canines and carnassial premolars, paws with sharp claws, cursorial, long snout, large ears, long tails

[Family Canidae of Order Carnivora; Family †Thylacinidae of Order Dasyuropmorphia of Infraclass Marsupialia; Subfamily †Hemicyoninae of Family Ursidae, Subfamily †Daphoeninae of Family †Amphicyonidae, Genera †*Mesonyx,* †*Pachyaena,* and †*Sinonyx* of Family †Mesonychidae, Genus †*Epicyon* of Family Canidae of Order Carnivora; Genus †*Andrewsarchus* of Clade Cetancodontamorpha of Order Artiodactyla; Genera †*Hyainailouros* and †*Megistotherium* of Family †Hyaenodontidae of Order †Creodonta]

73. Nicotype Vulpicis [Carnivorous fox-like forms]: Medium-sized carnivorous animals with long legs, digitigrade posture, short incisors, sharp canines and carnassial premolars, paws with sharp claws, cursorial, long snout, large ears, thick tails

[Genera *Vulpes*, *Alopex, Speothos,* and *Otocyon* of Family Canidae of Order Carnivora; Genera †*Hesperocyon*, †*Phlaocon*, and †*Leptocyon* of Family Canidae of Order Carnivora; Genus †*Sinopa* of Family †Hyaenodontidae of Order †Creodonta]

74. Nicotype Hyaenicis [Large carnivorous hyaena-like forms]: Large-headed and bodied with long thick neck scavenging carnivores with slower gait and sloped hind quarters, plantigrade, thick legs with claws, and secodont cheek teeth with carnassial pair, and short tail]

[Family Hyaenidae of Order Carnivora; Genus †*Harpagolestes* of Family †Mesonychidae of Order †Mesonychia; Family †Borhyaenidae of Order †Sparassodonta; Genus †*Andrewsarchus* of Clade Cetancodontamorpha of Order Artiodactyla; Genus †*Hyaenodon* of

Family †Hyaenodontidae and Genus †*Palaeonictis* of Family
Oxyaenidae of Order †Creodonta]

75. Nicotype Mustelicis [Elongated short-legged carnivorous weasel or
mongoose-like forms]: Elongated slender short-legged carnivores (to
omnivorous) with short incisors and secodont cheek teeth with carnassial
pair, tails
[Subfamilies Mustelinae, Ictonychinae, Helictidinae, Genus *Pekania* of
Subfamily Guloninae of Family Mustelidae and Genus *Poiana* of
Family Viverridae, and Family Herpestidae, of Order Carnivora; Genus
†*Cladosictis* of Family †Hathliacynidae of Order †Sparassodonta;
Genus †*Theriognathus* of Family †Whaitsiidae; Genera †*Prolimnocyon*
and †*Tritemnodon* of Family †Hyaenodontidae of Order †Creodonta;
Genus †*Piestictis* of Family †Miacidae and Genus †*Cynodictis* of
Family Canidae of Order Carnivora]

76. Nicotype Lutrinicis [Carnivorous semi-aquatic otter-like forms]:
Medium-sized carnivorous to durophagous forms with long canines, slim
body with webbed feet for swimming, and often a laterally flattened tail,
freshwater to coastal waters
[Subfamily Lutrinae and Species *Mustelis lutreola* of Subfamily
Mustelinae of Family Mustelidae, and Genus *Cynogale* of Family
Viverridae, of Order Carnivora; Genus *Potamogale* of Family
Potamogalidae of Order Afrosoricida; Genera *Chironectes* and
Lutreolina of Family Didelphidae of Order Didelphimorphia of
Infraclass Marsupialia; Family †Pantolestidae of Order †Cimolesta;
Genus †*Hapalodectes* of Family †Hapalodectidae of Order
†Mesonychia; Genus †*Potamotherium* of Family †Semantoridae and
Family †Enaliarctidae of Order Carnivora; Genus †*Liaoconodon* of
Order †Eutriconodonta; Genus †*Didelphodon* of Family
†Stagodontidae]

77. Nicotype Phocicis [Aquatic carnivorous flippered seal-like form]:
Large aquatic piscivorous mammals with long canines, homodont cheek
teeth, sometimes tusks, a streamlined body shape, reduced or absent ears
and legs, fore and hind flippers and reduced tail
[Families Otariidae, Phocidae, and Odobenidae of Order Carnivora;
Family †Enaliarctidae of Order Carnivora; Family †Ambulocetidae of
Order Artiodactyla]

78. Nicotype Delphicis [Aquatic dolphin-like forms]: Large aquatic piscivorous fusiform fast-swimming mammals with fluked tails, dorsal fins, and lateral flippers, many conical peg-like teeth or laterally flattened teeth, and breathing hole located on forehead
[Family Delphinidae, Iniidea, Lipotidae, Phocoenidae, Platanistidae, Pontoporiidae, of Infraorder Cetacea of Order Artiodactyla]

79. Nicotype Odonticis [Aquatic toothed-whale-like forms]: Extremely large piscivorous or invertebrate-eating aquatic mammals with unicuspid conical teeth, fluked tails, dorsal fins, pectoral flippers, and a breathing hole on forehead
[Families Monodontidae, Physeteridae, and Ziphiidae, and Genus *Orca* of Family Delphinidae, of Parvorder Odontoceti of Infraorder Cetacea of Order Artiodactyla]

80. Nicotype Balaenicis [Aquatic baleen whale-like forms]: Extremely large aquatic mammals with fluked tails, dorsal fins, pectoral flippers, and an extended toothless rostrum with baleens for filtering plankton and blowhole on forehead
[Families Balaenidae, Balaenopteridae, Eschrichtiidae, and Neobalaenidae of Parvorder Mysticeti of Infraorder Cetacea of Order Artiodactyla]

H. Sortal Hematophagum

81. Nicotype Desmodonticis [Small aerial hematophagous bat-like forms]: Small flying hematophagous to carnivorous mammalian forms with large ears, enlarged nose often forming snout, long forelimb bones with membrane between them forming wing, clawed short hind limbs, short tail, large sharp incisors, large canines, sharp premolars and molars
[Subfamily Desmodontinae of Family Phyllostomidae of Order Chiroptera]

We thus end up with 81 basic nicotypes, or basal mammalian forms that have evolved on Earth. This, of course, is a preliminary classification and some important decisions remain open to further reflection. It is sometimes difficult to know where to place some of the transitional forms, such as between artiodactyls and whales, or whether anagalids should be grouped with rabbits or not, and some of these could be placed in their own nicotype. One could also split off some of the forms that have their own novel traits into their own nicotype, as opposed to putting them into subnicotypes, or what we might call more specific *ecomorphic* groupings. For example, we might split off the walrus from seals, horned gopher from the gopher, sheep from goats, skunks from badgers, the platypus from other aquatic insectivores, fanged chevrotains and musk deer from other deer, pouched bats from other bats, sabretooth cats from other cats, and the proboscis monkey from other monkeys. Finally, there are decisions as to where to put repurposed forms such as maned wolves or shrew rats and whether to put them in their own nicotype, or with their original nicotype or the new nicotype on which they are verging. If one is a splitter rather than a lumper the number of basal nicotypes could approach or exceed 100.

BIBLIOGRAPHY

Christianity, Extraterrestrials, and the Cosmos

Andrews, Lewis M. "Christianity and the Space Program." *New Oxford Review*, No. 69 (2002): 14–24.

Antall, Richard. "Evangelizing E.T." *Angelus*, No. 5 (2020): 24–25.

Antonites, Alex J. "The Meaning and Challenge of the Quest for Extraterrestrials." *Studia Historia Ecclesiasticae*, No. 39 (2013): 71–91.

Arcadi, James M. "Recent Developments in Analytic Christology." *Philosophy Compass*, No. 13 (2018): e12480.

Bauckham, Richard. 2015. "The Incarnation and the Cosmic Christ." In *Incarnation: On the Scope and Depth of Christology*, edited by Niels Henri Gregersen, 30–45. Minneapolis: Augsburg Fortress, 2015.

Bertka, Constance M. 2013. "Christianity's Response to the Discovery of Extraterrestrial Intelligent Life: Insights from Science and Religion and the Sociology of Religion." In *Astrobiology, History, and Society*, edited by Douglas A. Vakoch, 329–341. Dordrecht: Springer.

Bertka, Connie, Roth, Nancy, and Shindell, Matthew, eds. *Workshop Report: Philosophical, Ethical, and Theological Implications of Astrobiology*. Washington: AAAS, 2007.

Bonting, Sjoerd L. "Theological Implications of Possible Extraterrestrial Life." *Zygon*, No. 38 (2003):, no. 3: 587–602.

Brague, Rémi. "Geocentrism as a Humiliation for Man." *Medieval Encounters*, No. 3 (1997): 187–210.

Brague, Rémi. 2004. *The Wisdom of the World: The Human Experience of the Universe in Western Thought*, translated by Theresa Fagan. Chicago: University of Chicago Press.

Brazier, Paul H. "C.S. Lewis: The Question of Multiple Incarnations." *Heythrop Journal*, No. 55 (2014): 391–408.

Carr, Anne. "Take Me to Your Leader." *Homiletic and Pastoral Review*, No. 65 (1964): 256.

Champlin, Joseph. "Church Architecture in the Space Age," *Liturgical Arts*, No. 37 (1969): 70–72.

Chela–Flores, Julian. "Fitness of the Universe for a Second Genesis: Is It Compatible with Science and Christianity?" *Science and Christian Belief*, No. 17 (2005): 187–197.

Clapp, Rodney. "Extraterrestrial Intelligence and Christian Wonder." *Christianity Today*, No. 27 (1983): 10.

Conklin, Daniel G. "Jesus and ET: Identity of Jesus the Christ in View of Ultimate Pluralism." *Bangalore Theological Forum*, No. 36 (2004): 101–121.

Consolmagno, Guy. 2000. *Brother Astronomer: Adventures of a Vatican Scientist*. New York: McGraw–Hill.

Consolmagno, Guy, ed. *The Heavens Proclaim: Astronomy and the Vatican*. Huntington: Our Sunday Visitor, 2009.

Consolmagno, Guy, and Mueller, Paul. 2014. "Would You Baptize an Extraterrestrial?" In *Would You Baptize an Extraterrestrial?: And Other Questions from the Astronomers' In–Box at the Vatican Observatory*, 248-286. New York: Image Books.

Cook, Alan. "Seeds of the Scientific Revolution." *Notes and Records of the Royal Society of London*, No. 51 (1997): 327–334.

Cooley, Dawn S. "Astrobiology as Contemporary Theology or Why Extra–Terrestrial Life Matters." *Religious Humanism*, No. 43 (2013): 27–57.

Cooley, Dawn S. 2018. "Astrobiology as Contemporary Theology." In *Theology and Science: From Genesis to Astrobiology*, edited by Richard Gordin and Joseph Seckbach, 3–24. New Jersey: World Scientific.

Connell, Francis J. 1967. "Flying Saucers and Theology." In *The Truth about Flying Saucers*, edited by Aimé Michel, 255–258. New York: Pyramid Books.

Considine, Kevin. "Does the Church Believe in Life on Other Planets?" *U.S. Catholic*, No. 77 (2012): 46.

Cook, Rob. "Would the Discovery of Alien Life Prove Theologically Embarrassing?: A Response to Paul Davies." *The Evangelical Quarterly*, No. 84 (2012): 139–154.

Corbally, Christopher J. "What If There Were Other Inhabited Worlds?" *Studies in Science and Theology*, No. 5 (1997): 77–88.

Coyne, George V. 2000. "The Evolution of Intelligent Life on Earth and Possibly Elsewhere: Reflections from a Religious Tradition." In *Many Worlds: The New Universe, Extraterrestrial Life and the Theological Implications*, edited by Steven J. Dick, 177–190. West Conshohoken: Templeton Foundation Press.

Crisp, Oliver D. 2007. *Divinity and Humanity: The Incarnation Reconsidered*. Cambridge: Cambridge University Press.

Crisp, Oliver D. 2009. *God Incarnate: Explorations in Christology.* London: Bloomsbury.

Crisp, Oliver D. 2008. "Multiple Incarnations." In *Reason, Faith, and History: Philosophical Essays for Paul Helm*, edited by Martin Stone, 219–238. Burlington: Ashgate.

Crowe, Michael J. "A History of the Extraterrestrial Life Debate." *Zygon*, No. 32 (1997): 147–162.

Crowe, Michael J. 2011. *The Extraterrestrial Life Debate, 1750–1900: The Idea of a Plurality of Worlds from Kant to Lowell.* Cambridge: Cambridge University Press, 1988.

Crowe, Michael J. 2008. *The Extraterrestrial Life Debate, Antiquity to 1915: A Source Book.* Notre Dame: University of Notre Dame Press.

Crowe, Michael J., and Matthew F. Dowd. 2013. "The Extraterrestrial Life Debate from Antiquity to 1900." In *Astrobiology, History, and Society*, edited by Douglas A. Vakoch, 3–56. Dordrecht: Springer.

Crowe, Michael J. 1994. *Modern Theories of the Universe from Herschel to Hubble.* New York: Dover.

Crowe, Michael J. 2001. *Theories of the World: From Antiquity to the Copernican Revolution.* New York: Dover.

Crysdale, Cynthia. 2007. "God and Astrobiology." In *Workshop Report: Philosophical, Ethical, and Theological Implications of Astrobiology*, edited by Bertka, Connie, Roth, Nancy, and Shindell, Matthew, 196–207. Washington: AAAS.

Davies, Paul. 1995. *Are We Alone: Philosophical Implications of the Discovery of Extraterrestrial Life.* New York: Basic Books.

Davies, Paul. "ET and God." *The Atlantic Monthly*, No. 292 (2003): 112–118.

Davis, Charles. "The Place of Christ." *The Clergy Review*, No. 45 (1960): 706–718.

Davis, John J. 2002. *The Frontiers of Science and Faith: Examining Questions from the Big Bang to the End of the Universe.* Downers Grove: InterVarsity Press.

Davis, John J. "The Search for Extraterrestrial Intelligence and the Christian Doctrine of Redemption." *Science and Christian Belief*, No. 9 (1997): 21–34.

Davis, Stephen T., Kendall, Daniel, and Gerald O'Collins, Gerald, eds. *The Incarnation: An Interdisciplinary Symposium on the Incarnation of the Son of God.* Oxford: Oxford University Press, 2002.

Davison, Andrew. "Astrotheology: Science and Theology Meet ET." *Theology and Science*, No. 16 (2018): 377–379.

Davison, Andrew. "Astrotheology: Science and Theology Meet Extraterrestrial Life." *Theology and Science*, No. 17 (2019): 143–146.

Davison, Andrew. "Christian Systematic Theology and Life Elsewhere in the Universe: A Study in Suitability." *Theology and Science*, No. 16 (2018): 447–461.

Delano, Kenneth. 1977. *Many Worlds, One God*. New York: Hicksville.

Delio, Ilia, "Christ and Extraterrestrial Life." *Theology and Science*, No. 5 (2007): 249–265.

Delio, Ilia. 2011. *The Emergent Christ*. New York: Orbis.

Delio, Ilia. "Revisiting the Franciscan Doctrine of Christ." *Theological Studies*, No. 64 (2003): 3–24.

DeSanctis, Michael E. "Thinking again of Mass on the Moon (and Other Dreams of the 60s)," *Ministry and Liturgy*, No. 32 (2005): 12–14.

Dick, Steven J. 1996. *The Biological Universe: The Twentieth Century Extraterrestrial Life Debate and the Limits of Science*. Cambridge: Cambridge University Press.

Dick, Steven J. 2000. "Cosmotheology: Theological Implications of the New Universe." In *Many Worlds: The New Universe, Extraterrestrial Life and the Theological Implications*, edited by Steven J. Dick, 191–210. West Conshohoken: Templeton Foundation Press.

Dick, Steven J., ed. *The Impact of Discovering Life Beyond Earth*. Cambridge: Cambridge University Press, 2016.

Dick, Steven J. 2001. *Life on Other Worlds: The 20th Century Extraterrestrial Life Debate*. Cambridge: Cambridge University Press.

Dick, Steven J., ed. *Many Worlds: The New Universe, Extraterrestrial Life and the Theological Implications*. West Conshohoken: Templeton Foundation Press, 2000.

Dick, Steven J. 1993. "Plurality of Worlds." In *Cosmology: Historical, Literary, Philosophical, Religious, and Scientific Perspectives*, edited by Norriss S. Hetherington, 515–532. New York: Garland.

Dick, Steven J. 1993. "Plurality of Worlds." In *Encyclopedia of Cosmology*, edited by Norriss S. Hetherington, 502–512. New York: Garland.

Dick, Steven J. 1982. *Plurality of Worlds: The Origins of the Extraterrestrial Life Debate from Democritus to Kant*. Cambridge: Cambridge University Press.

Dick, Steven J. 2018. "Toward a Constructive Naturalistic Cosmotheology." In *Astrotheology: Science and Theology Meet Extraterrestrial Life*, edited by Ted Peters, 228–244. Eugene: Cascade Books.

Dick, Steven J. 2013. "The Twentieth–Century History of the Extraterrestrial Life Debate: Major Themes and Lessons Learned" and "The Societal Impact of Extraterrestrial Life: The Relevance of History and the Social Sciences." In *Astrobiology, History, and Society*, edited by Douglas A. Vakoch, 133–174 and 227–328. Dordrecht: Springer.

Doege, Lisa. "Astrobiology or Why E.T. Matters?: A Response." *Religious Humanism*, No. 43 (2013): 59–65.

Donceel, Joseph F. "A Pangalactic Christ." *Continuum*, No. 6 (1968): 115–119.

Drees, Willem B. 1990. "Extraterrestrial Persons." In *Concepts of Person in Religion and Thought*, edited by Kippenberg, Hans G., Culper, Yme B., and Sanders, Andy F., 259–276. Berlin: Walter de Gruyter.

Dugan, George. "Priest Suggests Rational Beings Could Well Exist in Outer Space," *New York Times*, August 7, 1960, 14.

Duhem, Pierre. 1987. *Medieval Cosmology: Theories of Infinity, Place, Time, Void, and the Plurality of Worlds*. Chicago: University of Chicago Press.

Estes, Douglas. "The Exoplanets Declare the Glory of God." *Christianity Today*, March 14, 2017.

Fergusson, David. "Are We Alone?: And Does It Matter?" *Theology Today*, No. 72 (2015): 194–205.

Fergusson, David, and Christopher L. Fisher, 'Karl Rahner and the Extra–Terrestrial Intelligence Question." *The Heythrop Journal*, No. 47 (2006): 275–290.

Fisher, Christopher L. 2010. *Human Significance in Theology and the Natural Sciences: An Ecumenical Perspective with Reference to Pannenberg, Rahner, and Zizioulas*. Eugene: Wipf and Stock.

Francisco, Reginaldo, 1994. "Possibilita di una redenzione cosmica: Implicazioni teologiche circa una suposta vita extraterrestre." In *Proceedings of the Venice Conference on Cosmology and Philosophy, Ca' Dolfin, Venice, December, 1992, Origini: l'universo, la vita, l'intelligenza*, edited by Bertola, Francesco, Calvani, Massimo, and Curi, Umberto, 95–112. Padova: Il Poligrafo.

Funes, José G. "Canticle of Brother Extraterrestrial?" *L'Osservatore Romano*, No. 2048 (2008): 10.

Funes, José G. 2018. "The Road Map to Other Earths: Lessons Learned and Challenges Ahead." In *Astrotheology: Science and Theology Meet Extraterrestrial Life*, edited by Ted Peters, 56–73. Eugene: Cascade Books.

Galle, Griet. "Peter of Auvergne on the Unicity of the World." *Recherches de Théologie et Philosophie Médiévales*, No. 68 (2001): 111–141.

Galle, Griet. "The Relation between the Condemnations of 1277 and Peter of Auvergne's Questions on De Caelo." *Ephemerides Theologicae Lovanienses*, No. 91 (2015): 223–238.

Gascoigne, Laura. "Nod and a Wink from Outer Space." *The Tablet*, No. 260 (2006): 34.

Genta, Giancarlo. 2007. *Lonely Minds in the Universe*. New York: Copernicus Books.

Genuth, Sara S. 1992. "Devils' Hells and Astronomers' Heavens: Religion, Method, and Popular Culture in Speculations about Life on Comets." In *The Invention of Physical Science: Intersections of Mathematics, Theology, and Natural Philosophy Since the Seventeenth Century*, edited by Erwin N. Hiebert, Mary Jo Nye, and Joan L. Richards, 3–26. Dordrecht: Kluwer, 1992.

George, Marie I. 2002. "The Catholic Faith, Scripture and the Question of the Existence of Intelligent Extra–Terrestrial Life." In *Faith, Scholarship, and Culture in the Twenty–First Century*, edited by Alice Ramos and Marie I. George, 135–145. Washington: The Catholic University of America Press.

George, Marie I. 2005. *Christianity and Extraterrestrials: A Catholic Perspective*. Lincoln: iUniverse.

George, Marie I. "E.T. Meets Jesus Christ: A Hostile Encounter Between Science and Religion?" *Logos*, No. 10 (2007): 69–94.

George, Marie I. "Reasons for a Christian to Think That Intelligent Extraterrestrials (ETIs) Do Not Exist." *Faith and Reason*, No. 31 (2006): 336–364.

George, Marie I. "Would St. Thomas Aquinas Baptize an Extraterrestrial?, Revisited," *New Blackfriars*, December 27, 2019.

Gore, Charles. 1903. *The Incarnation of the Son of God: Being the Brampton Lectures for the Year 1891*. London: J. Murray.

Grant, Edward. 1979. *The Condemnation of 1277: God's Absolute Power and Physical Thought in the Late Middle Ages*. Los Angeles: University of California Press.

Grant, Edward. "The Condemnation of 1277: God's Absolute Power and Physical Thought in the Late Middle Ages." *Viator*, No. 10 (1979): 211–244.

Grant, Edward. 1996. *The Foundations of Modern Science in the Middle Ages: Their Religious, Institutional, and Intellectual Contexts*. Cambridge: Cambridge University Press.

Grant, Edward. 1999. *God, Science, and Natural Philosophy in the Late Middle Ages*. Leiden: Brill.

Grant, Edward. "How Theology, Imagination, and the Spirit of Inquiry Shaped Natural Philosophy in the Late Middle Ages." *History of Science*, No. 49, no. 1 (2011): 89–108.

Grant, Edward. "The Medieval Cosmos: Its Structure and Operation." *Journal for the History of Astronomy*, No. 28 (1997): 146–167.

Grant, Edward. 1994. *Planets, Stars, and Orbs: The Medieval Cosmos, 1200–1687*. Cambridge: Cambridge University Press.

Grant, Edward. "Scientific Imagination in the Middle Ages." *Perspectives on Science: Historical, Philosophical, Social*, No. 12 (2004): 394–423.

Grasso, Domenico, 1904. Die Sternewelt undihre Bewohner. Köln: J.F. Bachem.

Grasso, Domenico. "La teologia e la pluralità dei mondi abitati." *Civiltà Cattolica*, No. 103 (1952): 255–265.

Graves, Mark. 2018. "'E.T. Call Church!': Astrosemiotics and Shared Spirituality." In *Astrotheology: Science and Theology Meet Extraterrestrial Life*, edited by Ted Peters, 245–270. Eugene: Cascade Books.

Green, Brian Patrick. 2015. "Astrobiology, Theology, and Ethics." In *Anticipating God's New Creation: Essays in Honor of Ted Peters*, edited by Carol R. Jacobsen and Adam W. Pryor, 339–350. Minneapolis: Lutheran University Press.

Green, Brian Patrick. "The Catholic Church and Technological Progress: Past, Present, and Future." *Religions*, No. 8 (2017): 106–132.

Hart, John. 2013. *Cosmic Commons: Spirit, Space, and Science*. Eugene: Wipf and Stock.

Harford, James. "Rational Beings in Other Worlds." *Jubilee*, No. 10 (1962): 19.

Haught, John F. 2017. *The New Cosmic Story: Inside Our Awakening Universe*. New Haven: Yale University Press.

Haught, John F. "Theology after Contact: Religion and Extraterrestrial Life." *Annals of the New York Academy of Science*, No. 950 (2001): 296–308.

Hayden, Judy A., ed. *Literature in the Age of Celestial Discovery: From Copernicus to Flamsteed*. Dordrecht: Springer, 2016.

Hebblethwaite, Brian. "The Impossibility of Multiple Incarnations." *Theology*, No. 104 (2001): 323–334.

Hebblethwaite, Brian. 1987. *The Incarnation*. Cambridge: Cambridge University Press.

Hebblethwaite, Brian. 1979. "The Uniqueness of the Incarnation." In *Incarnation and Myth: The Debate Continued*, edited by Michael Goulder, 189–191. Grand Rapids: William B. Eerdmans.

Heffern, Rich. "Looking for Company Beyond the Skies." *National Catholic Reporter*, No. 43 (2006): 12–13.

Hess, Peter M. J. 2018. "Multiple Incarnation of the One Christ." In *Astrotheology: Science and Theology Meet Extraterrestrial Life*, edited by Ted Peters, 317–329. Eugene: Cascade Books.

Hewlett, Martinez. 2018. "Yes We Will Meet Them: A Scientific Argument for ETI." In *Astrotheology: Science and Theology Meet Extraterrestrial Life*, edited by Ted Peters, 146–159. Eugene: Cascade Books.

Hick, John. 1993. *The Metaphor of God Incarnate*. Louisville: Westminster Press.

Hick, John, ed. *The Myth of God Incarnate*. London: SCM Press, 1977.

Hume, Basil, 2000. *The Mystery of the Incarnation*. London: Darton, Longman, and Todd.

Iribarren, Isabel. "L'Empyrée et ses habitants au moyen âge." *Revue des Sciences Religieuses*, No. 91 (2017): 181–192.

Jaki, Stanley L. "Believe in Extraterrestrials?: You'd Be Better off Moonstruck." *National Catholic Register*, No. 74 (1998): 9.

Jensen, Alexander S. "The Unintended Consequences of the Condemnation of 1277: Divine Power and the Established Order in Question." *Colloquium*, No. 41 (2009): 57–72.

Kaiser, Christopher B. "Extraterrestrial Life and Extraterrestrial Intelligence." *Reformed Review*, No. 51 (1997–1998): 77–91.

Kleinz, John P. "The Theology of Outer Space." *Columbia*, No. 40 (1960): 28.

Keane, James T. "What Would a Chapel on the Moon Like Like?: Catholics in the '60s Had Some Ideas" *America*, July 10, 2019.

Keller, Catherine. 2017. *Intercarnations: Exercises in Theological Possibility*. New York: Fordham University Press.

Keretszky, Roch A. 1991. "Christ and Possible Other Universes and Extraterrestrial Beings." In *Jesus Christ: Fundamentals of Theology*. New York: Alba House.

Kevern, Peter. "Limping Principles: A Reply to Brian Hebblethwaite on 'The Impossibility of Multiple Incarnations'." *Theology*, No. 105 (2002): 342–347.

Knight, Christopher C. 2009. *The God of Nature: Incarnation and Contemporary Science*. Minneapolis: Fortress Press.

Kracher, Alfred. "Are We Special?: Humanity and Extraterrestrial Life." In *Issues in Science and Theology: Are We Special?: Human Uniqueness in Science and Theology*, edited by Michael Fuller, Michael, Dirk Evers, Anne Runehov, and Knut-Willy Seather, 27–42. Dordrecht: Springer.

Kracher, Alfred. "Meta–Humans and Metanoia: The Moral Dimension of Extraterrestrials." *Zygon*, No. 41 (2006): 329–346.

Lamm, Norman. "The Religious Implications of Extraterrestrial Life." *Tradition*, No. 7-8 (1965-1966): 5–56.

Lane, Anthony N. S. "Is the Truth Out There?: Creatures, Cosmos and New Creation." *The Evangelical Quarterly*, No. 84 (2012): 291–306 and No. 85 (2013): 3–18.

Lazzari, Edmund M. "Would St. Thomas Aquinas Baptize an Extraterrestrial?" *New Blackfriars*, No. 99 (2018): 440–457.

Le Poidevin, Robin. 2011. "Multiple Incarnations and Distributed Persons." In *The Metaphysics of the Incarnation*, edited by Anna Marmodoro and Jonathan Hill, 228–241. Oxford: Oxford University Press.

Leftow, Brian. 2004. "A Timeless God Incarnate." In *The Incarnation*, edited by Stephen T. Davis, Daniel Kendall, and Gerald O'Collins, 273–299. New York: Oxford University Press.

Lewels, Joe. 1997. *The God Hypothesis: Extraterrestrial Life and Its Implications for Science and Religion*. Columbus: Wild Flower Press.

Lewis, Clive Staples, "Religion and Rocketry." In *The World's Last Night and Other Essays*, 83–92. New York: Harcourt, Brace, and Company.

Lewis, Clive Staples. "Will We Lose God in Outer Space?" *Christian Herald*, No. 81 (1958): 7–10.

Lewis, James R., ed. *The Gods Have Landed: New Religions from Other Worlds*. Albany: State University of New York Press, 1995.

Lightman, Alan. "In His Image: Reflections on Other Worlds." *Books and Religion*, No. 13 (1985): 1–4.

Loos, Elizabeth. "Is Life Unique?: Perspectives from Astrobiology and Synthetic Xenobiology." In *Issues in Science and Theology: Are We Special?: Human Uniqueness in Science and Theology*, edited by Michael Fuller, Michael, Dirk Evers, Anne Runehov, and Knut-Willy Seather, 17–26. Dordrecht: Springer.

Losch, Andreas. "Astrotheology: Exoplanets, Christian Concerns, and Human Hopes." *Zygon*, No. 51 (2016): 405–413.

Losch, Andreas. "The Cosmic Christ's End: The Cosmological Meaning of Christ in an Interreligious Perspective, with a Focus on Jewish–Christian Eschatology." In *Issues in Science and Theology: Are We Special?: Human Uniqueness in Science and Theology*, edited by Michael Fuller, Michael, Dirk Evers, Anne Runehov, and Knut-Willy Seather, 43–54. Dordrecht: Springer.

Losch, Andreas, and Andreas Krebs. "Implications for the Discovery of Extraterrestrial Life: A Theological Approach." *Theology and Science*, No. 13 (2015): 230–244.

Losch, Andreas. "Kant's Wager: Kant's Strong Belief in Extra-Terrestrial Life, the History of This Question and Its Challenge for Theology Today." *International Journal of Astrobiology*, No. 15 (2016): 261–270.

Losch, Andreas. 2017. *What is Life?: On Earth and Beyond*. Cambridge: Cambridge University Press.

Lynch, John J. "Christians on Other Planets?" *Friar*, No. 19 (1963): 29.

Malloch, James M. "Do We Need a Space Christology." *Anglican Theological Review*, No. 39 (1957): 169–174.

Mangan, Terence J. "The Doman Moon Chapel." *Liturgical Arts*, No. 35 (1967): 3–8.

Manning, Heidi. "Yes We Will Meet Them: The Drake Equation Tells Me So." In *Astrotheology: Science and Theology Meet Extraterrestrial Life*, edited by Ted Peters, 56–73. Eugene: Cascade Books, 2018.

Mascall, Eric L. 1946. *Christ, the Christian and the Church: A Study of the Incarnation and Its Consequences*. London: Longmans.

Maunder, Edward Walter. "The Habitability of Worlds." *The Methodist Review Quarterly*, No. 69 (1920): 195–206.

McColley, Grant, and H.W Miller. "St. Bonaventure, Francis Mayron, William Vorilong, and the Doctrine of a Plurality of Worlds." *Speculum*, No. 12 (1937): 368–389.

McHugh, L. C. "Life in Outer Space?" *Sign*, No. 41 (1961): 28.

McMullin, Ernan, "Christianity and Extraterrestrials: A Catholic Perspective by Marie I. George," *The Thomist*, No. 70 (2006): 143–148.

McMullin, Ernan. 2000. "Life and Intelligence Far from Earth: Formulating Theological Issues." In *Many Worlds: The New Universe, Extraterrestrial Life and the Theological Implications*, edited by Steven J. Dick, 151–176. West Conshohoken: Templeton Foundation Press.

McMullin, Ernan. "Persons in the Universe." *Zygon*, No. 15 (1980): 69–89.

Mehl, Édouard. "La fiction théologiqe du ciel empyrée, de Luther à Descartes." *Revue de Sciences Religieuses*, No. 91 (2017): 193–210.

Michaud, Michael A. G. 2006. *Contact with Alien Civilizations: Our Hopes and Fears about Encountering Extraterrestrials*. New York: Copernicus.

Miller Smith, Cynthia A. 2011. *Extraterrestrials and Christ: The Theological Implications of Intelligent Life on Other Worlds*. Lexington: Cynthia Anne Miller Smith Publishing.

Milne, Edward A. 1952. *Modern Cosmology and the Christian Idea of God*. Oxford: Oxford University Press.

Mix, Lucas J. "Life-Value Narratives and the Impact of Astrobiology on Christian Ethics." *Zygon*, No. 51 (2016): 520–535.

Montgomery, John Warwick. 2012. "Did Christ Die for E.T. as well as for Homo Sapiens?" In *Christ as Centre and Circumference: Essays Theological, Cultural and Polemic*, 244–269. Eugene: Wipf and Stock.

Morris, Thomas V. 1986. "A Cosmic Christ." In *The Logic of God Incarnate*, 163–186. Ithaca: Cornell University Press.

Moritz, Joshua M. 2018. "One Imago Dei and the Incarnation of the Eschatological Adam." In *Astrotheology: Science and Theology Meet Extraterrestrial Life*, edited by Ted Peters, 330–346. Eugene: Cascade Books.

Moss, Christopher. "Extraterrestrials and the Love of God." *The Tablet*, No. 250 (1996): 100.

Mucci, Giandomenico. "Siamo soli nell'universo?" *La Civiltà Cattolica*, No. 166 (2015): 500–505.

Mullan, Dermott J. "Brother from Another Planet: Redeemed?" *National Catholic Register*, No. 78 (2002): 9.

Murphy, Nancey. "Jesus and Life on Mars." *Christian Century*, No. 113 (1996): 1028–1029.

Nelson, Thomas. 2010. *The Heavens Proclaim His Glory: A Spectacular View of Creation Through the Lens of the NASA Hubble Telescope.* Nashville: Thomas Nelson Publishing.

Nesteruk, Alexei V. "The Motive of the Incarnation in Christian Theology: Consequences for Modern Cosmology, Extraterrestrial Intelligence and a Hypothesis of Multiple Incarnations." *Theology and Science*, No. 16 (2018): 462–470.

Nesteruk, Alexei V., and Alexander V. Soldatov. "Christian Theology, Extraterrestrial Intelligence and a Hypothesis of Multiple Incarnations." *Humanities and Social Sciences*, No. 6 (2019): 1048–1071.

Nolan, Joseph T. "Bringing Liturgy Down on the Moon," *National Catholic Reporter*, August 27, 1969, 6.

O'Meara, Thomas F. "Christian Theology and Extraterrestrial Intelligent Life." *Theological Studies*, No. 60 (1999): 3–30.

O'Meara, Thomas F. 2014. "Extraterrestrials and Religious Questions." In *Space Exploration and ET: Who Goes There?*, edited by Jacques Arnould, 21–28. Hindmarsh: ATF Press.

O'Meara, Thomas F. 2012. *Vast Universe and Extraterrestrials: Threat or Mystery for the Christian Faith?* Collegeville: Michael Glazier.

O'Meara, Thomas F. "Vast Universe and Extraterrestrials: Threat or Mystery for the Christian Faith?" *New Theology Review*, No. 27 (2014): 1–7.

O'Murchu, Diarmuid. 2017. *Incarnation: A New Evolutionary Threshhold.* Maryknoll: Orbis Books.

Okwuosa, Lawrence, and Chinyere Theresa Nwaoga. "A Critique of John Hick's Multiple Incarnation: Theology and Christian Approach to Religious Dialogue." *Mediterranean Journal of Social Sciences*, No. 8 (2017): 159–167.

Oliver, Kendrick. 2013. *To Touch the Face of God: The Sacred, the Profane, and the American Space Program, 1957–1975.* Baltimore: John Hopkins University Press.

Osborne, Catherine R. 2018. *American Catholics and the Church of Tomorrow: Building Churches for the Future, 1925–1975.* Chicago: University of Chicago Press.

Osborne, Catherine R. "From Sputnik to Spaceship Earth: American Catholics and the Space Age." *Religion and American Culture*, No. 25 (2015): 218–263.

Pawl, Timothy. "Brian Hebblethwaite's Arguments against Multiple Incarnations." *Religious Studies*, No. 52 (2016): 117–130.

Pawl, Timothy. "Thomistic Multiple Incarnations." *Heythrop Journal*, No. 57 (2016): 359–370.

Pentin, Edward. "Alien Life Out There: Vatican Astronomer's Take on Extraterrestials." *National Catholic Register*, No. 84 (2008): 1 and 12.

Perego, Angelo. "Origine degli esseri razionali extraterreni." *Divus Thomas*, No. 61 (1958): 3–24.

Perego, Angelo. "Rational Life beyond the Earth?" *Theology Digest*, No. 7 (1959): 177–178.

Peters, Ted. "Astrobiology and Astrochristology." *Zygon*, No. 51 (2016): 480–496.

Peters, Ted. 2018. "Astrobiology and Astrotheology in Creative Mutual Interaction." In *Theology and Science: From Genesis to Astrobiology*, edited by Richard Gordin and Joseph Seckbach, 25–44. New Jersey: World Scientific.

Peters, Ted. "Astrotheology: A Constructive Proposal." *Zygon*, No. 49 (2014): 443–457.

Peters, Ted, ed. *Astrotheology: Science and Theology Meet Extraterrestrial Life*. Eugene: Cascade Books, 2018.

Peters, Ted. "Exo–Theology: Speculations on Extra–Terrestrial Life." *CTNS Bulletin*, No. 14 (1994): 1–9.

Peters, Ted. 2018. "Extraterrestrial Life and Terrestrial Religion: A Crisis?" In *Astrotheology: Science and Theology Meet Extraterrestrial Life*, edited by Ted Peters, 183–207. Eugene: Cascade Books.

Peters, Ted. "The Implications of the Discovery of Extra-Terrestrial Life for Religion," *Philosophical Transactions of the Royal Society A*, No. 369 (2011): 644–655.

Peters, Ted. 2018. "Introducing Astrotheology" and "The Tasks of Astrotheology." In *Astrotheology: Science and Theology Meet Extraterrestrial Life*, edited by Ted Peters, 3–26 and 27–55. Eugene: Cascade Books.

Peters, Ted. 2018. "One Incarnation or Many?" and "Extraterrestrial Salvation and the ETI Myth." In *Astrotheology: Science and Theology Meet Extraterrestrial Life*, edited by Ted Peters, 271–302, 347–380. Eugene: Cascade Books.

Peters, Ted. 2013. "Would the Discovery of ETI Provoke a Religious Crisis?" In *Astrobiology, History, and Society*, edited by Douglas A. Vakoch, 341–356. Dordrecht: Springer.

Piché, David, ed. *La condemnation parisienne de 1277: Texte latin, traduction, introduction et commentaire.* Paris: Vrin, 1999.

Popham, Peter. "Pope's Astronomer Insists Alien Life 'Would Be Part of God's Creation'." *The Independent*, May 15, 2008.

Pospíšil, Ctirad Václav. "La dimensione universale dell'opera salvifica di Gesù Cristo e gli ipotetici extraterrestri un esperimento mentale in cristologia." *Antonianum*, No. 77 (2002): 131–149.

Price, Robert M. [Enoch Bowen]. "Fields Unknown: A Thought–Experiment in Extraterrestrial Evangelism." *Journal of Faith and Thought*, No. 4 (1986): 9–16.

Pucetti, Roland. 1968. *Persons: A Study of Possible Moral Agents in the Universe.* London: Macmillan.

Putz, Oliver. 2018. "God's Self–Communication in a Cosmos Bound for Life." In *Astrotheology: Science and Theology Meet Extraterrestrial Life*, edited by Ted Peters, 160–182. Eugene: Cascade Books.

Race, Margaret S. 2018. "Searches for ET Life in the Solar System: Exobiology, Astrobiology, and the Big Picture." In *Astrotheology: Science and Theology Meet Extraterrestrial Life*, edited by Ted Peters, 109–123. Eugene: Cascade Books.

Rahner, Karl. 1966. "On the Theology of the Incarnation." In *Theological Investigations*, vol. 4, 105–120. Baltimore: Helicon Press.

Raible, Daniel C. "Men from Other Planets?" *Catholic Digest*, No. 25 (1960): 104–108.

Raible, Daniel C. "Rational Life in Outer Space?" *America*, No. 103 (1960): 352.

Randolph, Richard O, Race, Margaret S, and McKay, Christopher P. "Reconsidering the Theological and Ethical Implications of Extraterrestrial Life." *CTNS Bulletin*, No. 17 (1997): 1–8.

Regan, Hilary D., and Kelly, Terence J., eds. *God, Life, Intelligence and the Universe.* Adelaide: ATF Press, 2002.

Russell, Robert John. 2006. *Cosmology, Evolution, and Resurrection Hope: Theology and Science in Creative Mutual Interaction*. London: Pandora Press.

Russell, Robert John. "Life in the Universe: Philosophical and Theological Issues." *CTNS Bulletin*, No. 21 (2001): 3–9.

Russell, Robert John. 2018. "Discovering ETI: What Are the Philosophical and Theological Implications?" and "Many Incarnations or One?" In *Astrotheology: Science and Theology Meet Extraterrestrial Life*, edited by Ted Peters, 74–89 and 303–316. Eugene: Cascade Books.

Sarojini, Henry. "Are We Alone in the Universe?" *Bangalore Theological Forum*, No. 41 (2009): 167–178.

Schaab, Gloria L. 2012. *Trinity in Relation: Creation, Incarnation, and Grace in an Evolving Cosmos*. Winona: Anselm Academic.

Scharf, Caleb. 2014. *The Copernicus Complex: Our Cosmic Significance in a Universe of Planets and Probabilities*. New York: Farrar, Straus, and Giroux.

Shea, Mark P. "We're Hardly Alone in the Universe." *National Catholic Register*, No. 82 (2006): 9.

Shostak, Seth. 2008. "Other Intelligences." In *The Edge of Reason?: Science and Religion in Modern Society*, edited by Alex Bentley, 176–185. London: Continuum.

Smith, Howard. "Alone in the Universe." *Zygon*, No. 51 (2016): 497–519.

Spradley, Joseph L. "Religion and the Search for Extraterrestrial Intelligence." *Perspectives on Science and Christian Faith*, No. 50 (1998): 194–203.

Stevens, Clifford J. 1969. *Astrotheology: For the Cosmic Adventure*. Techny: Divine Word Publications.

Stevens, Clifford J. "The Cosmic Adventure: A Challenge for Theology," *Liturgical Arts*, No. 35 (1967): 10–11.

Swantek, David. "Counterpoint: Extraterrestrials May Well Be Out There." *National Catholic Register*, No. 86 (2010): C7.

Tanner, John S. "'And Every Star Perhaps a World of Destined Habitation': Milton and Moonmen." *Extrapolation*, No. 30 (1989): 267–279.

Tarter, Jill Cornell. 2000. "SETI and the Religions of the Universe." In *Many Worlds: The New Universe, Extraterrestrial Life and the Theological Implications*, edited by Steven J. Dick, 143–150. West Conshohocken: Templeton Foundation Press.

Teilhard de Chardin, Pierre. 1959. *The Phenomenon of Man*. New York: Harper and Row.

Thomson, Martin. "Extraterrestrial Life and the Cosmic Christ as Prototype." *Scottish Bulletin of Evangelical Theology*, No. 18 (2000): 160–178.

Torrance, Thomas F. 1974. "The Relation of the Incarnation to Space in Nicene Theology." In *The Ecumenical World of Orthodox Civilization: Russia and Orthodoxy*, edited by Andrew Blane, vol. 3, 43–70. Paris: Mouton.

Torrance, Thomas F. 2005. *Space, Time, and Incarnation*. Edinburgh: T & T Clark.

Vainio, Olli–Pekka. 2018. *Cosmology in Theological Perspective: Understanding Our Place in the Universe*. Grand Rapids: Baker Academic.

Vakoch, Douglas A., ed. *Astrobiology, History, and Society*. Dordrecht: Springer, 2013.

Vakoch, Douglas A. "How Should We Respond to the Stars?" *National Catholic Reporter*, No. 47 (2011): 21.

Vakoch, Douglas A. 2000. "Roman Catholic Views of Extraterrestrial Intelligence: Anticipating the Future by Examining the Past." In *When SETI Succeeds: The Impact of High–Information Contact*, edited by Allen Tough, 165–174. Bellevue: Foundation for the Future.

Van Driel, Edwin C. 2008. *Incarnation Anyway: Arguments for Supralapsarian Christology*. Oxford: Oxford University Press.

Van Huyssteen, J. Wentzl. 2005. *Alone in the World?: Human Uniqueness in Science and Theology*. Grand Rapids: William B. Eerdmans.

Vincie, Catherine. 2014. *Worship and the New Cosmology: Liturgical and Theological Challenges*. Collegeville: Michael Glazier.

Ward, Keith. 2015. *Christ and the Cosmos: A Reformulation of Trinitarian Doctrine*. Cambridge: Cambridge University Press.

Weeks, Andrew. 2005. "Cosmic and Terrestrial Aliens in the German Renaissance." In *Foreign Encounters: Case Studies in German Literature Before 1700*, edited by Mara R. Wade and Glenn Ehrstine, 255–264. Amsterdam: Rodopi.

Weintraub, David A. 2014. *Religions and Extraterrestrial Life: How Will We Deal with It?* Dordrecht: Springer.

Wiker, Benjamin D. "Alien Ideas: Christianity and the Search for Extraterrestrial Life." *Crisis*, No. 20 (2002): 25–30.

Wiker, Benjamin D. "The Truth Is Out There: Extraterrestrials, Probably Not." *National Catholic Register*, No. 85 (2009): 7.

Wilkinson, David. 1998. *Alone in the Universe?: Aliens, the X–Files, and God*. Downers Grove: Intervarsity Press.

Wilkinson, David. 2017. "Human Beings in a Cosmic Context." In *Issues in Science and Theology: Are We Special?: Human Uniqueness in Science and Theology*, edited by Michael Fuller, Michael, Dirk Evers, Anne Runehov, and Knut-Willy Seather, 3–16. Dordrecht: Springer.

Wilkinson, David. 2013. *Science, Religion, and the Search for Extraterrestrial Intelligence*. Oxford: Oxford University Press.

Winter, Harry E. "Anniversary of Communion on the Moon, July 20, 1969." *Ecumenical Trends*, No. 42 (2013): 14–15.

Wiseman, Jennifer. 2018. "Exoplanets and the Search for Life Beyond Earth." In *Astrotheology: Science and Theology Meet Extraterrestrial Life*, edited by Ted Peters, 124–132. Eugene: Cascade Books.

Zeller, Benjamin E. "Alien Worlds: Social and Religious Dimensions of Extraterrestrial Contact." *Nova Religio*, No. 12 (2009): 114–116.

Zubek, Theodore J. "Theological Questions on Space Creatures." *The American Ecclesiastic Review*, No. 145 (1961): 393–399.

Zweerink, Jeff. 2017. *Is There Life Out There?: A Christian Astrophysicist Answers Common Questions about the Search for Life–Friendly Planets*. Covina: RTB Press.

Science Fiction and Catholicism

Alsford, Mike. 2000. *What If?: Religious Themes in Science Fiction*. London: Darton, Longman, and Todd.

Anders, Lou. 2005. "Religion." In *The Greenwood Encyclopedia of Science Fiction and Fantasy*, edited by Gary Westfahl, vol. 3, 661–663. Westport: Greenwood Press.

Berman, Michael, ed. *The Everyday Fantastic: Essays on Science Fiction and Human Being*. Angerton Gardens: Cambridge Scholars Publishing, 2008.

Beswick, Norman. "Glimpses of Ecclesiastical Space." *Foundation*, No. 53 (1991): 24–36.

Brooke, Elise. 1977. *Theology and Fantasy*. Dublin: Mercier Press.

Busto, Rudy V. "Religion/Science/Fiction: Beyond the Final Frontier." *Implicit Religion*, No. 17 (2014): 395–404.

Cassutt, Michael, and Greeley, Andrew M., eds. *Sacred Visions*. New York: Tor, 1991.

Chase, Robert R. "Science Friction." *First Things*, No. 202 (2010): 29–33.

Clark, Stephen R. L. 1995. *How to Live Forever: Science Fiction and Immortality*. London: Routledge.

Clark, Stephen R. L. 2005. "Science Fiction and Religion." In *A Companion to Science Fiction*, edited by David Seed, 95–110. Oxford: Blackwell.

Clarke, Jim. 2019. *Science Fiction and Catholicism: The Rise and Fall of the Robot Papacy*. Canterbury: Gylphi.

Clary, Grayson. "Why Sci-Fi Has So Many Catholics." *The Atlantic*, November 10, 2015.

Clute, John. 1997. "Religion." In *The Encyclopedia of Fantasy*, edited by John Clute and John Grant, 808. London: Orbit Books.

Connor, Kimberly R. "The Speed of Belief: Religion and Science Fiction, an Introduction to the Implicit Religions of Science Fiction." *Implicit Religion*, No. 17 (2014): 367–377.

Consolmagno, Guy. "Religion, Science Fiction, and the Real Universe." *Argentus*, No. 3 (2003): 3–8.

Consolmagno, Guy. "Science Fiction and Catholic Sensibility." *L'Osservatore Romano*, No. 2507 (2017): 4.

Deignan, Tom. "Why Do Catholic Priests Keep Popping up in Sci-Fi?" *America*, July 11, 2019.

Elwood, Roger, ed. *Strange Gods*. New York: Pocket Books, 1974.

Engler, Steven. 2008. "Science Fiction, Religion, and Social Change." In *The Influence of Imagination: Essays on Science Fiction and Fantasy as Agents of Social Change*, edited by Lee Easton and Randy Schroeder, 108–117. Jefferson: McFarland & Company.

Geraci, Robert M. "Robots and the Sacred in Science and Science Fiction: Theological Implications of Artificial Intelligence." *Zygon*, No. 42 (2007): 961–980.

Geraci, Robert M. "There and Back Again: Transhumanist Evangelism in Science Fiction and Popular Science." *Implicit Religion*, No. 14 (2011): 141–172.

Greenberg, Martin H., and Warrick, Patricia S. 1975. *The New Awareness: Religion through Science Fiction*. New York: Delacorte.

Gregory, Alan P. R. 2015. *Science Fiction Theology: Beauty and the Transformation of the Sublime*. Waco: Baylor University Press.

Guthke, Karl S. 1993. *The Last Frontier: Imagining Other Worlds from the Copernican Revolution to Modern Science Fiction*. New York: Cornell University Press.

Hassler, Donald M. "Enlightenment Genres and Science Fiction: Belief and Animated Nature." *Extrapolation*, No. 29 (1988): 322–329.

Herrick, James A. "Sci-Fi's Brave New World: How the Genre Draws Us to Its Own Views of Redemption." *Christianity Today*, February 6, 2009.

Herrick, James A. 2008. *Scientific Mythologies: How Science and Science Fiction Forge New Religious Beliefs*. Downers Grove: IVP Academic.

Hrotic, Steven. 2014. *Religion in Science Fiction: The Evolution of an Idea and the Extinction of a Genre*. London: Bloomsbury.

Johannsen, Dirk. "On Elves and Freethinkers: Criticism of Religion and the Emergence of the Literary Fantastic in Nordic Literature." *Religion*, No. 46 (2016): 591–610.

King, J. N. 1977. "Theology, Science Fiction, and Man's Future." In *Many Futures, Many Worlds*, ed. Thomas D. Clareson, 237–259. Kent: Kent State University Press.

Kirby, Danielle. 2014. *Fantasy and Belief: Alternative Religions, Popular Narratives, and Digital Cultures*. London: Routledge.

Kreuziger, Frederick A. 1982. *Apocalypse and Science Fiction: A Dialectic of Religious and Secular Soteriologies*. Riga: Scholars Press.

Kreuziger, Frederick A. 1986. *The Religion of Science Fiction*. Bowling Greek: Bowling Green University Popular Press.

Lantero, Erminie H. "What Is Man: Theological Aspects of Contemporary Science Fiction." *Religion in Life*, No. 38 (1969): 242–255.

Leigh, David J. 2008. *Apocalyptic Patterns in Twentieth-Century Fiction*. Notre Dame: University of Notre Dame Press.

Machado, Carly. 2010. "Science Fiction and Religion: About Real and Raelian Possible Worlds." In *Religions of Modernity: Relocating the Sacred to the Self and the Digital*, edited by Stef Aupers and Dick Houtman, 187–204. Leiden: Brill.

May, Stephen. 1998. *Stardust and Ashes: Science Fiction in Christian Perspective*. London: SPCK Books.

McGrath, James F., ed. *Religion and Science Fiction*. Eugene: Cascade Books, 2011.

McGrath, James F. 2002. "Religion, but Not as We Know It: Spirituality and Sci-Fi." In *Religion as Entertainment*, edited by Charles K. Robertson, 153–172. Frankfurt: Peter Lang.

McGrath, James F. 2016. *Theology and Science Fiction*. Eugene: Cascade Books, 2016.

McKee, Gabriel. 2007. *The Gospel According to Science Fiction: From the Twilight Zone to the Final Frontier*. Louisville: Westminster John Knox Press.

McMahon, Christopher "Imaginative Faith: Apocalyptic, Science Fiction Theory, and Theology." *Dialog*, No. 47 (2008): 271–277.

Mendelsohn, Farah. 2003. "Religion and Science Fiction." In *The Cambridge Companion to Science Fiction*, edited by Edward James and Farah Mendelsohn, 264–275. Cambridge: Cambridge University Press.

Miesel, Sandra. "The Cross and the Stars: Catholics in the Field of Science Fiction and Fantasy." *The Catholic World Report*, May 15, 2011.

Mohs, Mayo, ed. *Other Worlds, Other Gods: Adventures in Religious Science Fiction.* New York: Doubleday, 1971.

Mort, John. 2002. *Christian Fiction: A Guide to the Genre.* Santa Barbara: Libraries Unlimited.

Nadeau, Jean-Guy. "Problématiques du religieux dans la littérature de science-fiction." *Laval Theologique et Philosophique*, No. 57 (2001): 95–107.

Nahin, Paul J. 2014. *Holy Sci-Fi!: Where Science Fiction and Religion Intersect.* New York: Springer.

Parrinder, Patrick. 1979. "Science Fiction and the Scientific World View." In *Science Fiction: A Critical Guide*, edited by Patrick Parrinder, 67–89. London: Routledge.

Pizzino, Christopher J. *Religion in Postmodern Science Fiction: A Case Study in Secularity* (University of Rutgers, 2008).

Possamai, Adam, and Possamai-Inesedy, Alphia. "Cultural Framing of Risk and Religion within Science Fiction Narratives." *Journal for the Academic Study of Religion*, No. 27 (2014): 94–113.

Possamai, Adam, and Murray Lee. 2010. "Religion and Spirituality in Science Fiction Narratives: A Case of Multiple Modernities" In *Religions of Modernity: Relocating the Sacred to the Self and the Digital*, edited by Stef Aupers and Dick Houtman, 205–217. Leiden: Brill.

Randall, David. "Ecclesiology in Space." *First Things*, March 21, 2017.

Ready, Karen. "Other Worlds, Otherworldliness: Science Fiction and Religion." *The Christian Century*, No. 90 (1973): 1192–1195.

Reilly, Robert, ed. *The Transcendent Adventure: Studies of Religion in Science Fiction and Fantasy.* Santa Barbara: Praeger, 1985.

Renard, Jean Bruno. "Religion, Science-Fiction et Extraterrestres." *Archives de Sciences Sociales des Religions*, No. 50 (1980): 143–164.

Rénard-Cheinisse, Christine. "Les problèmes religieux dans la littérature dite de science-fiction." *Archives de Sociologie des Religions*, No. 25 (1968): 141–152.

Roberts, Adam. 2009. "The Copernican Revolution." In *The Routledge Companion to Science Fiction*, edited by Mark Bould and Andrew M. Butler, 3–11. London: Routledge.

Roberts, Adam. 2014. "The Enlightenment." In *The Oxford Handbook of Science Fiction*, edited by Rob Latham, 451–462. Oxford: Oxford University Press.

Sammons, Martha C. 1988. *"A Better Country": The Worlds of Religious Fantasy and Science Fiction.* Westport: Greenwood Press.

Sleight, Graham. 2012. "Fantasies of History and Religion." In *The Cambridge Companion to Fantasy Literature*, edited by Edward James and Farah Mendelsohn, 248–256. Cambridge: Cambridge University Press.

Stableford, Brian. 1997. "God." In *The Encyclopedia of Fantasy*, ed. John Clute and John Grant, 412. London: Orbit Books.

Stableford, Brian. 2011. "Religion." In *The Encyclopedia of Science Fiction*, edited by John Clute, David Langford, Peter Nicholls, and Graham Sleight, 1000–1003. London: Gollancz.

Sturch, Richard. 2007. *Four Christian Fantasists: A Study of the Fantastic Writings of George MacDonald, Charles Williams, C.S. Lewis, and J.R.R. Tolkien*. Zurich: Walking Tree Publishers.

Theroux, Paul. "Christian Science-Fiction." *The Washington Post*, May 16, 1971, 280.

Tuckett, Jonathan. "Science Fiction and the Ideological Definition of Religion." *Implicit Religion*, No. 19 (2016): 525–551.

Udías, Agustín. "Jesuit Scientists in Science-Fiction Novels," *Journal of Jesuit Studies*, No. 6 (2019): 133–140.

Uhlenbruch, Frauke. 2015. *The Nowhere Bible: Utopia, Dystopia, Science Fiction*. Berlin: William de Gruyter.

Weinkauf, Mary S. "The God Motif in Dystopian Fiction." *Foundation*, No. 1 (1972): 25–29.

Winston, Kimberly. "Other Worlds, Suffused with Religion: A Hybrid with a Long History Seems to Be Gaining in Popularity." *Publishers Weekly*, April 16, 2001.

Woodman, Tom. 1979. "Science Fiction, Religion, and Transcendence." In *Science Fiction: A Critical Guide*, edited by Patrick Parrinder, 110–130. London: Routledge.

Yoke, Carl B. 1985. *Death and the Serpent: Immortality in Science Fiction and Fantasy*. Westport: Greenwood Press.

CONTRIBUTORS

Robert R. Chase is a former Chief Counsel of the Army Research Laboratory. He has published three novels, most notably *The Game of Fox and Lion* (Del Rey, 1986) and about three dozen short stories, mostly in *Analog Science Fiction and Fact* and *Asimov's Science Fiction*. He has been short-listed for both the Compton Cook and Theodore Sturgeon awards.

Janice Daurio, a native of Brooklyn, received her bachelor's degree in philosophy from Hunter College of the City University of New York. There she was influenced by Alice von Hildebrand, wife of Dietrich von Hildebrand. She continued her philosophy education at Claremont Graduate School (now Claremont Graduate University), receiving a PhD in 1994. She holds a Master's degree in religious studies from Mt. St. Mary's College (now Mt. St. Mary's University), Los Angeles. Her areas of specialization are ethics and the philosophy of religion. Her teaching experience includes Marymount High School and Loyola Marymount University, Los Angeles. She is currently Adjunct Professor of Philosophy at St. John's Seminary, Camarillo, California. Her work has been published in the *Downside Review* and the *Philosopher's Annual*, as well as being included in *A Political Companion to Walker Percy* (University Press of Kentucky, 2014). She is an oblate of St. Andrew's Abbey, Valyermo, California.

Carol A. Day is Tutor Emerita at Thomas Aquinas College where she specialized in math, physics and astronomy. Carol Day earned her doctorate in the history of science at Indiana University in 1986, after earning degrees in astronomy and astrophysics at Indiana University and the University of Michigan. In addition, she was formerly an astronomer at Sacramento Peak Solar Observatory and the National Radio Astronomy Observatory. She has published articles on stellar dynamics and spectroscopy in *The Astrophysical Journal* and *Astrophysical Letters*. She has also written an article on the ontological nature of elementary particles, "What Goes Around Comes Around: Elements and Elementary Particles," *The Aquinas Review*, No. 13 (2006): 53–79 and has lectured on various topics in mathematics and natural philosophy. She is an avid hiker and kayaker, and she has served for several decades as a volunteer wilderness ranger with the Forest Service.

Michael F. Flynn, a statistical consultant before his retirement in the US and abroad, has written more than 70 science fiction stories in *Analog Science Fiction and Fact*, *Asimov's Science Fiction*, and elsewhere, and 15 novels and story collections. He has been nominated several times for science fiction's Hugo award, including for his novel *Eifelheim* (Tor Books, 2006) which received Japan's Seiun Award and the French Prix Julie Verlanger. He has additionally received the Robert A. Heinlein Award for his body of work, the Compton Crook award, the Prometheus award (twice), and the Theodore Sturgeon prize for the short story "House of Dreams" (1997). His most recent book is the collection *Captive Dreams* (Phoenix Pick, 2012), six interlinked stories dealing with issues of morality and technology. He has just started a novel, *In the Belly of the Whale*, set in a multi-generation starship.

Marie I. George is Professor of Philosophy at St. John's University, NY. She received her PhD in philosophy from Laval University. She also holds Master's degrees in biology and in pastoral theology. An Aristotelian-Thomist, her interests lie primarily in the areas of natural philosophy and philosophy of science. She has received several awards from the John Templeton foundation for her work in science and religion, and in 2007 was co-recipient of a grant from the Center for Theology and the Natural Sciences (CTNS) for an interdisciplinary project entitled: "The Evolution of Sympathy and Morality." Professor George has authored two books, *Christianity and Extraterrestrials?: A Catholic Perspective* (iUniverse, 2005) and *Stewardship of Creation: What Catholics Should Know About Church Teaching on the Environment* (Saint Catherine of Siena Press, 2009]) and over 75 peer-reviewed articles, including "ET Meets Jesus Christ: A Hostile Encounter between Science and Religion?" *Logos*, No. 10 (2007), 69–94, and "Would St. Thomas Aquinas Baptize an Extraterrestrial?, Revisited," *New Blackfriars* (December 27, 2019).

Cyril Jones-Kellett is the host of *Catholic Answers Live*, the world's most widely listened to radio program of Catholic Apologetics. He is also the author of *Ad Limina* (March 7 Media, 2013), a science fiction novella about the first Catholic bishop born on Mars. Kellett served for more than a decade as editor of *The Southern Cross*, the newspaper of the Catholic Diocese of San Diego. He is a graduate of Boston College and the University of Massachusetts, a former high school religion teacher, and a former member of Boston's Catholic Worker community. Kellett and his wife Missy have three children.

Tim Powers is the author of sixteen science fiction and fantasy novels, including *The Anubis Gates* (Ace, 1997), *The Stress of Her Regard* (Tachyon Publications, 2008), and *Declare* (William Morrow, 2001). He has won the World Fantasy award three time, the Phillip K. Dick award twice, and the Mythopoeic award, in addition to receiving multiple nominations for the Nebula prize. His books have been translated into well over a dozen languages, and his novel *On Stranger Tides* (Harper, 1987) was the basis of the movie *Pirates of the Caribbean: On Stranger Tides* (2011). Powers lives with his wife, Serena, in San Bernardino, California.

Jennifer E. Rosato completed her PhD in philosophy at the University of Notre Dame in 2010 and currently teaches at St. John's Seminary in Camarillo, California. She has published articles on various figures in recent French philosophy, including Emmanuel Lévinas and Jean-Luc Marion. Rosato freely admits that she knew next to nothing about Catholic science fiction before working on this project and is grateful to have had the opportunity to learn. She looks forward to the day when her five children are old enough to enjoy Walter Miller's *A Canticle for Leibowitz* (J. B. Lippincott, 1959) and Michael Flynn's *Eifelheim* (Tor Books, 2006).

Alan Vincelette received a Master's degree in biology from the University of California, Riverside, and a PhD in philosophy from Marquette University. Previously he studied and wrote articles on fossil horses while working in the paleontology division of the San Bernardino County Museum in Redlands, California and teaching biology at Chaffee College. He is currently the Von der Ahe Chair of Philosophy at St. John's Seminary in Camarillo, California and Adjunct Professor of Philosophy at Holy Apostles College and Seminary in Cromwell, Connecticut. In philosophy he specializes in ethics as well as the history of Catholic philosophy, having written on such topics for the *New Catholic Encyclopedia*, the *Continuum Encyclopedia of British Philosophy*, and the *Bloomsbury Encyclopedia of Philosophers*. He is the author of *Recent Catholic Philosophy: The Nineteenth Century* (Marquette University Press, 2009), *Recent Catholic Philosophy: The Twentieth Century*, 2nd edition (EnRoute Books, 2020), and *A Reader in Recent Catholic Philosophy* (EnRoute Books, 2020).

John C. Wright is a retired attorney, newspaperman and newspaper editor, who was only once on the lam and forced to hide from the police. He is the author of some twenty-two novels, including the critically acclaimed *The Golden Age* (Tor, 2002), and *Count to a Trillion* (Tor, 2011). His novel *Somewhither* (Castalia House, 2015) won the Dragon award for Best

Science Fiction Novel of 2016. He has also published numerous short stories and anthologies, including *Awake in the Night Land* (Castalia House, 2014) and *City Beyond Time* (Castalia House, 2017), as well as nonfiction. He holds the record for the most Hugo Award nominations for a single year, and has also been nominated for the Nebula, John W. Campbell, Mythopoeic, and Seiun awards. He presently works as a writer in Virginia, where he lives in fairytalelike happiness with his wife, the authoress L. Jagi Lamplighter, and their four children: Pingping, Orville, Wilbur, and Just Wright.

Jeff Zweerink is Associate Project Scientist in cosmology at UCLA where he is involved in GAPS balloon experiments seeking to detect dark matter. He is additionally Senior Research Scholar at Reasons to Believe where he writes and speaks on the evidence for the legitimacy and rationality of the Christian faith in regard to such topics as exoplanets and the multiverse theory. He earned a PhD in astrophysics with a focus on gamma rays from Iowa State University and has been involved in the Solar Two Project and the Whipple Collaboration research projects. In addition to coauthoring more than 30 academic papers in cosmology he is the author the books *Who's Afraid of the Multiverse?* (Reasons to Believe, 2008), *Is There Life Out There?* (Reasons to Believe, 2017), and *Escaping the Beginning?: Confronting Challenges to the Universe's Origin* (Reasons to Believe, 2019).